ABCD... SGML

A User's Guide to Structured Information

Liora Alschuler

INTERNATIONAL THOMSON COMPUTER PRESS

I(T)P™ An International Thomson Publishing Company

London • Bonn • Boston • Johannesburg • Madrid • Melbourne • Mexico City • New York • Paris
Singapore • Tokyo • Toronto • Albany, NY • Belmont, CA • Cincinnati, OH • Detroit, MI

For more information, contact:

International Thomson Computer Press
20 Park Plaza, Suite 1001
Boston, MA 02116
USA

International Thomson Publishing Europe
Berkshire House 168-173
High Holborn
London WCIV 7AA
England

Thomas Nelson Australia
102 Dodds Street
South Melbourne, 3205
Victoria, Australia

Nelson Canada
1120 Birchmount Road
Scarborough, Ontario
Canada M1K 5G4

International Thomson Publishing Southern Africa
Bldg. 19, Constantia Park
239 Old Pretoria Road, P.O. Box 2459
Halfway House, 1685 South Africa

International Thomson Publishing GmbH
Königswinterer Strasse 418
53227 Bonn
Germany

International Thomson Publishing Asia
221 Henderson Road #05-10
Henderson Building
Singapore 0315

International Thomson Publishing Japan
Hirakawacho Kyowa Building, 3F
2-2-1 Hirakawacho
Chiyoda-ku, 102 Tokyo
Japan

International Thomson Editores
Campos Eliseos 385, Piso 7
Col. Polanco
11560 Mexico D.F. Mexico

International Thomson Publishing France
1, rue st. Georges
75 009 Paris France

1 2 3 4 5 6 7 8 9 10 QEBFF 01 00 99 98 97 96 95
Library of Congress Cataloging-in-Publication Data
(available upon request)

ISBN: 1-850-32197-3

Publisher/Vice President: Jim DeWolf, ITCP/Boston
Project Director: Chris Grisonich, ITCP/Boston
Production: Jo-Ann Campbell • mle design • 562 Milford Point Rd. • Milford, CT 06460 • 203-878-3793
Cover Designer: Dick Hannus Design Associates

To Judy, of blessed memory.
Although this book would not have fit
on the *nachas* wall,
I know it would have given you, a woman of letters,
much pleasure.

Contents

Chapter 5   **Who Needs It? Making the Case for SGML**

Chapter 6   **Where Is There? Document Architecture**

Chapter 7   **Where Is There? System Design**

Chapter 8   Getting There: Labor, Data, and Technology in Transition .281

Chapter 9   Being There: SGML-Based Production 303

Chapter 10   And Beyond: SGML Today and Tomorrow 325

Foreword
On the Inclusion of Panorama FREE

We are pleased to be able to bring to you a disk with a section of *ABCD... SGML in* SGML together with the first SGML browser for the World Wide Web. We included an SGML version of *Resource Guide A: Keeping Pace with SGML* with the viewer so that you can see how SGML really works.

What you can do with ABCD... and Panorama FREE

- If your computer can read ASCII text on a DOS disk, you can read the SGML source files.
- If you have Windows, but no Web access, you can view the files locally in Panorama.
- If you have Windows and Web access, you can view the files locally or you can get onto the Web and link to all of the HTML and SGML sites mentioned in the *Guide*.

We created a simple HyTime-compliant DTD for *Resource Guide A*, the first appendix in this book, then we added Panorama navigators and style sheets that show off SGML at its best including multiple views of the data, HyTime linking, and dynamic tables of contents—none of which would be available with an ordinary Web browser. With the *ABCD... Resource Guide* in Panorama you can:

- Navigate using hierarchial tables of contents as hypertext links
- Choose your view of the *Guide*—full text or organizations only
- Choose your method of navigation—table of contents, organizations, or SGML tree
- Link internal cross references.
- Link directly to all Web sites listed in the *Guide*.
- Link to, load, and view other SGML files available over the World Wide Web.

If you run Windows and have Web access

Install and take a look at the files included on the disk.* When you click on a link to an HTML document, Panorama invokes your HTML browser. Use your HTML browser as you normally would. When you click on or input a URL with the extension .sgm from either browser, Panorama will load the SGML document and its DTD.

The last section of the *Resource Guide—Archives Created in SGML/SGML on the Web*—has direct links to SGML Web document, and to lists of SGML documents. You can use these links as your starting point to explore SGML on the Web. There are also links to the Thomson Web Extras where you can find the latest version of the *ABCD... Resource Guides*, both the guide included on this disk and *Resource Guide B: Tools and Vendors* which provides direct links to all the vendors listed, plus additions and changes made after this edition goes to press.

Please send information to be included in updates to Guides A&B to the author c/o ITCP, 20 Park Plaza, Suite 1001, Boston, MA, 02116, or c/o itcp@thomson.com

If you run Windows, but have no Web access

Even without Web access, you can install Panorama FREE and use it to navigate the *Resource Guide* and the Panorama Manual included on the disk in SGML. The installation program expects to find a Web browser but if you don't have one, you can complete the installation as if you had a Web browser (select any one) and use Panorama with the supplied local files.*

And if you don't have Windows

The SGML files for *ABCD... Resource Guide A* are included on the disk as uncompressed ASCII files in the subdirectory SGMLONLY and the updated versions of both guides can be downloaded from the www.thomson.com Web Extras. You can view these source files in any application that accepts ASCII. You can load the files into any SGML-capable viewer following its load, compilation, and style sheet requirements. Also, check with SoftQuad on the availability of Panorama for other platforms.

International Thomson Computer Press on the Web

We will continue to update *Guides A&B* on the Web as Thomson Web Extras and may add additional material, such as a *Guide to Consultants* or an HTML version of the same files, so check the Thomson site. You can access the *Guides* directly using the enclosed disk or with any Web connection and a browser that can read SGML.

**Resource Guide A* loads each time you open Panorama FREE. If you switch to the Panorama *Manual,* you cannot go back to the *Guide* unless you re-open Panorama FREE.

Preface

SGML—Standard Generalized Markup Language—is an open, nonproprietary, international data standard governed by the International Organization for Standards. Its purpose is to encode information according to its structure and content. SGML does not change the underlying meaning of the information; it adds *markup* which becomes part of the text stream but which remains distinct from the original language. Markup of electronic text supplies information about the text that can be used by computer processing applications. A *markup language* sets up rules and standards so that a processing application can interpret the markup consistently.

This markup makes possible manipulation, analysis, storage, linking, and transformation of all media, starting with text. Flexible and heterogeneous sets of markup are defined for each type of information—corporate records, music, technical and scientific data, film and video, drama, poetry, scholarship, entertainment, and legal documents—as well as for the World Wide Web, which is an application of SGML. Text provides the backbone to which other media are attached.

SGML marks up language according to a data standard—a data standard designed, controlled, and owned by the information provider, not the software provider. This shift—from reliance on proprietary products with limited application to reliance on an open data format with multiple applications—represents a fundamental change in information management. With SGML-encoded data, a single information repository can be used for print publishing; search and retrieval; workflow and document management; online, electronic, and Internet publishing; and data archives. This repository is immune to changes in data format introduced by applications or operating systems.

Shifting the focus from single-purpose proprietary applications to multipurpose, locally-controlled and locally-defined data formats has repercussions throughout an organization, from traditional publishing to information science. SGML changes the rules for information management. It makes possible information-handling systems for language built on applications that specialize in input, management, and output functions replacing applications that control the information and format at every stage.

Before SGML, the only options for information management were data in databases or language in word processors and composition systems. The former was too rigid for most text, and the latter was too loose for anything except the output processing for print for which it was designed. With SGML, information science can control and process language, video, graphics, or any media or means of expression to the same extent that it has processed data in the past. SGML provides the flexibility to markup ideas, not just data, and the specificity to apply computer algorithms to all kinds of processing, not just to print on paper.

It is difficult to understand SGML and its application only if you come at it as just another publishing system. If you understand that this is no longer a computerized extension of printing technology but that it is computer technology with applications in publishing, communications, and information management, you have already taken the first step toward understanding SGML and SGML-based technology.

This book covers fundamental concepts of SGML-based technology from an integrated, systems perspective. It addresses these questions:

- What do I need to know about this data standard?
- Who uses SGML and to what purpose?
- What tools are used with SGML?
- How does SGML integrate into a wider information environment?
- How does a company plan for a successful migration?
- How does the work environment change when SGML is adopted?

The constant flow of facts, statistics, procedures, rules, dockets, proposals, data sheets, mailing lists, and records which the Age of Information heaves up each day is of no lasting value if it cannot be exchanged, queried, transformed, reviewed, and distributed. SGML shapes, crafts, and packages this mountain of raw information into an infrastructure that can support all manner of economic, social, and cultural activity.

This book is for all those who see this new technology approaching from over the horizon and who want to prepare for its arrival: it is for writers, production supervisors, programmers, publications managers, and managers of information systems.

With SGML, information science can control and process language, video, graphics, or any media or means of expression to the same extent that it has processed data in the past.

Acknowledgments

This book is delivered to you due to the hard work and support of my editorial and project team at this fresh, new imprint, ITCP. Many thanks to Jo-Ann Campbell, Barbara Tower, Chris Grisonich, and to my editor, Jim DeWolf. I also want to thank my first editors at Van Nostrand Reinhold, Dianne Littwin and Steve Levenson, without whose encouragement I would not have pursued this project, and I should not forget the International Thomson crew who kept things moving between VNR and ITCP.

My case study informants, and informants on all subjects, are named in the text of the book. My thanks to you all. You have each been most generous with your time and experience. I hope that you will pardon any unintended deviation from the story as you told it to me. I also want to thank my case study finders: Tom Brady, Lillian Ruston, Baird Foster, Joe Gangemi, Tommie Usdin, Barbara DeFelice, Yuri Rubinsky, Phil Pochoda, Mary Laplante, Bob Glushko, Gerry Fischer, Ken Holman, Linda Turner, Irina Golfman, Linda Burman, and Faye Merridith. I owe particular thanks to the vendors and consultants who put me in contact with clients and users of SGML. And especially those who so openly discussed the pros and cons, ups and downs of their implementations.

I owe more than I can say to readers who helped me through many earlier versions of all or part of this text including Bill Baschnagel, Susan Sellew, Debra Schneider, David Silverman, Bob Glushko, Kate Hamilton, Baird Foster, Mary Laplante, and Lloyd Harding.

Dick Vacca and all the students at my UW classes are due much gratitude for feedback and for giving me a fresh look at this material each time I teach.

I want to thank Frank Smith, Editor of *Technical Communication,* Journal of the Society for Technical Communication, for publishing the special series of articles on SGML in 1993 and to thank the nine fine authors with whom I worked on that series. You did such a good job that I realized that, valuable as the individual articles remain, there was still room for a book.

Thanks to Ted Jerome for setting up my newt and to Valley Net for providing a reliable community-run Web connection. Thanks to Cliff Stein and Fillia Makedon for helping me see the Web before Valley Net was ready.

I am grateful to SoftQuad, particularly Yuri Rubinsky and Lucy Ventresca, for producing and marketing the first, free SGML browser and for making it possible for us to distribute that browser with this book. While readers will find mention of Panorama along with other SGML viewers in the chapter on tools and in the Intel case study, the book was essentially complete before we included Panorama in our own distribution plans.

I didn't know that a noncommercial version would be available for the publication of the book and when I started this book, there was no ITCP, no Thomson Web site, and no Thomson Web Extras. I am all the more pleased that Thomson has provided the venue to offer the dynamic portion of this book, the *ABCD... Resource Guides*, as SGML files on the Web at www.thomson.com under Web Extras.

Very special thanks are due to Kate Hamilton not only for informing many of the passages of this book but for timely and, as always, cheerful, courteous, and skillful assistance with the DTD and the design of the electronic *ABCD... Resource Guides.*

I must express my gratitude to the providers of the SGML resources themselves—the same resources that I commend to the reader have been invaluable in the preparation of this book—so thanks to Eric Naggum, Robin Cover, Steve Pepper, the SGML Forum of New York, all the WebMasters of the Web sites and the list managers of the listservs and to all the contributors and participants on these public forums.

And I must acknowledge my debt, our debt, to all those who contributed to the genesis and propagation of SGML—to all those who wrote it, created the first tools, brought it through the standardization process and by doing so bequethed it to the public, and to those who continue to promote it so tirelessly. You deserve more credit than this book can convey.

To whom do I owe not only thanks, but allegiance? No one has been *that* helpful—no one has underwritten this book. SoftQuad provided a copy of Author/Editor 3.0, Frame a copy of FrameBuilder, and Microstar a copy of CADE Near & Far all of which helped illuminate the process of writing in SGML and writing a DTD.

Despite all this fine help, the words of this book are my own, entirely—with the possible exception of expressions such as }'*mx*rXS!W which are the unfiltered contributions of my cats who seem to like CAPS LOCK almost as much as catnip.

Am I an SGML fan, an advocate? Yes, but not a religious one. I have tried to be an advocate, an observer, and a reporter who recognizes the limits of technology and who would be the first to say, "This works and this doesn't work, or doesn't work in this context."

Personally, I want to thank all the friends who helped me take a break now and then—Laura ("Every break is a good break"), Kate, Wendy, Alan, and Teresa—and my family, Joy Colelli, and Debra Drown for constant support and encouragement. Thanks to the providers of all the venues that sheltered me as I wrote including William Child of Child's Pond and Julie, Ted, and Cynthia Arenson of Sunny Oaks Hotel. And, finally, there is no verb of gratitude good enough for Shalom and Daniel Goldman who remind me that there is more to life than ABCD and SGML—there are many seven letter words in Scrabble®, for instance, and there is pingpong and kadema and swimming and rowing and walking and talking and vacations, all of which I hope to do with them again soon, now that the book is complete.

The following have been reproduced with the permission of their respective copyright owners:

OmniMark error report and sample conversion script from Exoterica Corporation; Near & Far screen from Microstar Software Ltd.;

Author/Editor screen from SoftQuad, Inc.;

Adept•Editor screen from ArborText, Inc.;

Smart Editor screen from Auto-Graphics, Inc.;

FrameBuilder screen from Frame Technology Corporation;

Avalanche FastTag screen sequence from Avalanche Development Company;

Parlance Document Manager screen from Xyvision, Inc.;

OpenText screen sequence from Open Text Corporation;

DynaText screen from Electronic Book Technologies;

Passage Pro screen from Passage Systems;

NCSA Mosaic screen from the National Center for Supercomputer Applications at the University of Illinois at Urbana-Champaign;

Intel Component Technical data from Intel web site at http://www.intel.com/ ©1995, Intel Corporation;

Panorama Pro screen from SoftQuad, Inc.;

Netscape Navigator screen from Netscape Communications Corporation;

The Electronic Volcano from Barbara De Felice and Richard Stoiber;

Data provided by permission from Publications International Inc.; and

Explorer screen from SoftQuad, Inc.

1

Understanding SGML
And Where It Came From

THE IMPORTANCE OF SGML

If there is one single aspect that characterizes SGML—Standard Generalized Markup Language—it is that it puts the computing power of information technology behind the all-encompassing descriptive power of human language. It provides a system of notation that describes the structure of which we are all aware but which is seldom rendered in terms that a computer can process.

The sea change occurring around SGML emerges not from new applications requiring a new data format but from a new data format itself.

The impact of SGML has spread slowly and steadily over the last ten years until it is now an essential part of print and electronic publishing and information handling in fields as diverse as financial analysis, criminal justice, material science, and plain, old-fashioned paper book production. That it would come to play a large part in information technology was not always apparent; originally, it was just another way to set type.

Most of the profound innovations in information technology (IT) have come from new applications, new types of programs, not new data formats. The format of the data more or less went along with the application, and application-independent data formats tended to emerge out of existing applications. The sea change occurring around SGML emerges not from new applications requiring a new data format but from a new data format itself. New applications conform to the requirements of the data, and existing applications import SGML data into their internal format.

The origins of SGML go back at least 25 years to a publishing industry dissatisfied with the way computers were handling text. The original intent was to rationalize the publishing process so that data could be transferred easily between electronic typesetting systems. The impact of SGML on typesetting and typography is today overshadowed by the impact of SGML on electronic publishing and information processing. What started as a more efficient way to put words on paper has become a more efficient way to use a computer.

Before SGML, if you wanted to classify, compute, combine, and recombine, count, sort, and manipulate information, you had to cut it up in little pieces and stuff it into the pigeonholes of a database. Databases are fine for discrete, predictable pieces of information—age, height, weight, income, hair color, place of birth, part numbers, case numbers, ingredients, financial assets, and so on. They do not work for stanzas, scientific descriptions, engineering characteristics of new semiconductors, recipes, parts of speech, maintenance procedures, state statutes, legal briefs, and the 65–85 percent of the world's information that is today neither a number nor a piece of data but is part of a lump of text on a computer called a file or a document.

Most of the assets of the information age are in the form of language, not in the form of discrete chunks of data. Before SGML, handling this information was the province of publishing technology that used computers as handy electronic substitutes for lead type. Computers do a good job of this, but the computer has a higher calling in terms of language and text than as an efficient conduit to the printed page. Systems built on SGML occupy the ground between, and overlap with, both traditional publishing technology and information-handling technology, two fields that have shared the same computer hardware, but little else, during their short history.

What does this new processing power achieve? It achieves the original, publishing-based objectives, and a great deal more. SGML is the key to the technology that:

- Files, sorts, tracks, searches, and retrieves judicial case files, new drug applications, and tax returns;

- Teams up with traditional database technology to archive and retrieve documents, letters, descriptions, and reports; manage them; and publish them electronically, in print, or on demand;

- Creates new windows on existing information, inspiring and enabling spin-off products from a single set of information assets;

- Cost-justifies publication of scholarly text on-demand to a niche audience and cost-justifies publication of multimedia entertainment on CD-ROM to a mass audience;

- Publishes instantly the collaborative work of scientists and researchers at different sites in a form that is accessible on the Internet;

- Separates the job of writing and creating information from the job of designing and displaying information, creating efficiencies at both ends of the process;

> *What started as a more efficient way to put words on paper has become a more efficient way to use a computer.*

- Integrates information into customers' CAD/CAM simulators without rekeying or reformatting between the original engineer and the end user;

- Eliminates redundant formatting when printed works are published online or as CD-ROMs;

- Creates interactive electronic technical manuals that provide all the documentation needed, and only the documentation needed, for complex, on-site maintenance procedures;

- Pulls out just the right recipes from a collection of 40,000, records their use, tracks them through the publication process, and prepares them for print; and

- Spins the World Wide Web.

Each of these accomplishments is illustrated in one of the case studies presented in Chapter 4 of this book.

THE CONCEPT OF SGML

SGML notation models language. SGML wraps identifying tags, at least one set, around each segment of text in a document. The tags and the text they delineate constitute an SGML *element*. The elements form a model of structure and content that the computer can process. In this manner, SGML can mark up any level of detail or type of content and structure required. Thus, the sentences: "Come here, Mr. Watson. I need you!" might have a simple paragraph tag:

`<PARAGRAPH>`"Come here, Mr. Watson. I need you!"`</PARAGRAPH>`

or they might have tags conveying that:

- The paragraph is a direct quote (`<QUOTE>`).
- There are two verbs (`<VERB>`).
- The first verb is in the imperative mood (`<VERB mood=imperative>`).
- The verb in the second sentence is emphasized (`<EMPHASIS>`).
- "Mr." is a form of address (`<TITLE>`).
- "Watson" is a proper name (`<NAME>`).

Tags can also identify and convey information that is not part of the printed or displayed text:

- The speaker is Alexander Graham Bell (`<SPEAKER person="A.G. Bell">`).

The elements form a model of structure and content that the computer can process. In this manner, SGML can mark up any level of detail or type of content and structure required.

Other tags could supply the year, the place, an alternate version of the sentence, the media of communications, and so on. There is no limit to the information that can be contained in SGML markup; what is conveyed varies from application to application. Markup of a text for historical research may have nothing in common with markup of the same text for linguistic analysis. Markup of different types of information and for different purposes—case files, financial analysis, parts lists, and production inventory—may share some notation or none at all. That is the power and flexibility of SGML.

A file separate from the text—the all-important document type definition, or DTD—defines which tags can be used, the context in which they can be used, and what they mean. If you mark up parts of speech, your DTD contains elements for subjects, verbs, and so on. If you mark up classified material and track revisions, your DTD contains elements for security levels and versions. The DTD defines the relationship between elements and describes the content of the elements (Table 1.1). Thus like a database, but without requiring an inflexible table structure, SGML markup identifies information in terms that are unambiguous to a computer application.

Table 1.1 What the DTD does

THE DTD DEFINES:	FOR EXAMPLE:
Tag names:	CHAPTER is the name of the tag that indicates the start and end of a chapter.
Element content:	Chapters can contain an introductory paragraph and must contain one or more sections. (PARA?, SECTION+)
The relationship between elements:	The body element contains a series of chapters. (CHAPTER+)

Like any other publishing application, SGML identifies the parts of a document that are set off on the page or screen by distinctive typography—titles, running headers, emphasized text—but SGML identifies these by their structure and content instead of their appearance. SGML markup says: "This is a title" or "This is a computer instruction" instead of saying, "This is big, bold, and centered" or "Use 14 pt. mono-spaced type." Conversion and formatting applications then use the information about structure and content to render typographic characteristics: "If this is a title, make it big, bold, and centered in print; if this is emphasized text, make it flash green and purple on the screen."

Because its origins and many of its original applications lie in publishing technology, SGML is often compared to electronic writing and composition systems that show the user exactly how the text will format when printed. These are called "What You See Is What You Get," or WYSIWYG, systems and include popular word processors and electronic publishing tools with graphical user interfaces. Those in the know about SGML call these "What You See Is *All* You Get" systems, because restricting markup to what you can see on the page and restricting the screen to what will print on the page limits your view of the information and limits what you can do with it.

In a WYSIWYG format, the information that is computer-processible with absolute certainty is restricted to:

- File name, size, and format
- Alphanumeric characters and symbols
- Typography

WYSIWYG applications can distinguish a sentence, but not with certainty because any character string with a period (Here is myfile.txt ver.1.2.) is indistinguishable from a sentence. WYSIWYG applications that use styles and templates map appearance to certain aspects of document structure, like captions or footnotes, but there is no way to indicate the relationship between the parts or to verify that they follow a certain pattern.

In contrast, in an SGML-based application, the information that is computer-processible with absolute certainty is not restricted. It can include a sentence, a phrase, a paragraph, a clause, a section, an item, a list, a brief, a note, a figure, a version, a tool, an author, a title, a heading, a footer, a subsection, a stanza, a refrain, a song, a table, a column, a formula, or a lullaby. It can delineate a musical score or a frame of video or a coordinate on a graphic. It can indicate format directly or indirectly. And it can be used to sort and query and manipulate the text. Information in an SGML-based application can do this with or without a one-to-one mapping to typographic characteristics. And SGML parsers can verify that all the required and none of the proscribed parts are present and in the correct order.

WHERE IT CAME FROM

Computers were already sending men and monkeys into space orbit before serious attention was paid to the manipulation of language for its own sake. The year given for the first word-processing program at IBM is 1964, and word-processing applications did not become widespread until the nineteen-eighties. Today, nary a word gets into print that has not passed through a word processor at some point.

But somehow, and this history has not yet been written, text got pigeonholed in word processing and electronic publishing, as if the most that a computer could contribute to text manipulation was the page on which it is printed. What we have come to think of as computerized text is actually text with intricate formatting instructions intended for one, and only one, purpose: to make it look the way we want it to look when it is printed on paper.

Information about the structure and content of the text, not what it looks like, but what it *is,* is the heart and soul of SGML. SGML developed so that text on the computer would have a life apart from its eventual format in print.

But there was another problem with the way languages was treated in digital format. Not only was the computer unable to process text but, at the highest level of electronic publishing, markup systems were not interchangeable. Once a format was applied for typesetter A, the formatted text belonged to that system. If A went out of business, the publisher paid a data conversion fee; if the publisher wanted to combine elements of manuscript X and manuscript Y and they were in different formats, the markup applied to one manuscript, at least, was useless. The laborious and careful work of typesetting was used once and once only. As the information-based economy swung into high gear, the inability to reuse, manipulate, query, and search text became increasingly serious.

The idea of structured documents in an open, published format that could be exchanged and manipulated emerged in the late 1960s at more than one site.

The idea of structured documents in an open, published format that could be exchanged and manipulated emerged in the late 1960s at more than one site. A committee of the Graphic Communications Association (GCA) created GenCode to standardize typesetting codes, and IBM developed the Generalized Markup Language (GML) used for its internal publishing and later for its BookMaster product. The GenCode mandate was to develop generic typesetting codes that would allow clients to send their data to different vendors while avoiding conversion charges and delays each time they changed systems. They could then maintain an integrated set of archives, regardless of who originally set the type. The GML project was similar, but included structural manipulation and electronic delivery.

Representatives of both of these groups joined to form the American National Standards Institute (ANSI) Computer Languages for the Processing of Text committee. It was this committee that developed the first working drafts of what was to become a standard of the International Organization for Standards, officially known as ISO 8879:1986.[1] Although many individuals have distinguished themselves with their tireless effort for the development and adoption of SGML, the origin of the language was a collaborative international effort. The two key elements of SGML were the syntax, which stemmed primarily from the IBM GML system, and the semantics, which came from the typesetters through the GCA. These met the original intent of an interchange language that could be used to manipulate text—and much more.

---

[1] Interviews with N. Scharpf and J. Gangemi and "A Brief History of the Development of SGML" by the SGML Users' Group, reprinted in Goldfarb (1990) and elsewhere.

Application of the ISO 8879 standard, SGML, would not have progressed past the "Sounds Good, Maybe Later" stage without the development of the tools that put it to work. First, the *sine qua non* of SGML were the parsers that read a file and validate that it follows the rules of the standard. Next, came SGML-aware editors. There were editors for input only, that inserted markup into a text stream, and editors with composition and print capabilities. The next category to see commercial development were conversion tools and languages for manipulation and transformation, and then viewers and search engines. The most recent categories to see intense commercial development have been:

- Data and document managers built specifically for SGML
- DTD development and analysis tools
- Internet and World Wide Web servers and viewers for SGML
- Integrated production systems that incorporate all of the above

The development of tools for SGML received a huge boost in the late 1980s when the standard was adopted by the U.S. Department of Defense as part of the CALS initiative.[2] While the DoD initiative continues to develop and mature, other industry initiatives have leapfrogged over it in terms of impact on the tools market.

SGML has been implemented by many who deal with vast quantities of information. The Association of American Publishers, the Air Transport Association, the Government Printing Office, the Society of Automotive Engineers, and the semiconductor and pharmaceutical industries are all moving their document archives and production workflow to an SGML foundation. (*Resource Guide A* contains a more extensive list of users.)

SGML is becoming the format of choice for multimedia applications like Microsoft's Cinemania and for traditional publishers like Butterworth and Thomson Legal Publishers. SGML as a database population engine is becoming increasingly common. At least six states and large municipalities are adopting SGML for electronic legal filing, and Standard & Poor's updates and outputs its huge repository of financial analysis with SGML.

The most recent leap, and a great leap it is, is the World Wide Web. The Web is the fastest-growing application on the Internet. It is an international network of hypertext documents accessible through public domain and low-cost browsers available for all computer platforms. The data format that makes the originating and viewing platform and application nearly transparent is an application of SGML called HTML, which stands for hypertext markup language. The

Application of the ISO 8879 standard, SGML, would not have progressed past the "Sounds Good, Maybe Later" stage without the development of the tools that put it to work.

---

[2]While the CALS acronym dates from 1985, what it expands into has changed three times since its inception. The latest is Continuous Acquisition and Life-cycle Support.

Web demonstrates that SGML applications need not be complex: There are hundreds of new Web sites each week; anyone can learn to use it in an afternoon. Many of these implementations are covered in the case studies in Chapter 4, including two Web applications—Intel Corporation and the Electronic Volcano.

A CONCEPTUAL FRAMEWORK FOR SGML-BASED PRODUCTION

The Web demonstrates that SGML applications need not be complex.

SGML-based tools span publishing and computing functions and transcend old divisions of labor. For this reason, it is necessary to take a fresh look at how these tools map onto various production processes. This book builds a framework for understanding SGML-based production based on three concepts:

- Information processing is a three-stage process comprising input, management, and output.

- SGML markup creates "high-energy" information.

- Information is organized in different ways as it goes through the production process.

The first concept is the traditional view of information processing. The other concepts are explained below.

An Energy-Level Diagram

SGML markup conveys more information than do other systems of markup. It conveys the information required for typesetting *plus* the information required for data-handling.

We can use an energy-level diagram as an analogy. To move from a lower level to a higher level requires an input of energy. To move straight across requires no input or output of energy. And to move down a level implies a release of energy. It's easy to see how this works on physical systems: Charging up a battery requires an input of energy; do that and you can start your car, listen to the radio, or run your laptop computer. Let the battery run down and everything stops.

Adding computer-readable markup to your information requires effort. But the more computer-readable information there is in your document, the more uses it can have. Using this analogy, there is more computer-readable information in ASCII text than in bit-mapped text; there is more information in word-processor text than in plain ASCII; there is more information in word-processor or composition systems that use styles and templates; and there is yet more information in SGML-defined text (Figure 1.1).

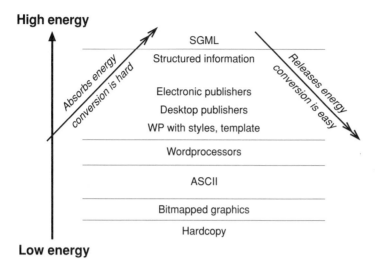

Figure 1.1 Energy-level diagram

Putting all that information into electronic form does take effort. But, when you want to use the information—for formatting, for viewing, for sorting, or for retrieving—all that energy is available to the computer. And unlike a physical system, SGML-encoded information can be cloned and maintained in its original state without loss through use or leakage. The image of up-conversion going into SGML and down-conversion going out of SGML is used throughout this book.

A Structure/Process Diagram

Information can take various forms and move through different energy-levels at different stages of the production process. The *x* axis of Figure 1.2 shows the processing stages of input, management, and output common to all information systems. The *y* axis measures the degree of structure or structural energy at any given stage in the process. This diagram shows SGML as more structured than WYSIWYG word processing and publishing formats and less structured than traditional databases.

Structure

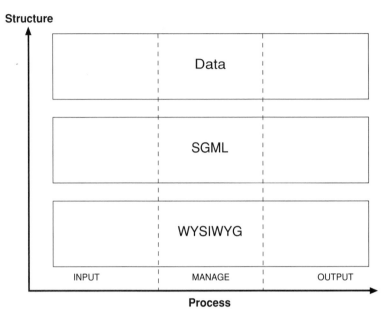

Figure 1.2 Basic structure/process diagram

This graphic device is used extensively throughout this book to illustrate how information takes on different energy levels at different points in the production process. The variations on the basic diagram illustrate how SGML is used, sometimes on its own, but most often in combination with word-processing and data-handling technology, to create, manage, and produce information.

BASIC CONCEPTS: INDEPENDENCE AND INSURANCE

The discussion thus far has placed SGML on the map between and overlapping data-handling and publishing, but there are other aspects of SGML that contribute to its impact on computing technology.

SGML and the Declaration of Independence

SGML is the information provider's Declaration of Independence. SGML-based information is:

- Output-independent—same source can be piped to print, online, CD-ROM;

- Version-independent—update and revise material without losing notation and annotation;

- Platform-independent—source files work across platforms;

- Application-independent—source files can be ported to any application format;

- Vendor-independent—source files not in proprietary format.

Output, version, platform, and application independence stem from the explicit structure and content of SGML-coded data. How this works in practice, and what a production and processing environment must supply to realize this, is the subject of much of this book.

Vendor independence is the result of a different aspect of SGML—that it is a nonproprietary, open standard administered and published by the International Organization for Standards, the ISO. This has a profound effect on the immediate and long-term value of information that uses this data format because *whoever owns the format, owns the information.* Regardless of whether or not it publishes the source code and calls it open, if an organization owns a proprietary format, it owns the information in that format and lets you use it through a lease arrangement. "Open" doesn't just mean, "I'll publish what I want of the standard, when I want to, and I'll let you use it." In this context, it means equally open to all, the property of none.

Your license fee for the application that unlocks a proprietary format is your lease payment for the privilege of using your own information. If the organization upgrades the format, you must pay another installment or you lose the value of the markup you have put into your information. If they do not upgrade, and you want to change formats, you must pay to convert your information to another format or lose its value.

With SGML, an ISO-defined data standard, you, the information provider, control the format. If you designate something as a "citation" or "tool name" today, that piece of information is a citation or tool name on any SGML-compliant system, regardless of application, for all time. Not only are you not at the mercy of someone else's upgrade schedule, but you can describe your own information in the way that you want it to be described, using a language that is independent of any vendor or platform or output or configuration. This makes for high-energy information, for long-term conversion insurance, and for long-term data viability.

The history of innovation over the last 40 years has demonstrated again and again that proprietary data formats have a very short half-life. If you doubt this, take the Jeff Suttor Challenge—try to read data stored ten years ago on eight-track tape, two-inch videotape, or WordPerfect 3.1 for DOS. Vendors routinely change a data format with the new release of an application, as Microsoft did with Rich Text Format (RTF) between Word 2 and Word 6. If you have not

With SGML, an ISO-defined data standard, you, the information provider, control the format.

declared your independence from proprietary data formats, then each time your application vendor upgrades a product, you are liable not only for the upgrade fees, but for the depreciation on your information assets, which are, overnight, in a down-level format.

SGML, Interchangeability, and Conversion Insurance

There are two fundamental ways to achieve interchangeability among systems: You can give applications common behavior so that they can work on each other's information, or you can give your information common characteristics so that it can be processed by any application. Standardizing applications is difficult and can inhibit the freedom of the application designer to reach creative and innovative solutions. When information is integrated at the application level, the applications must use complex, difficult to maintain routines on data created for another application. When information is integrated at the data level, each application can bring the data into its own internal format as long as the neutral standard is maintained for exchange. This is illustrated in Figure 1.3 where the shaded parts indicate proprietary formats and the white space an open format.

SGML advocates believe that standardizing data rather than applications offers greater flexibility and stability for information resources, as well as fewer restrictions over applications.

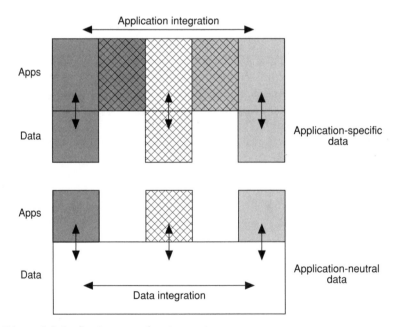

Figure 1.3 Application versus data integration

SGML advocates endorse the latter solution and believe that standardizing data rather than applications offers greater flexibility and stability for information resources, as well as fewer restrictions over applications. Over time, applications constantly improve and rise and fall in a natural flux controlled by the competitive software development market. Your data, your information assets, should not be subject to these fluctuations and should retain the value you have added to it with your markup, regardless of which application and which platform you choose for processing.

High-energy SGML data is not only application-independent, it offers *long-term conversion insurance*. When your information is at a high energy level, it can be down-converted into the format of whatever application suits your immediate purpose. Today, that format might be PostScript or HTML or RTF or a typesetting language or a multimedia viewer format. Tomorrow, it might be something else entirely. Putting in the extra effort required to create high-energy markup is like buying an insurance policy: You pay a small premium now, but you know that when you need it most, whatever is required of your data, the "insurance" covers your costs of conversion, maybe minus a small deductible.

Proprietary data formats do have their place, but that place is not in your data archives, not in the chief repository of your information assets. Data mobility is the only long-term survival strategy and high-energy SGML data is the best tactic.

Proprietary data formats do have their place, but that place is not in your data archives... Data mobility is the only long-term survival strategy and high-energy SGML data is the best tactic.

MORE BASIC CONCEPTS

So far, we have described the primary characteristics that distinguish SGML: It is structured like a database, but it models language like a publishing system, and it is an open, nonproprietary language controlled as an international standard. The fact that it is structured creates a new operating environment, with new possibilities, that requires new tools, new processes, and new procedures. The fact that it is open—nonproprietary and system-independent—releases it from the constraints of old systems.

There are other concepts, introduced here, that recur throughout this book. They are:

- *SGML works with other publishing technologies, not against them.* SGML tools complement, augment, supplement, and work with your existing tool base. They complement each other because they have different, albeit overlapping, functions. You do not have to throw out your database and your electronic composition system, although you may change the way that you work with them when you adopt SGML as a data format.

- *SGML is not a one-for-one swap with previous electronic publishing technologies.* Designing an SGML system does not begin or end with figuring out which SGML-aware editor should replace your word processor or desktop publisher.

- *Ask not how my print engine can give me SGML; ask how my SGML engine can give me print.* Most people start with the common, familiar tools of word processing and try to extend them to SGML. This is only one possible scenario.

- *Information drives your SGML application.* The shape, size, and demeanor of your SGML-based environment is based on the type of information with which you are working. The way that you model information in your application, what is called your document architecture, determines what you can do.

- *SGML does not* do *anything.* It is a descriptive language, not a processing language. Applications "do" things with SGML-coded data. If we say, "SGML does this or that," it is just a lazy way of speaking—what is meant is that SGML-based technology does this or that.

- *Purity is for purists, not for implementers.* It is important to understand the principles behind structured information and SGML. In practice, it may be equally important to compromise these principles from time to time where short-term production efficiency conflicts with long-term data integrity.

- *SGML spins the World Wide Web.* Information slides into a Web viewer because it is a form of SGML, *not* because of any special cleverness on the part of the applications. The text-handling aspects of the Web work because of data standards, not application standards. It is the common text format that, together with communication protocols, weaves the Web.

- *Technology must match jobs; jobs must match people and products; products must fit markets.* Technology-driven solutions create problems, not solutions. Market-driven (customer-centered) solutions work.

- *Most of the benefits of working with SGML are included in the following three benefits:*

  — Innovation: new products, without (totally) redundant labor and new features for current products
  — Efficiency: greater efficiency producing old products
  — Insurance: against outdated formats and expensive data conversions

- *SGML is for technical information... and* scientific information and entertainment and literature and business and government and law. And the boundaries are expanding all the time. SGML encodes aircraft maintenance procedures, catalogs active volcanoes, commemorates deceased actors, and quotes immortal poems.

• *SGML creates a strategic alliance between IT and publishing.* If it does not wipe out the border completely, SGML at least erases many of the distinctions that have barred free exchange between IT and publishing and, in many cases, erases the distinction entirely.

What SGML Is Not

SGML is not a way of *doing* anything. Structural notation, in and of itself, does not add value—musical notation did not write a single concerto—but the notation is what allows the value to be added, the applications to be written. In an SGML-based installation, the SGML standard, ISO 8879, defines the rules that define the markup that describes your data. Applications are required to turn that marked-up data into useful information, to print it or present it online, to sort it or revise it or insert change pages.

Much of the hard work attributed, in error, to SGML, such as "SGML reuses text in multiple contexts" or "SGML keeps track of versions and changes" stems from a misunderstanding of the SGML-based tools described in Chapter 3. SGML does not *do* these things; document and data management tools *do* these things with the hooks and handles that you design into your SGML-encoded data. If you mark up figure references with `<FIG_REF>`, you can search for them, link them, and process them as figure references, distinct from text that may appear the same—if, and only if, you have the search and retrieval and processing tools to do so.

What document and data management applications can do with your data depends on how well the applications are integrated and what they have to work with in your coded data. Does a paragraph just have a `<P>` tag or does it have tags that indicate the context, source, version, author, keywords, cross references, and parts of speech? Your SGML-encoded data will allow this "heavy lifting" if you have properly planned and integrated document and data management tools that capitalize on the structures encoded with SGML. The richer the metadata (all the information about your document that is not part of your document), the more management you can apply to it, given the proper tools.

What document and data management applications can do with your data depends on how well the applications are integrated and what they have to work with in your coded data.

WHAT'S IN THE BALANCE OF THIS BOOK?

How to make SGML-based systems work for you is the subject of the rest of this book.

Chapter 2, *What Is This Stuff?* explains SGML and SGML systems to the depth required for nontechnical implementers and is a good introduction for those who will go on to more technical work. This chapter presents the basic method of SGML coding and makes further comparisons among SGML and WYSIWYG publishing, traditional database technology, and other markup systems.

Chapter 3, *Who Buys What?* describes the technology available for various aspects of SGML implementation. It presents the universe of SGML tools and then describes each category of tool. Not intended as a shopper's guide, this chapter presents and clarifies terms and categories used throughout the book.

One of the best ways to understand the complexity, flexibility, and diversity of SGML is to look at the variety of sites using different aspects of this technology. Chapter 4, *Who Uses It?* is a series of case studies that examines this diversity. There are two levels of studies: portraits and sketches. The portraits cover a site in some detail, describing how it got to where it is, how decisions were made, and what plans are for the future. The short sketches round out the picture—each site illustrates an aspect of SGML-based solutions not covered in the full studies.

The portrait-length case studies are:

- Butterworth Legal Publishers—A legal publisher using SGML to manage, print, and publish on CD-ROM.

- Ericsson Inc.—An international communications technology firm using SGML for technical documentation in multiple formats.

- Columbia University Press—A scholarly press using SGML for traditional print publishing as well as for CD-ROM and multiple spin-off products.

- Standard & Poor's—Financial analysts using SGML as a user-friendly front end to their relational database.

- The Electronic Volcano—A research librarian and a professor emeritus from Dartmouth College team up to publish a guide to resources as well as updated reference works on the World Wide Web.

- Intel Corporation—The semiconductor manufacturer produces technical documentation in industry-standard SGML for direct incorporation into clients' CAD/CAM applications and for publication and distribution on the World Wide Web.

- Adams & Hamilton—Typesetters explain why they find that SGML is the key to efficient print production.

The sketches are:

- Microsoft's Cinemania—Describes how SGML is used to produce this multimedia, home-entertainment CD-ROM.

- The Women Writers Project—Researchers are creating an expanding database of women's writing in English from 1330 to 1830 used for on-demand publishing, scholarly volumes, and research.

- Utah Administrative Office of the Courts—The Utah courts are using SGML as the key to the automation of electronic case files.

- InfoUCLA and ICADD—A campuswide information system based on SGML enables multiformat publishing on-demand, including formats for the print disabled.

- Publications International, Ltd.—A commercial publisher uses SGML to manage a database of tens of thousands of recipes in the prepublication and publication process.

- Sybase—This software company uses SGML to produce electronic technical documents in a state-of-the-art, integrated, production environment.

- Canadian Code Centre—Canadian Code Centre of the National Research Council of Canada uses SGML and SGML-aware data design tools to help architects become "information architects" and produce thousands of pages of multilingual codes covering building, plumbing, fire safety, and farm construction.

SGML is a departure from current electronic or desktop data formats and the decision to adopt it is not just another "Which one to buy?" decision. After a decade of mind-numbingly fast progress toward more and better WYSIWYG, this chapter explains why anyone would want to put aside WYSIWYG for applications that do not consider "how things look" to be the central concern. Chapter 5, *Who Needs It?* presents a three-stage method that you can follow to answer that question for yourself. The first, prequalification, stage characterizes your information in terms of its suitability. The second stage looks at the internal, business case for SGML: What will it do to your production budget? What kind of investment does it require? The third stage looks at the impact of SGML on your place in the market.

In creating an SGML-based production system, the most important aspect of design is designing the data, a process called information architecture. Chapter 6, *Where Is There? Document Architecture,* describes the process of creating your own markup notation and document type definitions. Chapter 7, *Where Is There? System Design,* describes the process of designing your SGML-based production system.

Even when you know what your data and your production system will look like, the process of getting from here to there can seem daunting. Chapter 8, *Getting There,* describes the process of adopting SGML in terms of the three basic areas where the transition occurs: labor, technology, and data. It offers concrete suggestions and methods for designing a transition that fits your requirements.

SGML is not just a new coding technology. In its widest sense, it is a set of rules for organizing information that must transform the way information is managed. Chapter 9, *Being There*, describes what to anticipate in an SGML-based information environment in terms of new jobs and changes to old jobs.

Chapter 10, *Back to Basics*, summarizes the major concerns of someone considering SGML, looks again at the implications of adopting SGML, and looks toward the future of SGML tools and technology.

Appendices cover SGML resources, tools, and vendors, and provide a glossary and index.

SGML AND REENGINEERING

SGML makes possible a fundamental change in information handling and, therefore, is often mistaken for a technology-based solution.

Somewhere in the midst of writing this book, I read the book behind the reengineering word, *Re-engineering the Corporation*, by Hammer and Champy (1993). The reengineering message, in essence, is that it is time to rethink basic business processes and the division of labor that has been in place since the beginning of large-scale industrialization. The authors stress that technology can support and enable this process, but that you can't just throw technology at the problem and expect it to fix itself.

SGML makes possible a fundamental change in information handling and, therefore, is often mistaken for a technology-based solution. Nothing could be further from the case.

While the focus of this book is this new technology, the focus of any successful implementation must be an integration of new technology with new techniques and new processes. The lesson from Hammer and Champy that is essential to the application of SGML is that heavy-duty technological change cannot occur in a process vacuum, that to incorporate new techniques and use them to support new products, you must be open to changing the way work is organized.

So, while the reengineering book says that new technology should support and enable process changes, this book urges that process changes be considered as necessary concomitants of new technology.

ABOUT THE METHOD USED IN THIS BOOK

How did I get the information contained in this volume?

I have relied heavily, though not entirely, on cases researched specifically for this book. This research was carried out through on-site visits, e-mail, and in-person and telephone interviews with contacts at each installation. How did I substantiate the facts and processes related to me? Or, for that matter, those presented in an article or public presentation?

Where possible, I received confirmation from two sources within a company. I have also used indirect corroboration—indirect in the sense that if the situation were not as described, the pieces would not fit together. Some cases are corroborated by the experience of others. In most cases, material was reviewed by the subject of the case study, a procedure that has only increased the accuracy of the reporting.

In all cases, I have measured what I found in the case studies against what I know about the publishing process and the mixing of information and computers. In addition to the cases, I have relied on my ten years in technical publishing, on my investigation of hypertext systems, which started in 1987, and on my knowledge of SGML from an implementer's point of view, which goes back to the early days of CALS, when I consulted on the provision of technical documentation for one phase of the Joint STARS weapons system. And, of course, I have relied on the information provided to me in the course of my own practice, advising and implementing SGML solutions.

So, while I have relied in small part on being the SGML "expert," I have relied to a greater degree on being the SGML "reporter." In this regard, I have benefited from the same resources that I commend to you in *Resource Guide A*: the conferences of the GCA, the meetings of the SGML Forum, the work of SGML Open, comp.text.sgml, and all the other Internet lists, archives, and discussions.

2

What Is This Stuff
And How Does It Work?

In the strictest sense, SGML is an international standard that defines a language—a language that describes text. Just as you can take the same set of words from a dictionary and write poetry or produce a film, you can take the same set of SGML rules and constructs, codified in ISO 8879, and structure a seventeenth-century poem or a multimedia CD-ROM. The SGML standard *itself* does not describe paragraphs or line endings or chapters or stanzas or segues. ISO 8879 gives you the tools to define containers and objects that delineate and describe paragraphs, stanzas, and video frames.

SGML sets up an alphabet and a grammar—it does not restrict the vocabulary.

SGML sets up an alphabet and a grammar—it does not restrict the vocabulary. You can call a paragraph a PARA, a P, a PARAGRAPH, a GRAPH, or any other name that you want to use. You don't even need to define "paragraph" if it doesn't fit into your scheme. The exact mechanism for designating a tag name and defining and delineating the content and structure associated with that name is the stuff of SGML syntax, which is defined in the ISO standard.

The vocabulary, the range of words and the mode of expression for a specific document, to extend this analogy, is given in the DTD—the document type definition. And the DTD is a marvelous thing. Just how the DTD works and how it relates to your document are explained later in this chapter.

SO WHAT IS IT?

SGML as a System of Notation

SGML is a system of notation. It is a language in the same way that algebra is a language—it is not a language that communicates directly, a natural language like French or a computer language like FORTH.[1]

---

[1]Sperberg-McQueen and Brennan (1994).

Without a notation for structure, the best description that can be given to text, (not data, not statistics, but text) is BLOB, which stands for binary large object, as it is called in relational database systems. Without a notation for structure, you can extract pieces and divide pieces and establish relationships, but there is no systematic way of doing so. In unstructured word processing and electronic publishing systems, the operating system file is the one piece that holds together related information at its conception and throughout its useful life. Attempting to systematically revise, update, divide, link, condense, sort, search, and retrieve information with a word processor is like trying to specify an accounting system without mathematical notation.

SGML gets inside that BLOB, that undifferentiated mass of textual data, differentiates the structural pieces, and describes their relationships. And it does this in a system of notation that can be easily transported, stored, and translated.

At its simplest, SGML is *just* a system of notation. Other notations exist—MIF (FrameMaker Maker Interchange Format, RTF, PostScript Page Description Language, and so on. Why should SGML redraw the boundaries of information processing when these have not done so? Aren't these also a form of algebra?

These systems could not be called an algebra for text for two reasons: First, they are proprietary—someone owns the code, can change it, can charge for it, and can restrict its use. And, second, while these systems may describe some structural elements (they may identify a heading or a footnote), their primary purpose is to describe appearance. The structural elements that they do identify—a table of contents entry, an index item—are useful only within a specific application, and for manipulation conceived and preprogrammed by the designers of that application. When the underlying system of markup is for appearance only, only appearance markup is unambiguous outside the application and over time.

C.M. Sperberg-McQueen, co-editor of the Text Encoding Initiative, the group that is publishing standards for the use of SGML in the academic environment, distinguishes SGML this way:

> It allows the specification of a document grammar, and thus allows the validation of the document. It allows attributes and provides defaulting mechanisms... Its entity reference mechanisms provide hooks for document management and file storage, for boilerplate text, and for character-set independence. It provides a conceptually simple (though rarely implemented) method for allowing multiple hierarchical views of the data to coexist. And it actively encourages a declarative nonpresentational view of data.[2]

---

[2]Usenet post January 23, 1994, to comp.text.sgml; the distinction being made was between SGML and ODA.

Appearance-based Markup

To get a sense of what structure versus appearance really means, and how format-based markup is distinct from SGML and structural markup, let's look at an example of unformatted and formatted text. The text in this example defines the elements "Filename" and "PubsNumber." It is from the documentation for version 2.1 of the DocBook DTD, a public DTD for technical documentation developed by the Davenport Group.[3]

The unformatted text in Figure 2.1 looks as it might if received through e-mail. You get the words with punctuation, line endings, and that's about it. That is the lowest common denominator that can be reliably transmitted between machines running different software on different platforms as long as you rely on format-based, proprietary markup at either end.[4]

```
Filename The name of a file, including pathname if this infor-
mation is present. For the MoreInfo attribute see
"Application."
PubsNumber A number assigned to a publication, other than an
ISBN or ISSN or InvPartNumber. It contains plain text and has
common attributes.
```

Figure 2.1 Unformatted text

The formatted text in Figure 2.2 shows how the definitions might look when printed with a desktop publishing system. The format—specifically the use of two typefaces (Optima ExtraBold and Times Roman) and the indented paragraphs—make the definitions distinct and easy to read.

Filename
> The name of a file, including pathname if this information is present. For the MoreInfo attribute see *Application.*

PubsNumber
> A number assigned to a publication, other than an ISBN or ISSN or InvPartNumber. It contains plain text and has common attributes.

Figure 2.2 Formatted text

The markup used to create the formatted text in Figure 2.2 is RTF, or Rich Text Format, the markup system promoted, owned, and developed by Microsoft Corporation. The same paragraph with RTF, appearance-based markup is in

---

[3]This text, the SGML markup, and the DTD definitions are taken from DocBook 2.1. The current release of DocBook is 2.2, although these particular features did not change. For more information on DocBook, see Appendix A. In this example, I have used line breaks and indentation to indicate structure and hierarchy. These features, as well as the case of the tag name (`File`, `FILE`, or `file`) are not intrinsic to the markup.

[4]Carried to an extreme of all lower-case alphanumeric characters, the example, would look like this: filenamethenameo-fafileincluding… Ancient texts, in fact, resemble this crush of letters. Today, much that is format is taken for granted.

Figure 2.3. In this example, much of the detail of markup has been edited out (and people say that SGML is complex!).[5] The markup clearly defines the appearance of the text: it cites the font, the margins, tabs, line endings, paper widths, and so on.

```
{\rtf1\ansi \deff0\deflang1024{\fonttbl{\f0\froman Times New
Roman;}
{\f8\fnil Optim ExtraBold;}} ...
\paperw12240\paperh15840\margl2160\margr2016\margt1440\margb20
16\gutter0 \widowctrl\ftnbj\makebackup \sectd
\linex0\endnhere \pard\plain
\fs20\lang1033 {\f8 Filename
\par }\pard \fi-360\li360 \tab The name of a file, including
pathname if this information is present. For the MoreInfo attribute see
{\i Application}.
\par \pard {\f8 PubsNumber
\par }\pard \fi-360\li360 \tab A number assigned to a
publication, other than an ISBN or ISSN or InvPartNumber. It contains plain
text and has common attributes.
```

Figure 2.3 RTF markup

Structure-based Markup

Figure 2.4 shows the SGML markup of the same text. The SGML markup says nothing about how the text appears (typeface, type size, and so on) and it says everything about what it *is*.

```
<VARLISTENTRY>
  <TERM>Filename</TERM>
  <LISTITEM>
    <PARA>The name of a file, including pathname if this information is
          present. For the MoreInfo attribute see
<EMPHASIS>Application.</EMPHASIS>
    </PARA>
  </LISTITEM>
</VARLISTENTRY>
<VARLISTENTRY>
  <TERM>PubsNumber</TERM>
  <LISTITEM>
    <PARA>A number assigned to a publication, other than an ISBN or ISSN
       or InvPartNumber. It contains plain text and has common attributes.
    </PARA>
  </LISTITEM>
</VARLISTENTRY>
```

Figure 2.4 SGML markup

---

[5] The RTF file was generated by Microsoft Word 2.0; I have edited out the heading information for the file and left in the format information that applies to these paragraphs.

Translating this markup, it says that:

- This is an entry in a list of variables (`<VARLISTENTRY>`).

- Each entry includes a term and a list item (`<TERM>`) and (`<LISTITEM>`).

- "Filename" is a term.

- The list item includes a paragraph (`<PARA>`) that describes the term "Filename."

- At the end of the description is an emphasized word (`<EMPHASIS>`).

The term "PubsNumber" is another entry in the same list of variables and has its own descriptive paragraph. Note that this fragment nests several elements: `EMPHASIS` is within `PARA`, which is within `LISTITEM`. `LISTITEM` and `TERM` are within `VARLISTENTRY`.

Nesting and hierarchy are powerful features of SGML. They allow you to assign different properties to text in different contexts. As data is input, you can tag all book names as `BOOKNAME`. Then, in composition, you can give them different display and search values depending on whether they occur in notes or in paragraphs. If you were searching for the definition of "Filename," you could restrict your search to instances where the string occurs as a term within a list of variables.

With appearance-based markup, all italics are italics. With content and structure-based markup, titles are titles, emphasized words are emphasized words, and they can be rendered independently to suit the context and the media. In this example, the `EMPHASIS` tag has been interpreted as italics by a composition system. If this were a screen display, the `EMPHASIS` tag could be mapped to a font change or an underline or any other distinguishing characteristic.

Marking up content and structure with SGML makes it possible to distinguish any piece of delimited text with typography—it does not require that the typography carry all the information about the text.

Marking up content and structure with SGML makes it possible to distinguish any piece of delimited text with typography—it does not require that the typography carry all the information about the text. While some appearance-based format markup does map one-to-one with content and structure markup, there is no guarantee that this will be so. In fact, intentionally mapping format to content and structure puts an undue burden on the format—the page would look like the proverbial ransom note.

Yet, there are many items within a document that you may want to identify for ease of updates, searches, producing different versions, and database manipulation. For example, a user manual might contain definitions of error messages as they occur throughout a book. Typographically, the error messages are indistinguishable from other definitions. If the markup distinguishes between error messages and other definitions and notes, then an application can extract the messages and their explanations from the manual for an appendix. The error messages and their explanations can be maintained in a single database and inserted into user manuals, reference manuals, and online help, reusing the same text each time.

The DocBook DTD defines elements for all the computer terms in Table 2.1.[6] This may be more detail than you want to mark up. Defining special elements for these terms does not require that you always make use of them—it gives you a standard way of doing so when coding the information has a specific payback for your application.

Table 2.1 *Computer terms defined in the DocBook DTD*

action	hardware	property
application	interface	protocolrequest
classname	interfacedefinition	replaceable
command	keycap	returnvalue
computeroutput	keycode	structfield
database	keysym	sturctname
errorname	literal	symbol
errortype	mask	systemitem
eventstructure	medialabel	token
eventtype	msgtext	type
filename	option	userinput
function	parameter	

The key point is that these chunks of text, or whatever chunks make sense for your application—legal citations, stock quotations, marginalia—these are the pieces that can then be manipulated and processed by your application, whether that application assigns a typeface or sorts or rearranges or hyperlinks these chunks to other chunks of text.

SGML Syntax

There is a misconception among users of desktop systems that SGML markup is more complex than other systems of electronic publishing. This is not the case— just compare the SGML with the RTF markup above. Some SGML applications, like that used on the World Wide Web, are simple in the extreme. It is true— and this may be responsible for this misconception—that user interfaces which hide the technical details have been developed slowly for SGML-based tools. Perhaps another reason for the misconception is that, too often, the people explaining SGML have been technical implementers who have explained SGML in the terms in which they understand it—technical terms.

Using SGML does require some training, but not everyone who uses SGML-based systems—manages them, writes with them, publishes with them—need be equally proficient at a technical level. It is no more necessary to understand all the mechanics of SGML syntax in order to use SGML-based systems than it is to understand the mechanics of PostScript to use a PostScript printer, or to under-

Using SGML does require some training, but not everyone who uses SGML-based systems— manages them, writes with them, publishes with them—need be equally proficient at a technical level.

---

[6]DocBook 2.1.

stand the mechanics of RTF to use Microsoft Word. The case study of Columbia University Press demonstrates this—the press published its first five or six SGML-based products successfully, profitably, without a single SGML technical expert on staff.

It is necessary, however, to have a conceptual understanding of SGML and of structured information. If the exact mechanics of SGML markup are not of interest to you, skip to the next section, *SGML Compared to...* If you read the rest of the book, you will be proficient at a conceptual level. If you read this section as well, you will have a small introduction to the technical side of SGML.

We have already looked at the basic building block of SGML markup, the *element*. The following section defines elements more precisely, as well as the fundamental constructs of *attributes* and *entities*.

Elements and DTDs

The text in the example in Figure 2.5 is enclosed within two tags. The *start* and *end tags* are enclosed within angle brackets, <> (less-than, greater-than signs) and the end tag begins with a </. All this, the set of symbols that constitute the markup syntax, is variable according to the rules of the ISO 8879. This particular set of symbols is the default and is used in most instances. The start and end tags and the text they enclose constitute an element.[7]

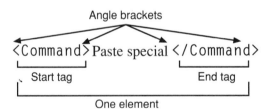

Figure 2.5 An SGML element

The rules for the elements—the name of each, what each means, where it can be used, and what it can contain—are in the *document type definition*, or DTD, which is stored separately from the document. The DTD is the set of rules by which SGML-encoded information lives throughout its various stages—input,

---

[7]The name of the element used in a tag is called a *generic identifier* in SGML terminology, but this book refers to both the element and its name as an element.

storage and management, and output. Your application, whether it is an editor, a search-and-retrieval engine, or an electronic viewer, if it is SGML-aware, knows how to interpret your SGML document because each of the tags in the document has been defined in a DTD. Figure 2.6 shows the DTD as a template for a series of clauses.

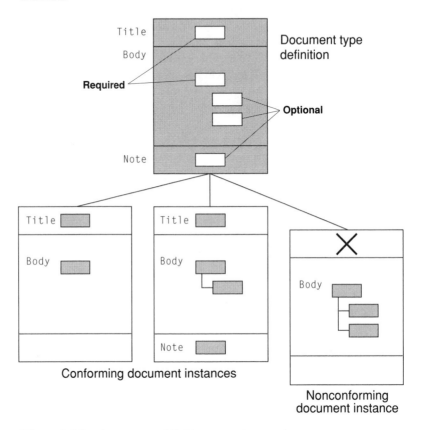

Figure 2.6 One document type definition, many document instances

In this example, each clause is a unit, in SGML jargon called a *document instance* (DI), although it need not be what we think of as a "document" in the common sense of the term. This particular DTD requires a title element and at least one body element, and defines other optional elements. The two DIs on the left are different from each other, but both conform to the DTD. The DI on the right does not have a title element, so it does not conform to the DTD.

The definitions for clause and body are:

```
<!ELEMENT CLAUSE - - (title, body, note?) >
<!ELEMENT BODY - - (section+) >
```

Each character or symbol in the DTD carries a specific meaning. The part of the definition within parentheses is called the *content model*. It specifies what the element can contain and what it must contain. The plus symbol means "one or more" and the comma between the entries indicates that they must occur in that sequence. In this example, CLAUSE must contain one and only one TITLE, followed by the BODY, followed by an optional NOTE. The next line says that BODY contains one or more SECTION. In a complete DTD, definitions for TITLE and NOTE would follow.

Entities

Entities are character strings that stand in for longer strings, groups of elements, special characters, or graphics. They are delineated with an ampersand sign (&) or a percent sign (%) at the start and a semicolon (;) at the end. The entity for the plus-or-minus sign (±) is:

&plusnm;

There are common sets of entities defined by ISO standards, for example, the Latin-1 set cited in ISO 8879 and used in the HTML DTD for the World Wide Web and ISO 8859/1m 8-bit single-byte coded graphic characters.

Entities can also replace more complex constructs. DocBook uses a type of entity called a *parameter entity* to create a category of elements or attributes. The DTD inserts a parameter entity into a content model instead of listing the individual components. In this way it can assign behavior to the group in a compact and precise fashion. The following statement defines the parameter entity docinfo and says that it contains the listed elements:

```
<!ENTITY % docinfo.content.gp "Author | AuthorInitials |
CorpAuthor | ModeSpec | OtherCredit | ProductName | ProductNumber
| RevHistory" >
```

Entities may be defined within the DTD where they are cited or within a referenced DTD. These are referred to as internal and external entities, respectively.

Attributes

Attributes modify elements the way an adjective modifies a noun. The attributes that an element can have are defined together with the element in the DTD. The value of the attribute can be restricted to one among a fixed list of values (yes or no) or can be indefinite and supplied in the document itself.

One of the common attributes allowed for almost every element in DocBook is role. It allows you to modify an element without creating a new one. If there is only one kind of list in the DTD and you need to distinguish lists of vegetables from lists of fruits, you can use the role attribute with the LIST element to distinguish them. This is how they might be used in a document:

```
<LIST role = fruit> Fruits of the Tropics </LIST>
<LIST role = vegetable> Vegetables Kids Like to Eat </LIST>
```

Note that attributes are included with the element name within the angle brackets.

DocBook figures use attributes to identify graphics files. A FIGURE element includes an id attribute, a TITLE element, and a GRAPHIC element. The GRAPHIC element includes three attributes: format, file reference (fileref), and id.[8]

```
<FIGURE id="FG-10">
    <TITLE>Window with resizing pointer.</TITLE>
    <GRAPHIC
      format="EPS"
      fileref="figs/1_10.eps"
      id="GC-10">
    </GRAPHIC>
</FIGURE>
```

Figure 2.7 shows the relationship between the elements and attributes in a figure call.

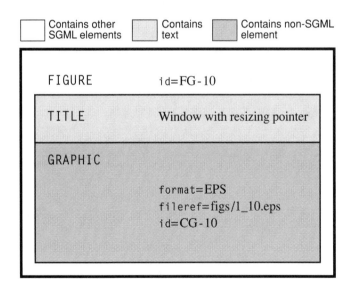

Figure 2.7 Figure structure

This markup can interface easily with a graphic or document management application because there are three separate identifiers for the graphic. The id attribute in the FIGURE element identifies the figure within a sequence in the document; the id attribute in the GRAPHIC identifies the figure independently of the document, and the fileref attribute identifies the file where the graphic is stored.

What This Explanation Leaves Out

There is a great deal more to the technical side of SGML that this explanation does not touch on. Technically speaking, SGML documents have three parts: in addition to the document instance and the DTD, there is a formal SGML declaration for technical syntax, which sets up the rules for both the DTD and conforming documents. The declaration determines if the default syntax—angle brackets and slashes and so on—are in force or if they are replaced with substitute characters. The declaration also states which of several optional features of SGML are included. For example, a declaration can allow or disallow the use of tag minimization, an optional feature that permits start or end tags to be omitted from markup when doing so would not be ambiguous.

Generalizing the rules that make possible this type of markup is what concerns the technical community that supports and surrounds ISO 8879. The balancing act has been, and continues to be, one of making a language powerful enough to describe all types of data without proprietary or system- or machine-dependent constructs.

Fortunately, there is a growing number of excellent technical reference books on the SGML language. For these and the latest technical developments, check the resources listed in *Resource Guide A*.

SGML COMPARED TO. . .

SGML Versus WYSIWYG Word Processing and Desktop Publishing

Proponents and opponents of SGML love to fight the "WYSIWYG Wars": Which is better, SGML or WYSIWYG? Should an SGML editing tool strive for WYSIWYG? Can true WYSIWYG with SGML ever be achieved and, if so, is it an admirable goal?

Like most seemingly intractable conflicts, this one is built on a narrow premise—that the SGML editor is a one-for-one swap for today's word-processor or desktop-publishing system. In fact, there is plenty of room for mutual coexistence between SGML and WYSIWYG publishing systems. As in so many relationships, the preconditions for peace are a mutual recognition of the rightful domain of each: SGML exists to structure information, WYSIWYG to format it.

But, there continues to be a great deal of confusion on this point, with partisans on both sides comparing SGML with word processing, particularly WYSIWYG systems, and so it is worthwhile making the relationship explicit. SGML should not be matched, head to head, with a word processor or desktop publisher. Doing so is like comparing the editorial features of a word processor with those of a database, or comparing the number-crunching abilities of a spreadsheet with those of a database. While many of the same operations can be performed in both, one type of tool is appropriate for one task and the other tool for another task.

WYSIWYG editors—desktop and electronic publishers—provide some tools for creating text and many tools for formatting and composing text in print. Systems built on SGML-based editors give you many tools for creating, organizing, and storing text. They provide a neat and efficient point of departure for format and composition tools.

When text is tagged according to its structure and meaning, it has many lives, including, but not limited to, a beautiful life in print. "Appearance is one possible use," is how typesetters and SGML experts Adams & Hamilton put it. Other uses include online publishing, hypertext, sophisticated search and retrieval, and platform and vendor-independent transmission and storage. This delineation sets up a neat division of labor:

- SGML-based tools organize, structure, manipulate, and store information.

- Appearance-based, WYSIWYG, word processors and desktop publishers *format* information for print.

But, this description glosses over most of the debate. The rub between SGML and non-SGML editors is that *both* seem to want to handle the information on both the input and output sides. The early forays into SGML publishing by the giants of word processing maintain an appearance-based word processor (theirs) as the input tool, then convert the data to SGML. The first call for SGML capabilities at WordPerfect (now part of Novell) was for an "output as SGML" capability as a menu item. The eventual product, Intellitag, maintains WordPerfect as the input tool with a complex conversion mapping to SGML. Conversely, some SGML advocates and toolmakers see no need for non-SGML composition systems. They use SGML syntax to describe output format without a WYSIWYG composition tool.

There is no one "right" side to this debate. There are many good solutions to specific situations. Most of them use a combination of SGML and non-SGML tools. Much of this book is about how to find the right balance for any given situation.

WYSIWYG editors provide some tools for creating text and many tools for formatting and composing text in print.

SGML-Structured Text Versus Database-Structured Data

On the other side, SGML is often compared with traditional systems of data manipulation in hierarchical, relational, and object-oriented databases. Here, too, SGML complements the earlier technology, it does not replace it. Just as several of the case studies show SGML-encoded data as the input to WYSIWYG systems, there are several instances where SGML data works hand-in-hand with traditional relational data. Some of the most exciting new implementations described in this book use SGML-structured text to populate a traditional database. These include Standard & Poor's and the Utah Administrative Office of the Courts.

Here, too, SGML complements the earlier technology, it does not replace it.

If you are going to a database-defined structure, what does SGML have to offer? Why not just put the data into the database and be done with it? SGML markup allows information to be input in its current and most natural form, as a letter, a report, or a poem, without being picked apart or pigeonholed into ill-fitting data structures. The metadata associated with the markup goes into the relational database—the text stays as text. In a traditional schema, either the data or the text would be distorted to attain this level of flexibility and verity.

A brilliant example of the distinct functions of text and databases is provided by the arguments given for use of SGML in the new electronic case-file system being introduced into the Utah Courts. Alan Asay, a developer with the Utah Judicial Information Services and a lawyer, argues persuasively that database systems fit administrative tasks well, where counting, tracking, and tallying are the objective, but that they do not fit case files, where evidence and values are weighted and on which decisions are rendered.

> The database notions predominating in information technology do not fit legal information well, mainly because open texture, policy- and value-laden ideas, the human experience captured in one's memory, and the richness of natural language are all inconsistent with a database approach. Databases process discrete, categorizable, concrete things, but such things are not the substance of much of the case file…
>
> In the case file, the law is a major, defining part of the content, and the [previous, relational] technological model cannot assume that any legal idea fits within any preconceived digital strictures. The arbitrary clarity of an artificial technical conceptualization cannot be superimposed on the law without severe distortion.
>
> Besides losing the ability to accurately handle open texture, a contrived system of categorized or "normalized" ideas would limit the richness, flexibility, and persuasiveness of natural language in expressing ideas and argumentation. Natural language is the principle means of communication in the case file, and not without reason.[9]

[9]Alan Asay, "Applying Information Technology to Court Case Files: Report of the Utah Electronic Filing Project," unpublished paper by A. Asay, Utah Administrative Office of the Courts, 230 South 500 East, Suite 360, Salt Lake City, UT 84102, alana@courtlink.utcourts.gov

SGML models the structure of natural language whether it is a casefile, a financial report, a technical manual, or a sonnet. It is not bound to a notion of structure derived from data-handling or mathematics. The next section looks at how it compares to other systems created to model text.

Generalized Markup Language (GML)

Generalized Markup Language (GML) is an antecedent of SGML. It was developed by Charles Goldfarb, Edward Mosher, and Raymond Lorie (GML, get it?) at IBM. The effort, led by Goldfarb, a lawyer by background and training, was based partially on the generic coding ideas being developed at the time by the GCA and was spurred by the need for better management of legal documents.

GML is the format for IBM's BookMaster and BookManager software. It was used in the bulk of their publications, even before the release of these products in 1987. Similar to SGML in many respects, it does not employ a separate DTD.

Open Document Architecture (ODA)

ODA (Open—formerly Office—Document Architecture), also an ISO standard (ISO 8613), is either an overlapping, competing, or complementary standard, depending on who you talk with. It was developed concurrently with SGML, with a broader mandate in terms of function—it was to handle format, graphics, and interchange directly, not by reference, as well as text—and a narrower mandate in terms of application, being aimed specifically at office-bound document handling.

While both ODA and SGML have mechanisms for defining structure, the critical difference between them is that, while SGML sets up a grammar for you to define your own structures, ODA goes ahead and defines those structures for you. If you need a structure that ODA did not define for you (Sperberg-McQueen's example is a tool for marking illusions to the poet Milton), or if you want to put your structures together in ways that ODA trees do not allow, you are out of luck.

ODA does not have wide application today in the United States except as the hub in a hub-and-spoke conversion scenario. A representative of SGML Open, the vendor consortium, speaking at the SGML Forum of New York, said that SGML has two competitors, and ODA is not one of them. The two he was referring to are the OpenDoc standard and "anything that Microsoft Corporation declares as a standard."

OpenDoc and OLE

But OpenDoc is not directly competitive with SGML.

OpenDoc and OLE (Object Linking and Embedding) compete with each other. Both want to become the dominant method for the exchange of processing objects. They set standards for the acceptance and manipulation of objects—they say nothing about what those objects are. Objects, here, are application-defined documents, graphics, spreadsheets, and data. In a compliant application, data inserted from another application can be manipulated as if it were in the original application.

They may sound similar to SGML—both are often cited as "vendor neutral" and "cross-platform"—but they approach these issues on different levels. OpenDoc and OLE are *application* standards; SGML is a *data* standard. OpenDoc/OLE-compliant applications ("apps") render some functions application-independent, not by making the data independent but by invoking application modules to manipulate (proprietary) data modules within an application.

OpenDoc and OLE are application standards; SGML is a data standard.

While the compound document architecture of OpenDoc and OLE does allow you to import and export data between applications—which is one of the functions of an SGML-based system—it binds you to those applications and to the data format of those applications. If OpenDoc and OLE are instances of moving from "computer-centered" to "document-centered" word processing, then SGML goes one step further to information-centered processing.

OLE is developed and supported by Microsoft, and OpenDoc is developed and supported by a consortium of other big players: Apple, IBM, Novell, and Lotus, who jointly support its developer, Component Integration Labs.

Rich Text Format (RTF)

Rich Text Format describes text format; it is appearance-based markup. It belongs to Microsoft Corporation and is used within their applications, Microsoft Word, Excel, and so on, as a means of exchanging format-based information. It is a handy way to exchange formatted text without use of binary files when both sending and receiving applications can read it.

As a replacement to SGML, RTF has little to offer because it does not define structure and because it is a single-vendor format. There is some security in the fact that it *is* backed by the largest software company in the world, but there is no insurance that the format will not change in arbitrary and unpredictable ways or that the data described by RTF today will be readable tomorrow. In fact, the RTF for Word 6.0 is not compatible with the RTF for Word 2.0. Microsoft itself makes extensive use of SGML in its multimedia products (Cinemania and Encarta) and has an SGML product called SGML Author for Word.

PostScript and Acrobat (PDF)

PostScript Page Description Language, while also owned by a single vendor, Adobe Systems Incorporated, has become a standard of a sort for the print world. It is a language that translates between diverse text and graphics systems and print output devices, such as laser printers. It has little basis for comparison with SGML, except for the fact that it has recently been expanded to the screen in the form of PDF (Portable Document Format), a modified PostScript used in Adobe's Acrobat viewer.

Acrobat with its PDF format is a screen painter in the same way that WYSI-WYG editors and publishers and PostScript are page painters. PDF makes it possible to exchange documents and to display them on-screen on disparate systems and to maintain the appearance of the page. As such, the markup languages present little direct overlap of function with SGML. There is some head-to-head competition between PDF-based viewers and SGML-based viewers, but the functionality and application of the two are quite different.[10]

Applications where appearance-type markup is sufficient or preferred are typically design- and layout-intensive and short, like an advertisement or a brochure. For the most part, PDF and PostScript are complementary to SGML as descriptive languages suitable for some print and screen output applications. There is a more extensive comparison between PDF and SGML viewers in Chapters 3 and 7.

HTML, SGML, AND THE WEB

Hypertext markup language (HTML) is an SGML DTD used for documents on the World Wide Web. The Web, as it is known, is an Internet application that allows users on *all operating systems* to view and navigate through and between multimedia documents stored all over the world, wherever there is an Internet server, using publicly distributed, high-quality, graphic and text-based browsers.

HTML has spread at an almost untraceable rate. Table 2.2 and Figure 2.8 show the growth in Web servers from June, 1993 to July, 1995. Estimates say that there are between 50 and 100 new Web servers each day.[11]

---

[10]Adobe has indicated that Acrobat will support some form of SGML markup in the future, but it is not yet clear what this support will entail.

[11]Figures on Web growth are from Matthew Gray, mkgray@netgen.

Table 2.2 Web growth

DATE	NUMBER OF SITES
June, 1993	130
December, 1993	623
June, 1994	1265
December, 1994	11,576
July, 1995	15,768

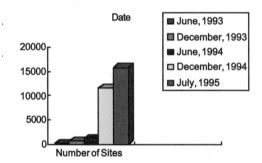

Figure 2.8 Web growth

The original HTML was not fully SGML-compliant, taking some syntactic liberties in the name of simplicity. Since that time, the advantages of full compliance—the ability to validate, to use SGML-based tools, to control conformance among them—have outweighed the (perceived) disadvantages. HTML2 is the current level of most Web browsers. The next version, HTML3, will be fully compliant with ISO 8879, adding strong support for math and tables, which will make SGML officially and without question the backbone of the largest distributed hypertext system in the world.

While most of the early applications of SGML were in large-scale government and industrial settings, the Web, sometimes called the largest vanity press in the world, has taken off as a grass roots phenomenon. The Web exemplifies much of what is most useful about SGML—cross-platform hypertext and multimedia—and it is no accident that this Internet "killer app" is SGML-based.

It is extremely important to understand that the cross-platform compatibility of the Web stems from standardization of *data*, not of applications. As long as the markup language used on the Web remains open, nonproprietary, and uniform, anyone can write a conforming application for any platform, and all data can be viewed and exchanged without translation. This equilibrium would be threatened by widespread use of nonstandard data types to extend the capability of a single vendor's application. A common data format maintains the level playing field on which the Web has thrived.

Two of the in-depth case studies in Chapter 4 look at Web sites, one a worldwide clearinghouse for volcanologists cataloging volcanic activity, research, and publications, the other, Intel Corporation's online component technical data.

HYTIME

HyTime, short for Hypermedia/Time-based Structuring Language, is an SGML application and an ISO standard, ISO 10744:1992. HyTime provides a common document architecture for time-based applications like music and video and for many aspects of text as well. "Common document architecture" means that all HyTime-conformant SGML documents approach certain design issues, like how to code hypertext links and how to describe video segments, in the same manner.

One way to look at HyTime is as a convention for good practice in the use of SGML.

This common approach allows applications to operate on conformant documents in a predictable manner. HyTime was created as a method of generalizing the linking and synchronization of multimedia within the framework of SGML. There is nothing contained in the HyTime specification that could not be accomplished in non-HyTime conformant SGML. One way to look at HyTime is as a convention for good practice in the use of SGML. While created to standardize the way music and time-based media are coded in SGML, HyTime also has application in hypertext.

Like SGML, HyTime is only slowly attracting tools and applications. Like SGML, the first HyTime tools were not end-user applications but HyTime-compliant parsers and processing engines. Like SGML, HyTime opens up whole new areas of interoperability and application and, like SGML, HyTime will undoubtedly develop in ways not foreseen by its composers. Finally, like SGML, simple HyTime applications and concepts are easily grasped, but its application to larger-scale products and implementations requires a greater investment in time. Fortunately, there are several new books and tools that make the standard accessible.

MAKING IT WORK

SGML differentiates pieces of text, imposing clear boundaries between flexible, unambiguous containers. With SGML, information can be described, manipulated, and associated in multiple, variant structures and storage units that have no predetermined relationship to the BLOB or to the container known as a "file." This notation permits a much needed differentiation in function, storage, and structure.

In current electronic and desktop publishing, you create content, you manage that content, and you format that content for print all in the same container—a file or group of files—using one tool or type of tool. SGML fractures this congruity and extracts from it specialized tools that create content, tools that manage content, and tools that output and format content.

The repercussions of this change reach from work group computing into distributed publishing into database management. With a notation to define and track entities—a formal construct in SGML, but here also used in its plain English sense—a work can be composed of pieces drawn from all types of media—words and pictures written, vocalized, and recorded over time.

It Is Not a Magic Pill

There once was a major aeronautics manufacturer whose staff understood all the advantages of SGML, having spoken to several vendors. They bought what they thought was the core of their system, in this case, an editor, and proceeded to customize it until they had the graphics and document handling, printing, and storage capabilities that they required. They were quite happy with the system and quite proud—as they ought to have been, having spent 3 million dollars on the "customization."

This is no fairy tale—they woke up one day to realize that they had created a product many times more complex than the one they had bought and their dream system, of which they were so proud, began to take on a nightmarish quality. As the demands of maintaining and supporting the system grew, they realized that they were not prepared to become full-time software developers.

This story is true, but it is already history—the off-the-shelf tools and the expertise available today are many times more sophisticated than they were then. No one needs to spend this kind of money on system integration any longer, but the moral of the story is still valid. SGML is a system of notation, and a powerful one. Acquiring one tool with SGML capability does not make a production system with all the features and advantages of a structured information-processing system.

SGML Tools

SGML-encoded data requires new types of tools, sometimes different from the tools of traditional publishing and data-handling applications, sometimes working in concert with them. We can project the new tools and the familiar tools of publishing and data processing onto the structure/process diagram to create a map of the universe of SGML tools (Figure 2.9).

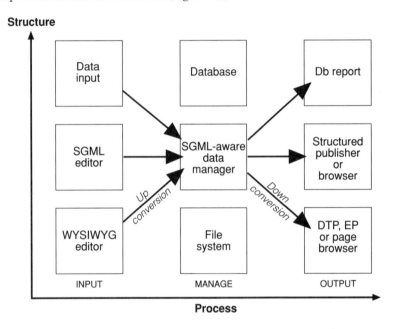

Figure 2.9 The universe of SGML tools

The "latitude" and "longitude" on this map are degree of structure (energy level), shown vertically, and the stages of the publication process (time), shown horizontally. The basic premise is that as information moves through the production cycle, it adopts various levels of structural complexity. Different tools map onto different sectors of the diagram. These are shown in greater detail in Chapter 3.

This idealized division gives us nine blocks on the map. As significant as the blocks themselves are the paths traveled between them. Starting with unstructured word-processing files, bringing them up to SGML, then outputting them from a composition engine would trace path 1 in Figure 2.10. Starting with native SGML, maintaining the information in SGML, and outputting it with an SGML-aware browser would trace path 2. A simple, actual system might look like Figure 2.11. Several other configurations are described in the following chapters.

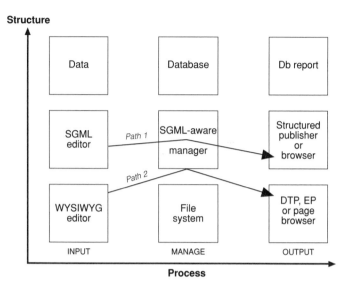

Figure 2.10 Structure/process diagram with paths traced

By splitting up the functions of content creation and content design—separating, once again, writing from page layout and traditional typography—structured information precipitates enormous efficiencies in production workflow. By transcending the file as the ultimate structure of a document, this movement towards format-independent processing lets the computer manage information with the same ferocity with which it has managed data and numbers in the past. The tools used to accomplish this are described in the next chapter.

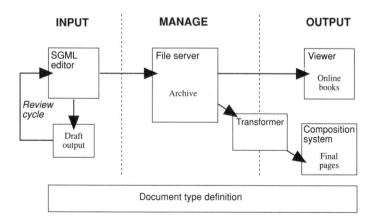

Figure 2.11 Simple system block diagram

3

Who Buys What?
Tool Types and Products

Warning: If you are going to read one chapter and only one chapter looking for an accurate picture of SGML, *do not* choose this one to read.

This chapter merely gives you the pieces. How to collect them and paste them together, how to decide whether to edit in native SGML or to convert from another format, whether to use current tools or to buy new ones, to incorporate a database manager or to set up a system based on file management—all this comes later. First it is necessary to understand the pieces, to understand the many new types of tools being created to work with SGML.

We can describe the universe of SGML tools as having the same regions as our structure and process diagram—regions that correspond to the input, management, and output phases of production and to the vectors that connect these regions.

Like all classification systems, the division into tool types in Figure 3.1 is only a convenience. No simple classification can be completely just to all tools because of the rapid evolution of the tool market. The companies known last year for excellence in one sector of the market—editors or browsers—are moving aggressively into the other sectors, adding products that complement their original line.

The expansion of capability in SGML-based tools is changing fundamental production processes and product definitions, not simply adding more widgets and fussier foobars to existing applications. New tools are coming out weekly and new tool types quarterly. Recent additions include editors that work on a database storage model and browsers that provide sophisticated queries; specialized converters that tailor SGML output for powerful composition engines; off-the-shelf products that use two-step conversion methodologies; and CASE-like tools for data design.

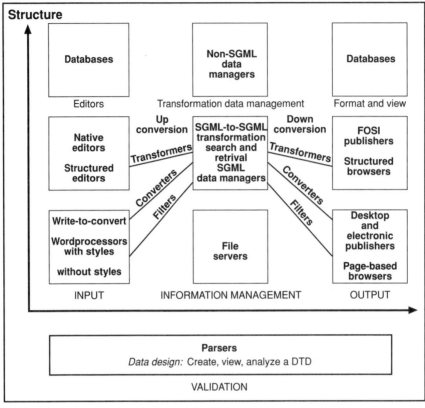

Figure 3.1 Tool map

Each category of tool in this list was, at one time, populated by just one or two groundbreaking applications—some still are. Certainly, the span of time between when I am writing this and when you are reading it will see new products introduced and a redefinition of product capabilities and categories. What follows is an explanation of the primary features of each type of tool mentioned in Table 3.1 and how each tool type fits into the larger picture of SGML-based production and data management.

Caveat: This is not intended as a thorough review of any product or as an endorsement of any product or of one product over another. Giving a rigorous, blow-by-blow, feature-by-feature description and comparison is the proper task of the weekly and monthly computer press. Some tools are mentioned by name and vendor here to illustrate specific capabilities or because they define the category; I have included a full list of tools and vendors with contact information, arranged according to this classification, in *ABCD... Resource Guide B*.[1]

---

[1] *ABCD... Resource Guide B*, the guide to tools and vendors, will be continually-updated on the Thomson Web site, see www.thomson.com under Web Extras.

***Table** 3.1 Tool types and their functions*

FUNCTION	TOOL TYPE
Data design and validation	
Validation	Parsers
Data Design	Create a DTD
	View a DTD
	Analyze a DTD
Input tools	
Editors	Native editors
	Structured editors
	Write-to-convert
	Database output
Up-conversion	Off-the-shelf
	Home-grown tools
	Service bureaus
Information management tools	
Transformation	SGML-to-SGML converters
Data Management	Search and retrieval
	Non-SGML-based managers
	SGML-based managers
Output tools	
Down-conversion	Filters
	Output converters
Format and View	Desktop, electronic publishing
	FOSI publishers
	Browsers
System integration	**Integrated tool sets**

The development of the DTD—the information architecture—affects the entire production process, so in this discussion, DTD tools are presented first. This is followed by the other tools, roughly going from input through output. There is a brief consideration of the role of integration products, consultants, and system integrators after the tool descriptions.

The newest category of tools is that designed to work with the World Wide Web. Initially, Web tools were HTML tools, by definition. Today, the demand for richer search and retrieval capability, more complex document types, and better navigation has led to tools that make *all* SGML, not only that encoded according to the HTML DTD, accessible over the Web. A short section on Web-specific SGML tools completes the chapter.

DATA DESIGN AND VALIDATION TOOLS

In this category, we will consider two types of tools—parsers and data design tools.

Parsers

An SGML parser is a software application that reads and processes both document instances and document type definitions. Parsers were the first SGML-based applications. In fact, presense of a parser defines an SGML application—without a parser, there is no SGML-based application.

There are two types of parser defined in the standard. A *conforming* parser is one that can process an SGML document without introducing errors. Paraphrasing Annex B of the standard, a conforming parser must:

- Distinguish markup from data

- Insert entities where referenced

- Interpret optional SGML features and variant syntax, if used

- Pass processing instructions to a processing application, if present

- Track element hierarchy within the document[2]

In addition, the ISO standard defines a *validating* SGML parser as "a conforming SGML parser that can find and report a reportable markup error if (and only if) one exists."[3]

When a DTD is parsed, the parser looks at the constraints in the SGML declaration, constraints such as the character set employed and the syntax applied—what characters can and cannot be used, what characters are reserved for markup itself—and capacity, a system for determining the memory required for process-

---

[2]Goldfarb, 1990, Sec. B.2, p. 20.

[3]Goldfarb, 1990, Sec. 4.329, p. 215.

ing a conforming document. When a parser looks at a document instance, it references the applicable DTD, then checks the document instance for conformance.

One output of a validating parser is an error report that points to invalid markup within the submitted file. Consider a DTD (`leroy.sgm`) that defines a document (`test`) with elements A, B, and C where the elements must appear in that order (`A,B,C`) in the document. Each element can contain parsed character data (`#pcdata`):

```
============== leroy.sgm ==============
<!doctype test [
<!element test o o (A,B,C)>
<!element (A,B,C) - o (#pcdata)>
]>
```

Then, consider a short document instance with an element out of place:

```
<A>A's text
<C>C's text
<B>B's text
```

OmniMark, a validating parser, reports the error when it parses this document against its DTD:[4]

```
===================== leroy.log ===================
OmniMark V2R5
Copyright, (C) 1988-1995 by Exoterica Corporation.
omnimark —
SGML Warning on line 6 in file leroy.sgm:
A start tag is not allowed at the current point, but will be
allowed through error recovery.
The element is "C."
The open elements are "TEST" and "A."
The following element can end: "A."
The following element can start: "B."
Text is allowed.
```

Translated, the report says that you cannot have an element C following an element A, that only the element B can begin at that point. The full parser report notes the complementary error—that element B cannot begin while element C is open—and reports errors in tag minimization, the rules that allow a document to skip the end tag (`</A>`) for certain elements. In addition to checking conformance, finding and reporting markup errors with no false positives, validating parsers can check a DTD for ambiguous statements, violation of capacity limits, and other syntactic errors.

---

[4]This example provided by Exoterica Corporation.

Note that the parser does not validate the *data* within any file. A parser can check that a memo contains AUTHOR and DATE elements and that there is data in each element but it cannot verify that a name is spelled correctly or that a date is current. SGML syntax identifies pieces of text and the relationships between those pieces so that applications can process the pieces without ambiguity. Applications use the second output of a parser, the Element Structure Information Set, to process the text.

Parsers vary in the clarity of their documentation and their reports, as well as in their speed and performance. There is currently no certification for parser conformity, although the National Institute for Standards and Technology is considering creating a formal testing and certification procedure.

Unless you are doing a high degree of system integration and customization, it is unlikely that you will purchase a parser as a stand-alone piece of software. Parsers are routinely bundled in SGML editors, converters, transformers, and data management tools. All the applications listed in *Resource Guide B* are SGML applications and, by definition, can process an SGML document. Those with a validating parser are noted.

Most parsers that are bundled into an application are either the Sema parser (Mark-It), the OmniMark parser from Exoterica, or the public domain parser sgmls, written by James Clark. sgmls is written in C and can be compiled to run on PCs and most Unix boxes. The source code and various compiled versions are available on the Internet from the sources listed in *Resource Guides A & B*.

Data Design and Validation

A DTD, like any SGML document, can be written with any editor that will output ASCII text. Today, most DTD programmers and analysts work with specially designed tools and utilities. These tools and utilities range from free scripts that embed HTML codes into a DTD to make it viewable in a Web browser, to sophisticated CASE tools that translate graphic structural representation into valid SGML code and SGML code into graphics. The collection is eclectic but can be categorized as tools used to:

- Create

- View

- Analyze

document type definitions.

DTD Creation Tools

So far, the only entrant into this field that is more specialized than a simple editor is CADE Near & Far from Microstar International. CADE stands for computer-aided document engineering and is a sort of groupware CASE tool for DTDs. The front end, sold separately, is a template for Lotus Notes that assembles and organizes input from diverse members of a production team. This body of knowledge is then passed to Near & Far, which suggests methods to organize the input into a corresponding DTD. Without Notes, the designers enter and manipulate the DTD directly, using the graphical tools to piece together and define a structure and content model in a tree diagram with dialogue boxes for the content model and attribute and entity definitions.

Near & Far defines symbols that represent SGML syntax down to the smallest detail. In Figure 3.2, the open and filled squares in front of date and keyword indicate that there can be one and only one date in a header and that a header must contain one or more keywords. The open dialogue boxes show the method of selecting and placing elements into the DTD.

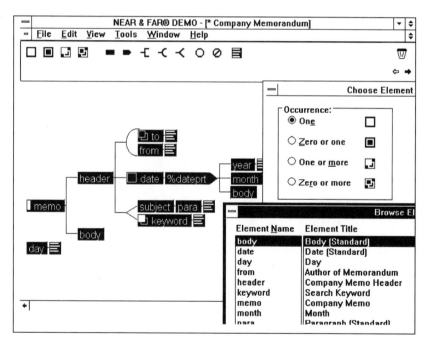

Figure 3.2 Near & Far showing memo DTD

DTD Viewing Tools

Viewing tools vary in the features that they offer and the elegance of the offering. The features that distinguish these viewers one from another are:[5]

- Number of elements visible

- Access to full element specifications

- Number of levels visible

- Attribute display

- Attribute values display

- Display of sequence and occurrence

- Display and expansion of parameter entity references and short references

- Print output

- Cut and paste capability

Some viewers provide additional navigation and analysis tools.

DTD Analysis Tools

Somewhere between tools that let you look at the DTD and tools that create and validate it are a large number of utilities that help you analyze the DTD. Many of these are home-grown tools using the Unix text manipulation utilities of perl, sed, and awk and are announced and made available free of charge on the Internet. An example would be true-dtd, a "modest tool implemented in perl" and announced in January of 1994 on comp.text.sgml. This tool analyzes the recursive elements in document type definitions and outputs a report listing the final set element and entity declarations.[6]

Debbie LaPeyre, of ATLIS Consulting, makes the point, however, that the largest number of these tools and utilities never make it into the public eye, that they constitute the custom bag of tricks that every consultant and DTD programmer brings to a job. Her very welcome, and public, contribution to this field has been to describe and categorize the types of tricks employed by a seasoned SGML analyst. These tools:

- Recognize patterns in documents

- Classify markup objects

---

[5]Adapted from LaPeyre (1994).

[6]Announced as available from ftp.ifi.uio.no as /pub/SGML/DEMO/true-dtd.pl.

- Count elements and attributes of the same name, recursive elements, and tokens

- Compute the depth of recursion and the degree to which an element is reused

- Warn the user of mixed content models and recursion

Other tools extract the information from DTDs that later forms the basis for DTD documentation. These reports document tag names, what elements can contain which elements and are contained by which elements, and how attributes are used. Most useful are indices and cross-references to a DTD (LaPeyre, 1994).

INPUT TOOLS

There are several ways to get your data into SGML. Since SGML-encoded data is, at its most basic, just a character stream, any editor that can output ASCII characters without extraneous, embedded codes will do. Editing SGML in an ASCII text editor can be effective in a development environment where the objective is to work directly on the markup itself. This is also practical in certain phases of production work.

Specialized tools for getting information into SGML range from native SGML editors to converters working in tandem with non-SGML editors. In the past two years, the territory between these extremes has been populated by a number of tools that provide some degree of structure and validation to material as it is written, then complete the process with a conversion or transformation.

Editors

Although the boundaries are shifting all the time, we will consider four distinct types of editors used to get new material into SGML:

- Native editors

- Structured editors

- Write-to-convert editors

- Databases

The distinction is made on the basis of SGML validation: How complete is it and when does it occur in relation to the writing process? Native editors provide complete SGML validation and immediate feedback on that validation during the writing process. Structured editors provide a high degree of feedback on structure during writing, although they do not meet the full standards of an SGML parser. Write-to-convert editors may constrain input in some fashion but do not validate input until the written document is exported or converted in a separate step. Database editors do not have internal SGML validation but provide complete control over output structure.

Some Web-specific HTML editors, those that were born of SGML editors, have a degree of validation and would fit into the first category except for the fact that they work only with the HTML DTD. Others are closer to a word-processing model and fit into the second or third category

Native Editors

Native editors are the best known of the SGML tool groups—for all the wrong reasons. Those new to SGML often ask: "Which editor should I buy?" and expect that the "right" answer will set them up with this new technology. For those who may have turned here looking for the answer to this question, it bears repeating that you cannot swap an SGML-based editor for your current composition technology and expect to go into SGML-based production.

These editors share only a superficial resemblance to word processors. WYSIWYG editors compress the input, management, and output functions. SGML editors, on the other hand, are input tools and are not designed to replace the output functions of word processors and electronic composition systems. While they have many of the text-handling capabilities of word processors, it would be better to think of them as text-base population engines or data editors. They share as many properties with a database as they do with composition tools like WordPerfect or Quark Xpress, with which they are more often compared.

What defines an SGML editor is that data can be validated against a DTD during the editing process.

What defines an SGML editor is that data can be validated against a DTD during the editing process. What this means is that the conformance of the data to a specific DTD can be checked and enforced as the data is input or at any time when checking (parsing) is invoked by the user.

These editors are structure-aware. The user cuts and pastes or types into a container defined by the start and end tags of an element and inserts objects (entities). All the while, the editor is checking the markup to make sure that it follows the rules of the DTD. One consequence of being structure-aware is context-sensitive tagging. Figure 3.3 shows a screen from Author/Editor from SoftQuad. The insertion cursor is between the nested tags for AUTHOR and SURNAME. The Insert Element window lists the elements that can be entered at that point in the document structure according to the document's DTD. The element for first (given) name is highlighted.

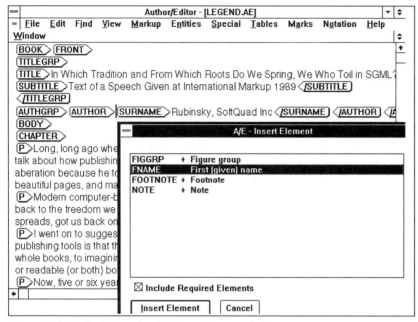

Figure 3.3 Author/Editor showing Insert Element window

While all commercial SGML editors use on-screen formats to give the writer visual feedback, on-screen format has no fixed relationship to the eventual format of the data. For example, a third-level head tag might show up on the screen as red, flush left, and italic to make it easy for the writer to see. In print, the third level head might be flush right, 18-point Gill Sans, or it might be in any variety of formats depending on the media. As far as the SGML editor is concerned, the screen format is a convenience and has no direct bearing on the output data stream. Figure 3.4 shows the Adept Editor from ArborText with on-screen format and SGML tags.

This validation and this indifference to format ensure conformity with the DTD and the format independence of the data. In addition, they enable an entirely new approach to data creation. Just what this feels like and what repercussions it has for writers and for production are discussed in Chapter 9 and throughout the case studies in Chapter 4. Here, suffice it to say that the ability to check data structures is the foundation in an edifice of new and important editorial capabilities.

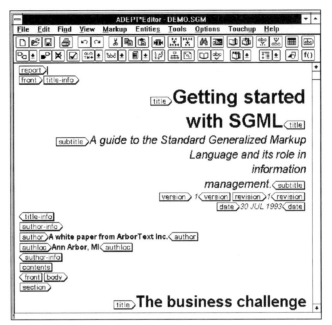

Figure 3.4 *Adept Editor with on-screen format and SGML tags*

Commercial SGML editors are highly competitive and are upgraded regularly. All include validation, but they vary in many respects, one from the other. Most of them include most of these features:

- Validation—The editor can invoke a parser to determine if the data conforms to a referenced DTD. It can interpret the parser's error messages, flag the offending passages, and provide reports and various assists to correct the situation.

- Context-sensitive tagging—The editor limits the selection of tags and objects (elements and entities) to those that are valid in the current context. The selection of valid tags changes dynamically as the document is edited.

- Accepts an arbitrary DTD—Some editors require that the DTD be compiled into an internal format, but any valid DTD can be used with the editor. This distinguishes SGML editors from Web-specific HTML editors. (See the *Special Note on Web Tools* at the end of this chapter.)

- Flexible on-screen formatting—Users can specify the on-screen appearance of elements and entities.

- Immediate or invoked parsing as a selectable feature—Immediate parsing is on-the-fly, as-you-type, structural validation; invoked parsing allows sections to be input without validation, then checked when the user is ready to have them checked.

- Customizable application program interface (API)—Users create site-specific defaults and routines that enhance the production environment. Sites use the API to define the Enter key to mean "insert an end-paragraph tag and a start-paragraph tag" mimicking the action of WYSI-WYG word processors.

- Edit multiple, simultaneous documents, records, or document fragments—Users edit on a database model, working on sections of a document without calling up and validating the entire document.

- Unlimited unique tag names, tagged elements, and levels of hierarchy—There are no internal limits on these beyond what the DTD defines.

- Graphics handling—By the rules of SGML, all editors allow inclusion of graphic elements by reference, but none are required to give the user any clue to what the graphic looks like or how it will be composed in an eventual publication. By the requirements of the marketplace, many commercial editors now launch a graphics browser or editor and allow the user to view the referenced graphic.

- Flexible table models—There is more than one way to slice and dice a table in SGML. Most editors allow the user to work with different, standard table models and render the model more or less easy to work with. See the discussion of tables and why they remain problematic in Chapters 6 and 7.

- Draft output—Although beyond the responsibility of any native SGML editor, competitive editors print hard copy for review, giving the user varying degrees of control over appearance.

The Database Model and the Word-Processor Model

One important feature of the SGML editor is its relationship to data management—how it handles files and documents. Most SGML editors work on the assumption that the immediately relevant collection of data, what one wants to edit at one time, will be in one file, that the single file will contain one document, and one single document will occupy one file. This assumption is so basic to word processing that it is only now being challenged by new SGML tools.

The challenge for implementers is to provide the editorial interface to data irrespective of the file storage structure or data management scheme. Many sites integrate separate editorial and data management tools. Smart Editor from Auto-Graphics offers an alternative to the file-centered approach to SGML editing.

Smart Editor (Figure 3.5) is an SGML-aware editor that can work on several records simultaneously, verifying the record structure of each against a DTD. These records may or may not be from a single file; they may, in fact, be stored quite independently. At this writing, the capabilities that Auto-Graphics has incorporated into the editor developed for Columbia University Press put it into a class of its own, sort of a hybrid browser and editor, where the DTD drives the user interface. Paul Cope, VP of Publishing Services at Auto-Graphics, does not think that Smart Editor competes with the other SGML-aware editors, but that it meets a different need. Smart Editor, for example, does not have the same capabilities to work with large pieces of text that the other editors do. (See the portrait of Columbia University Press in Chapter 4.)

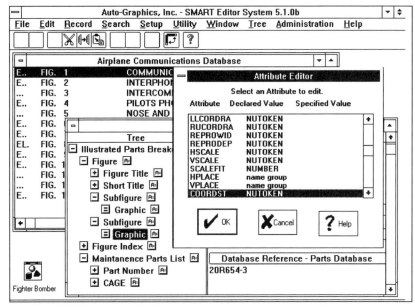

Figure 3.5 *Smart Editor showing database views and attribute editor*

Structured Editors

Structured editors are those that act nearly like native SGML editors on the surface but that, underneath, manipulate and store data in their own, non-SGML, format-based markup. Many of the native editors also translate SGML out of ASCII into other, internal formats for processing and manipulation, but the structured editors explicitly require input and output filtering and conversion for both DTDs and SGML documents.

Until recently, there was only one product in this category—FrameBuilder from FrameMaker[7]—a product that represents a compromise between native editor and unstructured word processor. Frame has built a structured document editor with its own, internal format that disallows some of the features of SGML in the name of greater utility while not compromising structure to the point at which output of fully compliant SGML is problematic.

FrameBuilder shares many of the features of the native editors, and improves on some of them. Instead of offering the either-or choice of rules-on or rules-off, FrameBuilder lets the writer write whatever the writer wants to write, indicating where the data complies or does not comply with the document model. Like the natives, FrameBuilder has context-sensitive element choices so that only valid elements are available. This does not prohibit invalid structures—the author is able to cut and paste at will—but it discourages them and lets the author know when one has been created. Figure 3.6 illustrates a FrameBuilder screen with a document structure window showing tags, text, and document hierarchy.

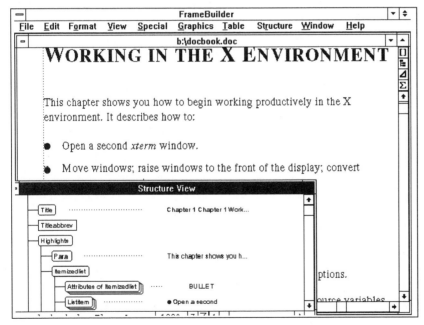

Figure 3.6 FrameBuilder edit window with structure view

---

[7]As this book was going to press, it was announced that Frame was repositioning its SGML entry as FrameMaker + SGML, a native SGML editor, to be released at the end of 1995. The characteristics of FrameBuilder, used here to define structured editors, still apply to the category of tool.

By working in the Frame/MIF (Maker Interchange Format) environment, FrameBuilder sidesteps the mapping of SGML to output—a stage that can add to the cost and confusion of beginning to work with SGML. FrameBuilder resolves elements-in-context and generates implied text on screen so that the writer sees exactly what the document will look like when printed. Another significant feature is the resolution of cross-references and footnotes so that the author sees how and where they will appear. And entities, which would appear in some native editors as character strings, are resolved in FrameBuilder so that instead of seeing `&plusorminus;` the writer sees ±.

This tool category differs from the structured editors... in the degree and timing of validation—how far you can go without feedback on what you are doing.

Tag Wizard for Microsoft Word 6.0 from NICE Technologies of France is an application built on top of Microsoft Word that loads an arbitrary DTD and allows the user to map a style template to the DTD via a dialogue box. The interface shows the open element and its content model; it expands parameter entities, and looks one element up and down the hierarchy to see what is legal to add. In fact, it is difficult to see why Word 6.0 with Tag Wizard should not be considered a native SGML editor, except that it stores the data internally in Word 6.0 format.

The recently announced, currently in beta, Near & Far Author from Microstar, which also works on top of Word 6.0, will probably fit in this category as well.

Write-to-Convert

This is a new category evolving product-announcement-by-product-announcement. Using these tools, the writer writes in a proprietary word-processing format using templates and style sheets to achieve some consistency of markup. Then the word-processing file is output (converted) to SGML, using a predefined set of rules called a *mapping*. This tool category differs from the structured editors not in the native storage format but in the need for an explicit output mapping and, perhaps more significantly, in the degree and timing of validation—how far you can go without feedback on what you are doing. Before the document is exported, a writer may get little more feedback from the tools in this category than he or she would from any word processor.

Both of the big players in word-processing, Novell (WordPerfect) and Microsoft, have thrown their hats into the SGML arena with such an entry. Novell has already replaced its first SGML offering with a product that moves closer to a structured editor. The first release, Intellitag, was little more than a two-way conversion template for the word processor. As this chapter was being written, the company announced a major upgrade to their SGML capabilities to be called WordPerfect 6.1 for Windows SGML Edition. The new product will supersede Intellitag.

The Microsoft product, SGML Author for Word, maintains the Word environment and data format for information creation. It requires DTD-specific mapping between source and target before a writer can create a document in SGML, as would any legacy conversion. The Word add-on gives the writer some guidance on which elements are valid at each point in the document. Then, during conversion, the program inserts elements to correct omissions and reports changes to the author. From that point, the author can import the document into any SGML editor or can rework the document in SGML Author for Word.

Several vendors of SGML-based technology have announced products that will work in concert with the Microsoft product. These include an SGML editor with a Word-like interface called Enactor from SoftQuad and a conversion program called SureStyle from Avalanche (Interleaf). Enactor cleans up exported SGML files and SureStyle prepares legacy documents for SGML Author for Word templates.

Database Output

It does not make much sense to go out of your way to write in a database in order to convert, ultimately, to SGML unless you have other compelling reasons to input into a database. In fact, as the Standard & Poor's case study and the Utah AOC sketch show, it makes more sense to use SGML as the front end to a database (because of the flexibility it offers to writers), than to use a traditional database to produce SGML. But, if you have compelling reasons to input into a database or your material is already in that format, then the output of that database can become your SGML input.

All major database products have output and report writing facilities that can wrap SGML syntax around the information on its way out of the database. While this offers no immediate SGML validation, the regularity of the database ensures that once a relationship between output and markup is established, it will remain valid.

Up-conversion

This is how word-processed, desktop-published, and typeset files get into SGML. It is a major topic in SGML-based production and figures heavily in the following chapters.

Basically, all conversion works using algorithms and recognition of implied structure in the source document. Together, these can be considered a conversion engine. Off-the-shelf or home-grown engines give you the required power, but you, the user, have to build the vehicle for the engine to drive.

The most exciting and significant developments in conversion tools over the past two years have not been from new engines, but from new vehicles that change basic conversion algorithms into efficient production machines. Some new tools use multistep conversion methods based on intermediate transformations. Others give writers immediate feedback on the results of the conversion and then help them change the source document.

Before describing these tools, let me clarify the use of the terms *conversion* and *transformation.* The SGML community has settled on conversion to mean bringing data from an unstructured state, usually in a proprietary word-processing markup, into a structured state. In this stage, conversion implies "up" conversion, adding to the energy level on our energy-level diagram (Figure 1.2). Transformation implies passing from one type of structured information to another. Using transformation tools in conversion recognizes that not all SGML markup has the same degree of structural energy. Figure 3.7 compares conversion and transformation in terms of structural energy levels.

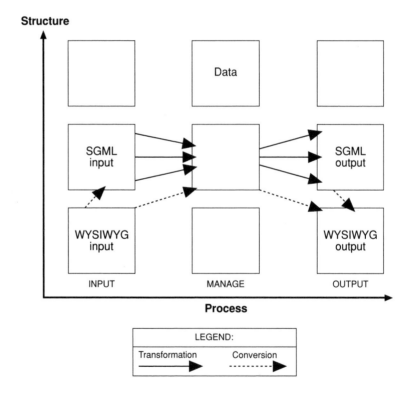

Figure 3.7 *Conversion and transformation*

Originally, transformation tools took SGML marked up according to one DTD and altered it to comply with a second, different DTD. The relative ease of this transformation, the relative ease of adding richer structure and deeper hierarchy through transformation tools led to their widespread application to the related problem of converting legacy documents into SGML—going from simple SGML markup to more complex and richer SGML markup, raising the energy level along the way.

This two-step or multistep conversion takes data with appearance-based markup, like RTF or PostScript, and maps it to a simple, intermediate DTD. The Rainbow DTD, created by David Sklar of Electronic Book Technologies, Inc., and placed in the public domain, is such a DTD.[8] The Rainbow DTD describes, in rigorous SGML, the appearance-based format of the original document, something like the way documents are marked up in HTML. This DTD is a relatively easy, hands-off conversion target from most word-processing markup.

There are various "rainbow-makers," conversion templates from popular formats, in the public domain. With the Rainbow markup, the converted legacy document has consistency and syntax that allow it to be manipulated as a structured document and transformed to a second, structure and content-based DTD.

This two-step methodology is in widespread use today, not always using the Rainbow DTD. OCLC (Online Computer Library Center) goes through Microsoft's RTF to achieve consistency, then into a simple SGML DTD, which it enriches with OmniMark.

Off-the-Shelf Software

Although termed "off-the-shelf," there is no conversion engine that you can buy in a box that can input your legacy data and output usable structured documents without effort comparable to a programming effort. None of the available products can be put into production without customization and configuration. Once this effort is complete, operators with no programming experience can invoke these converters, but don't expect to achieve that end without putting in the programming time required up front.

Some conversion products provide a user interface that can run the engine once the mappings are complete; others retain a command line interface. FastTag from Avalanche is an example of the first type (Figure 3.8) and the OmniMark programming language from Exoterica is an example of the latter (Figure 7.4, p. 261).

There are a growing number of conversion tools that provide some degree of programmed conversion and then provide some editorial access to either the source or target documents or to both to complete the conversion. Although very different one from the other in terms of their total capabilities and design, DynaTag from EBT, SureStyle from Avalanche (Interleaf), Passage Hub from Passage Systems, and some of the write-to-convert editors each perform this type of conversion.

---

[8]If format-based DTD sounds like a contradiction in terms, it is a sign that you understand what a DTD is supposed to be. The Rainbow DTD is for the transition to a structure and content DTD; it is not intended as a destination.

Figure 3.8 is a composite of five FastTag screens showing the application interface (1), the source text (2), the mapping of data design to visual objects (3), the actual converision program (4), and the resultant SGML file (5).

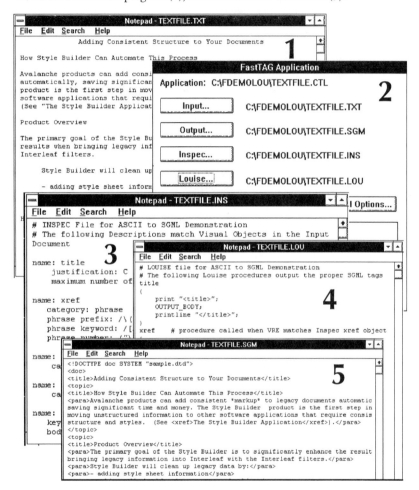

Figure 3.8 FastTag screen sequence

Converting your data is a major undertaking and a major expense, whether you do it in-house, with your own staff and resources, whether you invest in outside consultants and software, or whether you farm out the project to experts at a service bureau. Chapters 5 and 8 consider further the cost and methods of data conversion.

INFORMATION MANAGEMENT TOOLS

The relationship between SGML-defined data, databases, and document and data management is not easy to pin down and it is changing rapidly. SGML treads heavily on traditional database turf and the two overlap and blend in theoretical and practical terms. Here, SGML departs from the concerns of traditional publishing and reveals itself to be an information-handling language, not just a handy way to describe type to a computer.

It is difficult to categorize document and data management functions in relationship to SGML. The neat categories of data processing are not always the useful categories from a user's or system administrator's point of view. In this arena, relational and object-oriented models have more in common than not. What matters is the relationship of the data manager to the encoded data itself: Is the SGML placed in objects, stuffed into relational fields, held as BLOBs or defined solely by the SGML tagging itself?

Furthermore, distinct functions in the user's view might stem from a single tool in the system view. The functions of query, retrieve, route, view, and compile for export can be done by a single tool that stores data, has a search and retrieval engine, and manages metadata. Alternately, functions that appear as one to the user may result from the integration of several tools. For example, the directive to "find this and show it to me" can be handled in a single application, a browser with search capabilities, or by separate database, search, and viewer applications.

All these tools do some combination of finding and tracking, moving around, and managing data. In addition to transformation, the things that document and data managers do can be reduced to:

- Store
- Find (search)
- Fetch (retrieve)
- Identify, annotate, and track metadata about the document

These basic functions combine to produce workflow management, search and retrieval, and document management tools. The capabilities made possible by these basic functions include the following:

- Who, what, when of workflow management—this can be tracking jobs, tracking component pieces of a complex task, tracking the progress of the overall deliverable

- Revision control and tracking

- Check-in, check-out of any size chunk of information

- Document and text generation from stored elements

- Security and effectivity, including version control

- Link management within expanding circles of association: document, data collection, archive, network, and Internet

- Precise linking—to finer granularity than file or document

- Concurrent access to different parts of a document by multiple users

- Ability to work on part of document without retrieving the whole

- Information reuse; shared content

- Integration with SQL, other database managers

Although there is much overlap and many thin, gray lines between them, for convenience I have grouped the tools with these features and functions into the categories of transformation, search and retrieval, non-SGML data managers, and SGML-based data managers.

Transformation

Transformation tools manipulate, rearrange, and reconfigure SGML-coded documents. As such, transformation tools carry SGML further from the realm of a handy typesetting utility language and into the mainstream of information processing. They open the door to the larger possibilities inherent in SGML-to-SGML transformation tools. As Erik Naggum put it on the Usenet discussion group comp.text.sgml when commenting on the introduction of the Rainbow DTD, "... working *within* SGML is perhaps even more important than getting into, or getting out of, SGML." The Rainbow DTD and the rainbow maker utilities are just one category of transformation tool, designed to work on up-conversion rather than on lateral transformation.

What can an SGML transformer do? To demonstrate just this point, a workshop at SGML '93 (the Year of the Transformer) presented a set of problems to transformer developers and conducted a session examining their solutions. The problem set included:[9]

- Normalization—Take a document with markup minimization and apply full, non-minimized markup.

- Split entries—Take a dictionary and split it into files, one file for each dictionary entry; track entry file names.

- Collapse/expand hierarchy—Transform a hierarchical document, described by a hierarchical DTD into a flat instance, and then regenerate the hierarchical document. (In the hierarchical instance, levels are indi-

---

[9]Problems were submitted by the participants in the shoot-out: Electronic Book Technologies, Inc., Exoterica, Inc., AIS (Berger-Levrault). For vendor contact information, see *Resource Guide B.*

cated by nesting elements; in the flat instance, levels are indicated by explicit instructions.)

- Data-type validation—Provide additional validation beyond that required by an SGML parser. The example given was for typed cross-references, those that target a specific kind of information, like a figure or a table. A parser checks that there is such a reference, but not that the reference is the correct data type. A transformer can check the reference type. A transformer can also validate use of empty or floating references used to mark revisions or versions and resolve references to external documents.

- Table conversion—Different DTDs have different ways to designate tables. Transformers can convert one method of markup to another method. Another exercise called for the transformers to count rows and columns and insert that information in the text stream.

- Generated text—Automatically generate referenced text, such as references to section titles where the text is not in the document instances but is referenced explicitly in the markup. Control order, type, and format of generated numbers and dates using SGML attributes.

- Extract and sort text—The example given was to find, extract, and present in alphabetical order all figure captions.

- Line breaking—Determine document line length according to a simple rule set. This is easy for a transformer and renders all SGML editors potential database population engines.

- Comply with ICADD—Implement the SGML guidelines for DTDs from the International Committee for Accessible Document Design. Document instances compliant with these guidelines can be published in large print and Braille without further processing.

Some of these operations, like counting table rows and columns, have clear applications in publishing. Inserting the row and column data would be useful when exporting SGML text to a typesetter, for example. But the same exercise could have wide application in data processing if the items counted were significant not only for their eventual arrangement on a page but for their meaning as well. In a data-processing application like the Utah State Court system, rows in one table might be warrants issued and rows in another context might be warrants denied.

While the transformation function is clearly defined, the tools that perform transformations also tend to have other uses. Thus, the Balise language used for transformation also does data conversion and has operators for search and retrieval. Once mastered, OmniMark has many applications—it can be used for both conversion and transformation. It is one of those tools that becomes its own verb, as in "to OmniMark your data."

Search and Retrieval

Often mentioned as if they were one, search and retrieval are, in fact, separate functions. Once found, control over what is retrieved passes from the search engine to a data manager. For example, you might search for an occurrence of "framus" in a procedure, but that does not specify what you want to retrieve and what you want to do with it once you retrieve it. You might want just the word, the word in context of the sentence, or a paragraph section, chapter, or article, depending on whether you are doing a QC (quality control) check on framus references, writing a framus maintenance procedure, or researching the history of the framus.

This point was made by C. Michael Sperberg-McQueen (1994) in his talk on databases at SGML '94. In that talk, he listed the things that search engines do, split into two categories—those things unique to SGML-aware search engines and those that are common to all search engines:

SGML-based engines search on:

- Elements, attributes, and entities;
- These in context;
- Links;
- Sections marked with empty elements;
- Any combination of the above, plus keywords and character strings and proximity searches and each of these, in context.

Not-necessarily-SGML-based engines search:

- For proximity
- With Boolean operators
- Character string
- Full-text

Search engines vary greatly in how they implement these capabilities. The tools available for managing SGML data combine some measure of searching with the ability to extract and manipulate the identified piece or pieces. Combined with the ability to search and manipulate not only the data but the metadata, these basic functions make possible a tremendous variety of operations.

Non-SGML Data Managers

The file management system of default—your operating system file manager—is just fine for most word-processing and for some SGML applications. With the advent of open, nonproprietary text markup and exchange, an information storage and retrieval mechanism that is based on more than the file's name, size, format, and date of origin is often called for.

Not surprisingly, SGML-based data storage has turned to the prevailing data-handling systems for finer control over storage. Both relational and object-oriented database technologies have been applied successfully in-house and in commercial software. The basic design here is to manage through traditional object-oriented or relational means, while data is stored in arbitrary but well-defined containers. Figure 3.9 shows Parlance Data Manager from Xyvision with a window for metadata and sections of the publication on a desktop.

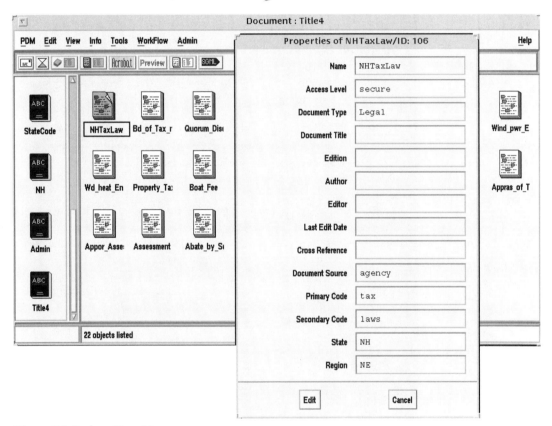

Figure 3.9 Parlance Data Manager screen

Relational databases handle SGML-encoded text as a series of BLOBs (for "Binary Large Objects"—their term, not mine.) Each BLOB corresponds to a unit of the text; it could be an element or an entity or a section between two pointers. Information about the BLOB is the metadata which is stored in a relational database and used to manipulate the BLOBs. Typical metadata would include the version, security, and change history for a segment of text.

Object-oriented databases index and store objects. They can store SGML-encoded text in these objects, adding a layer of structure over the SGML, or they can define as objects those entities and elements already defined by SGML syntax. The database manager controls these objects through the model of structure present in the SGML markup.

Both object-oriented and relational databases can store and manage SGML BLOBs or objects alongside other digital files containing text in another format or graphics, audio, and video in an integrated application.

SGML-based Data Managers

Explicit tagging of entities and elements adds functionality to search engines without trading performance or accuracy.

Data storage and handling programs that fit neither the object nor the relational paradigm have been designed to operate directly on the SGML-encoded data. Here, all transactions are mediated by queries and instructions to SGML elements, attributes, and entities. These support the hierarchical and contextual nature of SGML documents without breaking the data into other units or building tables based on metadata. Barry Schaeffer of ISI, which builds a data management system on top of software from OpenText, calls this "managing at the level of the data design."

The OpenText search software operates on the native SGML format, so that the strength of the search is dependent directly on the quality of the SGML markup, as well as the ability of the search engine. Encoding data in SGML has a significant impact on the trade-offs of a search engine, assuming that the search engine is able to take advantage of the SGML-encoded semantics. Defining the context of each part of a document takes much of the burden off the engine itself. Explicit tagging of entities and elements adds functionality to search engines without trading performance or accuracy. Figure 3.10 is a composite of three screens showing an Open Text query with the query screen (1), query results (2), and retrieved text (3).

Information Dimensions, Inc., has been in the information retrieval business since it released the first Basis Server in 1973. Recently, the company has added an SGML-based search engine, Basis SGMLServer, to its text search and retrieval products. IDI considers SGML component-level management in information retrieval to be a breakthrough in information management.

Yet another view of SGML storage states that SGML *elements* are the structural building blocks of a document while SGML *entities* are the natural storage units of a database. Hence, a new group of products is emerging called entity managers. Standardizing entity management facilitates direct, unmediated exchange across applications and across data repositories. Entity management is addressed by some HyTime applications and was the subject of the first Technical Resolution passed by the Technical Committee of SGML Open.

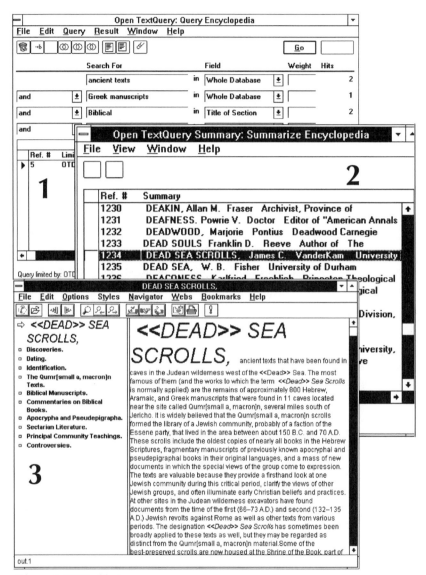

Figure 3.10 OpenText query sequence

OUTPUT TOOLS

Most output tools are "down and out" tools—they release the energy in structured SGML markup to create a markup that enables a specific function. The exceptions are output processes that are driven by SGML data directly, without cashing in any of the high-energy features of the markup. FOSI—format output specification instance—publishers are driven directly by SGML data as are certain on-screen viewers. FOSI publishers are described with the other print tools and the SGML-driven browsers are considered with the other on-screen tools, below.

Down-conversion

Down-conversion is a means to a specific end. While up-conversion is like putting your money into the bank—you don't necessarily know what you are going to do with it when you use it—down-conversion is like taking money out of the bank—you don't do it unless you have a specific end in mind. Consequently, there is very little call for general-purpose down-conversion tools; most of the tools that perform this part of the cycle are integrated with a specific type of output, like an online browser or print compositor. Most of the traffic in this area goes through home-grown converters and filters.

One exception is the product called SGML Enabler from SoftQuad which has just been released. Enabler takes SGML files and maps them to Quark External Style tags so that SGML-defined features can be quickly coded in the desktop publishing tool. The clear advantage here is that what goes into Quark already has all ambiguity removed.

For now, most sites use home-grown output conversion using the same tools as for input conversion, such as the one described in the case study on Adams & Hamilton in the next chapter.

Other than specialized tools like SGML Enabler, the choices for down-conversion tools are the same as they are for up-conversion, with the distinction that none of them are taxed so heavily in this direction as they are at input. The tools break down into these categories:

- Off-the-shelf filters, SGML transformers, and converters, including general-purpose conversion languages

- Service bureau conversions

- Home-grown filters and conversions

In the following sections on outputting to print and to screen, we will look at how these tools operate and at what is available.

Output to Print

The most important point to consider when you look at tools for print composition is that, if the tools you use today are sufficient, then they are probably the same ones that you want to use after you convert to SGML-based publishing. Assuming that you have no reason to change your composition system, there is still the question of preparing the files.

Service bureaus are beginning to accept and process SGML data—you give them your SGML-encoded data and your DTD and they typeset it for you—an arrangement that sounds like what was envisioned for SGML in the first place. Penta has announced that in response to demand from its client base, it has created interactive batch-processing of SGML in its DeskTopPro high-end publishing software, for which 80 percent of the users are service bureaus.

FOSI and style sheet publishers differ in certain respects, but the intention behind each of them is that you create a style mapping once and use it many times. FOSI publishers also resolve inherited styles, generate implied text, and apply format markup. They do this using a file written in SGML that translates each element and element-in-context to specific format parameters. In addition to the usual control of a batch publisher, FOSI publishers can impose element-specific conditions, such as "Keep all warnings on the same page as the step that follows."

Currently, the FOSI is required only for deliveries to the Department of Defense, although certain other publishers have chosen to use them. (See the Ericsson case study and the Canadian Code Centre sketch in Chapter 4 and the general discussion of FOSI publishing in Chapter 7.)

DSSSL was approved in early 1994. There are as yet no DSSSL products. Whether or not vendors move to support DSSSL, it is clear that the long delay in its publication has not held back the industry.

> *FOSI and style sheets publishers differ in certain respects, but the intention behind each of them is that you create a style mapping once and use it many times.*

Output to the Screen

Output to the screen from SGML means taking the encoded data and presenting it through a viewing or browsing application using local media on a local drive, on a network server, or through online services like the World Wide Web. In each case, the SGML data is mapped to a set of display characteristics and converted to the internal format of the browser. Browsers vary greatly in terms of the type of data they accept, what the user can do with them, how easy they are to use, and the cost of distribution.

This summary looks at only those types of browsers specifically designed to take advantage of structured documents. Suffice it to say that there is no single "best" tool for viewing SGML documents, that different tools are appropriate for different situations. Although browsers built for structured data have a higher level of performance than do those built to accept unstructured text, there is no reason not to port SGML to an unstructured viewer if that is what the situation calls for.

Browser Characterization

It is impossible to characterize this field without an expansive feature list, a sure sign that the field is rich and that consumer interest is high. What follows is a general characterization of browsers, with special reference to their SGML capabilities, in terms of:

- Support for structured documents, support for SGML
- Delivery platform
- Format conversion
- Navigation
- Display
- Search and retrieval
- Cost
- Other important considerations

Support for Structured Documents, Support for SGML

Indications of support for structure include structured navigation features such as tables of contents, cross-references, and other hyperlinks. Measures of support for SGML include the ability to support an arbitrary DTD, HTML, and HyTime linking and the ability to query SGML constructs directly.

You might expect a close relationship between support for structured documents and support for SGML, but this is not necessarily true here. Some browsers, without reference to SGML, build levels of structured navigation (for example, SmarText from Lotus); others, with nominal SGML, give no support to structured navigation (for example, NCSA Mosaic and other HTML browsers. See the *Special Note on Web Tools*). Folio Views builds tables of contents on the fly from headings, whether the input is from SGML or not. Oracle Book is a highly structured browser that is beginning to support SGML—this was their stated direction.

The Air Force classifies Interactive Electronic Technical Manual (IETM[10]) browsers in five levels according to their interactivity. At the lowest level is the bit-mapped page image, scanned pages with no capability higher than scrolling a static image. At the highest level is the "true IETM," which includes awareness of logic states and the ability to follow conditional statements (if/then/else). High-level IETMs are used for technical troubleshooting and maintenance. While commercial browsers have many of the capabilities of a Class V IETM, none has all these capabilities available without customization. Some, however, have been used off the shelf for Class IV IETM presentation.

---

[10]This is pronounced "I-eat-'um"—I guess there are so many acronyms in mil-spec publications that you have to do something truly extraordinary to get noticed.

Delivery Platform

None of the other tool characterizations have mentioned platform because it is clear that you must select tools that integrate into your production environment. But, for electronic distribution, availability of cross-platform support can be a major qualifying factor. You control the degree of homogeneity in your production environment but you do not have the same degree of homogeneity or of control across your users' platforms.

In this respect, browsers vary greatly. Some are limited to a narrow range of delivery platforms, others are available across a wide range of platforms.

Format Conversion

Online browsing products differ in how you get your material into their browser. Builders of these tools have learned in the last few years that they must clear a migration path if they expect the world to beat its way to their doorstep. The result is a growing number of tools provided by browser makers that help you get your stuff into their product for publication. The actual steps required to get into the browser can include conversion, compilation, indexing, and compression.

The general-purpose conversion tools used for up-conversion can be used for browser format conversion as well. In addition, there are special-purpose tools like the OmniMark Toolkit for Folio Views, that have just one target, in this case, the Folio Flat File.

Browsers differ in the degree of tinkering required to import data. Depending on the application, the degree of hands-on required for an electronic book build may or may not be a factor in choosing a browser. For many tools, once a mapping to a particular DTD is set up, any future document that conforms to that DTD can be imported directly.

At this writing, Explorer and Panorama from SoftQuad stand alone in that they load any SGML file without mapping, preliminary conversion, or tinkering. The document is loaded directly, together with its DTD, to a default or custom style sheet. In the browser, the user can then customize the display in a variety of ways.

Navigation

Although the idea of hypertext dates back to Vannevar Bush and the end of World War II, on-screen navigation in commercial software meant the "scroll the blob"[11] method of a word processor until HyperCard was introduced by Apple in 1987. Since that time, the notion that you should use the power of the computer to help you navigate a document has taken hold. Today, all online viewers must satisfy the user's desire to point, click, and be somewhere else. Yet, they must inoculate the user against the disorienting, lost-in-space cybersickness that comes from indiscriminate jumping around.

[11] Bob Glushko's image.

Browsers are getting to be very good at this, offering extensive linking and navigation with a stable frame of reference and a path back to where you were. Features include structured views of content that double as hyperlinks; annotations and user-generated bookmarks, both text and audio; and user-generated links. Browsers can be configured with navigational paths laid out by theme or topic, scripted by the producer or by the user. Browsers differ in the degree to which they support any of these features in graphics, across documents, in libraries of documents, and outside of document libraries. Some offer user-created annotations and paths stored in the file or associated with the file and automatically reattached during updates and revisions.

Figure 3.11 shows the DynaText browser from Electronic Book Technologies, Inc. The table of contents on the left can be expanded and contracted and used to navigate the document.

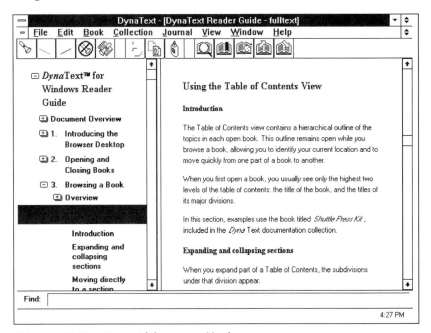

Figure 3.11 DynaText with hypertext table of contents

Display

All browsers, except those that work from display-only characteristics, like Acrobat, map screen styles, but they vary in how easy it is to do so. They also vary in the degree of latitude the producer and the user have in setting up the screen interface.

Display capabilities of an online browser include some of the same factors that characterize print composition:

- Independent control over type and layout for all elements;

- Inheritance of styles in context; and

- Generation of implied text, such as figure and chapter numbers.

Browsers differ in their ability to open multiple windows onto the same document and to display multiple documents simultaneously.

There is a large degree of difference in how browsers handle graphics. The greatest degree of flexibility is being able to choose to display a graphic or not; to place it in-line with the text or in a separate window, and to be able to size and crop and pan and zoom the graphic independently of the text.

Multimedia capabilities—the ability to display sound and moving pictures— also differ from browser to browser.

Search

Browsers can incorporate some or all or none of the characteristics of a search and retrieval engine. See the list of features given above under *Information Management Tools*. Browsers differ in their ability to retrieve arbitrary, multiple documents from a remote or local source and to display them on the fly.

Cost

Cost is not just a question of more or less, but of the pricing model itself. Some Web browsers are free, although professional, paid versions that include extra features and support are available. Others charge for the build but not for the run-times; others for the runtimes and not for the builds. Obviously, your usage model determines what pricing structure is workable.

Other Considerations

Other considerations that distinguish the wide range of browsers include:

- Reuse of style sheets
- Text editing
- Conditional views
- Customization
- Persistence of annotation and configuration across revisions
- Multi-language support

The ability to reuse an online style sheet for print is described below. The type of information that is useful in both media includes some forced page and line breaks, generated text, and resolution of inherited characteristics.

The browser might or might not support editing of files. Edits—as opposed to annotations—are reflected in stored and reexported SGML. Some browsers provide conditional views into the text, dependent on versions, security level, password protection, and levels of expertise. Some browsers provide an API so that the interface can be customized for individual applications.

Say you create links within your document and build paths through it and annotate it, and customize the style sheet and the display—what happens to all that when you do your next revision? Browsers vary a great deal in the degree to which customization, annotation, and linking persist across revisions.

And, finally, browsers differ in their support for languages other than English, particularly Asian languages that require two-byte characters for display.

INTEGRATION, CONSOLIDATION, AND CONSULTATION

There are three trends in integrated SGML software:

- Preconfigured, integrated products from more than one vendor

- Integrated product lines from a single vendor

- Integrated production systems built on modular products

Examples of the first type of integration are the Toolkit for Folio Views which includes an OmniMark script for transformation, and the integration of Avalanche's FastTag technology into a number of applications, including SGML Author for Word.

In addition to teaming up to provide better integration, all major SGML software vendors are moving toward integrated product lines. Avalanche, known for its conversion software, has been acquired by Interleaf; Electronic Book Technologies, known for its high-end browser, has introduced conversion and data management tools; SoftQuad, whose flagship product is an editor, has introduced browsers and composition utilities; and Frame, known for its editor and publishing software, also promotes its viewer and has acquired Curo Technologies, a developer of document management technology, as well as the high-end publisher Datalogics; Microstar, maker of the DTD design tool Near & Far, is introducing an editor; and the list goes on.

Integrated systems that cover some or all of the same bases are offered by a number of companies. All these build their integrated environment on top of applications, such as editors and conversion software offered by other manufacturers. They differ in the range of applications that they integrate and the quality of the interface that they offer.

The premiere example of this third type of integration is Passage Pro from Passage Systems. Passage Pro is an off-the-shelf integrated system that is the "glue" that holds together editor (WYSIWYG or native SGML), converter, database, and composition systems for print and electroic books. Unlike the others, it is an integration *platform* that can support tools from many vendors, not a single preconfigured tool set.

The Passage Pro interface is built with an understanding and appreciation for workflow integration and how that is affected by the move to SGML. For example, a writer using an SGML editor under Passage Pro can call up a browser or a composed picture of the finished page to get immediate feedback on the outcome of the markup they are creating with the editor. A writer using a WYSIWYG editor can use Passage Pro to convert and debug the document. During debugging, when a conversion filter detects an error, it writes an error message to the screen. The writer double-clicks on the error message and the editing position cursor goes to the error in the source document. This integration of technology and process masks the distinct tool types described in this chapter from the end user.

Figure 3.12 shows the Passage Pro desktop and query interface.

SGML tools are moving toward greater off-the-shelf integration of function and the vendor consortium, SGML Open, actively promotes interoperability.

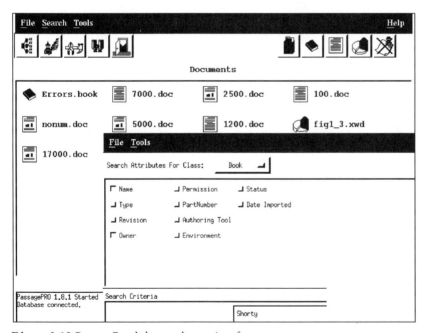

Figure 3.12 Passage Pro desktop and query interface

SPECIAL NOTE ON WEB TOOLS

Web tools fall into the same basic categories as other SGML-based tools with two distinctions: First, they are usually hard-wired for the HTML DTD; second, the sheer size of the user base changes the economics of production and distribution. Tools that were hard-wired to one document architecture were deprecated years ago in the SGML user community. How curious then that the size of the Web should revive demand for just such tools—editors and browsers that work with one simple document type, HTML.

Yet this situation has provided a great venue for SGML tool vendors to strut their stuff. Sort of like the impresarios of the Metropolitan Opera putting on a show at Madison Square Garden, SGML tool vendors have modified and simplified their products and made them available free or at low cost for the Web. SGML tools adapted for the Web have the advantage that, as HTML grows in sophistication, these tools are ready to exploit its added capabilities without relying on proprietary markup.

SGML tools adapted for the Web have the advantage that, as HTML grows in sophistication, these tools are ready to exploit its added capabilities without relying on proprietary markup.

SoftQuad's HoTMetaL is a scaled-down version of Author/Editor. While simpler than its SGML counterpart, it provides a richer feature set than many editors built from scratch to work with HTML. HoTMetaL could be considered a native *HTML* editor. It gives the author feedback on structural validity but works only with HTML, not with arbitrary DTDs.

Several SGML tool vendors now offer Web servers, which might be thought of as the document management tools for HTML. DynaWeb from EBT takes structured information from DynaText books and down-converts it to HTML on the fly.

There are several classes of Web browsers. While the Web browsers that read HTML alone cannot compete in strength of navigation and support for long documents with SGML-capable browsers, they add some essential features to the mix of tools available. These are low-cost, cross-platform support for retrieval of remote documents coupled with content-based, rather than page-based, structure. The more interesting browsers, from our point of view, are those that provide an Internet gateway for SGML data.

The announcement and demonstration of the Olias browser from HaL in early 1994 was the first attempt to integrate Web and SGML data through one port. Olias provided unified access to HTML and SGML from local and remote sources. Their usage model was, "Look it up on your local drive in an SGML-based browser; if you do not find it or if you find a link to a more recent source, click and go to a remote Web site and retrieve the update, or additional information, in HTML." All through one interface, transparent to users whether they were in a local SGML document or a remote HTML document.

The usage model for Olias is that you start out locally and invoke the Web as needed. In contrast, SoftQuad's Panorama, a subset of Explorer, is an application invoked by the HTML Web browser when it encounters an SGML document. In this model, you start browsing HTML Web data and, when you encounter SGML (a file with the .sgm extension,) your HTML browser invokes the local viewer to display the remote data. Figure 3.13 shows the NCSA Mosaic browser in the background and Panorama invoked in the foreground. The Panorama window shows document structure on the left and the document with SGML tags revealed on the right.

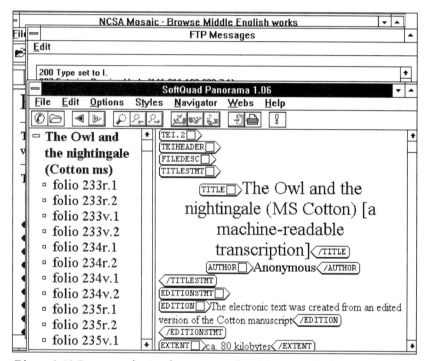

Figure 3.13 *Panorama showing ftp messages and Web browser in background*

Intel Corporation is one company taking advantage of this capability to capitalize on its investment in SGML component documentation. You can download the viewer from the Intel Web site and use it to browse Intel documents. See the Intel case study in Chapter 4.

Of ordinary, garden-variety Web browsers, without SGML capabilities, there are too many, and they are covered too well elsewhere, to devote space to them here.

For more information, Chapter 7 on system design includes a short section, *Getting on the Web*, and *Resource Guide B* lists Web tools that handle SGML as well as HTML-specific tools from SGML vendors.

4

Who Uses It?
Case Studies in SGML

If you are going to read just one chapter, it could well be this one. But here, too, there is a caveat:

Caveat: Anyone looking for a picture of a typical SGML implementation, look elsewhere.

These case studies represent the richness and diversity of real-world implementations, not a mythical norm. Their range shows the flexibility and adaptability of this language and the skill and creativity with which it has been applied. These cases were chosen because, through their diversity, they cover a great many of the areas being addressed by SGML today.

There are many criteria that characterize diversity. The measure I chose was the type of information handled because this, above all else, is the parameter with the most far-reaching consequences for those considering SGML. Three years ago, several full-length case studies might have represented the range of SGML application. Today, it would take dozens of studies to accomplish this. To give a sense of the range of application, I have supplemented the seven portraits with a series of less detailed sketches. Figure 4.1 illustrates the contrast in structure and process presented by some of these cases.

Inclusion in these studies does not imply endorsement of a methodology, a vendor, or a tool, and omission does not imply lack of it. Many vendors not mentioned here are as rich a source of expertise and technology as those that are. The primary criteria for balancing this list was the type of information and the industry, and then the production method—not the specific tools used.

Each case has at least one feature that is typical; each has a feature, or more than one, that could be considered unusual. There are budgets here in the millions of dollars and budgets in the hundreds of dollars. Butterworth is most typical in the use of tools—the staff there both convert and create SGML; they use a document manager designed for SGML and they have renovated—reengineered—their production process. They output to a wide range of formats from SGML files and they see the future in devices and delivery modes that we have not heard of yet. Does this match any of the other implementations described here? Not really.

Ericsson uses FOSIs* which, if you learned about SGML through the DoD, is the way one is supposed to do things. Does this make Ericsson typical? Hardly. Columbia University Press subcontracts a large portion of the data design and management, including parts of the process that are canonically done in-house. Intel teamed up with its competitors in the semiconductor industry; together these companies invested two years of time and energy and over $2 million in an industry exchange standard before beginning to design their internal SGML-based production systems. Adams & Hamilton are typesetters and designers, the kind of right-brain thinkers who are not supposed to get along with SGML, yet they think it is the best thing since movable type. And, to represent what is being done with HTML, I have chosen an Ivy League Professor Emeritus who has chosen to become a self-publisher.

Each of the portraits presented here answers a little differently the question "Who uses SGML and why?" The most compelling aspects of the full-length portraits are:

- Butterworth Legal Publishers—Output to multiple formats without redundant coding; sophisticated data management eases editorial work;

- Ericsson Inc.—Improved writer productivity; manufacturing-style workflow; international, cross-platform compatibility;

- Columbia University Press—Document database used to create new, spin-off products; subcontracted SGML technical work; produced successful commercial CD-ROM;

- Standard & Poor's—SGML as front end to relational database; information-handling application;

- The Electronic Volcano—World Wide Web HTML site; nontraditional academic publishing;

- Intel Corporation—World Wide Web SGML site; part of industrywide effort to provide electronic data directly to customers' databases and simulators without rekeying or conversion;

- Adams & Hamilton—Typesetters using structured information efficiently for traditional products.

---

*Format Output Specification Instance, a style sheet written in SGML, see Chapter 7 and the case study.

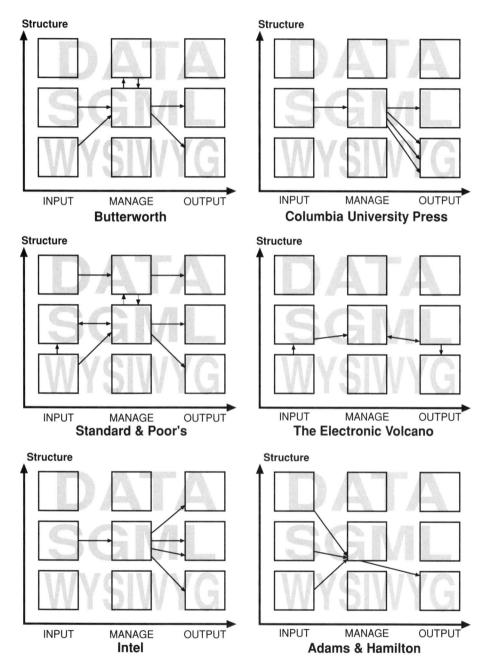

Figure 4.1 Contrasts in structure and process

The purpose of the sketches is to fill out the picture of who is doing what with SGML. The primary reasons for choosing these subjects are:

- Cinemania—Mass market, multimedia application using sophisticated production techniques;

- The Women Writers Project—Scholarly text archive with industry standard data type targeting niche research market;

- Utah Administrative Office of the Courts—Electronic case filing automates a new area in the courthouse, with a profound impact on users;

- InfoUCLA/ICADD—Use of SGML facilitates data conversion and provides improved access for those with print disabilities;

- Publications International, Inc.—SGML database used for streamlining commercial publishing;

- Sybase, Inc.—Smooth transition to use of SGML in multisite, cross-platform electronic technical documentation;

- Canadian Code Centre—Government application using state-of-the-art document engineering tools.

While the utility of the language has been established, we are, collectively, still in the early stages of experimental system design. It is much too early to say what is "proper" SGML workflow, data design, or system design. What might be a heresy in one system may lay the groundwork for a style of implementation that solves real problems in another environment. It would be misleading to read any single case, even if it is an implementation that closely matches your own, and to conclude that this is a standard way of doing things.

BUTTERWORTH PORTRAIT

Table 4.1 Butterworth Legal Publishers, Major Works Division

Industry	Legal publishing
Products	State statutes, rules and regulations, court decisions
Media	Print, CD-ROM, proprietary online
Key players	Michael Schwartz, Vice-President
	Mary McRae, Editorial Systems Manager
	Bev May, Manager of Typography

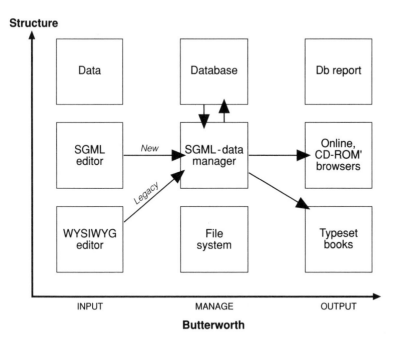

Structure

Figure 4.2 Structure and process at Butterworth

Basic Scenario[1]

Butterworth Legal Publishers is what the name says. Butterworth is part of the international publishing conglomerate Reed Elsevier; the Major Works Division is in northern New England. The editorial group, when interviewed, worked out of offices in Orford, New Hampshire, a small town on the Connecticut river, 110 miles north of the Massachusetts border.[2]

I told Mary McRae, Editorial Systems Manager,[3] that I was going to subtitle this case study "Getting There is Half the Fun," and she laughed and said "Getting there is *all* the fun. Once you are there, anyone can do it." Transition and conversion, merging and managing information in flux, are the constants of legal publishing, even more so when publishing electronically from a database, and even more so when the system itself is in transition.

---

[1]This portrait is based on visits to the Orford site and interviews with Michael Schwartz and Mary McRae.

[2]This office of Butterworth has since moved to Salem, New Hampshire, and, as this goes to press, is in the process of moving yet again, this time to Charlottesville, Virginia. How the group fared through the moves and why they moved are questions quite apart from the case described here.

[3]Since February, 1995, after this case study was completed, a consultant with Xyvision.

The structure and process, the whole rhythm of traditional legal publishing is built around the frequency of update and the frequency of publication. As rules and regulations are issued, the publisher issues supplements that accrue until a critical mass is achieved. Then a new volume is published with the supplemental information—additions, deletions, and changes—integrated into the existing text. Adding nontraditional products—CD-ROM and online delivery—changes the tempo and makes the orchestration of the whole more complex.

Butterworth has an exclusive contract with the State of Alaska to edit and publish rules and regulations. This became the company's first project to be published from an SGML database. The contract required delivery of hard copy plus a file for use with the state's own internal online database. The size of the print job is approximately 10,000 pages.

Butterworth had already issued one CD-ROM before the move to SGML, the 18,000-page New Hampshire state statutes. The markup for this disk was proprietary to the vendor who supplied the search engine, coded the data, and mastered the disk. While the disk met an urgent market requirement,[4] the data was not reusable because it was in the vendor's proprietary format.

To produce the first disk, Butterworth either replaced codes in the typesetting files or downloaded the files to a word processor, where new codes were inserted by hand.

To produce the first disk, Butterworth either replaced codes in the typesetting files or downloaded the files to a word processor, where new codes were inserted by hand. Both methods were time-consuming. Then they created a page-based format and joined these legacy data files with new material. Court opinions, unlike the statutes, are still cited by page number. To maintain these page-based points of reference, the CD-ROM had to include page break tags, which meant that every time a printer page ended with a hyphenated word, the word had to be moved to the next page. Sometimes these revisions generated *more* revisions by generating further changes in composition. None of this work was billable; it was just added production cost taken off the bottom line. Michael Schwartz estimates that one third to one half of the total project cost was eaten up in this format conversion and that substantial portions of this work would have been unnecessary if the data had been in SGML.

While this experience inclined the management at Butterworth toward SGML, it was their second non-SGML electronic delivery—the one for the State of Alaska—that made the business case sufficiently compelling. To deliver Administrative Codes for their Alaska contract, Butterworth had to comply with the state's in-house format and the format was idiosyncratic and problematic. It called for each line of text to have 72 characters—no more, no less—a blank space at the end of every line, and markup with what came to be know at Butterworth as the "seven deadly codes." Hitting such format requirements from

---

[4]A competitor had already produced a CD-ROM. The statutes themselves, being in the public domain, are not subject to copyright. Only the value-added editorial work, such as adding descriptive titles to numerical statutes, can be copyrighted.

a traditional markup system was costing Butterworth their profits, and then some. Schwartz estimates that the editorial and production work on the second format was equivalent to starting from the naked text, as if it retained nothing from the editorial and production work on the original print product.

There were two initial goals for the conversion to SGML: first, to eliminate the costly and redundant coding of information delivered in diverse formats; second, to maintain a competitive market position by offering timely, up-to-date publications in diverse media. The current aim is to deliver yearly supplements to the basic print volumes, quarterly CD-ROMs, and continuous delivery of online data. On CD-ROM, all data will be merged, not divided into basic volume and supplement as it is in print. Eventually, they would like to see clients have direct access to their database.

Tools

Table 4.2 In-house hardware and software

VENDOR	TOOL TYPE	TOOL NAME	QTY
Digital Equipment Corporation	Workstation; network servers	5000/240	2
(various)	Personal computers	486/66, 16 MB	13
ArborText	SGML editors	Adept Editors	13
Xyvision	Relational database	Parlance Document Manager (PDM)	13
Xyvision	Formatter	Parlance Publisher	6
Bridge Builder	Database manager; 4GL	Bridge Builder	1[a]
Exoterica	Conversion tool	Omnimark	3

[a]One developer's license; unlimited run-time licenses.

Butterworth uses a combination of off-the-shelf products integrated and customized for their environment and their data. Their primary consultant has been Xyvision, the provider of the document manager and typesetting software. Their data conversion vendor, Data Conversion Laboratory (DCL), is a second consulting resource and has worked closely with them to create the current production system.

The Bridge Builder 4GL was not part of the initial system design. It was brought in shortly after system installation when it became clear that Butterworth needed the "second door" into the data that this product offered.

About half the editorial staff have workstations configured for SGML. The others swap locations when a project calls for them to use ArborText or Bridge Builder or Parlance Document Manager (PDM). This is adequate at the current level of production. As they take on more SGML work for other offices, they will expand the number of workstations.

Table 4.3 Contract services

PROVIDER	SERVICE	QUANTITY
Xyvision	DTD writing, system integration and customization	Yearly maintenance; "many" weeks for DTD, database configuration, legacy data conversion
Data Conversion Laboratory (DCL)	Legacy data conversion	5–10 percent of Alaska project; working continuously to convert balance of legacy data
Xyvision	Training on editor	One week, four people

About 5 to 10 percent of the legacy data for Alaska was converted by DCL; the balance, less complicated and less heavily tagged, was converted by Xyvision. DCL has handled a larger proportion of later conversions. Butterworth bought three OmniMark licenses, one for Unix and two for PCs, to increase the in-house conversion capability, but the extra licenses were not in use when this case study was researched.

Butterworth is moving to Folio Views as a browser for CD-ROM delivery because Folio has become a de facto standard in the legal industry—customers are familiar with it and expect it.

At the time of the original interviews, the group was still working closely with Xyvision, although not under a formal consulting contract.

Getting There

Given the task of taking the division from lead type to electronic typesetting when he went to work at Butterworth in 1990, Michael Schwartz feels it was a natural next step for him to lead the company to SGML three years later. During the Magna interregnum (the move to electronic typesetting in the summer of 1990), Schwartz changed the traditional workflow, which paid off again later in the move to SGML. Both steps reshaped processes and the division of labor, as well as bringing in new technology.

Before he came, typesetting and proofreading had been done at the production plant. Schwartz changed the demarcation so that the break occurs where the collaboration occurs. He describes the new division of labor this way:

> As long as the "look" of the page is up for grabs in any way, it is editorial. All those who collaborate on the look of the final page are editorial, including coding and proofing. As long as the page is still dynamic, it is editorial.

The rest—putting the coded text on paper—is production. At the same time, Schwartz moved some traditional jobs from paper to the keyboard. When it was time to move to SGML, the editorial staff were already accustomed to working in a typesetting file.

A key element of the transition process was identifying a vendor whose product fit their needs and who provided critical consulting services. Three years before the move to Xyvision, Butterworth had considered a high-end SGML production system, but Schwartz felt that the intermediate step of an electronic typesetting system like Magna was needed. In addition, Butterworth considered the SGML system considered at that time to be prohibitively expensive.

Then Mary McRae heard about Xyvision, a company with an experienced consulting staff that offered a less expensive, open system which was easier to integrate into the Butterworth environment. Xyvision spent over six months in a process of sales, education, and consulting with the staff and management in Orford before Butterworth committed to the project and signed a contract. At that point, the group in Orford had several SGML assets, according to Schwartz:

- Knowledge
- The choice of Xyvision as prime vendor
- An infrastructure plan
- A project plan

McRae's own training in SGML was an essential part of the transition. After they began looking seriously at SGML, she had a week of training in SGML at Xyvision. She had already, in her words, "gotten Goldfarb and Bryan and tried to muddle through."[5] While she knew the gist of the system, she got more of a sense of it from the training class. According to McRae, however, it was the first document analysis process that was the turning point in her understanding.

The system was phased in. The first SGML database product shipped out on January 5, 1994, about five months after the Xyvision installation, a year and a half after the initial contact with Xyvision. The last material was received from the state on December 5, 1993, and the typesetting file went to production on December 15. Different views of the sequence are shown in Table 4.4 and Figure 4.3.

---

[5]Goldfarb (1990) and Bryan (1988) are technical references to the SGML standard cited in *Resource Guide A*.

Table 4.4 Transition sequence

Fall '92	Contacted Xyvision
Spring '93	Contract signed w/Xyvision
Summer '93	Completed initial DTD First data out for conversion Installation of dB
Fall '93	Data back, installation and training on ArborText Creation of output translation tables
Winter '94	First product from SGML dB shipped

Figure 4.3 Transition bar chart

Preexisting conditions included:

- Commitment of upper management to structured information;

- Identification and initial training of key technical staff;

- Selection of pilot project;

- Identification of key conversion vendor.

The core editorial staff was trained using the first data that came back from conversion. Two editors and two typesetters received four days' formal training on the ArborText Adept editor. Although this training was good, the true initiation came with the actual work on the Alaska project.

Xyvision ran the first document analysis with Butterworth people sitting in; then McRae took over the role of facilitator. She picked it up quickly and coded the subsequent DTDs for Puerto Rico and New Hampshire. The database specification for the Xyvision database was a collaboration among McRae, Bev May, Manager of Typography, and their editors, "those who know the data inside and out."

DCL, the data conversion vendor, was an integral part of the phase-in. The conversion of legacy data is an ongoing process at Butterworth. There are potentially hundreds of thousands of more pages to be converted. When DCL converts a section, they also parse it. Of course, "parsed" does not mean "corrected" and there is cleanup to be done after every conversion. Schwartz had read about other conversion projects, and so he knew that no conversion is "hands-off" and was comfortable spending time to clean up converted data, deciding what to code and what to catch in cleanup, and what to give to a contractor or do in-house.

The system is still in transition. As this portrait was being written, the cleaned-up database from DCL is being merged with supplements that came in and were entered during the time the data was being converted and the editors are taking over more responsibilities from the typography group.

Being There

Table 4.5 Workgroups

GROUP	JOB DESCRIPTION	NUMBER OF PEOPLE
Editorial	Edit, proof, code, compose, convert—everything up to prepress	6
Typography	Part of editorial, 1 does SGML coding, 2 work on composed print files	3
Production	From prepress to printing	Offsite

When McRae says, "We're reengineering the whole editorial process, and SGML is the technology that allows us to do that," she's not just tossing around a popular buzzword. Changes in the organization of the workforce had already begun before the introduction of SGML, so it was easier to create a workflow that made sense with SGML. For example, when the expanded editorial team first sat down to do document analysis, team members were already accustomed to working together.

The most salient changes from the preSGML work environment stem from working with the Parlance Document Manager relational database. PDM affects every aspect of production, from the time when documents are logged in until they are typeset or mastered for CD-ROM. For that reason, we will look first at the document manager, and then more closely at the resultant editorial and production environment.

Document Management

Unlike some other legal publishers who publish loose-leaf, replacing individual pages as required, Butterworth compiles changes into supplements, which are then merged into a new bound volume. This feature of their paper publishing influenced their decision not to build a database of pages as some others have done, but to use Xyvision PDM 2.0 as a database of document modules, where each module is a logical component of the document.

Each section of a given legal text has a register number that determines if and where it goes in a publication. In the Butterworth DTD, register number is an attribute of the CREDIT element. Tagged modules of text are stored as BLOBs in the database. PDM copies the reference numbers from the marked section of the text into the metadata, stored separately from BLOBs. The metadata indicates which modules to extract for which publications. In other words, information about the information is stored separately from the information itself.

Butterworth creates and maintains a separate database for each jurisdiction. The metadata applies to each database. Keeping the databases smaller improves system speed. A piece of the metadata for each BLOB points to which DTD to use.

Each time a publication is updated, PDM maintains a complete list of changes in the metadata. When users consult the PDM history function for a chunk of data, they see when it was imported into the database and from what source, they see each time it has been changed and by whom and, most significantly for editorial, they see the actual version as it was before the change.

With PDM, Butterworth can run standard query language (SQL) queries but not full-text or Boolean searches. PDM keeps track of where sections are, what revision levels are current, and the document hierarchy. According to McRae, "PDM is used to build, edit, parse, and store metadata; not to handle it." To handle the metadata, she uses standard SQL commands, C programming, 4GL or, for a less programmer-intensive approach, or Bridge Builder, a fourth-generation language with a graphic user interface (GUI) that brings the art of querying the database down to a less technical level.

Bridge Builder has an easy interface that McRae thinks of as a second door into the data. It gives direct access to the metadata with a higher-level language than SQL. Supervisors can generate reports that help manage the publications, for example, reports that list every module within the database affected by a certain register. This report—all the modules affected by a certain register—becomes a volume or edition of the printed publication. PDM can do the same, but requires programmer-level work.

Each time a publication is updated, PDM maintains a complete list of changes in the metadata.

Editorial Work

Frequency of update for print is yearly; for CD-ROM, twice a year. When the full database is ready, online publication will be continual, almost instantaneous. Now print and electronic outputs are synchronized in terms of frequency of update and, not insignificantly, also in editorial content.

Working with an incomplete, transitional database, production work is still geared, primarily, to the print schedule. Huge amounts of new material accumulate. About one month before the last piece is due in, the staff shifts their effort from conversion and cleanup of the core legacy data to integration of the new pieces into that legacy core. When all the core legacy data is in SGML, editorial will add new material to the database as it comes in, entering and loading it into the database immediately. The database will always be ready to publish, in print or in CD-ROM.

As new packages come in for the Alaska project, the staff enter control numbers, which are actually lists of affected sections, in a word processor. Then, the work package goes to the editorial group to make the actual changes. The editorial group consists of the publications manager, editorial assistants, and legal editors. Under the old arrangement of work, these changes were made by the typography group.

Editorial Data Management

Typically, the editorial sequence is edit, parse, then file in PDM. When new material comes in, if it is relatively short, it is input directly into the ArborText editor and tagged while it is cleaned up by an editorial assistant. If it is longer, it is scanned and then imported and tagged and cleaned up.

Working with the data manager changes editorial work. With PDM, a copy is not a copy is not a copy. Some copies are copies, some are links. The distinction is this: copies that are "copies" exist twice, independently. Copies that are "links" are in the database one time, although they may be used many times. Editors must understand the difference. They must know if the section to be copied will have a life of its own, independent of the original, or if it is a slave in perpetuity and should be a link, not a duplicate.

Modules are parsed as they are entered in ArborText. Ordinarily, the DTD would expect to see the entire publication, not just a single module. The solution is based on use of a module tag. The DTD spells out that a module consists of a certain number of hierarchical levels. When PDM sends a document fragment to ArborText for editing, PDM wraps a module tag around the fragment. The wrapper is removed when the module is sent pack to the database.

Sometimes an editor must save a section without parsing, if it is incomplete when work is interrupted or if it is a subsection that cannot stand on its own.

This is possible with PDM and, as a consequence, when information is in the Xyvision database, it is not always valid, parsed SGML.

Some metadata is built, autoextracted by the customized PDM; other metadata is manually entered. A register number, which is part of the SGML structure, is extracted by a PDM program script that runs each time the module is stored. An index entry that is not a recurring keyword is extracted by hand.

Editorial Markup

The reaction of the editors to the new system was positive from the start. Instead of a cryptic typesetting code, they see a tag with a name, like "history" or "annotation section," which remains consistent from publication to publication, independent of the type style applied. When the editors did format-based markup, the codes were associated with a typeface that changed for each job. The same piece of text, a section header, for example, might have been UF15 in one job and UF27 in another. Now, the tag name is based directly on content and is consistent from job to job, regardless of the final format.

The editors have a choice of three or four tags, not 150 codes. With the Magna system, the editors never saw anything formatted until the final output; now, their quasi-WYSIWYG is "more friendly, much more friendly." Editors working on publications that are not yet converted tell McRae, "I could do this so much easier if it was in SGML."

Editors use Bridge Builder to build tables from metadata. For example, the agency with the power to create rules to enforce a statute is listed at the bottom of the statute. But, to know that, a reader would have to refer to the statute. PDM extracts the citation and puts it with the metadata. To build a table of cross-references, the editors create a Bridge Builder report, then flip flop the report and correlate by statute number, not by administration code. This work would have been a tedious, manual, editorial task before SGML. The PDM database with the Bridge Builder interface saves time building tables.

Repeals—laws that are on the books, then are repealed—will also be affected by the new way of handling the publications. When a client state determines how long to carry old information with repealed status, Butterworth can use the database to search for and retrieve repealed sections, then delete them from the publications in which they appeared.

The merger of new data and converted legacy data remains a major task. Regardless of how efficient and effective the mechanical phase of the merger, a human editor will always be required to go through and rewrite notes and move data not flagged by the merger process. The problem is that some sections are duplicated in a printed supplement and in a legacy volume. One version, the published section or the supplement, may contain the full text while the other contains only changed paragraphs or changed references. The merger program can flag the fact that there are two copies of this section, but it is up to the edito-

To build a table of cross-references, the editors create a Bridge Builder report, then flip flop the report and correlate by statute number, not by administration code.

rial/production personnel to delete the proper section. Inasmuch as legal works are always being updated section by section, this part of the merger process will be ongoing, outliving the period of the initial merge although, once the core is in PDM, the database will track and manage duplication.

Proofreading

Texts are currently proofed from a draft printout, section by section. Each draft printout includes a DTD module in the format used for screen presentation. It is called a screen dump by ArborText, although one command prints the entire module, not just the section currently on-screen.

A feature of this printout is that, if the tags are shown on-screen, they are printed with the text. Proofreaders, working with the printout, can check each tag. For example, `register number` is an important attribute of the `CREDIT` tag. If the `CREDIT` tag is not right, the register number will not be set. If the register number is not set, the module will not be included in the output, whether CD-ROM or print. In this manner, each new section is checked each day. The staff feels that this method of proofing works well for small chunks of material.

The editorial staff is beginning to use the PDM history function for proofreading. The history function can do a "diff" comparison between versions, highlighting things that do not match. In addition to showing that all intended changes were made correctly, this comparison also catches inadvertent changes. While there may not be many of these, catching them without such a tool requires a laborious full proof of the text.

The goal is that the proofroom will compare the new file against the present file online, without printing it out. PDM will extract the meaningful unit, the publication, and the comparison will be made on this unit, not on database fragments.

Print Products

When a section is good, that is, with correct captions and free of typos, it is exported for typesetting. A second round of verification makes sure that the correct sections are actually there and checks for line and page breaks and format. From that point on, the only changes are in style and layout—theoretically. In practice, changes are made up until the last possible moment, which includes the proof layout stage. The current method is to do these twice: once in the print output file, once in the database. There is no reimport into the database from the typesetting format.

To print, Butterworth converts the SGML to Xyvision XPP. McRae worked with Xyvision to set up the first set of Xyvision styles; now she does it on her own. The conversion is set up once per publication, and then it runs hands-off, except for tables.

Electronic Products

The CD-ROM output is all-inclusive—all information relating to the law is contained in one source: the statutes, administration rules, supreme court opinions, and treatise volumes. The disk links references from publications to statutes and links opinions with the relevant references. The frequency and synchronicity of publication and the handling of merged sections, repealed statutes, and phrases denoting spanned sections ("sections a–c") are all different as a result of the switch to structured information.

The first products, when they were dependent on links coded by the CD-ROM vendor, did not link by case name and register, although the tags for doing so had been input by Butterworth. Now that they are using OmniMark, this linkable information is converted programmatically into actual hypertext links for the electronic products. For example, each statute/regulation section has an id attribute; each reference to a statute/regulation is tagged with a corresponding idref (id reference). The references are not resolved as long as the data is stored in different places, but when combined, as on a CD-ROM, they are resolved and the links put in place.

Implied content and spans—phrases like "highways, roadways, etc." and "sections 1–10"—are no longer functional in the new publishing environment because they are not easily converted into hypertext link anchors. For example, say that you want to go to the referenced section 5, but the link is from the anchor "1–10." How do you indicate that it is the fifth or first or last of these that you want to link to? What do you do with the span if section 5 is deleted?

The Butterworth goal is to list spanned sections individually. The condensed form was largely to save paper. Now, they question if that is still a justification. They revisit these issues with each publication because anything that affects page count can be a billing factor.

DTD and Validation

The overall data design focuses on product groups and on jurisdictions (client states). McRae estimates that 85–90 percent of the statutes, opinions, and rules and regulations DTDs is reusable from state to state. She maintains data and element dictionaries and relies on them to dictate what things should be called and how they should be defined. She asserts, however, that some degree of state-to-state variation is inevitable and desirable because basic requirements differ. Should it be necessary, at some point in the future, to coordinate elements and structures that are not identical, McRae is confident that OmniMark can handle the SGML-to-SGML transformation.

The reuse of data structures means that now there are fewer debates about what to call something and how to structure it. Yet, each new project requires document analysis, coding, tagging, de-bugging, and review.

The original DTD, for Alaska, was created with the help of Xyvision. A key feature of the DTD is the use of content tagging to track the history of a section. For example, the null tag has an attribute analysis that points out if the section was repealed, recodified, or omitted. Entity management is not a major factor in the design because of the use of a relational database to track and manage the data. Although they tagged cross-references in the new material input at Butterworth, they didn't fix and tag everything that was converted.

Pictures, Tables

The Alaska project has much information in tables. The staff at Butterworth use the ArborText CALS WYSIWYG table editor for entering tables. And they cheat.

Using unique tags, not CALS table tags, they could get perfect output. But there was no way to edit the material and see the effect of what they were doing on the table because the ArborText WYSIWYG table editor worked only on CALS-type tables. Alternately, they could use the CALS table tags, have great WYSIWYG editing, and lose control over print format.

What they needed was nested rows, but these are not allowed under the current version of CALS tables. Butterworth opted, in fact, for a third solution. They are using CALS-type table tags and inserting processing instructions—Xyvision typesetting codes—as attributes into the tags. The actual file is not machine-independent—it contains some codes proprietary to the Xyvision system, but "it works." McRae's feeling is that, while she regrets the "impurity," they can skip these processing instructions when an alternate output is needed, as they do for their CD-ROM.

Pictures are not a common requirement in legal publishing and Butterworth has no canonical method of dealing with them. On the occasion when they are required to insert a chart or a logo, editors place a note that the graphic goes "here," with the final size, and leave it to production to strip in during prepress.

Conclusions

Michael Schwartz expected results two years from the initial contact with Xyvision. The move to Salem will complicate things, although he says that the key people are going. The only problem he anticipates is that there may be a lack of people skilled in legal publishing who know the ins and outs of their data structure for the extra effort of cleaning up large amounts of legacy data.

As is common, the transition period has no crisp boundaries. Among the current questions that are being considered at Butterworth is how to refine decisions made about what to automate and what to do by hand, not only for one-time legacy conversion but for the ongoing merger of supplements and published sections. And when to do the cleanup and the merge: When the material comes back from conversion? When the new sections come in? At publication?

To avoid double entry of last-minute corrections, they would need one of the following: a round-trip conversion into Xyvision typesetting codes then back to the source SGML so that changes entered into the typesetting file are echoed in the source or a totally hands-off formatting conversion so that changes could be entered into the SGML source and immediately set into type.

Not all the publications are online yet. The feeling at Butterworth is that they will work out the final production kinks at that time.

For the future, Schwartz is convinced that CD-ROM is not the ultimate delivery media, that there will be future methods that make CD-ROM look "clunky." And he does not want to be in the same situation when the next new media comes along. He believes that "the best shot at supplying any new format without prohibitive re-work is SGML."

The most important lessons about adopting SGML are, according to Schwartz:

- Prepare your staff: publishing from a database demands a level of sophistication.

- Upper management must not leave strategic technical decisions solely to technical staff.

- Top management must know and support the changes and be able to answer when the bean counters want to see a quick return.

- Know that conversion is never hands-off.

At Butterworth, bringing in SGML was not just a change in technology but a change in the organization of work, and in the marketing of their product. They no longer see themselves as book publishers, but as providers of information in whatever form required—online and off-line, electronic and printed books—and they are confident that they will not be in same situation again, supplying a quirky format by expensive rework.

SGML Elsewhere in Butterworth

The Orford/Salem office is part of a large multinational publisher. It is instructive to look at the effect of the pioneering work done in Orford on the other offices.

In terms of technology transfer, the most contact has been between the New Hampshire and the Canadian offices. According to McRae, the Canadians seem to be looking for technical changes only. And, as often happens when a technical fix is sought without accompanying education and reorganization, they are not willing to invest in the changes.

Until Orford adopted SGML, the Australian office had been at the forefront of technical innovation within Butterworth. Their move to SGML was delayed for a time while the roles to be played by production and editorial departments in the new system were worked out. However, by February of 1995, Australia and New Zealand were using SGML, as were many other Reed Elsevier companies.

The Salem office is working with the Puerto Rican office of Butterworth to update the technology used in the publications for the Territory of Puerto Rico. Previously, one publication had been handled in New Hampshire for print and a second one on the island for a local, proprietary online database. To populate the database, the staff either rekeyed from the printed books, or, if a typesetting tape was available, put it through the "washing machine"—taking out the initial coding so that it could be replaced.

Working together, the two offices are expanding their deliverables and will offer a CD-ROM as well as the online format from a new Puerto Rico SGML database. A key to the new, Spanish-language SGML database is a complex merge program from DCL. In the Spanish database, there are no paragraph numbers at the head of each paragraph, so the position and identity of replacements must be inferred by detailed analysis of the text. A typical problem in this type of merge is that, in a given section, paragraphs 1–4 do not change, while paragraph 5 does. The merge program compares the text, makes a best guess, inserts the addition, marks the material to be deleted, and tags the entire section so that human eyes make the final comparison. When complete, there will be between 70,000 and 80,000 pages, including laws, supreme court decisions and opinions in the Puerto Rican database.

The merge program compares the text, makes a best guess, inserts the addition, marks the material to be deleted, and tags the entire section so that human eyes make the final comparison.

On the other side of the Atlantic, the English Butterworth has been resisting use of SGML, pointing to the cost and difficulty. This office has been comparing the ease of use of SGML not with typesetting codes but with a graphic WYSIWYG editor. In terms of cost, the English say an SGML editor is ten times that of a word processor. McRae points out that, 15 years ago, a dedicated word processor cost five times the price of today's SGML editors, yet the advantage was clear and the industry no longer uses typewriters. But, she adds, this is only part of the debate because, in the type of installation Orford has chosen, the database is the major expense.

Another difference between the Orford office and other Butterworth offices is that it is difficult to see the advantages of the new system where typesetting is subcontracted outside. To get the benefit, you must work with the files. And the type of product matters. In Orford, they feel that you cannot get a good CD-ROM product from word-processor styles and that, when other offices start to compete in the new media, they, too, will need more control over their data.

ERICSSON INC. PORTRAIT

Table 4.6 Ericsson Inc.

Industry	Systems for the telecommunications industry
Products	Technical manuals
Media	Print, CD-ROM, tape
Key Players	Renée Swank, SGML Specialist
	Steve Chapman, Manager for Procedural Documentation

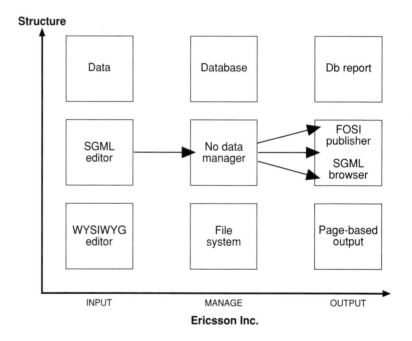

Figure 4.4 Structure and process at Ericsson Inc.

Basic Scenario[6]

Ericsson is an international manufacturer of telecommunications systems with headquarters in Stockholm, Sweden. The initial SGML development work was done there, but the Richardson, Texas, group soon became involved and has become an international corporate center for SGML documentation and services, creating a revenue stream for the division within the company. In 1993, the Richardson group produced over 15,000 pages of SGML-encoded documentation for other Ericsson groups.

For the most part, the setup is classic CALS-type production: SGML editor, no document management tool, print output by FOSI publisher. In addition, Ericsson converts its documents to a variety of electronic browser formats. Which one is used depends on the delivery platform. Two other aspects of the Ericsson implementation stand out:

- Careful tracking of the impact of SGML on technical writer productivity;

- Explicit tracking and administration of what they call their "working environments" or WEs, which are composed of sets of DTDs, FOSIs, and writing tools.

Ericsson's account of writer productivity, reported in early 1994 and based on production of over 30,000 pages, demonstrates that productivity improved more than 33 percent as the time required to produce a page decreased from 4.3 to 2.7 hours. Like Butterworth, Ericsson also realized a dramatic decrease in the cost of CD-ROM production. How the company got to this point and how they operate in the new environment are detailed in this portrait.

Tools

Table 4.7 Hardware and software

VENDOR	TOOL TYPE	TOOL NAME
Sun	Workstation	SparcStation 5, 1 per writer
ArborText	FOSI-based composition	Adept Publisher, 30 licenses
Knowledge Set	Browser for PCs, Macs, some Unix systems	KRS
Electronic Book Technologies	Browser for PCs and Suns	DynaText
Internal	Text-based browser	DocView

[6]Research for this case study was conducted through interviews at Bellcore and by e-mail. I have also drawn on the case study presented by Swank and Chapman (1994), pp. 170–174.

Ericsson produces documentation in an ArborText environment, using the Adept series editor and FOSI-based publishing system to go to print from the native SGML files. A variety of browsers are used, depending on the end user. On a trial basis, some clients have taken delivery of the SGML source data on tape without output processing.

Getting There

Conversion to SGML has had high-level corporate support from the outset. The documentation group in Stockholm hired a consulting group to help with the first document analysis and to develop the first WE, which was for procedural documentation. Then, the legacy procedural documents were converted and, when the documents and data design were in place, the first group of writers was trained.[7]

A year later, the Richardson group created the Working Environment for descriptive documentation. For the most part, the descriptive WE was based on the procedural WE using common elements and common format specifications. The group modified the conversion tool developed in Sweden, used it to convert their legacy documents, then trained their technical writers.

The legacy documents were in FrameMaker. Renée Swank reports that in the old environment, writers used a set of rules that established consistency between documents, although the source files were not as consistent as they would have been using a structured writing tool and a template. The group is pleased with the operation of the conversion tool which requires some manual cleanup of the converted files.

The Richardson group developed printed training material for writers and provided an SGML Help Desk to answer questions on tools, data design, and procedures. Swank reports that it takes a writer about a month to get up to speed.

After working with the procedural and descriptive documents for two years, the Richardson group initiated a new WE for user guides. This development process differed significantly from the previous two. The WE for user guides was developed *without* a model document—the first document and its DTD and FOSI were developed simultaneously. This changed the WE development method in several respects.

Since there were no prototype documents, the document analysis was a steadily evolving process. The initial design called for troubleshooting sections to contain only procedural structures, but the writers found that they needed a place to insert the general information supporting a procedure, and so a container for general descriptive sections was added.

---

[7]"Procedural" and "descriptive" are Ericsson terms describing the type of document—Maintenance Procedures, Feature Descriptions, and so on—and should not be confused with the distinction often made between procedural and descriptive markup.

Unlike previous development efforts, the group:

- Did not release the WE until the documents were released; all were in process at the same time;

- Used entities to incorporate subdocuments so that more than one author could work on a document at the same time; and

- Used multiple FOSIs so that a writer could print and check a section of the larger document.

In their paper on the subject, Chapman and Swank (1994) conclude that they had underestimated the number of major changes required because of the unstable nature of the document type being created. In spite of the bumps along the way, the user guide WE has been successfully incorporated into their document production process and is being extended to other sites around the globe.

Being There

The Richardson Customer Documentation staff includes about 50 people, of whom 25 are writers. Renée Swank is currently the only one with SGML technical expertise in the Document Development area.

The initial response of the writers to SGML was that they were "going backwards," giving up a state-of-the-art WYSIWYG editor for an SGML editor. As a result of this feedback, Ericsson increased the training and resources available to writers. A more recent poll of writers showed that they understood the structure of the documents better and had begun to see certain advantages in the new tools. They reported that the SGML-based editors eliminated certain mistakes and reduced the time required for mundane format details, like changing font styles.

The workflow itself is very straightforward: Writers write, preview on-screen, and send documents to print with the Adept Publisher, which has the same editor as Adept Editor in addition to FOSI-based composition. Documents are written and stored with no more elaborate storage and retrieval than the operating system file server.

Production time for the CD-ROM has been reduced by 50 percent because redundant coding is avoided. Previously, it took two to four weeks to prepare a library of documents for electronic publication. Now the same process takes one to two weeks, so that overall lead time is decreased as well as the absolute time spent on production.

Work for Other Divisions

The expertise in SGML at the Richardson Customer Documentation center has created additional work for the department, which is funded by other Ericsson units.

Center staff write and maintain WEs and produce finished SGML documents. When they introduce a new WE, they install the software, train the writers and support them after installation. Support includes phone and e-mail support for operational questions and maintenance of the WE. In 1993, they completed projects for branches in Japan, Australia, and Latin America that totaled over 15,000 pages.

FOSI Publishing

Ericsson uses ArborText's Adept Publisher, a FOSI-based composition system, for print publications. The Center develops one or more FOSIs for each type of document. For example, a Working Environment might include a DTD plus one FOSI that formats the document for U.S. letter-sized paper, and a second FOSI that formats it for European A4 paper. The Adept Publisher has a FOSI manager that switches FOSI for the output desired.

The FOSI itself is like a style sheet but has the rigor, definition, and structure of an SGML document. As such, it extends the structure of the SGML source to the final stage of production. The primary motive given by Ericsson for FOSI publishing is that you can change the appearance of the document without changing the document itself. This feature, however, does not require FOSI-based publishing—it is equally available for those who choose standard composition tools and maintain their data in SGML. For a general discussion of the pros and cons of FOSI publishing, see Chapter 7 on outputting to print.

WE Maintenance

Swank and Chapman (1994, p. 172) explain the need for maintenance of the WE in this way:

> DTDs and FOSIs are never complete. As new structures are encountered or as elements are organized and presented on a page in a new way, changes are required.

For this reason, the Center established a tracking system for change requests and trouble reports. When a request or report is received, it goes into a log. Next, the SGML specialist assigns a classification code to the item:

- Class A—A change that could invalidate existing documents, for example, removing an element from a DTD.

- Class B—A change that adds functionality and is backward-compatible, for example, adding an element.

- Class C—Minor corrections with no effect on the end user, for example, a change to a comment.

Once classified, the change is submitted to the Working Environment Review Board, composed of five writing and support managers. If approved, the change is implemented.

There is a data dictionary for each working environment, which defines the elements, their content, and their attributes. The Center reuses element definitions whenever possible to simplify overall design and to promote reuse between document types.

Conclusions

While writers complained, initially, that they were "going backward," the figures show that the adoption of SGML is a net good for the company. The initial complaints, placed against a background of a dramatic increase in writer productivity and a greater role for the department, highlight the need to join individual, departmental, and company goals.

The use of SGML is spreading to other divisions throughout the global Ericsson corporation. Some design engineers have already started to write in SGML; other design groups are in training. When all the design engineers are trained and using SGML, the documentation center will modify each WE to make direct reuse of the material easier. Swank has already started this with the user's guide, building common links (file entities) between the engineers' and the writers' environments.

SGML is relatively well established at Ericsson—the company has a track record built on tens of thousands of pages written and converted. The Richardson group has attracted contracts throughout the international company, in effect becoming an internal SGML service company.

Yet, even here, it is possible that use of SGML is just in its infancy and that much more sophisticated uses and applications are still to come.

COLUMBIA UNIVERSITY PRESS PORTRAIT

Table 4.8 *Columbia University Press*

Industry	Reference publishing
Products	*The Columbia Granger's® Index to Poetry, The Columbia Granger's® World of Poetry CD-ROM, The Columbia Granger's® Dictionary of Poetry Quotations, The Top 500 Poems, The Classic Hundred*
Media	Print, CD-ROM
Key players	James Raimes, Assistant Director for Reference Publishing
	Edith Hazen, Editor
	Baird Foster, Vice President, Publishing Sales, Auto-Graphics, Inc.
	Paul Cope, Vice President, Auto-Graphics, Inc.

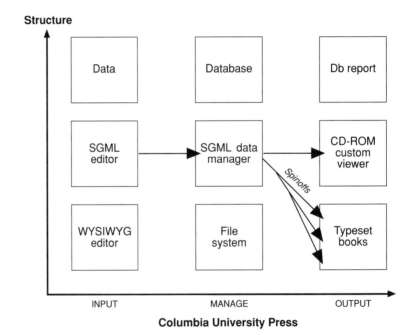

Figure 4.5 *Structure and process at Columbia University Press*

Basic Scenario[8]

Columbia University Press publishes a weighty and distinguished list of reference publications. The list includes *The Columbia Granger's Index to Poetry* (*Granger's*), a locator of anthologized poems which, in each edition, indexes over 65,000 poems in 400 separate anthologies. *Granger's* was first published in 1904 and the Press is now working on the eleventh edition and the second CD-ROM release.

New poetry anthologies are published every week. The Press identifies them, evaluates them, and selects those that merit inclusion in *Granger's*. According to James Raimes, Assistant Director for Reference Publishing, the process of evaluation and selection is the foundation of the enterprise. The adoption of SGML by the Press, then, should be one that would go by the book. Little except the success of the venture has done so.

One point of departure between this and other SGML implementations is their choice of technology and technology vendor. Auto-Graphics is a service provider to the electronic and print publishing industry—before SGML, its strong suit was bringing library card catalogs online and publishing large, structured reference works from document databases. When the company began to port its typesetting data to SGML in the mid-1980s, it brought a different set of requirements than did publishers and software vendors starting with a word-processing model. The people at Auto-Graphics did not assume that an editing tool should work on one file holding one complete document. From the start, they integrated the question of data editing with data storage and data management, never assuming, as did those with a word-processing model, that the file system was the default storage and management tool.

The document architecture, the data design, created by Auto-Graphics for the Press has more in common with pre-SGML databases than with pre-SGML documents. These products do not have an all-encompassing DTD built for a single book that covers front and back matter and that validates a volume as a single unit. The DTDs each structure a database—one DTD for an author database, one for a subject database, one for an anthologies database, and so on. A final product is culled from pieces of several linked databases. Material that is not highly structured and that has low potential for reuse, like a preface, is not maintained as SGML or as a database but is produced and typeset independently from the body of the reference work.

Another point of departure is that through several production cycles, the staff at the Press knew only the highest-level concepts surrounding SGML—there was not an angle-bracket techy in the place. All initial DTD design and data mainte-

> *Another point of departure is that through several production cycles, the staff at the Press knew only the highest-level concepts surrounding SGML.*

[8]This portrait is based on a site visit; interviews with James Raimes, Edith Hazen, Baird Foster, and Paul Cope; and on the cited correspondence and articles.

nance was done off-site by Auto-Graphics. In spite of this, SGML has become a major factor in the introduction of several new products and in the transformation of their workplace and workflow.

Tools

Table 4.9 In-house hardware and software

VENDOR	TOOL TYPE	TOOL NAME
Auto-Graphics	SGML editor	Smart Editor 4.0, customized
(Various)	Personal computers	x86/8066s
Auto-Graphics	Conversion	Quick Change; offshore keying
Auto-Graphics	Search and retrieval and browser	IMPACT, customized

In addition, the primary contractor, Auto-Graphics, uses proprietary database management tools and Xyvision's Parlance Publisher (XPP) composition system.

The staff at the Press input new material using customized, networked copies of Smart Editor 4.0; then they upload their entries to Auto-Graphic's central database. The Press manages the local database for input and editorial work. Auto-Graphics manages the master database for production output.

Auto-Graphics created Smart Editor because it determined that none of the existing SGML editors supplied the data entry model that their clients' reference products required. Their clients needed a *record-* or data-oriented editor, as opposed to a *document*-oriented editor. The editor works efficiently with this data model in which each entry in the book is formally an SGML "document instance" although not what we usually consider to be a "document." Multiple operators can edit multiple entries (records) simultaneously, irrespective of the file structure of the entries (Figure 4.6). (For further distinctions between SGML editors, see Chapter 3.)

Editing the *Granger's* database with an SGML editor built on the word-processing model requires that each entry be in its own file unless the editor works with an SGML-aware data manager that feeds data back and forth between editor and database. Changing the data design so that the entire work becomes one document instance eliminates the possibility of multiple, independent editors working on different pieces of the same document at the same time. Working on the database model, Smart Editor combines related records into one file, indexes the file, and manages it as a relational database.

Data-model editing

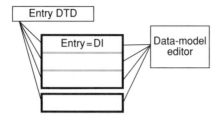

Multiple entries, single editor, arbitrary file structure

Document-model alternatives

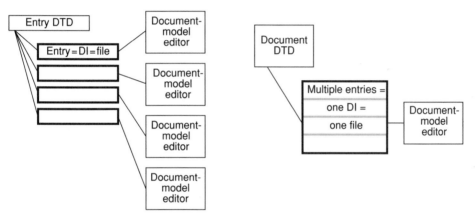

Multiple entries require multiple editors or single file

Figure 4.6 Data- and document-model editing

The DOS edition of Smart Editor does not accept arbitrary DTDs and is not available as an off-the-shelf item. While it can be adapted to accept other DTDs, this remains a custom process. Auto-Graphics plans an off-the-shelf Windows version of the editor that will accept arbitrary DTDs.

In addition to new material input with Smart Editor, significant quantities of legacy data have been converted by Auto-Graphics using programmed conversion or off-shore keyboarding. For print products, Auto-Graphics converts the SGML to Xyvision typesetting codes. For CD-ROM, it imports the files into a customized version of its IMPACT browser/search engine.

Getting There

The story of how *Granger's* came to be published in SGML takes a few lines from the story of how SGML came to be SGML.

In the early 1960s, the typesetting firm ROCAPPI was started by John Seybold, who started the Seybold conferences. According to Baird Foster, who worked for ROCAPPI and then for Auto-Graphics, ROCAPPI developed and implemented a "fairly generically" tagged file format, as much as was possible at the time. It was an early attempt at an independent tagging scheme and one that fed into the effort to create SGML.[9] ROCAPPI had typeset the eighth edition of *Granger's* in this generic format.

Ninth Edition

When James Raimes arrived in 1987, the Press was about to produce the ninth edition in the traditional way, on index cards, which were later composed as a computer-typeset file. Through a trail that twists around acquisitions, reorganizations, and misunderstandings, ROCAPPI came to be no more and Baird Foster went to Auto-Graphics, taking with him a sizable piece of the reference publishing client base.

Auto-Graphics is a supplier of database publishing services with strengths in two areas: large-scale reference works and electronic library card catalogs. Auto-Graphics convinced the Press to compile the book as a database so that future editions would be easier to produce. Columbia entered the material new to this edition in a word processor set up to accept fielded information but with none of the validation or flexibility of SGML. Given the time constraints of the project, Auto-Graphics could not complete the conversion to SGML and the Press had to settle for data that was tagged with SGML-like tags but not validated. Auto-Graphics then merged this new data with the tape inherited from the eighth edition.

By all accounts, the merger was not a pretty process but was long and treacherous for both parties, partly because the original ROCAPPI tape had been stripped of much of its structured generic tagging. Auto-Graphics inherited some understanding of the basic task, but none of the advantages of the generic file. Whatever the impact of those changes, both parties own up to their own piece of the responsibility for the problems in this joint venture. On the Auto-Graphics side, they did not grasp how subtle distinctions in content had an impact on the form of the typeset book. On the Press side, the staff was not prepared for the adjustment in editorial procedure that comes with database publishing.

---

[9]Joseph Gangemi, ROCAPPI VP of Systems and Programming, was part of the GCA GenCode Committee, whose work, combined with the GML syntax developed at IBM, grew directly into the International Standard for SGML. See Chapter 2 and the Standard & Poor's case study.

Foster describes the snags this way:

> The sort rules were very complex because they had to account for numbers, roman numerals, hyphens "pretending" to be spaces, and so on. In some cases, there was a separate sort field but this was not consistent. Because of a severe schedule crunch, Auto-Graphics did the best we could to organize the sort information, mostly on larger records, and we sorted and produced sample pages which were composed to spec. The Press examined the pages and approved them. Hindsight now indicates that the samples were viewed as typesetting samples only—not content, and with better understanding, this problem will disappear in the future. (Private correspondence, May 25, 1994; my emphasis)

According to Foster: "When you have a database, you do not really have a source document. When you work with a traditional typesetter, you always have the last version to check against." Without that, it is hard to visualize the final outcome. Errors that should have been caught in an interim proof were not detected until the final typesetting runs. At that point, changes had to be keyed into the composed file.

When the ninth edition was completed, both sides agreed that they would not and could not endure a similar process again.

CD-ROM

But the next *Granger's Index* publication was not to be the tenth edition, it was to be the first *Columbia Granger's World of Poetry* on CD-ROM, and this was produced from a fully compliant SGML database. The cost of the CD-ROM was in part offset by the fact that the database already existed. Of course, not everything on the CD-ROM was drawn directly from the previous book. The Press added the following information to distinguish it from the print edition:

- Information on poetry anthologies
- The full text of 8,500 out-of-copyright poems
- 3,000 quotations from 1,500 more poems in copyright

In this effort, Auto-Graphics was again typesetter, software vendor, and primary consultant. The Press put its effort into the customization and design of the browser/search engine interface.

Auto-Graphics's IMPACT search and retrieval and viewing software is the basis of the electronic product. It was chosen, among other reasons, because it was known by librarians as a user-friendly tool for card catalog automation. The Columbia University Press version includes not only subject, author, and title references but indexed first and last lines and full text and Boolean operators. It was clear from the outset that the tool would be customized for *Granger's*, but the process of customizing the user interface and the search functions was more demanding than anticipated. Raimes writes that, in the months before product launch, three staff members worked full-time to write help screens, test searches, get technical help, and get feedback from librarians.

His list of lessons learned are sound ones for any software project—and the Press was creating software—but perhaps the key to the success of the final product was this piece of advice, which Raimes (1994) passes on:

> Keep getting fresh opinions on the screens and on the way searches work from new people. We noticed a tendency in ourselves, and in anyone who played with the software for any length of time, to forgive its difficulty as soon as it was understood, to forgive anything annoying when someone defended it. Difficulties and annoyances must be fixed. Nothing should be puzzling or irritating, even to novices. We kept getting fresh pairs of eyes to react to our screens.

This extra effort has paid off as review after review cites the ease of use, clarity, and simplicity of the user interface.

Spin-offs

"At the center of the enterprise is the fact that the database can compile statistics" says Raimes. While the Press ventured into database publishing and then to SGML to make the mechanical pieces of production easier, the product line itself has been transformed by the reorganization of the data.

With the database, the Press can track and compare how often each poem has been anthologized. For the CD-ROM, they used these statistics to decide which out-of-copyright poems to show in full text and which copyright poems to quote. From the same statistics, they produced *The Columbia Granger's Dictionary of Poetry Quotations* and collections of the most anthologized "top 500" and "top 100" poems—*The Top 500 Poems* and *The Classic Hundred*. Other spin-offs are in the works.

The staff saw the potential for new publications as they were doing the CD-ROM, when they started to use the power of the structured data format to collect information. As with the CD-ROM, *The Top 500* and other spin-offs are not just subsets of the electronic product but again add value, with introductions by William Harmon and with poems in copyright that are not on the CD-ROM.

As with the print *Granger's,* there is no product-specific DTD for the spin-offs. The text is extracted by Auto-Graphics from the appropriate database and merged with the new editorial material.

Tenth Edition

The objective, when work started on the tenth edition, was to have Columbia enter the new material using an editor developed by Auto-Graphics. Developing the editor took longer than anticipated and began to have an impact on the production schedule, so Auto-Graphics took on the keyboarding that would have been done by the Press if the editor had been available.

The process for creating the tenth edition, while in fully compliant SGML, was not markedly different than for the ninth, a process that called for tremendous coordination and communication between the typesetters and the editors. And many of the same problems came back. The staff at the Press still had difficulty proofing in the new form. They thought, when they went into the tenth edition production phase, that the database was set up so that proofing could follow the usual editorial pattern. It did not. They had to go through the same two stages—proofing preliminary input, then proofing a final run.

The workload was not spread in a way that the Press was equipped to handle. The job was rushed and, in their words, "not satisfactory." Between Auto-Graphics and Columbia University Press, there was some "friendly friction." Both sides report a lack of communication at some crucial stages. Both sides politely refuse to blame the other—entirely. Both sides are optimistic about the next edition.

According to Edith Hazen, in the ninth edition production cycle, the editorial staff did things manually in the proof stage and expected those changes to hold for the tenth. For example, the early database had not identified roman numerals, but the manual corrections to the ninth edition meant that Four, IV, and Fourth were associated properly. Unfortunately, there was no reconciliation of corrections made at the end of the ninth edition run. And they had not allowed time to redo that material for the tenth.

The listing for Sir Philip Sidney's *Astrophel & Stella* is an example of one that "got by" the process. The sonnets in this collection are identified by roman numberals, as are psalms and Shakespeare's sonnets. The songs are identified by ordinal numbers—First Song, Third Song, Eleventh Song, and so on. The ninth edition, corrected by hand, lists the numbered sonnets and then the songs, each in sequence. The tenth edition ignored the ordinal numbers and conflated the roman numerals with first lines, producing:

> "Because I oft, in dark abstracted guise"
> C. "O tears, no tears, but rain from beauty's skies"
> CIV. "Envious wits, what hath been mine offense"
> "Come sleepe, O sleepe, the certaine knot of peace"

In addition to processing errors, Hazen says the editing software was "not good about assigning incidental information." Chantey and hymn all got put with music. It missed subtle differences between song and ode. Because the tenth was again keyed in by Auto-Graphics, the staff at the Press was not asked which was appropriate. If the Press had understood more about the types of errors to anticipate, they "would have hand-held a little differently."

They thought, when they went into the tenth edition production phase, that the database was set up so that proofing could follow the usual editorial pattern. It did not.

Being There

The Press is currently working on the second release of the *Granger's* CD-ROM (publication date: 1995), the eleventh edition of *Granger's Index,* and a new, unannounced, spin-off product. The Smart Editor from Auto-Graphics has been installed on a local area network and is in full use. The Press manages its data input and editorial work while Auto-Graphics does the large-scale manipulation required for new products.

Input

Using their own PC editor, the staff at the Press feel in "much fuller control, now." Training on the PC editor is quite rapid, they report, and easily accomplished in one to two days. While there have been bugs, they are generally pleased with the operation of the software. Four people keyboard full-time; two additional staff members edit with access to the authority files. The documentation for the editor was rewritten from the Auto-Graphics original by a Columbia University Press staff person, but even now, in this accessible form, it is not needed because the editing software is so easy to use.

The editor prompts the keyboarder to fill in fields and prompts for duplications in the database. Unlike a word-processor template, which might look the same to the user, Smart Editor has fields that correspond to real SGML constructs. When creating a new entry, the keyboarder can check the database to see if the author is already in the database and to make sure that the entry is consistent with existing text. Extensive pieces of text and quotations are sent offshore to be keyed and coded.

Once new data is entered, the Press uploads updated files to Auto-Graphics. Auto-Graphics takes the material keyed offshore and the new and updated files from the editorial staff and plugs them together.

Revisions, Editorial Work

Some errors in the first CD-ROM and tenth print editions were introduced by the automated process, and some were pre-existing and only came to light with the additional capacity of the electronic edition. For the eleventh edition, the PC editor accepts the designation "roman numeral" and the output will be adjusted accordingly.

Not all errors are from the data processing; some had been hiding in the printed edition, coming to light only in the electronic product. For example, the Shakespeare attributions were inconsistent in print—one time the author was given as "William Shakespeare," one time simply as "Shakespeare," another time as "W. Shakespeare." No big problem when the listings are pages apart. With the computer compiling the list of authors, these inconsistencies stand out. As a result, there are some isolated instances where, to a trained eye, the CD-ROM "looks messy" according to the editor, Edith Hazen. There was no time allotted to fix these for the first CD-ROM or for the tenth edition. They are fixing them now with the database as an aid.

Markup, Design, Layout

According to Foster, once data is in SGML, "people tend to forget about output, as if it were trivial, but it is almost a data translation." Columbia contracts all the typesetting to Auto-Graphics, which uses its proprietary, in-house Quick Change conversion software to go from SGML to Xyvision. From there on, the focus on format and typography is the same as for any project.

The Press does anticipate that use of computer-assisted typesetting will affect the look of the page. Complicated formats, like the one for the entry on *Astrophel & Stella*, which are not easily reduced to rules processed by the computer, could be simplified in the next print edition.

DTD, Validation, and Archiving

The Press controls the data repository by limiting access to the authority files to two editors. Everything that is added, deleted, or changed is checked by one of these editors. Auto-Graphics still manages the master databases.

Auto-Graphics designed the DTD in conjunction with the Press and has updated and maintained it. Although they started work on the project after completing work on the Houghton-Mifflin *American Heritage Dictionary*, third edition, an SGML-encoded database, Foster says of the DTD process: "We backed into it." The time factor and the fact that the customer did not have a deep understanding of the concepts were impediments. "A DTD needs those who understand the editorial content of the piece."

Auto-Graphics considers this DTD to be an *entry* DTD, not a *publication* DTD. The distinction is that it validates data as it is input. Any given publication can be drawn from any slice of the data, but the publication as a whole is not validated.

The original *Granger's* database has hundreds of unique tag names. According to Paul Cope, he would not have broken it down that far, but he can see why it was done. It was this precision in data identification that allowed the Press to create the later, spin-off products.

Although those involved think and speak of it as one DTD, there are actually separate DTDs for each database. There is a database for authors, a database for anthologies, a database for subjects, and so on. Unlike some relational database managers used with SGML, Auto-Graphics maintains the data as SGML elements, not divided up into BLOBs. While defined as SGML elements, fielded data in Smart Editor is not actually tagged during editing; the tags are applied at export. Auto-Graphics uses awk and C to output from the databases.

The Press is participating actively in the revision of the DTD while Auto-Graphics is taking a role closer to that of document analysis facilitator.

Balance Sheet

The costs of doing the CD-ROM include the cost of mastering, keyboarding, and licensing the technology—all costs incurred over and above the production of the ninth edition. The CD-ROM sells for $699, it is doing well, and the Press has made money on the product.

Foster says that there will be a saving on typesetting costs for the eleventh edition because the Press is doing its own keyboarding. It will save on revisions because the Press will do its own corrections instead of paying the compositor. Foster expects that composition and page makeup will cost the same as for previous editions.

Summary and Conclusions

The Press has plans for more additions to this family of poetry references, including a major new publication in about two years. It has a five-year plan for the whole product line.

Is Raimes concerned that libraries will not buy the print book if they have the CD-ROM? He says there is "a bit of that," but, the editors enhance each edition of both print and CD-ROM. The tenth edition indexed 12,500 "top" last lines that were not on the CD-ROM to maintain the appeal of the print edition. These will go into the next CD-ROM, which will have "a lot more of everything": full text poems, quotations, and new search features. The new features will include broader categories than subject. For example, a teacher putting together a syllabus can search for children's poems (broad category) about nature (subject).

Future plans include expanding the use of SGML to other Columbia University Press reference titles.

Division of Labor

Raimes still introduces himself saying, "I'm not a techy," and this is not likely to change. Pleased and proud with what they have done with the *Granger's* database, he says that primary among the lessons "is that computers alone just do not make everything easier." The Press has recognized that more technical expertise is needed in-house. A new staff member is being trained on the technical side of SGML. The Press and Auto-Graphics have regular e-mail communication to keep things on track.

From the vendor's side, Foster says that Auto-Graphics would encourage the Press to participate more, to learn SGML, and to get more involved in DTD design. With other clients, this has happened more quickly. How easy it is for a client to do this, he feels, depends on the temperament of the editor.

At the Press, pleased as the staff are with the collaboration, for future projects, they will consider all their options in terms of editor, database manager, and typesetter. "We are thinking about whether we should assume total control of the whole of the *Granger's* database—technical as well as administrative and editorial." They see the decision as being just like that for a fleet of trucks: Should we have a mechanic on staff, or should we use a service station? The considerations are the same: cost, time, and the feeling of total control. If they do take over, they see the period of subcontracting to Auto-Graphics as a successful transition rather than as a failed methodology. The experience with SGML, to date, has not dampened their enthusiasm for new techniques.

Lessons

Regarded in the light of other SGML projects, it seems at least possible that the complexity of the project, from editorial to layout and design, might have appeared less daunting if document analysis had taken a more canonical approach and if the editorial experts had maintained closer contact with the designers of the DTD and the database. This is changing and may take a new direction as technical expertise is brought in-house.

The Press did not follow the conventional wisdom regarding document analysis, control of their data, and training and education—but it worked. If they proceed to bring more of these functions in-house, the experience will have been, in essence, just a different way to phase in the new technology. They will have made a transition that started with editorial work and then added technology, with expertise coming last.

This was the latest stage in a long collaboration between the people at Auto-Graphics and Columbia University Press. At the Press, they say that they see this vendor not as a vendor but as a collaborator. Did it work solely because of the special nature of this vendor-client relationship? Perhaps. But there are many such relationships, and there is no reason to think that this division of labor cannot be effective, at least as a transitional strategy, for other vendor-client pairs.

Exclusive reliance on subcontracting during the transitional period did give the Press the option of saying: "This stuff doesn't work for our data, even our vendor can't make it work. Let's cut our losses and get out." They would have been no worse off than if the data had been put into a proprietary format. But the first projects met minimal production goals, and later projects streamlined the process, raised the quality of some aspects of editorial work, and allowed the Press to expand its product line using current resources.

The Press did not follow the conventional wisdom regarding document analysis, control of their data, and training and education—but it worked.

STANDARD & POOR'S PORTRAIT

Table *4.10 Standard & Poor's*

Industry	Financial Analysis
Products	Standard Corporation Records,
	The Electronic Prospectus
Media	Print, CD-ROM, online
Key Players	Bill McDade, Vice President, Technical Services
	JVG Consulting Services, Joseph V. Gangemi, SGML Consultant

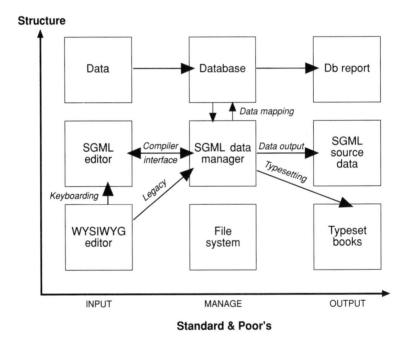

Figure *4.7 Structure and process at Standard & Poor's*

Basic Scenario[10]

Standard & Poor's is a well-known information provider to the financial community. At the highest level, S&P's is a simple information flow: The company receives information from multiple, outside sources; editors analyze it, adding value by their commentary and editorial work, and by drawing on company archives. The company distributes its products on a daily basis to brokers, banks, and others who follow the financial markets, and it compiles the *Standard Corporation Records* which is distributed semimonthly. Underneath this top level, the movement and control of information is quite complex.

Before the introduction of SGML, all material, regardless of the source, was transmitted by fax or paper and rekeyed by S&P's typesetting vendor, who maintained the Standard & Poor's database in a typesetting format. In this form, this massive repository of financial information was primarily a series of paragraphs and tables—meaningful only when compiled in print and accessible only by the vendor.

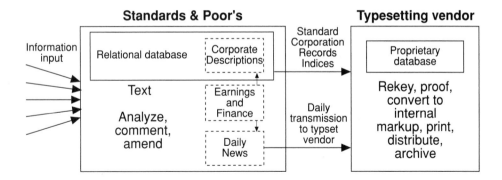

Figure 4.8 *Information flow before SGML*

The use of SGML with an Oracle relational database allows Standard & Poor's to take control of its data resources in-house, to query and reuse this resource for new, spin-off products and, through these new offerings, to open new markets. From the units converted to SGML, the company provides tagged electronic data to the typesetting vendor. Savings on redundant, external keyboarding were the main justification for the project. Figures 4.8 and 4.9 illustrate that the fundamental publishing process remains unchanged with the introduction of SGML. What is changing is that, as units are converted, S&P's controls more of the data archive internally and redundant keyboarding is eliminated.

---

[10]This portrait and all quotes within it are from interviews and correspondence with J.V. Gangemi that took place between June, 1994, and January, 1995. The portrait was reviewed by Standard & Poor's.

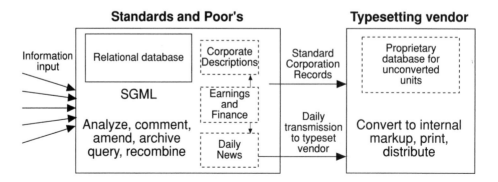

Figure 4.9 Information flow with SGML

Each of the three sets of data described here contributes to the *Standard Corporation Records*, a compendium of financial information on approximately 12,000 publicly traded companies that is a primary Standard & Poor's product.

The *Corporate Descriptions* are data. Each description is composed of segments—a segment may be a discrete date or number, like "number of employees," or, it may be a block of text of indefinite length, like a chairman's letter to stockholders from the Annual Report. Over 300 types of segments can be stored in *Corporate Descriptions* for each company.

Earnings and Finance is a set of elements, such as quarterly and annual reports, that is added both to the *Daily News* and *Corporate Descriptions*. When it comes in, *Earnings and Finance* is added to that day's *Daily News* and is stored in the *Corporate Descriptions* database.

The *Daily News* is what it says—short items of corporate financial news distributed daily. A Standard & Poor's business or financial analyst compiles a single story from several sources and may add commentary about the company's history, market, or other industry-related news. Each *Daily News* item is a new story, written for that day's publication. The typesetting vendor dials in each day, downloads the file, then composes, prints, and distributes the *News* overnight to paid subscribers.

The Oracle database is the information repository for these products. SGML is used to populate the database because SGML editing tools provide the best interface for writers and financial analysts. At the same time, the SGML format provides the structure needed to map large, irregular blocks of text to the database without ambiguity. This mapping would be impractical with word-processing formats. The databases are maintained and queried in the standard fashion. In addition, SGML is used to extract data from the database for final production because the format can describe the data for the typeset publications. Creation of new, spin-off products is an added incentive for the project.

Tools

Table 4.11 In-house hardware and software

VENDOR	TOOL TYPE	TOOL NAME
SoftQuad	SGML editor	Author/Editor
SoftQuad	API	Sculptor
Oracle	Database	Oracle SQLnet
Ultrix or OSF/I	Workstation	DEC Unix equivalent
DEC	Minicomputer	VAX

The most significant software in this implementation is custom-written for Standard & Poor's by in-house and contract programmers working in SGML, C, and SQL (Standard Query Language). This includes code for two-way data conversion, database read/write routines, eight primary DTDs, a conversion DTD, and various SQL queries.

While SoftQuad, the vendor of the SGML editor, provided some initial configuration consulting, the essential SGML resource has been JVG Consulting Services. Joseph V. Gangemi is a consultant whose association with SGML goes back to the initial days of the standard. Gangemi worked with ROCAPPI on its structured typesetting system and later with the GCA committee that merged into the ISO committee that wrote ISO 8879. (See Chapter 2 on the development of the standard.)

Getting There

Gangemi introduced SGML to Standard & Poor's and has written all the DTDs and the conversion software. The Oracle relational database is the standard database for Standard & Poor's and this has not changed with the introduction of SGML.

The data design process differs here from other SGML sites because one target—the Oracle database—is highly structured. For this reason, document analysis must consider the relational target as well as the unstructured sources and the formatted outputs. The resulting analysis specifications determine the eventual DTD and are also handed to the Oracle programmer who maintains the relational database. He uses the DTD as the basis for the relational design. The design specifies each element's meaning within the system, its conversion requirements, and any special processing considerations.

The legacy database is being converted in units, each unit corresponding to one of the eight eventual DTDs. The first unit was *Daily News*, the second

Earning & Finance, then *Bond Descriptions*, then *Preferred and Warrant Stocks*. So far, four have been converted and are in production. Once converted, the unit is maintained in-house at Standard & Poor's with updates sent to the typesetting vendor. After the conversion is completed, there will be only S&P's in-house database.

> To convert the material, Science Press, the typesetting vendor, translates the data in its internal markup to a data stream with embedded SGML tags that correspond to a conversion DTD. The role of the conversion DTD is similar to that of the Rainbow DTD and other, intermediate, exchange DTDs. The purpose is to put the data in a form easily reached from the source markup that can be further processed when in-house at Standard & Poor's. This is data stream A in Figure 4.10. The same intermediate DTD is used in the reverse direction—from Standard & Poor's back to Science Press—and is described further under *Typeset Output*.

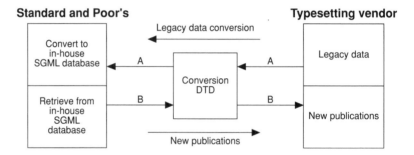

Figure 4.10 Conversion data streams

Once in-house,

> Keywords and phrases, relative positions of data elements, and existing tags are used to recognize elements that currently have no unique code identifier. SGML tags are generated in accordance with a [second] DTD specification. Like all complex conversions, a manual assist is required before the data is ready for database load. An SGML editor (Author/Editor from SoftQuad) is used to review and edit the data to achieve conformance with the DTD structure.

The first conversion effort, for *Daily News* production, started in the last quarter of 1992 and was completed and online within seven months. Within the next year and a half, by August of 1994, four units had been converted. The three remaining units are scheduled for completion by the end of 1995.

The conversions have been done in parallel with production, so that delays and extended development deadlines did not affect product delivery schedules.

Being There

Input

Information comes into Standard & Poor's in every imaginable medium—electronically via the major news wires, by paper and fax, by phone, and by mail. Before SGML, a compiler—a person, not a computer program, who is usually a certified financial analyst—would have typed his or her story on a typewriter or printed it from a word processor. It was then faxed to the typesetting vendor and rekeyed into the proprietary system's format. Today, working on data for one of the converted units, the compilers input directly into SoftQuad's Author/Editor.

A senior editor provides the compiler with all relevant hard copy. The compiler can display electronic data in a second window, for reference, but there is no direct transfer to SGML from outside electronic sources. Archival SGML data is pulled from the converted database and appears on the screen as formatted data in Author/Editor.

> ... the Compiler Interface software extracts the relevant company data from the Oracle database and creates an SGML file. Only the data requested is selected. For example, if the compiler is updating the Bond Descriptions segment, only the elements in the bonddesc DTD are extracted from the database and written to the SGML file. The Compiler Interface software launches Author/Editor and passes the name of the SGML file to the program. Author/Editor presents a formatted view of the document to the compiler.

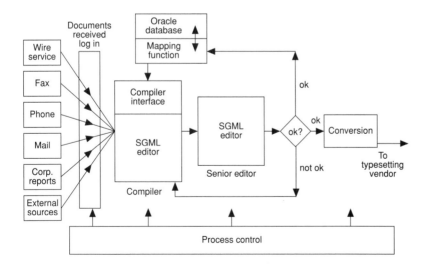

Figure 4.11 Workflow at Standard & Poor's

Data Design

Overall, there are eight DTDs, each corresponding to a type of archival data, in addition to the conversion DTD, which is used as an intermediate markup between Standard & Poor's and the typesetting vendor. The DTDs specify order, iteration, and hierarchy for the free-form text elements that are part of the *Corporate Descriptions.*

Each DTD has two types of elements: block elements and embedded elements. Block elements are stripped of their SGML tags and then stored as a relational database field in Oracle. Each SGML element can be retrieved with normal SQL statements. Elements embedded within the blocks are stored with SGML tags intact.

The embedded elements are of two types: those with and without query value. Those with query value may include a date or title. This information is extracted and stored in a fixed-format relational field to support SQL queries. This information, then, is stored twice in the database: once in context with SGML tags and once as a relational field. Embedded fields without query value include those that are useful for format only, such as an embedded fraction that will be set in distinctive type.

In addition, some elements in the DTDs support the data and workflow management software.

Management

There are two aspects to data management at Standard & Poor's: workflow and the data itself.

On receipt, information is logged into a document receipt system. This system tracks each document by company: an annual report for CBS, a profit statement for Disney, and so on. A process control system tracks each company's data as it moves through editorial and production areas. A senior editor assigns work to staff editors and compilers. Documents progress from receipt to assignment to a compiler, review by a senior editor, possible revisions, storage in the Oracle database, and then to conversion for typeset production. The process control software was written in-house by Standard & Poor's.

The data itself goes through several transformations that are transparent to the compilers and editors working on the Author/Editor interface. Figure 4.12 shows the successive mappings that occur between the compiler interface and the Oracle database. On the SGML side, Gangemi wrote a series of read/write routines that move the SGML data to and from the C data structures that function as internal maps between the SGML and the relational databases. This system-neutral C format is an easy translation to and from both the SGML and the Oracle data.

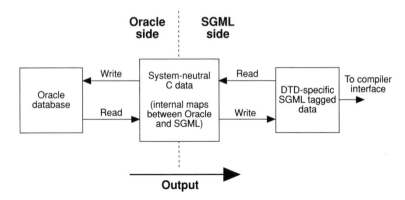

Figure 4.12 Data mapping at Standard & Poor's

On the Oracle side, the in-house Oracle programmer wrote a complementary series of read/write routines. The data is retrieved with SQL statements embedded in the program code. Write functions can be adapted for each type of derived output format. Each expert works in his or her own area of expertise. According to Gangemi "The internal map is our neutral turf that is easily understood by a reasonably competent C programmer."

Typeset Output

The transmission of data to Science Press uses the intermediate DTD that was developed for the transmission of legacy data to Standard & Poor's. (See data stream B in Figure 4.10.)

> The [output] conversion data stream consists primarily of tags that identify paragraphs and tables. Segment tags identify units of data that go together. Converting to the transmission data stream consists of removing "intelligent" SGML tags and dumbing them down to simple paragraph and an occasional heading tag. The set of tags that describes a table is also uniform for all tables and consistent with Science Press's typographic needs... Special functions were written to take the data needed for transmission (not all elements are sent) from the internal map, arrange them in the proper order, apply the appropriate tags, and write the data to the transmission file.

Other than to support a load of its own internal database from the transmission data stream, the vendor's production is unchanged, although the number of Standard & Poor's people working on-site at Science Press to rekey and to proofread the material is dwindling, as increasing portions of the data are transmitted electronically.

Electronic Output

Using SGML-encoded data, Standard & Poor's has brought out *The Electronic Prospectus* which includes details from the SGML descriptions in the *Standard Corporation Records*, plus data from existing relational databases—*Bond Guide* and *Stock Reports*. The data is distributed as an SGML-tagged electronic file.

> The purpose is to sell the data to a value-added vendor. The vendor would either add the data to existing products, or develop new products that complement existing ones... Standard & Poor's may develop additional products of their own, but right now they are just exploring the value of the data.

The data is extracted by queries based on customer-specified selection criteria. The data is extracted in order, tagged, and written to an output file.

In addition, Standard & Poor's has produced an electronic version of the *Standard Corporation Records*; it presents the data on screen, such that the user can choose a company and scroll through the data. The company has plans for additional electronic products.

Conclusions

The introduction of SGML into the production system at Standard & Poor's has gone smoothly, for the most part. According to Gangemi,

> Schedules have been missed because the work effort in some instances was underestimated. Nothing new to projects of this size. Because conversion parallels production, the missed schedules did not affect production of the products. However, production savings were not realized as early in the project cycle as budgeted.

He reports that, given the chance, he would have spent more time on a broad evaluation of the existing database and on content validation. Content validation will be addressed later, as resources become available.

In contrast to other sites where SGML editing tools have replaced WYSIWYG editors, at Standard & Poor's, the SGML editing tools replaced a direct interface into the Oracle database. In this light, the SGML editors have been received as relatively "relaxed" and easy to use.

There are no immediate plans to incorporate data from EDGAR, the Securities and Exchange Commission's SGML electronic data initiative, directly into the Standard & Poor's database, although compilers can load EDGAR data into Author/Editor to use as a reference as they write their reports.

The immediate benefit to Standard & Poor's from their SGML conversion is the reduction in typesetting costs due to the elimination of redundant keyboarding. In addition, they have gained greater control over their extensive corporate database, which can now be queried and mined for new products, without sacrificing ease of input.

   And they have bought conversion insurance for the future. As Gangemi puts it, "The system hardware and software may change over time, but Oracle, or its equivalent, and SGML will keep the data transportable and separate from the system environment."

THE ELECTRONIC VOLCANO PORTRAIT

Table 4.12 The Electronic Volcano (Dartmouth College, Department of Earth Sciences)

Industry	Scientific Research
Products	The Electronic Volcano, *Catalog of Active Volcanoes of Central America*
Media	The World Wide Web
Key players	Richard Stoiber, Professor Emeritus, Dept. of Earth Sciences
	Barbara DeFelice, Librarian, Dept. of Earth Sciences, Kresge Library
	Andrew J. Williams, Manager, Kiewit Computer Resources Center; Internet Specialist and WebMaster

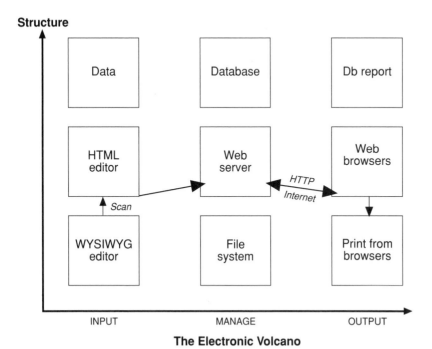

Figure 4.13 Structure and process in the Electronic Volcano project

Basic Scenario—The Web[11]

The World Wide Web is not quite like anything else—anything else described in this book, or out of it. The World Wide Web, or "world *wild* web" as one of my informants called it, or WWW or W^3 or, most commonly, the Web, is a set of technologies for creating, viewing, and distributing linked multimedia documents—documents that include sound, pictures, video, and text. Some estimates say that the WWW is growing at the rate of 11 percent per week. There are no natural or technical systems that grow at this rate—except bacteria and some volcanoes. (See the figures and graph on Web growth in Chapter 2.)

The Web substantiates much of the stuff of dreams of instant, universal electronic publishing. Before the Web, it was hard to make text and graphics look as intended when retrieved from the Internet to a variety of platforms and applications. With the Web, anyone with a Mac, Windows PC or X-windows-compatible computer can bring up a formatted page using a point-and-click, graphic interface. Any character-based interface, including mainframes and MS-DOS, can access non-pictorial material through a simple, menu-driven interface. And, if a page contains pointers to other Web pages, readers can point and click or choose a menu item and get there.

"Get there" is an interesting way to express switching documents, as if the *viewer* were moving, not the document. The Web abounds in such physical, geographical imagery, most important of which is the "home page." The home page is a Web publisher's base document. The document has an address known to others on the Web. From your home page, you can point to related documents at any address. These other documents might be in the same path and directory as your home page or on a Web server on the other side of the world. To the end user who points and clicks, there is no distinction (Figure 4.14).

Four key technologies make this possible:

- A DTD called hypertext markup language (HTML);

- The Internet and Internet file transfer protocols, including hypertext transfer protocol (HTTP) designed for the Web;

- A system of universal addressing called the uniform resource locator (URL);

- Universally available cross-platform viewing and browsing software, the original such software, NCSA Mosaic, having been followed by many commercial and noncommercial applications.

---

[11]This portion of the portrait is based on interviews and e-mail correspondence with Andrew J. Williams; the Electronic Volcano portion of the case study is based on site visits and interviews with Barbara DeFelice and Richard Stoiber.

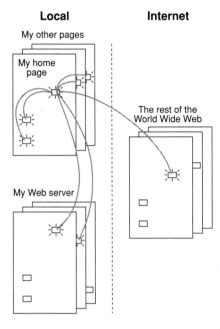

Local   **Internet**

Figure 4.14 Interconnected Web pages

Basic Scenario—The Electronic Volcano

The Electronic Volcano is, in the words of one of its creators, "Mostly a giant index for someone who might want to use the library." It encapsulates the library science knowledge of Barbara DeFelice and the earth sciences knowledge of Richard Stoiber. The primary orientation of the Electronic Volcano is to help people find resources, to guide them to information. The secondary orientation is to provide actual online sources that are not easily available elsewhere, particularly noncopyrighted, rare material available only in print.

Figure 4.15 shows part of the Electronic Volcano home page in the Netscape browser with a window open on the HTML source code for the page. It is the HTML coding, a simple application of SGML, that allows the source to be reproduced on multiple platforms and multiple browsers.

Both Stoiber and DeFelice have other Web projects. Stoiber is updating the Central American portion of the *Catalog of Active Volcanoes* in collaboration with William Rose of Michigan Technical University, Michael Carr of Rutgers University, and Stanley Williams of Arizona State University. DeFelice is working on the Kresge Library home page as part of the Dartmouth College Library Home Page project and on a guide to climate resources that will be a part of this project.

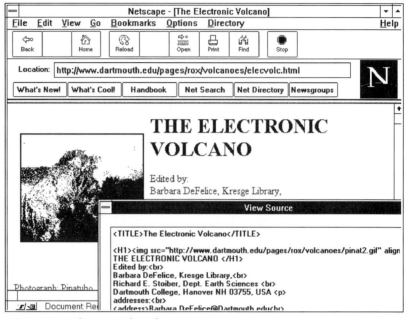

Figure 4.15 *Electronic Volcano home page*

Richard Stoiber, Professor Emeritus of Earth Science and volcanologist, is related academically to a very large number of those practicing in his field—either because they were his students or students of his students. His career has been dedicated to his research, his field expeditions, his publications, his colleagues, and especially to his students. Since he received his Ph.D. from MIT in 1937, he has more than 110 publications to his credit.

What then would motivate him to reissue the *Catalog of Active Volcanoes,* which has not been systematically updated for 30 years, and to produce the Electronic Volcano? And why do both on the Web, when regular academic publishers could provide the traditional route to publication?

The Central American section of the *Catalog* has not been updated since the early 1950s, although some sections date from the nineteen-seventies. Of the current volumes, each has its own format and its own set of hard copy updates. Dartmouth students and professors, under Stoiber's guidance, have done much of the research related to Central American volcanoes, and so bringing this up to date, "collecting the debris that has accrued relative to active Central American volcanoes" is a natural step. The Electronic Volcano codifies and distributes DeFelice's expertise at a time when it is increasingly difficult for her to devote her time to this area.

There is a strong element of personal commitment and belief in the need for a central clearinghouse, evidenced in the introduction and dedication included in the languages of many of the countries that have active volcanoes. (The screen and HTML source code for this page are reproduced in the next section.)

So, why put this important update on the Web? Stoiber's collaborator, Rose, has had a Web home page on the Michigan Tech server since early 1994. There are several reasons why he was able to convince Stoiber and DeFelice to choose the Web as their publisher instead of a traditional academic press. These are encapsulated in the fact that Web publishing is:

- Instant
- Collaborative
- Partial

What they publish is immediately available worldwide and is easily updated over time. Colleagues from several locations produce and maintain separate documents that appear as one seamless whole to the user. And they can make the information available before it is complete, without degrading the publication as a whole. Publishing the same work in print would require a more polished product. In contrast, as Barbara DeFelice says, "All Web publications seem to be works-in-progress."[12]

What they publish is immediately available world-wide and is easily updated over time.

Through the Web, Stoiber and DeFelice have eliminated the traditional role of publisher. This evokes a sense of relief, of settling an old score, balanced with a sense of loss. While they have successfully eliminated the middle man standing between them and their readers, they have lost the publisher's aid in such things as cover and page design and finding the proper market. In exchange, they can update the material as they are able, using a piecemeal approach that would be anathema to a traditional publisher.

Stoiber adds a sense of urgency to these motives from his feeling that he may not have time left in his career to see the completion of a work of this magnitude. He is of the age, as he puts it, when he "does not buy green bananas." Through incremental publishing on the Web "Nothing is lost except what you didn't do."

They considered alternate electronic formats, but none were as far-reaching as the Web: T_EX is portable only if not fancy; the Internet Gopher could not be read well on-screen; Acrobat did not have readers for all platforms; and plain text, without pictures, was unacceptable.

---

[12]As if to illustrate this point, the first set of screens that I captured from the Electronic Volcano contained a prominent typo that would not have been overlooked in a traditional publication process. While mistakes are easy to make on the Web, happily they are also easy to fix and the typo was soon remedied.

Tools

Table 4.13 Tools used

VENDOR	TOOL TYPE	TOOL NAME
Rick Giles, Acadia University	HTML editor	HTML Editor for Macintosh
laCie	Scanner	laCie scanner
Apple Computer	Personal computer	Mac Classic II, Si, Quadra 700
Apple Computer	Web server	Work group Server 8150 running MacHTTP 2.0
Netscape Communications Corporation	Web browser	Netscape

Stoiber and DeFelice selected their tools from those available on the public directory of the Dartmouth server. Dartmouth is an all-Macintosh site. Staff people at Kiewit, the college computing center, download new tools, test them, and add them to the public directory on the server if they feel that the tools will be useful.

The editor that Stoiber and DeFelice use is called HTML Editor. It is an editor that lets you see what the document will look like in a Web browser as you edit it.[13] They had tried earlier editors, but prefer HTML Editor. They also insert tags directly by hand in a word processor.

To bring printed documents online, they scan them and run OCR software. Their scanner is from laCie. Their OCR software is OmniPage Direct.

By definition, any HTML Web browser can be used to view the Electronic Volcano. The one used by Stoiber and DeFelice for their own previewing and editing is Netscape from Netscape Communications Corporation, a group that includes many of the original programmers who wrote Mosaic at the University of Illinois National Center for Supercomputer Applications (NCSA).[14]

Web tools are proliferating too fast to survey for this publication. *Resource Guide B* lists Web tools that are SGML-aware, most coming from SGML vendors. In addition, *Resource Guide A* lists Web sites that maintain updated lists of Web- and HTML-specific tools.

---

[13]The editor is available off the net without charge from: ftp://cs.dal.ca/giles/HTML_Editor_1.0.sit.hqx. For more information on the editor, see: http://dragon.acadiau.ca:1667/~giles/HTML_Editor/Documentation.html.

Getting There

Publishing on the Web is a multistep process: First, you must have access to an Internet server, and that server must establish a Web server and must provide you with the address of your home page and related pages. Once you have access to a server that will house your home page, the major portion of "Getting There" is conceptual—the design of your page and related documents. The minor pieces are technical—learning HTML, scanning the pictures, and coding the documents. This is end-user SGML.

The Server

The complete description of Getting There should include the story of how the infrastructure was created at CERN, the European Laboratory for Particle Physics in Geneva, Switzerland, and how the first multiplatform, public domain, graphic browsers were created at the University of Illinois' National Center for Supercomputer Applications—it could go back to the ARPANET and the creation of the Internet. Since these are documented elsewhere (Ford, 1994; Flynn, 1995), this Web publishing story will pick up after these technologies were in place, with the establishment of the Dartmouth College Web server.

Andrew J. Williams, of the Kiewit computing center, put up the Dartmouth home page on his own initiative, to his own specifications, and according to his own design in early 1994. By May, there were 12 home pages and about 4.3 Mbytes of Web documents connected to the home page, and the college was beginning to take notice. Eight months later, there were approximately 80 home pages and at least 100 Mbytes of related material—text and graphics—and an administrative superstructure to rule on appropriate use and related questions of access.

The college home page might be called an electronic brochure, pointing to information on how to get to Hanover, New Hampshire, and what to expect for weather when you get there. There is no thematic connection between this page and the Electronic Volcano, but the Dartmouth Web server set the stage for the Electronic Volcano by providing the required Web server as well as a direct link to the page.

---

[14]For information on Netscape, see http://mcom.com. For information on NCSA products, see http://www.ncsa.uiuc.edu

The Electronic Volcano

Given the existence of the Dartmouth Web server and a campuswide Ethernet, becoming a Web publisher was no more complicated, initially, than coding a page of information with HTML and getting Williams to allocate an appropriate server address. The Electronic Volcano can be reached via the Dartmouth Home Page (http://www.dartmouth.edu) under Research. The URL for the Electronic Volcano itself is http://www.dartmouth.edu/pages/rox/volcanoes/elecvolc.html

The first part of the locator indicates that the material can be retrieved through HTTP. The last part indicates that the file format is HTML. In between, the information given includes the server, its location, and the location of the file on the server.

Neither DeFelice nor Stoiber had any formal Web or HTML training before they began work on the Electronic Volcano.

Neither DeFelice nor Stoiber had any formal Web or HTML training before they began work on the Electronic Volcano. Although various parts of the college—computing, library service, individual departments—now offer seminars in HTML, Williams reports that most of those working on home pages are figuring it out for themselves using online resources. DeFelice reports that it was no different than learning other software. Much of her self-training came from looking at other Web sites. Stoiber's academic background has few direct ties to publishing, but he calls HTML coding "almost childlike in its simplicity." D. Randall Spydell, Associate Director for Consulting, Computer Services at Kiewit, helped Stoiber get started on the project. He set up the system for loading updates and new material.

There was no prolonged period of tools analysis and purchase because all tools used are available from the public Internet tools section of the college server. The only local change in technology was the acquisition of a scanner.

Being There

The home page has an introduction, dedication, and menu listing the main categories of information available. These appear as:

A. Catalogs of Active Volcanoes

B. Datasets for Literature Citations Relative to Active Volcanoes

C. Electronic Versions of Published Text Material Available in The Electronic Volcano

D. Journals with Articles Relative to Active Volcanism

E. Visual Information

F. Maps of Active Volcanoes

G. Volcanic Observatories and Institutions

H. Theses Relative to Active Volcanism

I. Volcanic Hazards

J. Current Research Projects.

K. Volcano Name and Country Index (those in Electronic Volcano)

The Electronic Volcano is composed of about 15 primary documents, each a separate file. Menu items A–K are each separate documents as is the Electronic Volcano home page and a few others large or significant enough to be managed more easily as separate documents. The pieces are connected with HTML links. The destination of an HTML link is an anchor which can be a URL or a designated point in any file.

Each translation of "The Electronic Volcano" in the Introduction below (DER ELEKTRONISCHE, EL VOLCAN, and so on) is a hypertext link anchor to a different file and is highlighted on the screen. The uniform resource locator for each file is an HREF attribute in the A (for anchor) element.

The HTML source code for the Introduction and Dedication is reproduced in Figure 4.16a.

```
<H2>INTRODUCTION</H2><P>
The Electronic Volcano is a window into the world of information on active volcanoes.
From here you can find many types of materials on active volcanoes worldwide, such as maps, photographs and full texts of dissertations
and a few elusive documents.
The Electronic Volcano will guide you to resources in libraries or resources on other information servers<P>
<H4><A HREF="http://www.dartmouth.edu/pages/rox/volcanoes/IntroGer.html">
DER ELEKTRONISCHE VULKAN
</A> — Introductory material in German  </H4><P>
<H4><A HREF="http://www.dartmouth.edu/pages/rox/volcanoes/IntroSpa.html">
EL VOLCAN ELECTRONICO
</A> — Introductory material in Spanish  </H4><P>
<H4><A HREF="http://www.dartmouth.edu/pages/rox/volcanoes/IntroIta.html">
IL VULCANO ELETTRONICO
</A> — Introductory material in Italian </H4><P>
<H4><A HREF="http://www.dartmouth.edu/pages/rox/volcanoes/IntroFre.html">
LE VOLCAN ELECTRONIQUE
</A> — Introductory material in French </H4><P>
<H4><A HREF="http://www.dartmouth.edu/pages/rox/volcanoes/IntroRus.gif">
THE ELECTRONIC VOLCANO
</A> — Introductory material in Russian </H4><P>
We are grateful to the many who have assisted us.<P>

<H4>DEDICATION</H4><P>
The Electronic Volcano was created in memory of volcanologists, friends, from Colombia, France, Papua New Guinea, Russia, United
Kingdom and United States of America who have died on volcanoes.<P>
```

Figure 4.16a *Electronic Volcano dedication—source code*

All the material between each <A HREF and </A> is a hypertext link end, but only the text outside the angle brackets appears on the screen. Figure 4.16b shows how this looks full-screen in a Web browser.

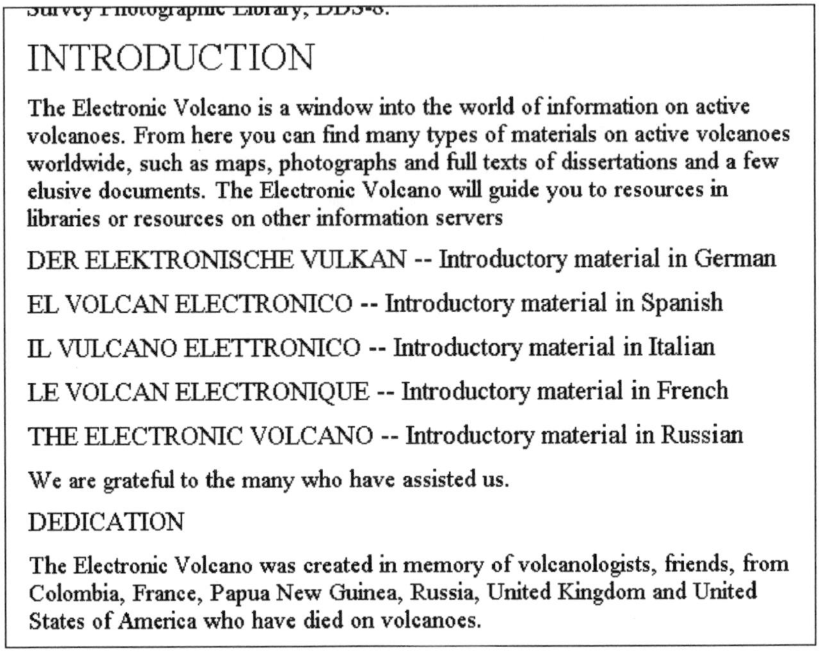

Survey Photographic Library, DDS-8.

INTRODUCTION

The Electronic Volcano is a window into the world of information on active volcanoes. From here you can find many types of materials on active volcanoes worldwide, such as maps, photographs and full texts of dissertations and a few elusive documents. The Electronic Volcano will guide you to resources in libraries or resources on other information servers

DER ELEKTRONISCHE VULKAN -- Introductory material in German

EL VOLCAN ELECTRONICO -- Introductory material in Spanish

IL VULCANO ELETTRONICO -- Introductory material in Italian

LE VOLCAN ELECTRONIQUE -- Introductory material in French

THE ELECTRONIC VOLCANO -- Introductory material in Russian

We are grateful to the many who have assisted us.

DEDICATION

The Electronic Volcano was created in memory of volcanologists, friends, from Colombia, France, Papua New Guinea, Russia, United Kingdom and United States of America who have died on volcanoes.

Figure 4.16b Electronic Volcano dedication—screen capture

Much of the text in the Electronic Volcano is taken from print sources. These are scanned, then converted to text using optical character recognition. The text is brought into Microsoft Word for the Mac for cleanup. When free of scanning errors, the text is exported as ASCII into an HTML editor or tagged by hand in Word.

Several public domain editors are available on the Dartmouth server; DeFelice and Stoiber use HTML Editor when they use a specialized editor at all. Now that they are familiar with HTML, it is often easier just to insert the required tags directly into a word processor and export the file as ASCII. The process goes smoothly with no surprises, although they do not have as much control over format as they would wish. For example, HTML list items are always interpreted as bulleted or numbered list items. They can work around this but would prefer a simple list tag that is not formatted with a bullet.

They insert tags in a word processor or specialized editor, then preview the results in their local browser, then edit, then preview again. When a file is ready, it is transferred to the file server, given a file name/URL, and the URL is inserted in the appropriate places in related files.

Pictures are scanned, from which process they emerge as TIFF files, which are then converted to GIF format using a converter from the public tools directory on the college system. There have been some problems with this procedure, which can become complex when all the variables—resolution, size of original graphic and of bit-mapped image, number of colors, and size of file—are considered. There are occasional system problems in translating and transferring large, color pictures. Stoiber and DeFelice do this infrequently, and so part of their problem, they report, is that they must relearn the procedure each time.

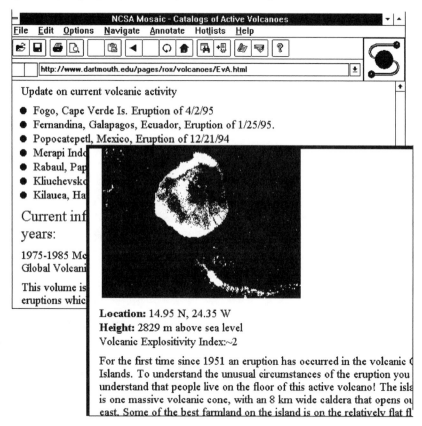

Figure 4.17 Current information on the Electronic Volcano

In terms of design and layout, the coding permitted by the current level of HTML and the format capabilities of the browsers limit what can be done. For example, there is no provision for text to flow around graphics. The choices are to break the flow of text and position a graphic on the left, center, or right of the screen or to insert the graphic in-line in the text as one would insert an icon.

Some browsers, including Netscape, enhance the layout capabilities of basic Web documents using special, nonstandard tags, called extensions to HTML.

While the immediate results may be pleasing, the danger is that documents will lose vital properties when viewed in browsers that do not read these extensions. Greater latitude in future versions of HTML will provide a more satisfying and long-term solution than single-browser HTML.

Data management has several layers for a Web site like the Electronic Volcano. At the highest level, the system of URLs and Internet address protocols provides a data management framework. Beneath that, the college Web server provides another layer by allocating file space, local paths, and directories. The most immediate level of data management is the way the authors use file storage and URL pointers to build and manage their piece of the Web.

Initially, during the design and first stages of implementation, Stoiber and DeFelice had a paper document that recorded what was on the Electronic Volcano and how the pieces were connected, but the paper document is no longer up-to-date and their web is growing "organically." The organization itself owes much to the library science of DeFelice. She notes that any fellow librarian accessing the Electronic Volcano would recognize the principles on which it is designed.

The HTML DTD

The original release of HTML was ambivalent in terms of its SGML origins. Tim Berners-Lee, the creator of the original HTML, wanted to use the syntax and the cross-platform compatibility of SGML while keeping the rules for markup so simple that no theory or knowledge of structured information processing would be required. In this last endeavor, he was wildly successful. The first version of HTML was loose with SGML syntax and loose with its own boundaries—there was no single statement of what was and was not "legal" HTML. There was no mechanism for parsing HTML, the test being "if it looked good in Mosaic." While this had certain advantages—it was easy to accomplish and forgiving of errors—it threatened to put the interoperability of the Web back in the hands of a single application instead of an application-neutral format.

In the years following the release of Mosaic, the proliferation of HTML around the globe has pushed the advantages of a higher degree of standardization and sophistication to the fore.

In 1994, as a preliminary step toward extending and standardizing the language, current practice was collected and defined in what is called HTML2. The next version, called HTML3, is under discussion; it is expected that it will be adopted by the Internet Engineering Task Force in 1995. HTML3 will introduce standard ways to code and present tables, math, complex placement of graphics, and other features, and it will allow applications to be parsed to ensure conformance. *Resource Guide A* details how to find out the latest on HTML3.

Conclusions

The Electronic Volcano was announced on two volcanologist listservs (geonet-l and volcano), which are Internet mailing lists sent to people interested in volcanoes. It has begun to attract notice and a modest amount of traffic. The responses have been positive and have shown evidence that the site is fulfilling its purpose. DeFelice is using it this term as she teaches the research techniques section of Earth Sciences 7, Myths and Volcanoes, a freshmen seminar. The authors' own assessment is indicative of the limits of rapid, HTML-based publishing at the present time.

Stoiber and DeFelice both feel that the inability to navigate through the material based on a theme, topic, or subject is a limitation. For example, it would be nice to ask for all material available on lava flows and be shown the relevant connections. In theory, they can create these connections now; in practice, building the paths by hand and anticipating what will be requested and maintaining the whole, once established, is not practical with HTML Web technology.

Stoiber also wants two windows open at once onto the same document. He says that, like a child, he wants to click on two places at once and he offers further observation on the changed quality of browsing.

The *Catalog* is hierarchical. It lists the five countries in Central America that have active volcanoes and the volcanoes in each. Using this system, you can go directly and efficiently to the information you want. This is a good feature, but Stoiber adds that there is another side of the coin:

> You miss the pages in-between. You do not see the pictures of the other volcanoes, so you have no feeling of the relative size, significance of your volcano versus the other volcanoes. Something is missing. It is bad that you can't browse (in the old fashioned sense), that you go immediately to what you want, that you don't have to look at anything else. It is naughty.

What people call browsing on the Internet, according to Stoiber, is more accurately labeled surfing, where one bobs from topic to topic in an apparently aimless pattern. Surfing is distinct from old-fashioned browsing which passed rapidly, lightly, over related material. He doubts that the delight in "surfing the Net" is conducive to scientific research. "People are so happy to be surfing, but in so doing they are fighting the best feature of the thing—that you can go somewhere directly."

Much of the Web, in Stoiber's opinion, is like light conversation; it holds your interest for a time but is not gripping, not the stuff of hard science. And he wonders if serious researchers have time to browse and if browsers have time for serious research. He wonders if the Web will grow up and if the focused approach will become its virtue. There are suggestions that part of the Web is doing just that.

Stoiber and DeFelice both feel that the inability to navigate through the material based on a theme, topic, or subject is a limitation.

In terms of their original objectives, Stoiber and DeFelice are pleased that the Electronic Volcano provides a more global compendium than other volcano-related online resources, which tend to reflect their own location and their own research interests. While their indexing is not the guide they would like it to be, it is better than most indexing available online today.

Of course, it is just the type of sophisticated, directed search and index they seek that SGML-capable browsers can provide. The reconciliation of HTML with SGML which, in early 1995 seems assured, and the introduction of the first SGML-capable Web browser profiled in the next portrait, means that Web authors and Web users can look forward to a vastly greater set of tools and capabilities in the near future. Already, since the first part of 1994, when it seemed that HTML and SGML might go their separate ways, at least half a dozen major SGML tool vendors announced Web-compatible products. In the future, the ability to integrate SGML browsers into the Web may provide the answer to the light-weight-versus-hard-science question posed by Stoiber.

INTEL CORPORATION PORTRAIT

Table 4.14 Intel

Industry	Semiconductor manufacture
Products	Integrated circuits, microprocessors, and related component datasheets
Media	Print, Web, CD-ROM
Key players	Melanie Yunk, Program Manager, Intel representative to Pinnacles Group
	Bob Yencha, Senior Systems Analyst, National Semiconductor representative to Pinnacles Group, Pinnacles Group Program Manager
	The Pinnacles Group

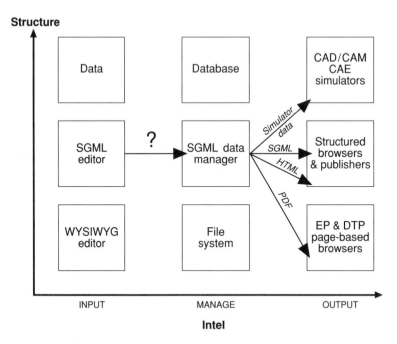

Figure 4.18 Structure and process at Intel

Basic Scenario[15]

Intel moved decisively to adopt SGML in 1992 as a member of the Pinnacles Group—originally four, now five, semiconductor manufacturers who took the initiative to develop a common electronic information exchange format for their industry. The vision then, as now, was to provide technical data in electronic form that can be incorporated directly into customers' databases, CAD/CAE (computer-aided design/computer-aided engineering) applications, and engineering performance simulators. Electronic technical data that can be imported directly into their customer's applications will be more up-to-date, more accurate, because it is not rekeyed, and cheaper to distribute.

A *White Paper* issued by the Pinnacles Secretariat in October, 1994, stated (p .5):

---

[15]This case study is derived from interviews with Melanie Yunk of Intel and Boy Yencha of National Semiconductor and the cited *White Paper*. While Yunk is the current Pinnacles Group representative, Pat O'Sullivan was the Intel representative during the formative stages of the Pinnacles work.

Pinnacles Group member companies believe that EDBs [Electronic Data Books] will increase the quality of product information by improving its accuracy, accessibility, and timeliness, as well as enabling CAD integration. Such improvements will help customers realize benefits in product identification and selection, reduced design-in and qualification cycle-times, enhanced product life-cycle management, and many other areas.

The EDBs not only eliminate keyboarding, they also include information not found in the printed books, such as voltage calibration values that are needed for CAD simulation.

Intel wants to start the use of SGML at the design engineer's desktop, where the information is created. According to Melanie Yunk, Program Manager and an engineer,

The goal is to transfer the information through Technical Marketing for revision and rewriting, and finally into editing, production, and printing without rekeying or converting any of the information, regardless of application or platform.

Currently, the information may be converted and rekeyed several times before publication. The Corporate Information Technology-approved word processor is not effective or efficient for 1500-page documents that include complex tables with spanning columns that shift from 3 to 5 to 4 columns, spread over 10 pages. Without SGML, data could be transferred between five different formats between the Intel engineers who create the information and the customers' engineers who use it. With SGML, the data stays in the original format from its inception until it is loaded into the client database or CAD/CAE simulator. Figure 4.19 shows the basic information flow with the current desktop technology and that projected with SGML.

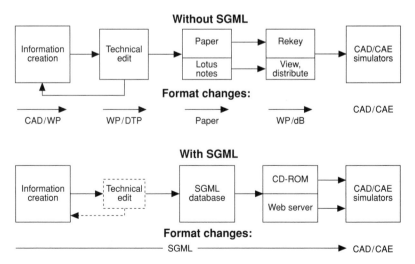

Figure 4.19 Manufacturer to customer information flow: with and without SGML

Even though Intel is not yet in production with its SGML component data system, it has a firm commitment to SGML and two years of experience with the language through participation in the Pinnacles Group. When the World Wide Web came to the attention of upper management as a means to distribute technical information, Yunk was asked to provide a Web gateway for the component information because she acts as consultant and PCIS expert to SGML-related projects within the component technical data group. A pilot Web system that contains abstracts and tables of contents and points to documents in both PostScript and Acrobat formats was installed and operational within four months.

This portrait tells the story of Intel's Pinnacles-related and internal DTD development and data design. It stops short of the tool-building and installation phase that is just now under way but describes the developing requirements.

Getting There

The Pinnacles Initiative and the internal SGML effort at Intel began at the same time. The idea of an all-out effort to develop interchange standards for Electronic Data Books sprang up synchronistically at each of the five sites—Hitachi America, Ltd., Intel, National Semiconductor, Philips Semiconductors, and Texas Instruments Semiconductor Group.

Bob Yencha, the original Pinnacles Group representative from National, recalls bumping into representatives from his competitors/business partners, including Pat O'Sullivan, Manager, Strategic Publishing Processes at Intel, at SGML meetings and forums, hearing their questions, speaking with them, and realizing that each had come to the same conclusion—that they needed more power and flexibility than they currently had in their publishing systems and that a joint effort would solve more problems more efficiently than if each worked in isolation.

Pinnacles Motives

The Pinnacles Group members share the conviction that "the resulting standard will be more robust, have wider applicability, and remain valid over a longer period" than if each company developed its own standard. As individual companies, it would take longer, they would draw on less experience, it would take more iterations, and it would be harder to fix at a later time. Together, they felt that they could do a better job of creating a standard that would satisfy their customers and help them share information in their various business partnerships. The joint effort would:

- Look good in the eyes of their customers;
- Project them into a leadership position;

- Create a groundswell of support for the standard, giving it a better chance of survival ("one standard is better than five"); and

- Cost more overall but less per company because they would share fixed expenses.

Individual companies added their own rationales for participation (*White Paper*, page 4):

- "… to get its current information to customers faster, providing them with accurate data to speed up design cycles and get products to market faster";

- "… to help its customers reduce costs";

- "to enhance [its] internal information creation and management processes";

- to give customers "the freedom to mix and match semiconductor products from several vendors…"

An additional selling point that helped create high-level buy-in for the project was that "the other guy" was doing it. The fact that all were on the same track at the same time made the entire effort more attractive and credible to upper management.

The Pinnacles Process

The Pinnacles *White Paper* explains that a neutral interchange standard is "difficult and time-consuming to derive in a volunteer setting without expert assistance" and so it was decided to fund a fast-track, consultant-led effort. After approximately six months of member-company buy-in, ATLIS Consulting was selected as the Pinnacles vendor in March of 1993.

From the beginning, the Pinnacles effort has been characterized by an exemplary emphasis on planning and training. The participants were constantly defining, redefining, and refining their common goals, the scope of the project, and what was outside the scope of the project. Before document analysis began, training was held so that all representatives would begin work with the same level of technical competence. The initial, week-long training session included a mini-analysis of documents that provided a final proof of concept. This was taken back to management at the individual companies to demonstrate the achievable nature of the joint goals.

The first document analysis workshop, held in May of that year, planned successive document analysis workshops to be held at the member companies (*White Paper*, p. 9):

The Pinnacles Group used a company-by-company serial analysis of the information contained in typical semiconductor component product datasheets, data books, and application notes. Each company hosted a week-long analysis session during which its information and publications experts examined the structure, content, and relationship of data elements contained in its product literature. Observers from the other sponsor companies, as well as consultants and tools suppliers invited by the host company, monitored the process. Each successive analysis session built upon the work of the prior sessions.

The overall process called for:

- Document analysis

- Architecture definition

- Joint architecture review

- DTD(s) and tag set creation, Version 1.0

- Supporting documentation development

- Invited comment and review session

- Revision of the DTD and release of Version 1.1

- Period of support for implementation and development by sponsor companies and suppliers

- Planning of follow-on phases

During the process, members of the group made every effort to include not only their own documentation requirements, but also those of companies not represented in Pinnacles. They analyzed and reviewed documents from several other semiconductor manufacturers and, where available, consulted with their experts.

The serial workshops concluded in November of 1993, and the draft was submitted for review at the beginning of 1994. The review proceeded throughout the year, and the draft standard—the Pinnacles Component Information Standard, PCIS 1.1—was released at the end of 1994.

The cost of the Pinnacles effort is put at between $2.5 and 3 million, which includes the cost of internal salaries, travel, and other expenses, as well as outside consulting for all five participants. Cost of salaries includes approximately 50 percent of the time of the primary representatives for each company for over a year, plus the time spent by company engineers. The joint effort involved 180 engineers, each devoting between 40 and 120 hours to the project.

At Intel

The initial SGML implementation at Intel covers component technical data—the supporting documentation for its microprocessors and for embedded microcontrollers and microprocessors. After the initial implementation for component data, Intel plans to bring SGML to its network products, which include boards and software.

They plan to initiate SGML at the source, with design and technical marketing engineers who will create the information using SGML-aware applications. The expectation, according to Yunk, is that these authors will "no longer have to worry about how it looks; that they will just concern themselves with accurate content."

At first, Intel expects to retain a technical review cycle. The hope is that later, when the process is well established, the authors will not need a separate review stage for hard copy or online documents because the documents will be composed of information that they, the engineers, have entered directly into the database. Although others will be responsible for distribution to customers, the published products will reflect the engineers' input without alteration.

Intel is currently designing a request for proposal for authoring tools. They feel that the PCIS calls for a tables/forms-based input metaphor, rather than a document-based metaphor for entering component characteristics and parameters. The initial goals of the Pinnacles Initiative stated that the standard should be implementable with existing tools but this was altered during document analysis and testing as the partners realized that they needed to include constructs that were not well suited to what was available in the marketplace.

The document architecture of the PCIS includes a source and reflection mechanism using the SGML constructs of ID and IDREF. Parameters are entered once into a document and tagged as a source, which can then be reflected to many locations within the document without reentry. Intel wants tools that will allow an author to write a parameter once and then designate where it is used, in which standard documents, and under which conditions. They want to offer authors a choice of standard table templates or custom tables based on defined elements. Intel wants immediate preview capability of the printed and online documents from the authors' desktop.

The SGML source material will go from the authors into a database. From the database, the production group will extract and publish on CD-ROM, paper, the Internet, and other online services, both internal and external to Intel. The current method of distribution is by printed books and datasheets and online datasheets and application notes. In addition, some documents are distributed via Lotus Notes.

In the future, Intel plans to cash in on the regularity of SGML using a rules-based composition system to go to paper, although the outlines of the system are still in flux.

Intel wants tools that will allow an author to write a parameter once and then designate where it is used, in which standard documents, and under which conditions.

Data Design

The primary characteristic of the PCIS design is that it is for information interchange, not for document production. (Chapter 6 contrasts PCIS with several other industrywide data designs). It specifies content, therefore, and does not specify large-scale structure and order. The PCIS describes what information can, and must, be contained in an element, but not which elements must be collected together or what order they must follow in a document. Yunk explains the reasons for the distinction this way:

> One company might place the functional description before the electrical specifications of a chip and another manufacturer publishes it the other way around... The Pinnacles Group did not want to force the way each does internal documentation to change. The interchange DTD can have the information in any order, and everything is optional.

Customers receive data from various suppliers. They, too, have different requirements for structure and order. Like the suppliers, the customers can reorder the information for their own use. But the exchange information itself, the primary data required by each company's customers, is fully specified by PCIS and goes beyond what they have been able to deliver on paper:

> For example, a customer's CAD designers who use our datasheets, manuals, and application notes want to have our database to search online and view parameters. They do not care about the paper document, they just want the AC characteristics of the Pentium processor.

> The PCIS-defined data will contain information not typically published. The value of V_{ol} and V_{os} (voltages) for example—there may be three definitions of these defined by three different standards organizations. Which one is used when measuring a parameter is not normally printed in a document, but will be identified as part of interchange information to be used by CAD systems and simulators. What will be printed will be different information.

The emphasis on electronic delivery is one of the characteristics of the PCIS that developed only during the document analysis and testing process. Yencha recalls that one of the original goals was that it be easy to publish on paper from the specification. As the analysis progressed, the participants altered their position to include constructs that make it easier to provide electronic delivery, regardless of the impact on paper output. As Yencha puts it, "The clear benefits are in the electronic area," and that eventually took precedence.

With the publication of PCIS 1.1, the data design effort at Intel has switched to its own internal requirements. The Intel DTDs will be a super-set to PCIS, for creating internal documents. For internal document analysis, Intel hired its own consulting vendor. The company expects the process to take about three days for each session. There will be some preliminary training because not everyone who will take part has been through the PCIS document analysis.

PCIS does not require any information, but, in practice, each supplier will include certain information, like chip pin-out. Internally, the DTDs developed by Intel and the other member companies will require specific types of information in a specified order. The Intel DTDs will also contain information for internal use, such as author's name, revision information, and workflow information, that is not part of the exchange specification.

The Web Server

In addition to print and CD-ROM, Intel is putting its component technical information onto a World Wide Web server. Initially, the service was implemented internally and is now available online at http://www.intel.com under PC Developer Support, Component Technical Documents. It offers PostScript and Acrobat versions of sample documents in a pilot project designed to solicit input from design engineers and programmers. Selected SGML documents are now available as well using the Panorama SGML Web browser from SoftQuad. Panorama is a subset of SoftQuad's Explorer browser designed for the Web and available in a free version and a paid version. Panorama works in conjunction with NCSA Mosaic and other HTML browsers. When the HTML browser encounters an SGML document it invokes Panorama much as it would invoke a graphics viewer or audio recorder.

The original pilot plan called for 25 popular technical documents to go online in PostScript and Acrobat (PDF). (PostScript is required for readers on Unix platforms until an Acrobat reader for Unix is released.)

During the planning stages for the pilot system, the group considered converting the documents themselves to hypertext markup language, but decided that the limited HTML DTD was not easily converted up to PCIS and was not robust enough for searching. The Panorama viewer from SoftQuad made it possible to provide full SGML markup through the Web. As soon as the viewer was announced, it was added to the plan, which is now to take part of the Pinnacles DTD, tag the same 25 documents that are available in PostScript and Acrobat, and put them online with Panorama.

The non-SGML files can be searched via the World Wide Web or a WAIS index, which provides a list of abstracts with tables of contents so that the user can then download or view the document. Users can scroll through the document but searching is limited.

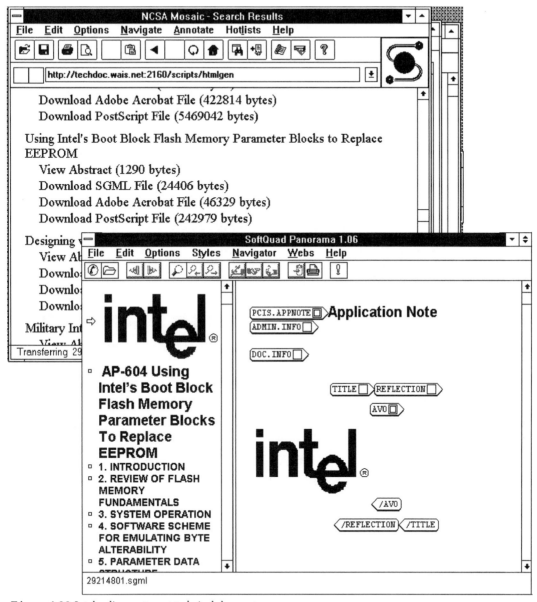

Figure 4.20 Intel online component technical documents

Figure 4.20 shows the Intel HTML page listing documents in different formats in NCSA Mosaic in the background and an Intel SGML document open in Panorama in the foreground. The SGML document was selected, and Panorama invoked, from clicking on the active link in the HTML document.

In contrast to HTML Web browsers, Panorama has a navigator displayed next to the document. The navigator in Figure 4.21 is a table of contents which shows the structure of the document and links to each section. With Panorama, you can build multiple paths through the document based on the markup. For example, if you want to see AC characteristics, you can build a custom path or navigator based on the corresponding tag. Since the DTD has more than 200 tags, the navigation possibilities are extensive. The capabilities of the browser and the richness and detail of the markup combine for an extremely powerful search and retrieval environment. Figure 4.21 shows the table of contents navigator and a section of the document with a pop-up window with and without some tags revealed.

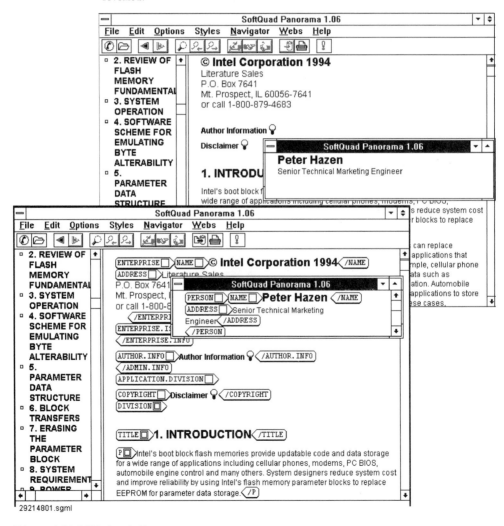

Figure 4.21 PCIS data in Panorama

The ease with which complex technical documentation can now go onto the Web has given visibility to SGML within Intel. The Web had already caught the attention of upper management as a marketing and communications medium. When management was shown how they could use SGML on the Web, they figured that they were getting "good bang for their buck." Yunk noticed them beginning to use "the SGML word" at the same time.

The pilot will survey users and get feedback comparing the PostScript, Acrobat, and SGML documents. An additional goal of the survey is to find out whether the designers and programmers who are Intel's target audience will come to the World Wide Web to view technical documents.

Conclusions

While PCIS is still a draft standard, all the Pinnacles participants are thick into the initial stages of internal adoption. Several challenges await Intel in the coming implementation.

Intel has set high goals for an all-SGML environment. When the plan was first presented to the technical marketing managers—a plan that includes the use of SGML authoring tools—they accepted it but said that they wanted intuitive tools that they could figure out how to use in seven minutes or less. Is this doable? Melanie Yunk thinks so, but only if technical marketing is committed to learning about the structure and the organization of the information before they start the clock ticking.

There are organizational challenges, as well as technical challenges. Yunk feels that teaching authors that "you do not own the information that you create—the company owns it," will be a critical test for the system. "Today," she reports, "they write it and stick it on their desktop." On the desktop, no one else has access to it. Overcoming this protectiveness is part of their training in SGML.

The hope and vision among the Pinnacles veterans at Intel, all unabashed SGML advocates, is that with the survey and roll-out of the SGML Web browser, the Acrobat and PostScript versions will go away. If not, they are prepared to generate these formats from the source SGML.

This case study illustrates the adaptiveness of SGML: Two years ago, at the inception of the Pinnacles Initiative, there was no Web and no thought of Internet distribution. With the advent of the Web and SGML-capable Web browsers, the investment in SGML has even greater potential payback.

A measure of the success of PCIS data design is that at the final reconciliation meetings attended by engineers from each company, the analysis and criticism did not break down along company lines, but along lines drawn by technology. According to Yencha, the main divisions were between "the analog guys and the microprocessor guys, the digital and memory guys. Everyone got into the spirit, looking at it from the *information* point of view."

The Pinnacles Group plans to extend the standard and to place it with an international standards body that will promote and support it. Even though much lies ahead for both Pinnacles and the individual member companies, Yencha says (*White Paper,* p.8): "There's value just in going through the process... It has given our people a chance to look at documentation from the customer's perspective on how to make it clearer and more consistent across the corporation."

ADAMS & HAMILTON PORTRAIT

Table 4.15 Adams & Hamilton

Industry	Typesetting and design
Products	Books, catalogs, pamphlets
Media	Print
Key players	Kate Hamilton
	Nelson Adams

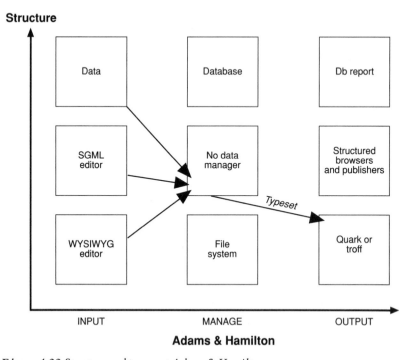

Figure 4.22 Structure and process at Adams & Hamilton

Basic Scenario[16]

Nelson Adams and Kate Hamilton design and typeset books. They consider SGML to be the key enabling technology in a process that remains the same from project to project, although the exact tools used may vary.

As Hamilton puts it, once information is in SGML, "appearance is one possible use." Files created in SGML or converted to SGML are filtered/converted to a composition engine such as troff or Quark. The SGML file remains the master file. Once printed, the file with the output markup becomes a throwaway file. Other designers "think the Quark file is the product; it is, in fact, designer-added value." These designers, Hamilton and Adams, clearly get the bigger picture—information is more than its appearance—but have sacrificed nothing as crafts-people along the way.

According to Kate Hamilton, SGML makes typesetting into the process that it was always supposed to be—the pure application of design. Without SGML, Hamilton and Adams claim that typesetters and designers allocate more time to clearing up what exactly that squiggle means and whether they have found every instance of a nested bullet than they allocate to the business taught in school as typesetting and design.

As designers, Hamilton and Adams work in their composition engine in the ordinary way, but with files imported from SGML markup. Unlike files imported from unstructured editors, they know that a file imported from SGML is consistent. They know that it is clean because it parses, it conforms to a certain shape. Without SGML, much of the work done by typesetters and designers is actually cleaning up after an author whose file arrives with unspecified quirks that are individual to that author.

The SGML source files give them a hook for each appearance that they want to create. On the chapter title hook, for example, they hang a style sheet for chapter titles in Quark or a macro for chapter titles in troff. The files are predefined, although not necessarily predesigned.

As designers and typesetters who work on contract, they are not concerned with long-term storage, reuse, and elaborate production workflow, although multiple outputs and revisions can enter into the picture. Most commonly, they take SGML-coded master files as input and produce a specific output. While this approach makes for a sleek and elegant production process, the rub—if there is one—comes when the throwaway file is tweaked in ways that might also have enduring value.

> *Unlike files imported from unstructured editors, they know that a file imported from SGML is consistent.*

---

[16]Portions of this case study have already been published by Schettini and Alschuler (1994). The case study was derived from interviews and correspondence with Kate Hamilton and Nelson Adams.

Tools

Table 4.16 Software

VENDOR	TOOL TYPE	TOOL NAME
Santa Cruz Operation (SCO)	Operating system for 386, 33 MHz PC	SCO Unix
Microsoft	Operating system or Windows 486 PC	Microsoft Windows
SCO	Unix text utilities	sed, vi, awk
SoftQuad	Output conversion	SoftQuad Publishing Software
In-house	Output conversion	"Kate's Converter"
Quark	Composition	Quark Xpress
Unix utility	Composition	troff

The critical tools in their repertoire are the converters that take the SGML source files and apply the formatter tags or macros. Going to troff, they use SoftQuad Publishing Software (SQPS); to Quark, they use what we will call Kate's Converter, a home-grown piece of software written in awk (mawk, actually, a variation on awk), a Unix utility, using a simple trick of its syntax. Kate's Converter was written on her own time—originally, it was just an exploration of issues while working as a typesetter at Coach House Press, a small Canadian publishing house well known for technological innovation, typography, camera work, and press work. It was designed to produce Quark input formats, from either Mac or MS Windows SGML files (the difference is in how each platform handles non-ASCII characters).

Typically, Adams and Hamilton convert SGML to Quark external style tags or to troff macros and do a minimum of tweaking once the file is in the composition format. They do only about 5–10 percent of their work with Quark, the balance with troff. In choosing the composition tool, they prefer Quark if there are many pictures, while troff handles regularity well, so they choose it when they do not require a final WYSIWYG stage. A capability to go to Frame was designed into the converter but never developed.

Getting There

Adams and Hamilton's initial exposure to SGML came while they were at Coach House Press, now CHP Printing, which has had a long association with

SoftQuad, a company that has been an innovator in SGML software for a decade. Hamilton says that CHP has had a lively, active interest in what SoftQuad does and was an early SoftQuad site. She describes Coach House as a "very small place for that kind of technology. But they didn't need heavy programming; they just needed a little persistence."

Nelson Adams's experience with type goes back to 1969, to the days of hand-set lead type for posters that were printed on a hand press. Along the road to SGML, he has known and used every twist of the technology from film to paper type to the Mergenthaler Linotype Machine; to typesetters driven by punched paper and cassette tapes that took hours to load each chapter. Adams and Hamilton used to use vi and troff primitives; then they used the GCA's GenCode, a precursor of SGML, to mark up literary parts. They used sed and awk to go to troff.

When they first encountered SGML files, they took them into troff, which they had already been using for over ten years. At that time, they did not yet have the choice of a WYSIWYG Quark composition engine. They have been converting SGML to troff and Quark since then, doing about 60–120 titles each year.

> We could not wait for the big software houses to bring out the perfect product; we were interested in whether there could be something that would make the work easier... The advantage seemed so great. We were struggling with word-processing files—it was really a lot of work—this looked like it could get us away from that.

Of the actual writing of the Quark converter, Hamilton says it took about a week of her so-called off time, although the week included two weekends and stretched into one year of clean-up.

Being There

As Nelson Adams describes their workflow: "You start with a design problem. You proceed to think about its use, to think about your constraints: page size, trim, output device—low/high resolution, fonts, capacity of formatter and so on." If this sounds the same as it would in any typesetting shop, well, it is. And that is the point. The basic parts of the design work itself do not change. What does change? Adams and Hamilton make several generalizations about their work that stem from the SGML-ness of the environment in which they work.

"More of the work has to be done up front, while more decisions can be put off to the end," is a refrain that runs through their descriptions.

> The process separates text-processing from page layout, so the designer does not have to worry about preparing the text and the typesetter does not have to worry about the art: All are happy, because each has control over the work that belongs to them.

For authors and editors, there is some initial discomfort—more of their work has to be done up front. They have to think about it before giving it to the publisher for typesetting instead of afterwards.

The SGML files that the firm typesets originate as native SGML files in Author/Editor, or they are converted to SGML from an unstructured format. They go primarily, but not exclusively, to print.

When the SGML file does get to the design stage, the designer gets a sense of all the different parts he or she has to take account of. Between the SGML and the formatter the file is converted to Quark External Style tags or troff with macros. This conversion, being by nature a down conversion, is relatively hands-off.

The converter produces a style name for each SGML tag-in-context. Before conversion, a paragraph within a note would have the same tag as a paragraph within a chapter; after conversion, the two types of paragraphs would have two different tags. They could be typeset to look the same or to look different. With some minor optimization for each run, the converter maps entities as well as elements, including character entities from either Mac or Windows character-sets. On simple books, the whole conversion process, including setup, is done within 15 minutes.

Figure 4.23 graphs the "need to tweak" against the production workflow. As the project progresses, the need to make minor adjustments in the file decreases.

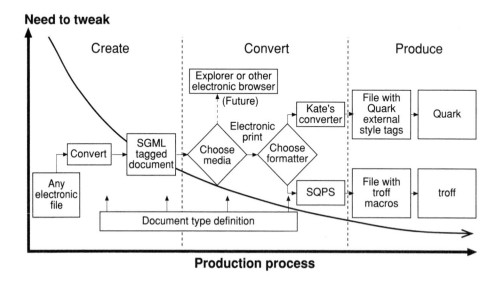

Figure 4.23 Need to tweak and the production process

In terms of the limits of her conversion tool, Kate Hamilton is very clear: It is a production tool, one of which, as a nonprogrammer, she is proud. It is *not* a commercial product—it does not have the error handling, usability, or features of a commercial product. It does not address SGML-marked sections, attributes, and omittag. They get around the lack of these features by running preconversion routines that normalize the files. A full-blown output conversion product would require analysis and manipulations that are beyond the simple Unix utilities that they use for this tool.

In general, Hamilton and Adams try to work out what's in a page before they begin typesetting. They may start with a generic style—in fact, they reuse many parts of their basic design. Kate's Converter brings files into a default Quark style sheet. Each part of the file is tagged, and the designer knows the full parentage of each tag—what part of the SGML file is contained within the style tag. They can bring the file in with known styles or they can bring it into plain vanilla styles.

If they want to work with plain vanilla—without their default design characteristics—then the format of each named tag is not specified or is given only minimal characteristics. On a WYSIWYG screen, the text will look as if it were not formatted. In fact, it is completely marked up with styles—but these styles have not been assigned design characteristics. As the design is created, the format is applied to every instance of the style.

Generally, Hamilton and Adams know up front what the book will look like. They apply what they know to a style, pull in the file, and tweak. Once the material is in the formatter, the designer works in the ordinary way. The difference is that, since every instance of a style is now tagged, any changes apply to all instances and the effect of a change is immediately apparent. Without SGML, they pulled in a file, tweaked here, then had to go back and readjust there. With files that come in from SGML, they can see all instances of a typographic feature, like a chapter title, from the start, so they can design for the whole book, not just a sample section.

After that, the actual working out of a design is the same as it is without SGML.

> There are only a few ways to do standard pieces such as a bibliography, or list. Once you know the trim, decide on type, measure columns, leading, then most things fall into place. It's a matter of knowing what goes together nicely more than being ingenious every time.

After input, they can change any part of the style that they wish—changes that ripple through the whole book or local changes that affect one section only. "It turns out to be lovely for the designer to have the batch part done when they go to do the hand work."

And the preparation of the text and the preparation of the design are independent. The designer makes the choices about the output file. The decision about output software can be made late in the process. At conversion, the design may or may not have been done. The author can create an entire SGML file without any thought about design.

On the other hand, the author must be unambiguous about content, which is his or her job, after all, Hamilton emphasizes. For example, if an author has used a Sanskrit character, *a* with a bar underneath, without SGML it would exist in the transmitted file as an asterisk (maybe with a note, maybe not) or as a workaround, as italics or an underlined letter *a*. Ideally, she says, the author is responsible for parsing the file and must define that entity in the correct character-set before jetting off to Delhi, leaving the typesetting crew wondering what he meant by that squiggly line.

> The textbook leaves out all the stuff about a-bar-under—but, that's what takes time. You don't know he (the author) has gone to India until you call two days in a row and don't get him, then you find out that he isn't available and this is what causes delay. Publishers do not like delay.

A DTD and a parser holding an author to unambiguous content make typesetting proceed like the books say it should.

Pictures

If the placement of the illustrations is regular—top right corner of every right-hand page—there is no need to preview the file before printing, so Hamilton and Adams position them with troff. If the placement is not regular, they use Quark or Frame. They scan the pictures in and position them in the composition engine by hand. "In theory, after you get the position set, you can put the size back into the SGML file as an attribute for an archive. If the size and position were known up front, it could be read in from the SGML file." While aware of the theoretical basis for automating this aspect of layout, Kate Hamilton sees no practical advantage for their firm at the present time.

Archives

Hamilton and Adams have not been concerned with the larger issues of data management and reuse. For them, each project is discrete. The Adams & Hamilton workflow makes no provision for re-export of Quark or troff to SGML. Nevertheless, to safeguard the integrity and lasting validity of the source file, their policy is to make all changes in the SGML source file because their customers are concerned with the long-term viability of their files. I asked if that applied to all changes, and Adams and Hamilton answered in unison, "*ALL* changes. We do not tweak the troff."

When they do a database extraction directly to a typeset input, the galleys may be the first opportunity to proofread it in anything close to the final form.

Then, if changes are required, there are two places to make corrections—the database and the SGML file—unless a new extraction is done. Of course, this double correction hassle is common with non-SGML source files, too.

DTD

Native SGML files come to them with a DTD in tow. For commercial trade books that are converted from an unstructured editor, they use a DTD they wrote themselves. Hamilton says, "We're on version 30 now—it is a well-polished tool."

They had looked at early versions of ISO 12083, the AAP DTD for books, but found that their own DTD fits their purpose more closely. Their own DTD has been refined through the process of doing about 500 books of poetry, plays, fiction, and college texts.

Conversion

Hamilton and Adams recognize that conversion of legacy data is a messy business—authors write dashes differently, use different symbols for nonstandard characters, and so on.

They use a commercial conversion house to prepare nonnative files, to tag them according to their in-house DTD, and to replace the funny characters with SGML constructs. Once the files are converted, the typesetters give little thought to the file's origin. They will look at the file for general sense and do a quick proof; otherwise, they rely on the conversion house. In general, by the time files come to them, Hamilton and Adams find that the nonnative files can be slightly better than some native files because of the high quality of work by the conversion house, where the files are proofed and extra checks carried out.

Alt In

In terms of alternate input sources, Adams says, "Database publishing is a natural for SGML typesetting; we'd like to do more work of this sort with library archives. The win for them is that they do not need to know the SGML, they just need to describe their existing database."

What do they do if using the output from a database? First, they talk to the client about the kind of output available. They look at the data export options. "In most cases, it is enough to have them stick text at the head of each field. They do a data 'dump' with structure and then we have it converted. On the whole, the earlier [the pieces of structure] are put in, the better the converted file."

Alt Out

In terms of alternate output, which for Adams & Hamilton means anything other than regular print, several of their books have had multiple uses. Hamilton did some of the early work on the SGML source file for *Christopher Columbus Answers All Questions*, which was eventually published in regular and large print by The Porcupine's Quill. Because the source file had been marked up with the International Committee for Accessible Document Design (ICADD) SGML extensions, it was published simultaneously in Braille by the Canadian National Institute for the Blind and in electronic form by Recording for the Blind. (See the InfoUCLA/ICADD sketch.)

Canada Writes! which they typeset, may go online. They are well aware of the potential for longterm reuse by going online, archiving, publishing in different formats, selectively republishing books or sections, and pulling out sections or summaries.

Conclusions

Of this continual evolution in typesetting technology, Nelson Adams says that he had the most fun in the first 10 years, doing posters in wood type for political demonstrations, but that was because of the scene, not the technology.

Adams says quite plainly: "I think we've found that typesetting books with SGML is easier than any other system we've used" and Hamilton adds, "incomparably easier." They know that an author's file has been tidied up in the conversion to SGML. "The typesetter is no longer getting 500 files in a word processor with the author's ideas about how to do a list. When the file goes to the typeset process, it is clean." For bigger overall savings, she explains "You can get non-typesetters to do cleanup. When you get the messiness out before you (the type-setter or designer) look at the page, you save a lot of time. It gets cleaner as is goes through the process and goes to higher and higher skilled workers." Looking at it from this point of view, "The most skilled 'worker' is the program that converts the file to PostScript. You want it to be real tidy by then."

Hamilton and Adams acknowledge that some designers and typesetters fear the assembly line—that all the publications will look the same. In fact, there is no intrinsic reason for files that originate in SGML to look more alike than files that originate in any proprietary or unstructured markup. The determining factor, here as elsewhere, is the eye of the designer. Their experience gained helping other typesetters and designers convert to SGML is that, once people see how it works, they appreciate it. They realize that the same information is involved, it is just injected earlier. SGML prevents the handoff of incomplete information, which is great for the publisher who has a schedule to meet.

Because of the length of their experience with SGML and their close association with SoftQuad, Kate Hamilton and Nelson Adams are not typical typesetters.[17] Can you generalize from their experience? Not every typesetter is prepared to write even a modest conversion tool, but they have worked successfully with other designers who lack their depth of experience. They prepare the files, and the designers, who know no SGML, do whatever handwork they want to finish the product. They report that, for these designers, "the regularity of the input file (as it came from SGML, not from the author) saved them hours of work per book."

They have also used their skills as consultants with others who are looking at SGML for the first time. They report that it took a while for the others to get the idea of batch production:

> A designer works on a page at a time, whereas SGML is about doing the preparation first. So they could not understand, initially, why we spent "so much time" on setup. They did not understand it until the files just slid into Quark, all formatted and typographically correct. No going through to pick out every place the author used two hyphens instead of an em-dash, for instance.

As for their own plans to enhance and expand their process, they did sketch out how to do the same conversions in perl. They have thought how it could be done in Windows. They would like to do a true archive with graphics included. They do not experience the lack of an export from the composition system into SGML as a problem because, unlike a traditional system, the content is settled before the piece is composed, and the composition process is so rapid that there is not a great time span during which changes accumulate. That the designer works on stable content pages has changed the entire timing of the process. Changes can be made in the SGML file much closer to publication time because the design phase itself is so rapid.

The current process works well enough that future enhancements are likely to come from those whose business is providing better software tools, not from further programming on their part. Software tool developers would do well to study how far these typesetters have gone in rolling their own software.

---

[17]After these interviews were conducted, Hamilton was named Product Manager for SoftQuad's Explorer, an SGML browser. She is now a consultant with Passage Systems.

SKETCHES

Microsoft's Cinemania[18]

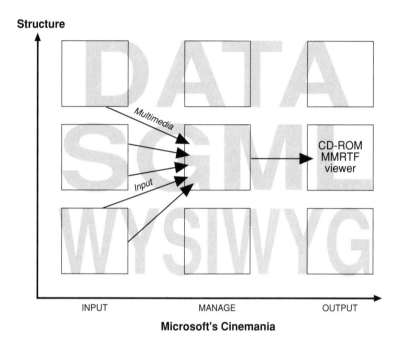

Figure 4.24 Structure and process, Microsoft's Cinemania

Microsoft's Cinemania demonstrates the use of SGML in the production of mass-market, multimedia entertainment. The 1992 Cinemania is composed of:

- Five print publications, including an encyclopedia
- 19,000 movie listings
- 3,000 biographies
- 1,245 articles and reviews
- 1,000 photos
- A glossary and other miscellaneous features
- 22 Mbytes of text and markup
- 1.6 million discrete SGML elements, an average of 10 characters per element

---

[18]This case study is based on presentation notes of John McFadden of Exoterica, and interviews with members of the Cinemania production staff at Microsoft and Exoterica. It was reviewed by Exoterica but not by Microsoft.

While the task of assembling this material in itself is daunting, the task of coding and maintaining it over time, through successive releases and updates, would be overwhelming if it were not automated to a high degree.

Hollywood, mass-market, and multimedia change the economics of production. In this case, the cost of writing and editing the material is relatively unimportant compared to the cost of permission to use film clips and stills, the cost of the intellectual property itself, and the potential profit. Microsoft estimates that the cost of text preparation for Cinemania is less than 10 percent of the total, while the cost of licensing of the media is 60–70 percent, the remainder being the cost of automation and mastering.

Hollywood, mass-market, and multimedia change the economics of production.

Where production costs do make a difference is not in the writing and editing, but in the tying together of the multimedia database, the tracking and linking of its constituent parts. Here, the structured, programmatic approach made possible with SGML makes the critical difference in the creation and maintenance of the data.

The process takes the disparate sources, codes them and combines them, adds the navigational data, and converts the whole into the format required by the chosen viewer. The browser used in Cinemania is Microsoft's Multimedia Viewer (MMV), which uses a variant of rich text format called MMRTF, although the choice of browser and format is not critical for the production process.

Microsoft produced the CD-ROM in close collaboration with Exoterica, using the latter's consulting services and Exoterica's OmniMark programming language for part of the work done at Microsoft. The division of labor was roughly thus: Exoterica took the source text, converted, tagged, and edited it to create the basic SGML database called a knowledge base. Staff at Microsoft did a final edit on the knowledge base, then wrote their own OmniMark scripts to link, combine, and format the data for the MMV. They created the look of the ROM in an iterative process, working alternately on the data and on the viewer interface.

Exoterica reports that OmniMark was used to do the following:

- Organize information into units;

- Create a hierarchical table of contents;

- Separate and access large tables and figures;

- Create a master index;

- Create hypertext links between and among documents; and

- Format text, tables, and graphics.

This degree of programmatic control is only possible because the documents are structured and identified explicitly with SGML. They use a project-specific control file that encompasses what is known about the application. The control file manages the viewing units, creates new topics, adds them to the table of contents, transforms the information for the viewer, identifies and links the graphics, and creates the script files that do the processing.

The type of linking employed is the implicit programmed linking described in Chapter 6. Another important feature of the markup used for Cinemania was the use of optional SGML features and OmniMark to reduce the markup overhead, the ratio of markup to text, and to improve the readability of the source. In this simplified markup, the string:

```
[The Mick = Mickey Rooney]
```

replaces the nested sequence:

```
<PERSON>
  <CALLED>
    <NAMEPART>
```

The Mick

```
    </NAMEPART>
  </CALLED>
  <ALSO>
```

Mickey Rooney

```
  </ALSO>
</PERSON>
```

The short sequence:

```
<movie c hv 1.5 pg>
```
Lightning, The White Stallion (1986: Drama): 95
```
<d>[William A. *Levey]
```

identifies a color movie with a 1.5 PG rating. It describes the movie as a 95-minute drama released in 1986, and gives the director's full name and family name. When expanded, the same information resolves to 13 elements and four attributes.

The nested content and structure elements make possible the programmed linking that ties together the CD-ROM without tedious, error-prone, and erratic hand-linking procedures. The condensed form of markup makes it possible to work in a simple text editor. Microsoft uses Word for Windows or a DOS editor with search and retrieval capabilities to edit the text. Quality assurance and debugging of the text are carried out directly in the multimedia viewer. They check for things that are not always amenable to programmed composition, such as film titles that use special characters and proper designation of remakes that share a title.

John McFadden, President of Exoterica, summarizes the advantages of using SGML for Cinemania:

- Editors concentrate on content, not format.

- Data is target-neutral—it can be ported to any multimedia viewer.

- Indirect linking is done with a program and is therefore more complete.

- The database as a whole is cheaper and easier to maintain and easier to modify and manipulate.

- The data design itself provides a high level of quality assurance.

- Presentation and linking are flexible and can change in response to user requirements without changing the data.

Cinemania demonstrates the versatility of SGML—it is equally suitable for this example of mass-market, multimedia entertainment as it is for technical manuals or scholarly research. More on this latter type of application in the next sketch.

The Women Writers Project[19]

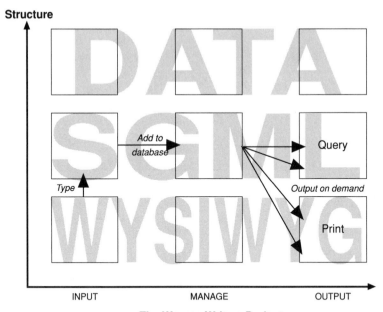

The Women Writers Project

Figure 4.25 Structure and process, Women Writers Project

---

[19]This case study was compiled from interviews and correspondence conducted with Allen Renear, Carole Mah, Textbase Coordinator, and Carol DeBoer-Langworthy, Director, Women Writers Project. Contact information for the Project is given at the end of *Resource Guide A*.

Quite at the other end of the spectrum from Cinemania lies the Women Writers Project (WWP). The two implementations form an interesting contrast: Where Cinemania puts a premium on capturing the latest trend and linking the hottest stars, the WWP values and guards the unchanging nature of its texts; where Cinemania lives to reach a wide, mass-market audience, the WWP prides itself on filling the requirements of even the smallest audience, a class of students or a single researcher; where Cinemania emphasizes delivery and the user interface, the WWP emphasizes the data and the intellectual content of the textbase. Much of the value of Cinemania is in presenting small pieces of sought-after contemporary works; much of the value of the WWP is in making available the entire text of neglected, forgotten, or obscure pre-modern writing.

Cinemania uses multimedia to bring mass culture to a mass audience; the WWP uses scholarly text encoding to bring rare works to the academic community.

Cinemania uses multimedia to bring mass culture to a mass audience; the WWP uses scholarly text encoding to bring rare works to the academic community. Cinemania uses highly sophisticated production techniques that automate critical parts of the process; the WWP uses no automation, relying entirely on handwork by highly trained individuals. When you understand how completely at odds the objectives and how disparate the means of these two projects, and that one data representation scheme made both possible, you have to appreciate how SGML coding delivers the value of the basic material home to its natural audience.

The Women Writers Project, affiliated with Brown University, is transcribing and coding all literature (fiction and nonfiction, poetry, and drama), and all writing, (journals, diaries, handbooks, and compositions), in English by women between the years 1330 and 1830. According to Allen Renear, a former acting director, the Project originally focused on texts of interest to literary and cultural historians. Later, the target audience was expanded to include linguists, social historians, and others.

Renear has a long and continuing association with electronic text and its place in academia. The articles he co-authored in the late nineteen-eighties helped to create the theoretical basis for the expansion of descriptive markup into scholarly text processing (Coombs et al., 1987; DeRose et al, 1990). He was part of the group that convinced Harvard to use SGML for the Perseus Project, one of the first large-scale applications of SGML to historical texts and images. Renear is currently Director of the Scholarly Technology Group, where much of his work is what he calls "functional data design—writing DTDs and creating document architecture that reflects how the texts will be used, that matches the opportunity and the technology to the method and the discipline." The Group works in hypermedia and heterogeneous media and specializes in transcription of early texts and the application of text encoding to pre-modern books. The Women Writers Project is among the prototype projects of this kind.

The Products

The primary product of the WWP is the text base itself. The Project assembles and codes the raw material; when complete, the material will be released for others to search and query and for others to build derivative products. There are, however, several current uses for the textbase.

Each year, the Project distributes about 200 works, each work assembled on special request, each a literal transcription of otherwise unavailable texts. Occasionally, they receive requests for anthologies or for unique formats, for example, "Suppress the stage direction, print in 30-point type," but the usual requests are for an entire work with a uniform look. This is essentially on-demand publishing of master copies, from which, they estimate, approximately 5,000 copies are distributed in classrooms. These orders are not edited and composed in the usual fashion, but are batch-processed from the SGML source. Renear says that the only problem with the batch process is that the pages "look too good," leading people to think they are edited, finished products instead of literal transcriptions.

The Project is also in the midst of publishing 30 volumes in scholarly editions with Oxford University Press (OUP). Unlike the special orders, these volumes are carefully edited and typeset. Volumes published in 1993–4 include *The Poems of Aemilia Lanyer: Salve Deus Rex Judaeorum,* edited by Susanne Woods, *The Poems and Prose of Mary, Lady Chudleigh,* edited by Margaret Ezell, *Fall River: An Authentic Narrative,* edited by Patricia Caldwell, and *The Letters of Arbella Stuart,* edited by Sara Jayne Steen. The eighth volume in the series has just been issued.

The ultimate goal of the Project, however, is not print, but electronic publishing. Renear states that several more pieces need to fall into place before that is possible. They must establish version control, not in the temporary sense of most document production systems, but in a secure system with digital signatures that guard the integrity of a work in the same way that print fixes an edition for all time. And they need a system for managing changes in the tag set and the encoding system.

Renear expects the full electronic project to be public in about three years. The electronic release will fully exploit the sophisticated markup that the Project has developed for this material. It will provide online delivery with hypertext and annotation as well as the raw files.

The Project is evaluating the ultimate means and methods of publication. Renear expects that it will be over the Web via an SGML Web server, but no decision has been reached. While a delay of several years would be intolerable in a commercial environment, it is not so unusual in the scholarly community.

In the interim, the electronic files are already in limited use. Individual linguists have access to the collection to study grammar and spelling. The *Oxford English Dictionary* is using it to broaden its source of citations, to revise word

> The *Oxford English Dictionary* is using it to broaden its source of citations, to revise word entries, to discuss changes in usage, and for instances of first uses.

entries, to discuss changes in usage, and for instances of first uses. Because these writings are exclusively the work of women, this represents a significant expansion of the basis of this authoritative work on the English language.

How Produced

Production of the Women Writers Project is relatively low-tech, as might be expected in an academic setting where the emphasis is on the long-term quality of the data and where the source material is primarily handwritten and pre-machine manuscripts.

Graduate and undergraduate students from Brown transcribe the manuscripts, adding the SGML markup as they go. Each student receives a full week of formal training covering the basics of SGML and the specific objectives of the WWP. Renear and Carole Mah, Textbase Coordinator, report that it takes anywhere from three weeks to three months to get fully up to speed. Project staff carefully supervise all aspects of the encoding. After the initial inputting, there are at least two cycles of proofreading and corrections; sometimes the electronic text is read aloud while a listener compares it with the original.

Renear says that everyone asks him about scanning texts, but he says "the intellectual aspects of the process dwarf what scanning can add to the Project." The Project's current platform is an IBM mainframe running CMS. They use Xedit with custom scripts that condense lengthy tag sequences into short key sequences. The SGML coding is verified with the public domain sgmls parser. The WWP has licenses for several structured editors, but is waiting for a general upgrade of the client/server infrastructure before bringing structured editing tools into production.

The time required to input a page using this method varies with the type of text (prose is fastest, then poetry, then drama), the condition and age of the manuscript, and the experience and speed of the transcriber.

The unedited, on-demand products are produced hands-off from script files with sets of macros that apply the script format to SGML. While there may be isolated cases of bad page breaks, most text comes through the process looking at least okay, at best as if it had been professionally typeset. Some material suffers more than others from this treatment—double-column pages and tables present the greatest difficulty.

The OUP volumes, on the other hand, are produced from FrameMaker and receive more attention before they are finalized. They use a set of macros to take the SGML into "maker markup language" or MML. From there, the text goes into a set of predetermined templates in Frame. Once the material is in Frame, the time required for processing varies from one or two days to up to two weeks. The text undergoes several editorial and revision cycles before the composed pages are camera-ready.

Document Architecture

The primary emphasis of the Women Writers Project, unlike that of many commercially motivated projects, is not on production methods (how they get there), but on where they are going (document architecture). The goal is not only the transcription of these texts, but the addition of codes that add value. Markup can clarify terms and practices that format alone does not define. Punctuation in a historical text may mean something that is not obvious to a modern reader. For example, double quotation marks may be used for emphasis as well as for direct speech. The Project distinguishes between the different usage with SGML tags, and this markup adds value to the text.

The WWP markup distinguishes between quotes used in text and quotes used as epigraphs. This sets epigraphs apart for typesetting layout and design, and it allows a researcher to extract and compare quotations used in different contexts. By identifying the author and language of the quote, a researcher can use statistical analysis of a large work to determine the percent of quotes from each author or each language both in the epigraphs and in the body of the text.

Carole Mah, Textbase Coordinator for the WWP, provided these three epigraphs excerpted from Sydney Owenson's *The Lay of an Irish Harp* (1807). In these excerpts, each EPIGRAPH element contains a citation (<CIT>). The citation contains the actual quotation (<QUOTE>) and bibliograhic reference (<BIBL>). Language is indicated by lang="IT" (Italian) or lang="FR" (French) with English as the default. Note the ALIGN attribute and the line break (<LB>) and emphasis (<EMPH>) elements used for page layout and format.[20]

> *The goal is not only the transcription of these texts, but the addition of codes that add value. Markup can clarify terms and practices that format alone does not define.*

```
<EPIGRAPH align="center">
  <CIT>
    <QUOTE lang="IT">Che s'altro amanta na piu destra
    <LB>Mille piacer ne voglion un tormento.
    </QUOTE>
    <BIBL align="right">PETRARCH.
    </BIBL>
  </CIT>
</EPIGRAPH>
**
<EPIGRAPH align="center">
  <CIT>
    <QUOTE lang="FR">De pouvoir sans nous ennuyer
    <LB>Eterniser la bagatelle.
    </QUOTE>
    <BIBL>DE MOUSTIER.
    </BIBL>
```

---

[20]I have deleted the attributes odel="“" cdel="”" which indicate that the open and close delimiters are left- and right-hand quotation marks. Otherwise, the excerpts duplicate the source markup.

```
   </CIT>
</EPIGRAPH>
**
<EPIGRAPH align="center">
   <CIT>
      <QUOTE>The pensive pleasures sweet
      <LB>Prepare <EMPH>thy</EMPH> shadowy car.
      </QUOTE>
      <BIBL align="right">COLLINS.
      </BIBL>
   </CIT>
</EPIGRAPH>
```

The first work on the Women Writers Project pre-dates the Text Encoding Initiative (TEI). In fact, the first work was done using GML with script processing commands. During the course of the Project, this was changed to SGML, which was then adapted to successive releases of the TEI guidelines—P1, P2, and now P3. The WWP's experience contributed to the creation of the TEI and, while the current WWP DTD is not exactly TEI-conformant, it could easily become so.

The WWP has augmented the markup specified in the TEI P3 because the TEI is geared toward modern, printed text, whereas the WWP deals exclusively and exhaustively with pre-modern text and therefore has special concerns. TEI rules for what must be on a title page do not have the flexibility to cover every work in the Project. The WWP also allows some attributes not included in the TEI, such as attributes that specify the exact placement of a note relative to the main text.

Impact of the Women Writers Project and the Text-Encoding Initiative

The WWP and projects like it are laying the foundation for profound changes in academic research and publishing. Unpublished work in special collections that used to require on-site examination is being indexed and disseminated electronically. Conclusions that were once based on years, maybe decades, of close reading and observation can now be altered or verified in hours. Before the entire corpus was available in searchable electronic form in the Thesaurus Linguae Graecae, an authority could claim that a certain kind of locution in classical Greek was used in letters, but not in funeral orations. "Now," says Renear, "every undergraduate can log on and verify or dispute this assertion. Now, we have a bounded corpus that before was based on memory and acquaintance."

An aspect of the TEI that holds much promise for the future is the common ground established between cutting-edge technology and the traditional liberal arts. It is refreshing to have people trained in philosophy designing technology and people trained in programming writing programs for academic research.

Utah Administrative Office of the Courts[21]

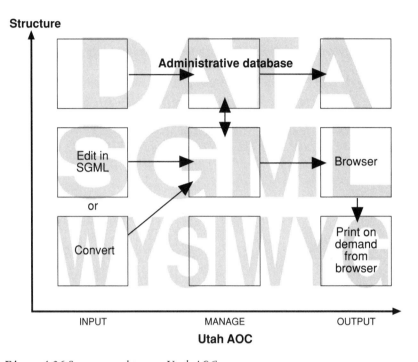

Figure 4.26 Structure and process, Utah AOC

The Electronic Filing Project (EFP) of the Utah Administrative Office of the Courts (AOC) allows all participants in civil and criminal justice cases to submit and to search electronically all of the testimony, briefs, warrants, and other documents that constitute a case file. This project, which has been piloted and beta-tested but is not yet in full implementation, establishes SGML as a technology that can open new areas to automation, areas not covered by computerized data-handling or by traditional publishing.

Until now, these documents were written with word processors and tracked in an administrative database but were submitted and handled on paper. Paper handling means that couriers often hand-carry time-sensitive documents; lawyers searching the file must flip through stacks of documents looking for the right one, then search within the document for the information required. The current administrative database lists what has been submitted to the case file, but it does

---

[21]This sketch is based on interviews with Alan Asay, his unpublished papers, and the Practicioner's Guide to Electronic Filing in Utah Courts prepared by the Utah AOC. A full treatment of this study is being published by SGML Open.

not track the actual order of documents in the file and it has no record of what is actually in each document.

With the EFP, documents can be written in the usual manner (most law offices today use word processors), and can then be converted to a simple SGML markup provided by the State of Utah, or they can be written in an SGML editor. Marked-up documents can be submitted through the Internet or dial-up remote connections. At the courthouse, the submitted document is archived, checked for viruses, and verified to make sure that the SGML coding is valid and that basic data, such as court name and case number, are present. Once the document has passed through these checks, data for the administrative database is automatically extracted from it and the full document is added to the case file, eliminating tedious filing procedures for courthouse staff (Figure 4.27).

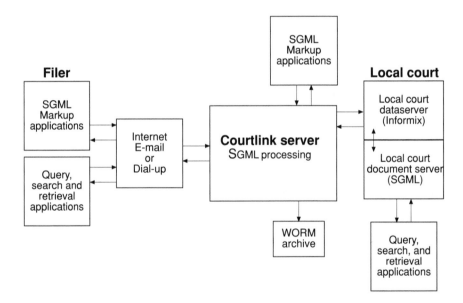

Figure 4.27 Utah AOC Electronic Filing Program block diagram

The electronic case file will be searchable through browsers available on-site at the courthouse or by Internet or dial-up remote connection. This improves case-file access by eliminating the need to go to the courthouse and also makes it possible to do full text, in context and Boolean searches.

Time savings through electronic filing and search and retrieval will allow all those involved with the system, lawyers and courthouse staff, to use their time more efficiently and effectively and may produce long-term savings for the public.

The reasons why SGML was chosen for this project are instructive. The essential feature of the SGML-based EFP is that the content of the documents in the case file is not restricted in any way by the document-handling system. The SGML codes identify the information in the document, but the document content, order, structure, and format need not change in any way. The SGML markup models the structure and content of the language but leaves it unchanged. A traditional database would require that the information be made to fit a relational table model. While word processing imposes no restrictions on a document, it offers no advantage for document processing once the page is printed.

InfoUCLA and ICADD[22]

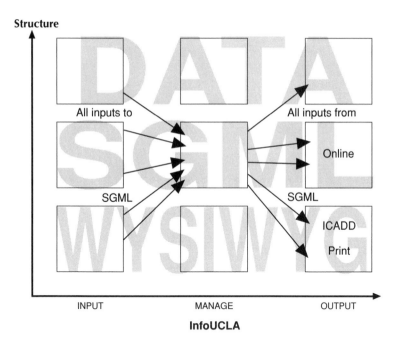

Figure 4.28 *Structure and process, InfoUCLA*

---

[22]The sketch is based on information available from the UCLA Gopher as well as interviews with George Kersher, of Recording for the Blind, and a talk given by Jeff Suttor, of UCLA and Passage Systems, when he described the system at the Chicago WWW '94 Conference. *Resource Guide A* lists contact information for ICADD and RFB.

InfoUCLA is the University of California at Los Angeles' campuswide information system. It distributes information such as the schedule of classes, the bookstore inventory, and the campus directory. This material is produced in innumerable formats and is distributed to a widespread and diverse community located both on and off campus. Before SGML was adopted, each format translation required a separate effort; whenever a format was upgraded, every translation to and from that format had to be upgraded.

InfoUCLA brings all source material into SGML. From there, every translation is a simple down-translation. With SGML, when a format changes, only one vector need be adjusted.[23]

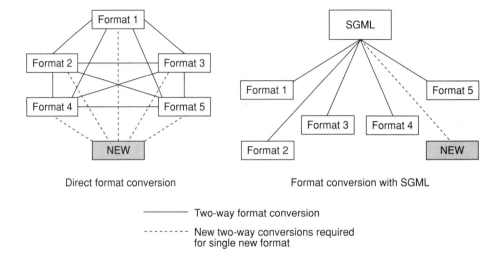

Direct format conversion   Format conversion with SGML

——————— Two-way format conversion

- - - - - - - New two-way conversions required
for single new format

Figure 4.29 Format translation through SGML

InfoUCLA simplifies conversion and exchange between common print and display formats and makes it easy to distribute information to sight-impaired people and to anyone who has difficulty with print or normal-size on-screen type. It translates the SGML source into Braille, large print, and voice output using an intermediary DTD designed for this purpose by the International Committee on Accessible Document Design called the ICADD DTD. The ICADD DTD is much like HTML2 and the Rainbow DTD. It has become standard input for systems that translate into Braille, voice synthesis, and large print.

InfoUCLA translates the detailed SGML markup used internally to the simple, appearance-based markup of ICADD. Table 4.17 compares InfoUCLA SGML markup with ICADD markup for a section of the campus GRAPES (Graduate and Postdoctoral Extramural Support).

---

[23]These contrasting pictures are adapted from Jeff Suttor's presentation.

Table 4.17 InfoUCLA and ICADD markup of the campus GRAPES.24

GRAPES as SGML:	GRAPES as ICADD:
`<FELLSHIP DSPName="09/27/93` `FULBRIGHT GRADUATE STUDY` `ABROAD PROGRAM (INSTITUTE OF` `INTERNATIONAL EDUCATION):'>`	`<LITEM>`
`<DEADLINE>09/27/93 </DEADLINE>`	`<B>09/27/93 </B>`
`<UPDATE>6/93</UPDATE>`	
`<PROGRAM>`FULBRIGHT GRADUATE STUDY ABROAD PROGRAM (INSTITUTE OF INTERNATIONAL EDUCATION):`</PROGRAM>`	`<H1>`FULBRIGHT GRADUATE STUDY ABROAD PROGRAM (INSTITUTE OF INTERNATIONAL EDUCATION):`</H1>`
`<DESCRIPT>`Approximately 900 fellowships for graduate study or research abroad. Fellowship amounts vary depending on country. Awards are for one academic year.`</DESCRIPT>`	`<PARA>`Approximately 900 fellowships for graduate study or research abroad. Fellowship amounts vary depending on country. Awards are for one academic year.`</PARA>`
`<ADDRESS>`1252 Murphy Hall, Campus; `</ADDRESS>`	`<PARA>`1252 Murphy Hall, Campus; `</PARA>`
`<ELIGIB>`	`<LIST>`
`<FIELDS>`All fields.`</FIELDS>`	`<LITEM>`All fields.`</LITEM>`
`<CITIZEN>`U.S. citizens.`</CITIZEN>`	`<LITEM>`U.S. citizens.`</LITEM>`

While InfoUCLA translates its material from SGML into ICADD, others achieve the same result by incorporating what are called SGML disability attributes (SDAs), sometimes called the ICADD extensions, into their DTDs. This set of attributes can be added to any DTD. Any document marked up with the SDAs can be converted into ICADD using standard translations.

Many public DTDs, such as DocBook and HTML2, allow use of the SDAs. Adding accessibility has practical value for many publishers, especially textbook publishers. The Texas Braille Bill mandates that all textbook publishers doing business with the state provide ICADD files for their books. According to George Kerscher of Recording for the Blind, including the SDAs shows a commitment to people with disabilities and adds social value to information markup.

ICADD simplifies the production of Braille and other formats, but it does not automate the entire process. Textbooks submitted in ICADD require some work before being published in Braille. For example, editors must add explanations to figure references and must translate graphs and charts to tables.

Kerscher is confident that future versions of ICADD will extend the material that can be translated without human intervention. He reports that Recording for the Blind is looking closely at the encoding of math in HTML3 for inclusion into the disability standard. Eighteen to twenty states have programs similar to the one in Texas, and more tools are being developed that take advantage of the ICADD format.

The dissemination of standards for translation into forms accessible by the print-disabled emphasizes the value of the information itself, rather than the delivery mechanism, and speeds the flow of information to those who have lost some or all of their ability to use print.

Publications International, Ltd.[25]

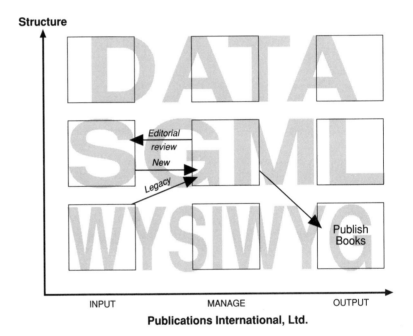

Figure 4.30 Structure and process, PIL

Publications International, Ltd. (PIL) is a $120-million-per-year trade and promotional publisher using SGML in a document database that supplements its traditional writing and composition tools. In this implementation, SGML was chosen, not in competition with desktop publishing, which is still in use, but in competition with document management software. In PIL's cost-benefit analysis, SGML came out the lower-cost, lower-impact solution.

---

[25]This information was provided by Rich Franco of PIL and Kate Hamilton in her capacity as Explorer product managr for SoftQuad.

The primary requirement at PIL was to create a searchable database for their 65,000 recipes to feed into a streamlined production system. Full-text or keyword search alone would not provide the rapid, accurate picture of the data required for pre-production evaluation. Finding "low-fat recipes for couples" requires that nutritional information and yield be fielded data.

As this book goes to press, a subcontractor is converting the legacy recipes. New recipes are entered in word-processing format, stripped of their codes, then hand-tagged in Author/Editor. The initial database of SGML-coded recipes is searchable in the Explorer browser from SoftQuad. When the full 40,000 recipes have been converted, PIL may add a specialized, SGML-based search engine for faster performance.

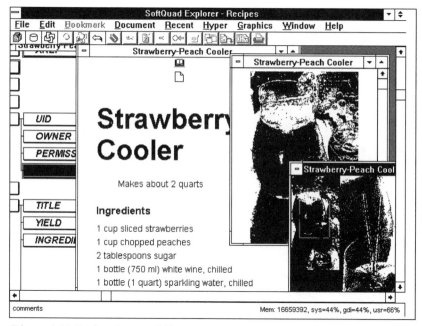

Figure 4.31 Explorer in use at PIL

Editors query the database to determine the feasibility of a new recipe collection. If the prospective collection is given the go-ahead, the recipes are brought into Author/Editor for editing and to update the publication history of the recipe using non-printing fields. The revised recipes are stored, then exported from the database using a beta version of the SoftQuad Enabler, which converts SGML into Quark Xpress, resolving elements in context, replacing entities, and converting SGML tags to Quark's internal markup language.

While the primary requirement for the document database was to use search and retrieval for editorial work, PIL expects a significant reduction in production lead time. They are experimenting with metadata in the form of Explorer "layers" to provide job tracking and workflow management. Since the current production method takes word-processing files directly into Quark, the new processes are being phased in without disrupting the old workflow.

Although still in the initial stages, PIL illustrates use of SGML as a low-cost, low-impact alternative to document management systems.

Sybase, Inc.[26]

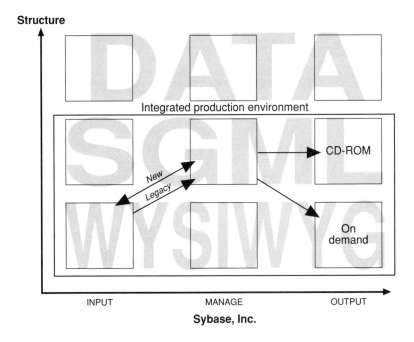

Figure 4.32 Structure and process, Sybase, Inc.

Sybase uses SGML to create the technical documentation for its relational database software, which runs on a wide variety of platforms. According to Steve Goodman, Manager, Online Information Systems, Sybase has saved money, cut the time required to produce and deliver a document, and pleased their customers by the shift to SGML and electronic documents. He reports that the sav-

---

[26]This information was relayed by Steve Goodman in interviews for this book and as part of the University of Wisconsin Extension Engineering and Professional Development course on Creating Structured Information.

ings for Sybase are "substantial" and they continue to increase as more documentation is produced and delivered as online electronic books. He estimates that the time required from project start to delivery of a CD-ROM has been reduced by about 40 percent. More importantly, Goodman reports, customers are very satisfied with the electronic SyBooks, customized versions of the EBT DynaText browsers. Feedback from customers indicates that information is more accessible in the electronic books, and few of them have requested paper documents.

There are twelve technical writing groups, most of them located at headquarters in Emeryville, California, with others spread around the country. In the past, each group wrote and edited books independently, then delivered them to a central unit, which produced and shipped the final product. Before adopting SGML, Sybase packaged a PostScript version of its manuals on CD-ROM for customers who need to print large quantities. Today, they are producing manuals in SGML while the production process continues to evolve.

Passage Systems has filled two roles in the Sybase transition: First, as subcontractor, Passage produced an initial set of books under a relatively short deadline; then, as software vendor, the company customized the Passage Pro integrated production environment based on Sybase requirements and guided Sybase through the transition to independent SGML production.

The Sybase Passage Pro environment integrates FrameMaker for word processing and print output with DynaText for electronic books, using OmniMark scripts for conversion and an SQL server for document management. Writers use FrameMaker for draft hard copy and also for final hard copy, if that is requested and paid for by the customer. They can mark sections as conditional text—for use either in print or online. OmniMark converts the FrameMaker documents to SyBooks. Passage Pro provides "interactive debugging" and preview so that a writer can see the effect of his or her coding on the final output. If there are validation problems, the environment invokes the word processor and guides the writer to the proper spot in the document to make the correction.

Sybase decided that writers should continue to use a familiar WYSIWYG editing tool, with all its features, so they integrated FrameMaker into Passage Pro. Writers must follow a carefully designed template or the document will not translate properly to SGML. They are assisted by paragraph and character catalogs in Frame. Writers convert their books from Frame's internal format to SGML, fix any problems in the converted text using the interactive debugger, and view the effect of what they do on their electronic books, all within one integrated environment. Sybase could switch to a structured editor and integrate it within the same environment in the future, if the software company sees significant advantages in doing so. Goodman reports that maintaining the conversion templates does require some effort.

A major effort for Sybase has been writing the cross-platform delivery and installation program for the CD-ROM. Sybase distributes one CD-ROM to all customers, regardless of platform. The installation program adds, replaces, and

He estimates that the time required from project start to delivery of a CD-ROM has been reduced by about 40 percent. More importantly, customers are very satisfied...

deletes electronic books from the SyBooks collection already installed at the customer's site. In addition, the Writers' Tools group provides scripts to help writers convert source documents from previous FrameMaker templates to the SGML-compliant templates. While the scripts are effective, much of the work cannot be automated and is done by hand.

The transition to strict use of a template in a write-to-convert environment was relatively easy because Frame templates have been used for some time. Some writers are excited by the new technology, some are not. Those who are not, observes Goodman, tend to be those technical writers who assumed that people were reading their paper books, instead of just using them to find information. While writers like using the WYSIWYG FrameMaker word processor because they like to tweak the format, Goodman feels that, when they "stop looking at paper as the product," they may choose to migrate, of their own accord, to structured editors that give them more direct control over the electronic book. They already like what DynaText does with their products and this is changing how they think about the writing process. On the other hand, FrameMaker is a mature product that offers advantages over comparable structured editors.

"Getting folks behind the process" is a primary focus now. This is the job of Bea Deering, the project lead of the Writers' Tools group, which provides support for, and modification of, the electronic publishing environment.

She had primary responsibility for the Frame template and is now taking over ownership of the DTD from Passage. Supporting and modifying the FrameMaker templates, the OmniMark conversion utility, the DTD, style sheets, and administration of the Passage Pro environment constitute a major effort. Future plans include Sybase-specific modifications to the DynaText browser.

Sybase illustrates the smooth, gradual approach to systemwide SGML. In the words of Bob Glushko, Chief Scientist at Passage Systems, Sybase is the company that is "doing everything right." What he means when he says this is that the process part and the technical part of the transition to SGML-based technical documentation has been carefully designed and coordinated at each step.

Canadian Code Centre[27]

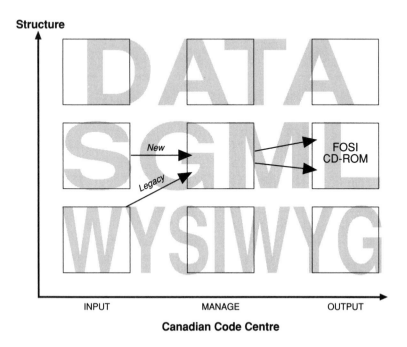

Canadian Code Centre

Figure 4.33 Structure and process, Canadian Code Centre

Every five years, the Canadian Code Centre of the National Research Council of Canada publishes four sets of codes, a set being an English and a French edition, covering building, plumbing, fire safety, and farm construction. Starting in 1995, the codes will be published in print and on CD-ROM from a single SGML source. The codes are complex documents that total over 1,000 pages in each language.

The data from the 1990 edition was converted to SGML over a period of a year and a half. New material is entered and editorial work is done in the ArborText Adept editor. All print composition is done with a FOSI in the ArborText Adept Publisher; the electronic edition uses the DynaText viewer from Electronic Book Technologies.

The initial data design was done on contract. Although the Centre still relies on contract assistance as a guide to SGML syntax, they now use a graphic tool for

---

[27]Sketch derived from interviews with Jamie Worling.

document analysis, Near & Far from Microstar, which has given the Centre more input into data design. Jamie Worling, who leads the SGML effort at the Centre, is an architect by training with a visual orientation to design. He says that, with the graphic tool, he could understand the structure, what related to what, and in what order. According to Worling, having a graphic tool for data design

> allows you to concentrate on document analysis and structure and (temporarily) ignore syntax. You still have to do document analysis, but the graphic tool allowed better discussions because everyone could see the structure. It was invaluable as a way of getting people involved.

He says that the Centre still needs an SGML expert as a guide to document analysis, not to write DTD syntax.

The justification for the project was to make possible same-source publishing for the Centre's CD-ROM. They have found some additional benefits in editorial work and composition. A preliminary version of the electronic text is used to proof the source and to search for terminology to ensure consistent usage. Centre staff can incorporate modifications up to the last-minute, even new paragraphs at the start of a book, since the creation of a table of contents and index is completely automated.

Worling says that the transition has gone "not too badly." The current source of delay is authors working in their traditional environment, with no connection to the SGML conversion. The Centre is working with ArborText to develop more flexibility in the FOSI output—the complexity of the publication has pushed the rules-based composition system to its current limit. While composition and printing take only an hour and a half—on the previous, pre-SGML cycle it took three months—the effort required to reach that stage is not reflected in these figures.

Tables and equations present the biggest problems, all of which are complicated by a two-column format. The original FOSI specification, written for military technical documentation, did not include features such as running footers, which are standard for more elaborate composition. Worling looks forward to the adoption of the DSSSL[28] specification by toolmakers and expects that this will give him the flexibility required for composition, along with all the other benefits of SGML publishing.

Worling says it is easier to create a style sheet for electronic publishing because there is more latitude with the electronic format than with print. There are no user expectations of how the browser should look because the electronic product is new.

Centre staff can incorporate modifications up to the last-minute, even new paragraphs at the start of a book, since the creation of a table of contents and index is completely automated.

---

[28]Document Style, Semantic, and Specification Language. See Chapter 7, *To All-of the Above*, p. 270.

LAST WORD ON THE CASES

Have I covered all the major flavors of SGML use? Certainly not. New—completely new—initiatives are starting all the time. Have I described the typical user? No, because there is no typical user.

Information-intense industries with the foresight and insight and creativity to revamp their use of information will be the heavy users of SGML in the coming years. The State of Utah Administrative Office of the Courts, which is not even a publisher, may become the "typical" user in the future.

If you do not see your needs directly reflected in any of these cases, it doesn't necessarily mean that SGML does not apply. The uses for SGML are too diverse to be covered in any compendium of cases. The next chapter looks at the features that characterize the successful adopter and presents a method for determining if your needs would be met by SGML.

5

Who Needs It?
Making the Case for SGML

The truth is, not everyone needs it.

Whether the change makes sense for you depends on the type of information you publish, your current infrastructure, the type of production system you create, and what you stand to gain at the end of the process.

Ideally, you should be able to design your new system, look at the price tag, then figure out if and when the new system will pay for itself. In practice, needs assessment is an iterative process that looks at needs, costs, and design requirements, successively refining the picture until all elements are in balance. Businesses rarely adopt SGML-based production without expanding their product line and their capabilities, so SGML needs assessment is not just about a new technology, meaning a new way to do the same old things. It is that, and it is a new technology employed to new and greater ends.

Perhaps, in the future, there will be some metric that looks at information, the where-from, where-to, and how-handled of it, that measures the life-cycle requirements plus the amount of information plus complexity and speed of handling, and spits out a profile of your structured information requirements. Such a metric might be calculated by a function that looks like Figure 5.1.

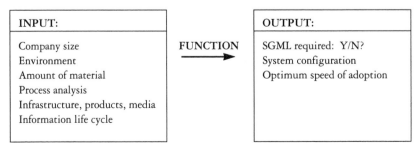

Figure 5.1 Information metric

But this kind of metric is not yet possible. In its place, this chapter presents the bare-bones outline, a template, for what you will need to consider when doing your own needs analysis, a process that can take weeks or months. There are three steps in this process:

- First, a prequalification step based on information analysis;

- Next, a consideration of the internal costs and benefits;

- Last, a consideration of external market benefits.

Information analysis means a consideration of the great life-cycle questions: Where does my information come from? What is it doing here? Where does it go? While this alone may not justify a project, it can certainly justify interest, defer the idea to a later time, or prompt you to go ahead with a detailed examination of costs and benefits.

... ultimately the most profound impact of converting to structured information may be on the products you produce rather than on the methods you use to produce them.

The internal business case looks at the "Getting There" costs—converting legacy labor, legacy technology, legacy data—and the "Being There" costs and benefits—the costs versus savings of SGML-based production. The external market case looks at how structured information affects your competitiveness and your ability to offer new products and services.

If you are subject to an industry or government or corporate requirement, you have no choice about *if* you convert but much choice about *how* you convert. How the criteria and arguments presented in this chapter fit your situation may determine how you look at the conversion, as a necessary evil or as an opportunity to expand and improve your information-handling infrastructure.

There is no strictly technological justification for converting your information to structured information. The decision to convert to SGML is not based on acquiring a better mousetrap or mousetrap builder. Converting to structured information is comparable to reengineering your corporation, where you look at the current division of labor and the technologies employed to support that division and ask yourself if there is a more rational method to get things done and if today's information technology can support that method.

INFORMATION ANALYSIS

Considering SGML from an information perspective rather than from a technology perspective is a valuable exercise because ultimately the most profound impact of converting to structured information may be on the products you produce rather than on the methods you use to produce them.

Does your information have the characteristics that make it a likely prospect for structured information? There are three sets of questions, the answers to which characterize information assets and build a profile of an organization likely to benefit from structured information.[1] The three sets are:

1. The life-cycle questions

2. The data characterization questions

3. The data environment questions

Let's look at each set of questions.

The Life-Cycle Questions

- Where does it come from?

- How does it get here?

- Do you control the output format?

- Is it revised, archived, reissued?

- Where does it go?

- How long does it take to travel through the pipeline? How critical is the production component of this length of time?

- What is the data life expectancy?

What these questions are driving at is a characterization of the insularity and fluidity of your information. Can you afford to live on a data island? This is not a loaded question. Let's look at an extreme case, a business whose business is information that can nevertheless afford to be an information island.

I am thinking of a small public-policy consulting firm[2]—successful, yet small by Fortune 500 standards. The firm's primary value-added is its own intellectual product. And this product does not mix, match, and recombine freely with that of other sources.

The firm controls its own information infrastructure. Data purchased or taken from public sources comes in as paper or ASCII or, at worst, something else that can be stripped down to ASCII. Each project receives individual attention and

---

[1]The arguments presented here are my own. I have been influenced by the talk delivered by Baird Foster, Vice President Publishing Sales, Auto-Graphics, at the Boston Bookbuilders Advanced Seminar. "SGML: Is It for You?" May 12, 1994, and by Bob Glushko's talk on preparing for SGML at the SGML Forum of New York, May 9, 1994.

[2]My model is, in fact, my brother's firm. He asked me what my book was about. I told him. He asked me why a business would use this technology. I told him. We agreed that there was no need for his firm to look into SGML any further at this time.

each project is unique. The sets of conclusions, the graphs and charts that constitute a report on a site for housing development in South Carolina take nothing from their counterparts for a mall in Northern New Jersey.

Information leaves the firm in single copies going to clients who have paid highly for it. It is not likely to be integrated into a public, and therefore perhaps SGML, database. Turnaround time is contingent on factors that far outweigh production efficiency. Once issued, the report becomes history. As an archival object, it stands alone, with no need to be referenced and recombined with other reports. The information does not need to be searched, sorted, queried, or viewed with a dynamic online browser.

Now, let's look at a case at the opposite end of the spectrum, an organization that can no more afford to be an information island than it can afford to give its product away free. In this case, I am modeling my example on an academic journal published by the University of Chicago Press, but it could just as well be Lexis/Nexis or any other publisher or organization. (The distinction between publishers and others being only this: Everyone publishes; publishers don't do anything else.)

The Press gets its data from thousands of different suppliers each year. The formats cannot be fully synchronized at the source, but some uniformity can be attained if the proper tools and guidelines are supplied. Material is submitted in any format under the sun, from handwritten pages to L^AT_EX. The manuscript goes to peer review, is copyedited and converted into one or more output formats for print and electronic distribution to thousands of readers. The time elements that are under the control of the publisher—coding, copyediting, tracking—are critical, all the more so since so many elements—peer review and submission—are not under their direct control.

The information published in the journal has definite value as an archive. While each article, as published, must remain intact for the historical record, it should be linked to complementary sources within and beyond the realm of the publisher.

This is clearly a profile of a user who cannot afford to be an information island. Evan Owens, Information Systems Manager, Journals Division, University of Chicago Press, explains the use of SGML for the *Astrophysical Journal* based on the need for:

- Multiple delivery formats;

- Retrievability;

- Shortened production cycle; and

- More generality and control over format than offered by L^AT_EX or by the Press's own internal system.

The decision was *not* based on ease of revision and reuse of units smaller than an article since the material must stand as is for the historical record (Owens, 1994).

These are two extreme cases with much, superficially, in common. In both cases you could say that information is their business. Both have highly intellectual products. Both gather information, add value, then return it to clients or subscribers. Yet, in terms of the life-cycle questions that determine suitability for SGML, they are a world apart. These two extreme cases are generalized in Table 5.1.

Table 5.1 The life-cycle questions: high- and low-suitability profiles

THE QUESTION	LOW SUITABILITY	HIGH SUITABILITY
Where does it come from?	Select sources not within your control.	Multiple sources you have some influence over them
How does it get here?	Data comes in limited formats	Can arrive wearing anything dressed up as a format
Do you control the output format?	You control the output format	You must conform to format requirements
Is it revised, archived, reissued?	Simple file format is suitable for archive; updates are not complex	File format not suitable for archive; recombination is desirable
Where does it go? How is it used?	Small audience; simple access requirements	Large, diverse audience; may have complex access requirements
How critical is production time relative to project time?	Not very	Very
What is the data life expectancy, in this form or in another form?	Rapidly becomes outdated; cannot be recombined and reissued	Long or, if short, can be recombined and reissued

The Data Characterization Questions

What are the:

- Quantity;
- Complexity;
- Potential output formats; and
- Number and type of potential products?

What these questions are driving at is a characterization of data on its own terms—not in terms of what is done to it, but what it *is*—the existential life-cycle questions. Are there characteristics inherent in the data itself that render it suitable, or unsuitable, to structured information?

First, let's look at quantity. Some projects that otherwise have the earmarks of a structured information project; may be disqualified on this criterion alone: They are small, a structured information project, typically, is big. It may be perfectly suitable to hook together hypercard stacks or handcraft hypertext links to demonstrate a concept, but scaling up makes entirely different demands on your technology (Glushko, 1989, 1992).

Complexity counts, too. If your data, your information, fits in the traditional database model, like a parts list or an inventory, a traditional database with fixed field lengths may do just fine. If there are no fixed limits to field lengths, if full-text searching in context is required, if nested hierarchy and optional inclusions are the rule, a relational database may not suffice. Complexity, in this context, includes nested hierarchy and all the multiple, variant forms that human language can take.

The third characterization question is: How suitable is this material for multiple output formats? In other words, can it be distributed both in print and in an electronic format? Can the same material be output in two different print editions or displayed on multiple electronic viewers?

An example of data with limited potential for multiple outputs is ..., well, is increasingly difficult to find as the flexibility and diversity of electronic presentation and delivery take away all excuses for not having some version of a text available online. But there are still examples. Private notes and records, high-security classifications, medical reports, specialized reports delivered to a small audience, and format-intensive marketing and advertising copy might fall into this category.

The fourth data characterization question addresses the potential for recombination (both internal and external), the potential number or type of derivative products, products that differ in more than format. What is the innate potential of the data to be made into new and different products?

This characterization is resistant to measurement and quantification because it relies on the imagination, on the creation of something where nothing was before. Look, for example, at the Columbia University Press project and its spin-offs described in Chapter 4. The Press did not go into structured information to create spin-off products; it went into SGML-based production for production efficiency, to cut costs. The editors had not yet seen lurking in their data the potential for alternate useful combinations. They did not see the spin-off books, *The Columbia Granger's® Dictionary of Poetry Quotations, The Top 500 Poems, The Classic Hundred,* and the *Guide to Anthologies,* until after the database for the CD-ROM had been compiled.

Will the creation of your database yield statistics that were previously unavailable? Might this new information be valuable enough to warrant treat-

It may be perfectly suitable to hook together hypercard stacks or handcraft hypertext links to demonstrate a concept, but scaling up makes entirely different demands on your technology.

ment on its own? It was the new *information* about the database that spurred the Press to publish the spin-offs, not the technical ability to do so.

Indications that by-products may be hidden inside our data might come from the chunking size—"chunking" is hypertext slang that refers to the granularity, the relative size of the basic units that are linked together in a hypertext web. Are there discrete units that can easily be pulled apart and therefore recombined in new and interesting ways? An encyclopedia entry is an obvious candidate for later, multiple, recombination. A discussion of a mathematical proof that proceeds incrementally is a less likely candidate. A collection of proofs, on the other hand, could be sliced and diced and served up in multiple contexts.

And a final note on potential for recombination: What you can actually do in terms of recombination depends on your data design. The same data, treated differently, will have varying degrees of recombination likelihood. The variables here are how astutely the data was designed and how thoroughly it was tagged. If the DTD for *Granger's* had defined only those elements that were required to reproduce the original book, if it had used (heretical thought) an HTML-like emphasis tag instead of a content-based tag for anthology titles, it would have been difficult, if not impossible, to create the spin-offs.

The more a scheme adheres to the principle of tagging everything, the more likely it is to generate spin-offs. Minimal tagging, however, can always be enhanced. HTML can be an initial step to the data richness that can generate creative and useful recombination of data. The data characterization questions and answers are summarized in Table 5.2.

Table 5.2 *The data characterization questions: high- and low-suitability profiles*

THE QUESTION	LOW SUITABILITY	HIGH SUITABILITY
Quantity of material?	Small	Large
Complexity of material?	Simple, suitable for database	Complex, not suitable for database
Is it suitable for multiple outputs, including electronic delivery?	Single-medium sufficient	Multiple outputs, within or across media, desirable
What is the potential for re-combination? New products?	Big chunks, low potential for new information to come out of database statistics	Divisible; thoroughly tagged; high potential for spawning new information from statistical analysis

The Data Environment Questions

How important is:

- Interchangeability across platforms, languages, operating systems; and
- Complex linking with other data?

The final set of questions is environmental. How well can and should your information move across platforms, through computer and human languages, and between operating systems? How intertwined is your information with other text and databases?

The ability to link your data with other data relates directly to the adoption of structured information. While any format, even an unstructured bit map, can be the end point of a link, if the file is the only container recognized by the computer, then the file defines the granularity of the link. For example, if this chapter were formatted in PostScript and put on the World Wide Web as a PostScript document with its own URL (Web address), then browsers could point to the address, call up a PostScript viewer, and link to the chapter, but there would be no mechanism to link to this section, this paragraph, this sentence, or this word.

To get a greater granularity of linking, you must have a greater granularity of structure. The greatest, that is, the finest, granularity of linking comes with the "finite coordinate space" concept of HyTime, which can link to any point in a document or, for that matter, in a piece of music, a graphic, or a video.

The importance of complex linking varies, depending on the type of information and the information environment. Again, to use the example of the relatively small, self-contained think-tank type of atmosphere, here the control over the computing environment is almost total, the contribution of technology to the value of the final product is relatively small, and the demands for linkage to other information and interchangeability are almost nil.

For broad-based, heterogeneous environments, the ability not only to deliver information across platforms but also to link that information together may be of prime importance. The data environment questions are summarized in Table 5.3.

Table 5.3 The data environment questions: high- and low-suitability profiles

THE QUESTION	LOW SUITABILITY	HIGH SUITABILITY
Importance of interchangeability across platforms, computer languages, and operating systems	Homogeneous, controlled computing environment renders this a low priority	Open, heterogeneous environment gives this great importance
Linking requirements	Not complex	Complex at several levels of granularity

Summarizing Information Analysis

If SGML enhances your competitive situation, you need it. How do you know? You can look at the information in question as a prequalification step. If it has a high-suitability profile for most of the life-cycle questions, data characterization questions, and data environment questions, then it is worthwhile examining the internal and external business cases.

INTERNAL ARGUMENTS FOR SGML

How much money will structured information add to, or subtract from, your bottom-line production costs?

There is no one number or proportion for the cost of SGML-based production, any more than there could be a single number for the cost of non-SGML-based production. One of the difficulties in finding such a number is that it is rare for nonpublishers to track publishing costs as closely as they ought to—an unfortunate part of the legacy of the preinformation economy.

Even where detailed preconversion costs are available, the scope of publishing enlarges with SGML. Instead of delivering formatted pages with a limited life span, publishing departments are delivering online documents and customer support over the Internet with their efforts, they are buying conversion insurance and are enabling spin-off products and multiplatform distribution.

One organization that does track documentation costs is the Department of Defense (DoD), which estimates that approximately 25 percent of the cost of new weapons systems is documentation. The Navy estimates that it takes the equivalent of 1,000 full-time sailors all year each year to insert change pages, at an estimated cost of $30 million. In an operation this size, any change to greater efficiency of operation will have far-reaching benefits, although overall costs may remain inflated in comparison to civilian costs—$400 pages are not monitored as closely as $600 hammers.[3]

Since 1985, when it first published the CALS guidelines, the DoD has claimed that adopting structured information and integrating it throughout a product's life cycle would save business 20–30 percent across its bottom line for document production and distribution. As yet, experience in the CALS world does not bear this out. What is clear is that compliance requires an up-front investment in training and technology and shifts costs around so that a cost comparison is not a simple process.

> *There is no one number or proportion for the cost of SGML-based production, any more than there could be a single number for the cost of non-SGML-based production.*

---

[3] Lawrence Beck, from Grumman, gave an excellent talk on the reasons for inflation of costs for mil-spec documentation at SGML '94, published as "The Reality of Military Document Analysis," Lawrence A. Beck, *Proceedings, SGML '94.*

Let's look at another number. A well-known consultant in technical publishing, not one who works with structured information or with SGML but one known for his work with online technical documentation, regularly primes his clients with the number 300. This, he claims, is the percentage increase in the cost of creating and producing a full-featured hypertext document on top of the cost of a complex technical document.

At the same time, the case studies in Chapter 4 document an increase in writer productivity of 33 percent (Ericsson), money saved on elimination of redundant keyboarding and coding for CD-ROM (Butterworth, Columbia University Press, Standard & Poor's, Sybase, and others), improved editorial efficiency (Butterworth, Ericsson, Columbia), improved production efficiency (Adams & Hamilton), and reduced time-to-market (Sybase).

Minus 30, plus 300... What is to be made of these numbers and how can you find the number that will truly represent your cost differential? More work, I am afraid, than plugging a number into a formula. What follows can guide you through the process of doing your own cost projection.

But, first, two caveats:

- It matters where you start from.
- It matters where you are going.

> *If the processes that manage your data are convoluted, distorted, and unworkable before you adopt structured information, they will be more so afterward.*

It matters what your technical infrastructure contains. Your projected savings and costs are compared to a baseline that is your current production process. If this is archaic, it will be relatively easy to cost-justify the transition. It may not sound fair, but there is an advantage to those who have done nothing for 10 years. If you are working in lead type or if you are producing CD-ROMs with entirely redundant coding and you go to SGML, you should save money immediately. If you have recently upgraded to a state-of-the-art, unstructured, format-based publishing system, it may be more difficult to do so. If your production process already enforces conforming styles and is highly tuned and optimized and if a second output is not required, other areas will have to pay for the transition.

It also matters what your *process* infrastructure contains. If the processes that manage your data are convoluted, distorted, and unworkable before you adopt structured information, they will be more so afterward. Count on it. If your processes and procedures are smooth and efficient before you start, you must ask yourself if this is the right time to make the cultural and process and infrastructure changes that must accompany this new technology.

And it matters where you are going. If you are looking at SGML as a method of structured input, storage, and output; if your data management requirements are steep; if you tag your data thoroughly; if you want no limitations on future output formats, then you need pure, format-independent markup. In this case, your data requirements and your transitional cost will be higher and the time to payback may be longer than if you are content with only some of these features.

Given these caveats, let's look at the elements of a cost and savings assessment. The costs I divide into two groups:

- One-time or temporary costs associated with the transition to structured information, called the "Getting There" costs;

- Ongoing costs associated with an established structured information system, called the "Being There" costs.

This is a preview of the next four chapters, which describe the process of designing your system, making the transition, and living with it once it is established.

The Getting There Costs

There are three groups of transitional costs to consider:

- Legacy labor—training and reorganizing your labor force;

- Legacy technology—upgrades and purchases for input, management, and output; and

- Legacy data—creating a data design and converting existing data.

Legacy Labor Costs

Training is expensive. Not training is more expensive. Chapter 8 describes three types of training: conceptual, operational, and technical.

Plan to provide some conceptual training at all levels of the organization. Reading this book may suffice but, in some cases, a seminar that teaches basic concepts and focuses on your industry and your own business issues will be a more effective use of time. Rates for custom seminars vary, but expect to spend at least $500 for a half-day presentation if you need to bring someone in from outside. More, if you expect the presentation to be customized for your environment.

Budget for operational training on new tools. For the past several years, if you knew one word processor, you could pick up enough of any new word processor to get started on your own without formal training. Do not expect to do this with the new tools that you acquire when you convert to SGML.

The degree of technical training required varies but, in most cases, you will need to train at least one staff member as an SGML technical expert unless you plan to hire one from outside. A thorough knowledge of the technical aspect of the standard is a demanding occupation, one that benefits from some initial formal training and much on-the-job time to work with documents, editors, parsers, and conversion tools. Providing a route to Internet resources is an inexpensive way to give your in-house expert access to the larger community of experts. The cost will, of course, depend on what Internet access you have already built into your work environment. (*Resource Guide A* lists Internet resources for SGML.)

An additional skill that you must feed, fertilize, and nurture is the ability to lead and facilitate document analysis. There is no school for this. There are articles available, at least one book is on the way, and courses of varying quality are offered. The tried-and-true method is to expose your staff to the process by bringing in an expert to conduct the first round—and giving your staff time to learn this skill.

The training costs can be summarized as follows:

- Conceptual overview, executive and midmanagement level;

- Conceptual overview, staff level;

- Job-specific tool training;

- SGML technical training; and

- Document analysis training.

And there is another cost in converting legacy labor: the cost of the process realignments that will make or break your adoption of new publishing technology. What these costs are is impossible to generalize. They may be no more than changing some minor details of workflow. Or they may be big-ticket items like moving or disbanding a department, reassigning workers, and changing the reporting hierarchy. Chapters 6 to 9 describe the new work environment, but only a thorough knowledge of your current environment can point to what you will need to change.

So, pull out your copy of Hammer and Champy. And look at it this way: If reengineering your work process is something that you have needed to do but have not been able to cost-justify, maybe SGML will tip the scales in your favor.

Legacy Technology Costs

This is where most people expect to look for costs and expect to find hard numbers. But upgrading technology is not a predetermined cost. If you have a minimally competent microprocessor with an up-to-date operating system, there is exceptionally good public domain software available that will do all that you need to do to create fully compliant SGML. Often more time has been devoted to the engine than to the interface. You will spend staff time in place of license fees. If you are in a commercial establishment, you probably will want to invest in commercially supported licenses and you may need to upgrade some hardware to get the processing power you want for the new technology.

As of this writing, the preponderance of software tools for SGML are offered for workstation-grade processors. This does not mean that you cannot integrate microprocessors with a workstation as server. The trend, as elsewhere, is to migrate the more powerful programs onto the PC platform as clients or as stand-alone applications. The balance between the cost of living with diminished performance and the cost of buying new processing horsepower is one that should be familiar from other spheres. Expect to meet it here as well.

The pieces of technology that may show up on your transitional budget are categorized and described in Chapter 3, which maps the universe of structured information tools. Be aware of the caveat at the start of that chapter: Everyone probably needs some of these, no one needs all of them, and few need one from every category. As elsewhere, costs are falling in a competitive atmosphere. The following chapters describe how to put the pieces together. To summarize the elements that *might* show up on your budget for converting legacy technology, look at the list of tool types from Chapter 3.

Hopefully, by the time this book is in your hands, the computer press will have started to cover SGML tools with the tenacity and rigor reserved for desktop publishing and e-mail systems. If they have not, you will need to devote your own time or hire a consultant to price-shop and compare options. And, if you are accustomed to high-tech purchasing, you know to look askance at *a number* say, on a data management system. The variables are too great. Once you know at least the outlines of your system requirements, there is no way to avoid a full request for proposal and bidding cycle. The purpose of this chapter and of this book is to prepare you for that cost-evaluation process, not to do it for you.

The range, if one must be given, is the cost of data transfer over the Internet, if public domain software is your choice, to the cost of creating and designing your own production and data environment. The usual price differentials exist between workstation and microcomputer licenses. For those who will feel cheated without numbers, here are some ballpark numbers:

- Editors—$180 per license for write-to-convert editors to $4,000 per license for native editors.

- Up-conversion—Off-the-shelf software can start as high as $1,000 per license and to this you must add the cost of filters, training and labor to create, upgrade, and maintain the tool. Estimates go up to $60 per page for initial pages for in-house and external conversion.

- Transformation—Up to about $2,500 for a license, plus the cost of a technical employee to configure and maintain the tool.

- Data design—Any ASCII-capable editor is the baseline tool; CASE-like tools start at $800 for DTD creation; $115 for viewing in a graphic environment.

- Document and data management—The cost of setting up any database: primarily the cost of the time invested in the design and management of the data. Tools already customized for SGML data management are changing too rapidly to ballpark.

- Down-conversion—The tools and methods are similar to an up-conversion, but the process is less complex.

- Print composition engines—Desktop and electronic publishers. You may want to take advantage of batch composition or, alternately, add an interactive WYSIWYG composition engine or stick with what you have now.

- Browsers—Anywhere from free (Mosaic et al.) to expensive, almost pay-per-view licensing.

- Search and retrieval—Varies too widely to estimate. Most free Web browsers can search for a text string in an open file. Site licenses for high-end search engines cost tens of thousands of dollars.

- System integration—Consulting costs vary. How much time you need depends on the complexity of your system and the amount of in-house expertise you buy or develop.

Legacy Data Costs

Legacy data costs vary widely but are relatively easy to quantify once you know the chief variables: quantity, quality of source material, and complexity of target format. Per-page prices drop sharply with volume due to the high cost of system setup and configuration. Getting information to HTML is one type of conversion. Getting it to fully compliant SGML with meaningful content tags and a rich data structure is a more expensive proposition. In the first case, any italic becomes an emphasis tag; in the second, somehow, by algorithm or by brute force, italics must be sorted into foreign language, emphasis, cross-reference, and so on.

Ballpark conversion costs for outsourcing conversion range from less than $1 per page to over $15 per page, depending on quantity and complexity. Ballpark conversion costs for doing it in-house are similar, when you consider the cost of training and labor in addition to an initial software license. Setup costs are as high for commercial software as for service bureau conversion. In addition to these cost factors, your decision on whether to develop your own conversion capability will depend on whether you are developing a tool for ongoing, in-house data conversion or just converting legacy material.

Detailed analysis of costs and cost factors is provided in Chapter 8. Here, suffice it to say that, for sites with significant quantities of legacy data, conversion up to SGML will be your major expense. Of course, not everything needs to be converted, and everything that does need to be converted does not need to be converted right away.

A final note on the Getting There costs: Speed and pace count. You can vary the pace and course of adoption to fit your production cycle, market, and business imperatives. Doing a little now, to gain some in-house expertise, to see how your data design works out, and to learn more about what the market potential is, can minimize your initial outlay and save over the long haul, although you will not have the benefits that accrue to the parts of the system that you defer.

The Being There Costs

Any consideration of costs and savings is based on a comparison. But, in this case, what are we comparing? SGML versus no SGML for current processes and products? For new products? SGML versus hand-set type? SGML versus top-end, proprietary electronic publishing? Are we looking at efficiencies and savings going to print, with multiple versions? Or are we looking at going to print and screen with single versions of each, with identical content? Or with variant content?

Everyone has his or her own idea of what an apple is and which orange they wish to buy. But everyone's produce is different. What I can do here is break down some of the cost factors, tell you what some people have experienced in terms of these factors, and tell you what factors to add up to make a projection that will work for you.

What follows here is a summary for your initial assessment of the financial impact of SGML on the ongoing costs of operation. The conclusion of this chapter and the chapter on system design summarize the cost factors that will shape how you put your new system together. This presentation looks at what happens to old jobs from a cost perspective and then looks at the new jobs in the same light.

In a structured information environment, what happens to the old jobs, to the cost of:

- Writing?
- Editing, copyediting, proofreading?
- Quality assurance?
- Production and design?

We will look only at the changes affecting the bottom line, not ongoing costs. The new jobs are:

- Creation and maintenance of document type definitions and, in most cases, also output specifications, templates, and conversion filters;

If you adopt a document and data management system, add:

- Maintenance and management of a text archive or database;

and, if you introduce electronic products, add:

- Specification and maintenance of a user interface and design;

- Creation and maintenance of search and retrieval strategies.

Your working environment will have shifted one step further away from the old world of leaden type and wooden trays and one step closer to the world of beta releases and engineering change cycles.

Whether or not your products are heavily electronic, your working environment will have shifted one step further away from the old world of leaden type and wooden trays and one step closer to the world of beta releases and engineering change cycles. Is this added overhead or does it pay for itself in increased efficiency?

As with raw technology costs, the costs of your new production environment vary so widely, depending on the skill of your design and how well it fits your product and your workforce, that the most honest answer I can give to these questions is: It depends. The discussion that follows gives you some idea of the variables and how to prepare yourself to make your budget estimates and design decisions.

Old Jobs

On the Internet, a writer complained that her SGML editor constantly interrupted the flow of her writing, beeping and refusing her input. An editor, interviewed for this book, complained that, using a document database, she was never given hard copy to proof, did not see errors until they were in galleys, and was forced to accept bad copy in the final publication or pay for costly last minute changes. Elsewhere, editors line up to complain to the production supervisor that they cannot meet deadlines *unless* the text is brought into the SGML system. Designers with a deep background in SGML argue that this is what typesetting was always meant to be that SGML, finally, lets them do the typesetting job they were trained to do.

The anecdotal evidence says both that traditional jobs get more efficient and that they get less efficient. Real-life experience "proves" that these processes are enhanced and expedited and it "proves" that these processes become entangled and bogged down in endless complexity. Which is correct? What is the real impact of SGML on traditional jobs like writing and editing? Chapter 9, *Being There*, examines these questions in detail.

In terms of your initial assessment of the cost of working with SGML, the question is not "How much can it possibly cost me if I really screw up?" The question should be "What will it cost and where can I save if I basically do things right?"

If you do not train your workers, if you do not get their input into data design, if your equipment is not suitable for the task and if you make major errors in system design, if you don't adapt your production process to the new technology and don't choose technology that works with a production process that is right for you, your process will get worse, as it does whenever an automation goes awry. It is not terribly useful to catalog all the mistakes that can gum up your production process, leach away your profits, and destroy your production schedule. If you follow the principles laid out here, and those of reputable consultants, you will avoid this list of woes.

Ongoing Training

Increased training costs are a given for this system throughout its life, not only in the initial, Getting There, period. You need to increase the skill set and awareness across the full range of employees working with the system. This cost is manifest every time you bring in or transfer a worker. You will need to recruit people with a higher skill set and to train employees to a higher level. The change is comparable to the increase in skill level that accompanied the change from traditional filing and typing to word processing and database entry.

Moving the Target

"Moving the target" means asking your writers and editors to produce more when they work with a structured information system than they did without it. The target moves if you add new products, reuse text in different contexts, or raise standards for quality and consistency at the same time that you adopt structured information. If you add new products, such as an online version of your publications or a help system, you cannot expect your staff to give you two for the price of one just because you give them new tools. If you design your data for reuse of text for multiple outputs, you add complexity to your writers' job.

Consider, for example, how the target is moved by changing the nature of your product and putting it online. This was the case with the Shakespeare references in the *Granger's Index*. Decades of conscientious, careful editing never revealed that some references are to William Shakespeare, some to W. Shakespeare, and some to Shakespeare. Using the database to create new indices on the fly, the first edition of the CD-ROM laid bare this inconsistency. Overnight, the editors were subject to quality concerns that had never surfaced before. While the structured text provides many new ways to perform old jobs, like enforcing stylistic consistency, it also ups the ante, raising the stakes to be won or lost.

For subsequent editions, the Columbia University Press staff used the CD-ROM and the database to ensure a consistent and high editorial standard. They

If you add new products, such as an online version of your publications or a help system, you cannot expect your staff to give you two for the price of one just because you give them new tools.

budgeted the time required to verify and validate the database for greater consistency of content and structure.

Applying the structural rules of the DTD makes a document more consistent in certain respects, but this higher level of consistency does not come free. A parser checks that the rules of the DTD regarding usage and construction have been followed—that the right pieces are assembled and that they are in a permissible sequence and hierarchy. It does not say anything about the *content* of the pieces. Structured information makes it possible to build a higher degree of automation into your applications, but these applications must still be built.

Using SGML and structured information applications to produce two products costs less than producing the two products independently, without structured documents, and much less than *maintaining* the two products separately. Structured documents enable and facilitate multiple outputs; they do not wave a magic wand and produce them out of thin air. Ultimately, structured information tools are efficient, although your costs will be higher than if you were writing for a single output only. Your tools, their integration, and the processes that you build around them determine the cost and benefit from the higher level of structural integrity in SGML-conformant publications.

Converts and Natives

A major cost factor to consider when looking at the effect of SGML on writing and editing is whether you write-to-convert or use a native SGML editor.

If you chose to retain your unstructured word processors as your primary input device, you will have less investment up front in equipment. You will have the same need for conceptual training. While employees do not need to learn a new tool, they do need to learn the structural concepts and to learn to use a new, more rigid, template. You also have the new responsibilities of creation and maintenance of a template and a conversion algorithm.

Writing-to-convert will always add at least one loop to the workflow, compared to the same process using a native SGML editor unless it is within a context of very tight process and tool integration, such as that pioneered by Passage Systems, which minimizes this effect. It is too soon to tell if the WYSIWYG/structure tools just becoming available will also change this part of the equation. In general, and this point is reiterated and expanded on in Chapter 7, the earlier in the production process your data acquires its structure, the greater the payback from that structure.

New Jobs

SGML-based production requires new jobs that create and maintain what Ericsson calls its WE, or working environment. This environment includes the codification of the "s" in structured information: the document type definition, the output specification, the text base or data manager, the output conversion filter, and the data transformation tools. If your data management requirements are complex, you need a database and a skilled person to manage the database. If you output electronically, add creation and maintenance of the user interface and the search and retrieval tools and interface. If you write-to-convert, you must add creation and maintenance of a word-processing template and conversion filter to someone's job description.

The Cost of Data Design

How much does it cost to write a DTD? Obviously, the cost depends on the complexity of the information: How extensive is it? Can you model it on a single document or a set of documents, or do you need to take a broader view of your information requirements? How much in-house expertise do you have? Are you developing a companywide architecture? Do you reuse fragments and modules from a DTD library?

What holds today as a good rule for data analysis and design will still be valid in a year's time. Nevertheless, ongoing enhancement and maintenance are as much a part of data design as they are of application design. Chapter 6 describes the process of document analysis. Here, we will look at the costs.[4]

Up front, let's consider the possibility that you can use someone else's DTD off-the-shelf. This was, in fact, an early model for industrywide standardization around SGML. The idea was that one DTD for an industry-specific class of documents—say, jet engine troubleshooting and repair—would fit all. The idea here is not only to save the cost of DTD development to individual companies but to ensure standardization and information interchangeability. While standardization and interchange are still powerful and prevalent concepts, the notion of what it takes to achieve them has been refined through extensive trials and tests. The original concept—that one could simply load up the specified DTD and be ready to roll—has been superseded by a more complex and detailed understanding of how data design works.

Today, taking a ready-to-wear DTD, loading it up, and starting to tag a new type of document is not the norm or the normal expectation. When an off-the-shelf DTD is taken as a basis for data design, experts caution that time spent modifying and customizing the structures and naming conventions for your own environment is necessary. Even when an industry-standard DTD is adopted, it may cover data structures important for *exchange*, leaving data structures for publishing, archiving, and other uses up to the individual companies.

---

[4]Much of this analysis comes from a presentation made by Debbie LaPeyre, of ATLIS Consulting, to the SGML Forum of New York, January 18, 1994, and clarified in subsequent conversations. For dissuading me from the notion that most people are better off modifying an existing DTD than doing their own, I am indebted to Eve Maler of ArborText.

This is the model of the Pinnacles Component Information Standard described in the Intel case study in Chapter 4. The PCIS specifies the description of chip pin-outs, but not whether chip pin-outs come before or after normal voltages in a publication. PCIS participating companies will use and modify the elements specified by the standard when they build their own internal document type definitions.

In any data design, whether working with an industry-standard specification or from scratch, there are two stages to the process: document analysis and DTD coding. The analysis stage produces a detailed description of the data elements and the relationships and parameters that will be encoded in the DTD. Document analysis is the full specification of the DTD, which is then coded in SGML.

Assuming that you will need to prepare, or substantially modify, a DTD, these are the costs you will need to consider:

- Document analysis—facilitator (optional, depending on size of project), an SGML expert and your own document experts; and

- DTD writing—SGML programmer.

The major expense in DTD development should be the cost of involvement of your own staff. Not the cost of in-house, SGML-trained *technical* people, if you have them, but the cost of *document* experts. Who are your document experts? All those with a hand in making and using that document: writers; editors; subject matter experts; quality control, production, and design staff; and systems analysts. They may need to spend up to a week in document analysis.

Outside experts bring this knowledge to DTD development:

- The SGML language;

- What mistakes others have made;

- The implications of certain types of data design; and

- How different products use the structures.

Depending on the size of your effort, you may or may not also need a facilitator to supervise and expedite the project. Add to this the cost of tagging and parsing a sample document and using it to test the DTD.

So, what does this cost in real dollars? The least-expensive-reasonable document analysis (*not* coding, just analysis) is a two-day affair for four people, plus $2000–5000 for outside SGML expertise. If there is a meaningful average, it might be three or four days of analysis and review by internal staff and $5000–15,000 for outside experts, assuming that you are starting out and your in-house knowledge of SGML is not extensive. These numbers are for the document analysis. Coding the DTD will take several days of a programmer's time, as a minimum, depending on its length and complexity.

This up-front expense is a new cost that comes with structured information. The spending of money on up-front analysis is a hallmark of SGML. It is cost-effective compared to the cost of not doing that up-front work. SGML without good document analysis will not do what it has been commissioned to do. Poor document analysis means constant updates and revisions that will inject added costs throughout a production cycle and throughout the life of the data.

In addition to the initial costs at system start-up, and the initial costs at project start-up, there are ongoing costs of maintenance and revision. The DTD is, after all, software. On the other side of the balance sheet, as you gain expertise, the need for outside help for maintenance and revision diminishes.

The Cost of Data Management

For some installations, the file system may be a sufficient data manager. For others, it may be an effective interim strategy to keep down the cost of the transition. For those with large-scale, wall-to-wall SGML requirements who want to realize the full benefits of structured information, data management can be a major consideration.

The cost of SGML-based data management is comparable to the cost of any data management system. It varies depending on the complexity and extent of the data, the person who will program and manage the database, and the initial investment in tools. As with any other database or data management system, there is an inverse relationship between the amount invested in the user interface and the training and background of the workforce—workers with fewer database skills require a greater investment in the user interface.

The good news is that this area of SGML tools, which lagged the other areas initially, is expanding rapidly.

The Cost of Data Output

The print output specification is a recombination of old functions with new skills and requirements. The need for page and document design does not change. If the production cycle is optimized to receive SGML input, typesetting and output coding can go exceedingly smoothly. This is nowhere more evident than at the firm of Adams & Hamilton, profiled in a case study in Chapter 4.

Essentially, Adams and Hamilton take the knowledge of structure and content derived from the SGML element and entity lists and use that to implement a design, theirs or someone else's, with full awareness of what all the ramifications will be. Training your design staff in the key concepts of structured information can turn this into an area of savings, where some of the investment in structured information begins to pay off.

Between the design and the source files lies the job of output translation. This is usually the job of in-house technical staff creating proprietary translation tables from SGML tags to various batch and page composition systems. Unless there are overriding reasons to upgrade composition systems, it is quite feasible to retain your investment in your current composition system and with it your in-house expertise in this system. Reasons to upgrade can include the need for more processing power—for example, some desktop systems are limited in the number of unique tags per file—or the need for interactive WYSIWYG composition.

In terms of the skills required, creating an output translation from SGML to a composition engine can be compared to creating a custom printer-driver—you don't need to be a programmer, but you need to be able to work like one.

The various write-to-convert options being released for popular word processors offer a writer more direct control over output at the price of less direct control over structured input. How these tools will integrate into production environments remains, at this writing, to be determined.

The cost of developing and using SGML syntax to translate directly to an output product with a format output specification instance (FOSI) is somewhat akin to document analysis, but dearer for the fact that it is rarer, fewer people choosing to go this route.

For electronic output, the skill set is more varied, but here, too, it begins with design. The design of your electronic page, which is not a page at all, takes as much from user interface design as it does from page layout. Page design developed over the centuries; screen design has been given much less time. New budget items include extensive time for user testing, getting a fresh supply of users all the time.

The degree of flexibility, the extent of this job, and the level of skill, beyond design acumen, depend on your choice of browser and search engine. Delivery engines provide fewer or greater options for customization requiring more or less programming skill. The range is wide. When you price output options, you must consider the degree of customization possible as well as the skill set required, whether you must contract for this or build the skills in-house.

Whatever your choice, it should be clear that this is a cost of porting your information to the screen and that cost includes design, testing and implementation.

The Cost of Essential "Extras"

These extras—graphics, math, tables, audio, video—which are not extras at all, will add dimensions to your budget for data design and management and increase the demand on your applications and on your basic infrastructure, whether or not you use SGML. They are extras only in the sense that SGML production systems can be built with or without them, although this, too, is changing. Much of what used to be customization, for example, an in-line view of graphics launched in separate application, is now available in off-the-shelf SGML-based editing software. In the near future, HyTime-based applications should do more to standardize and reduce the cost of multimedia.

If this is your first integration of these elements, if you are going to a graphic-intensive publication or to multimedia coincident with the adoption of SGML, there are cost items to consider that have nothing to do with SGML—storage, data conversion, management, compression.

These elements are mentioned here, not because their costs are related directly to SGML but because it would be a mistake to assume that their costs were covered automatically by a structured information production system.

Cost Summary

This section summarizes the costs of adopting SGML and producing structured information and looks at the areas that can pay you back for the investment. The primary areas in which to look for increased cost when moving to SGML, summarized from the discussion above, include:

- Training and hiring to a higher level, initially, and throughout the life of the system;

- Data conversion, both legacy and, in some cases, new material;

- Data design, an initial and an ongoing expense;

- System design;

- Tools for data input, management, transformation, and output, although not all these are specific to or necessary for SGML;

- Working to a higher standard of data structure and quality; and

- Creating new products made possible by structured information.

Training, new equipment, system design, data design, and data conversion are the five large areas of expense in the transition process. Of these, training and data conversion can dwarf the cost of new equipment. Add to these the cost of initial data design and it becomes apparent that the major expenses in shifting to SGML are not for the tools themselves.

Many of these costs would apply to *any* new publishing production system. The costs specific to SGML (or a comparable system of structured information, if there were one) are the costs of:

- Data design;
- Training; and
- Increasing document structure, either through conversion or structured editing.

These are the issues that are inherent in raising the energy level of your data. They are the inescapable cost increases that come not from increasing the scope or quality of your publications but from the inherent nature of structured information.

Specific areas of production where you can save are elimination of:

- Redundant keyboarding;
- Redundant and inefficient writing, editing, formatting; and
- Errors due to poor data management.

You will also save as a result of:

- Rapid, streamlined production due to a better distribution of work: writers write, editors edit, typesetters set type, and designers design.

If you use structured information to eliminate paper deliverables, you can save on:

- Printing
- Binding
- Shipping

Of course, these costs would also be eliminated if you went to electronic distribution without SGML.

How much you save depends on where you start from and where you are going. If you add complexity, raise the quality stakes, and add new products, you will pay more to produce them, although not as much as you would pay without SGML. What you can expect depends on the following:

- Starting point
- Target product(s)
- Quality goals
- Investment in infrastructure
- Customization of infrastructure

The payback on SGML can come with elimination of only one area of inefficient production, as illustrated in the Chapter 4 case studies:

- Rekeying data (Standard & Poor's)
- Elimination of redundant formatting (Butterworth)
- Increased efficiency among writers (Ericsson)

In none of these cases was the cost saving on production the sole justification for the switch. Standard & Poor's needed a friendlier interface to populate its database; Butterworth and Ericsson needed to keep up with emerging industry standards for information interchange. Shipping less paper to customers, which comes with any electronic document, is also a major cost incentive. Intel and Sybase wanted to produce more effective online documents and reach their clients more effectively than they could have without structured markup.

Two additional aspects of the payback for SGML do not map onto any specific area of production but nonetheless can have a big impact on the bottom line. These are:

- Data conversion insurance; and
- Long-term vendor independence

How do you put a value on data conversion insurance? One method is to look at the cost of previous data conversions—find out what your lack of coverage has cost in the past. What has your company paid to migrate from Selectric to Wang to Wordstar to Multimate to version X of whatever you use now? Mark Gross, who founded Data Conversion Laboratories in 1986, estimates that 40 percent of the cost of converting to *any* new technology is the cost of data conversion.

Data conversion insurance plus vendor independence provide a large measure of protection from information asset devaluation.

In a heterogeneous computing environment, data must be easily converted to multiple, arbitrary formats. The conversion insurance inherent in high-energy data itself will justify the switch to SGML.

How do you put a value on the independence of your data format? When a company owns the format in which your data resides, it controls the value of your business assets. For many, this is a very compelling argument, leading them to place the "open" in SGML at the forefront of reasons to adopt the standard. Data conversion insurance plus vendor independence provide a large measure of protection from information asset devaluation. If you do choose to transform your data, you can do so according to your own timetable and with minimal cost.

EXTERNAL ARGUMENTS FOR SGML

The external, market-driven reasons for adopting SGML are the ones that really shed light on why SGML is not just another data format. Here, we examine how SGML has an impact on what you can offer to the world outside your company. Let's consider four different areas where using SGML can shape your information products:

- New product, old media—spin-off products of the same general type but with a different focus or organization;

- New or old product, new media—alternate presentation or distribution media such as CD-ROM, the Web, and other online vehicles;

- Quality—faster time-to-market and, therefore, more up-to-date product; greater accuracy, consistency; better search and retrieval capability; better online navigation; and

- Industry standardization—mandates that the data itself be in SGML for interchangeability.

At virtually every site I have studied where SGML is the established data format, some form of new product is in production or under consideration. Some are inspired by the relative ease of production. When the cost of production is low or has been absorbed by the primary product, information providers can afford to create new products to sell to small niche markets, as the Women Writers Project is doing. Other products, like the Columbia University Press spin-offs, appeal to a wide audience but were not feasible without a statistical analysis of the data itself.

The ability to go into new media, without a high conversion cost, is another way to expand what you offer your market through SGML. Electronic information delivery is still in its infancy and there is little indication of what formats or media will provide the most popular delivery channels as it matures. When your data is in SGML, it is ready for output and delivery in any format required. This may have the ring of a theoretical justification, hard to see on the bottom line, but it has been borne out by recent experience with the World Wide Web.

When your data is in SGML, it is ready for output and delivery in any format required.

Instead of scrambling to add yet another incompatible format to their data archives, those with data already in SGML can derive HTML in a simple down-conversion. Perhaps the largest payback for this investment in markup is that the Web options for SGML are not limited to simple, flat, page-based files. SGML adds value to Web-ready data by making it easier to present richly structured data directly with an SGML Web viewer like Panorama or indirectly by search and retrieval of SGML data presented through HTML browsers.

Perhaps the most profound effect on product quality is on the type of electronic online book made possible by different levels of structured data. Any unstructured document can be brought into a page-based browser. Without adding structure, navigation in a page-based viewer is limited to scanning and scrolling. This is fine for small documents, but can be like reading a newspaper through a periscope for large documents. Table of contents links add structure and functionality. These links, however, are input directly into the output forma and so they cannot be created and maintained in the source or applied to any other media. Any time there is a change in the data, the value added by the links is lost.

In contrast, structure-aware browsers offer multiple vehicles for navigation, including tables of contents, indexes, cross-reference links, and special paths through the data, all based on the markup in the source.[5] This markup can be altered and maintained and changes passed through to the structured viewer. Structured documents in structured viewers offer the greatest variety of navigation and search and retrieval options without added markup overhead.

Quality comes into play in SGML deliverables in a number of other ways as well. A document type definition can be designed to enforce a level of uniformity that is difficult to achieve without the ability to parse document grammar.

---

[5]See your electronic *Resource Guide* for a demonstration of this principle.

Indexes generated on the fly from the data itself make it possible to see consisten-
cies (and inconsistencies) in the data to an unprecedented degree. In addition, the
sheer speed of SGML-based production helps publishers like Sybase get their
information in front of users more rapidly than is possible with other technology.

And, of course, if your market is asking for structured information in an open,
nonproprietary format, then you had better be ready to provide it. Intel (PCIS),
Ericsson (TCIF), the Women Writers Project (TEI), and InfoUCLA (ICADD) are
all examples of meeting a market demand for information complying with an
industry standard.

Bob Glushko of Passage Systems has guided more than one company through
needs analysis and the transition to SGML. He argues that market-based factors
are the *only* factors that carry a concern through to the end, that a customer-centered justification for converting to SGML is the best predictor of a successful
implementation. According to Glushko, if clear, concrete customer-centered
requirements are at the core of a conversion effort, there is "less incentive to cut
corners" than a reliance on cost justification alone. It is "easier to sustain support"
for a project and, importantly, the project is more likely to make something of
real use to the market. If real customer requirements are being addressed, the
customer is less likely to accept anything less than a full-scale implementation.[6]

Whether or not market considerations are your *sine qua non* of SGML, it is
imperative that you assess where your industry and your market are going, in
other words, how SGML will affect your competitive situation and what your
market is asking for.

How do you know what they want? Ask them. Market surveys have proven to
be valuable tools, not only in determining if SGML should be adopted but in
determining much about the eventual data design. Exactly how and when to
carry out your survey of market requirements is not within the scope of this
book, but it may be useful to look at the market surveys done by others.

Glushko and Kershner (1993) describe how their needs analysis and market
survey for Silicon Graphics (SGI) taught them things that they did not know
beforehand. Glushko and Kershner report:

The results clearly spelled out four requirements:

— Don't use proprietary technology.

— Develop a system that also works on other platforms.

— Add additional functionality that takes advantage of Silicon Graphics'
digital media capabilities.

— Use production methods that developers can use as well.

---

[6]This section reflects Bob Glushko's talk on preparing for SGML at the SGML Forum of New York, May 9, 1994. See
also Berkner (1994) which follows the Raimes article on the development of the *Granger's* CD-ROM, profiled in
Chapter 4.

This survey helped establish the basis for adopting SGML as the data format for the Iris Insight Viewer, which is now bundled with all SGI machines.

The decision at Columbia University Press to produce a CD-ROM, which was the basis for later spin-offs, was based on a solid survey and analysis of the library market for this type of electronic reference product. The Press found, among other things, that the acceptance of the electronic product would hinge on two factors: first, on value-added material, "something that differentiates this product, makes it unique, and makes it even more useful than the printed book." (Berkner, 1994, p.117).

And second, the Press projected that "once the added value has been provided, if the CD-ROM is too complex, it will not be well reviewed or bought widely." This did turn out to be the case. When a competitor brought out a CD-ROM that was priced lower than *Granger's,* Berkner reports that the competing ROM did

> appeal to a segment of the market, until they tried it and judged it less worthy than ours. In fact, the competitor finally lowered its price even further, but the sales of the Columbia CD-ROM continued to rise as the positive reviews poured in and our promotion took hold.

But the market does not always speak up so clearly, even when asked. SGML is transparent to the client for Butterworth's first SGML product—the State of Alaska's Fish and Game Regulations. As Michael Schwartz put it, they "might as well be marking it up with assembler codes." Nethertheless, Butterworth is looking to the future when SGML may prove to be a competitive edge. If and when the state moves to new, client/server technology, they may be able to use the SGML-coded files directly.

The market may say only, "Give us online books with a powerful, yet easy-to-use interface." It is up to the analyst to put together the requirement with a knowledge of what is reasonable to expect from structured and unstructured information, and what it will cost not only to produce, but to maintain the data over time. Is a "scroll the blob" interface sufficient, or do I need real dynamic electronic books with navigation and search and retrieval?

When the market does not speak unequivocally, and cost–benefit analysis cannot be done to a high degree of certainty, there are still some ways to consider the question of SGML.

LAST WORDS ON "WHO NEEDS IT?"

Everything said up to now regarding cost–benefit analysis and market analysis is important—critical—to an understanding of the impact of SGML, but there are reasons to consider SGML that your market may not articulate and that your cost–benefit analysis may not quantify.

How important is it for you that SGML renders information vendor-independent and platform-independent? That it is an open standard, controlled by the International Organization for Standards, as opposed to a private, proprietary profit-making enterprise?

It is quite difficult to place a monetary or risk value on a vendor- and platform-independent International Standard. While it does make sense to be independent of shifts in vendors, this *on its own* is not a driving force. Business has never shied away from doing business with business, and there is no reason now to believe that, all other things being equal, any industry would rush to endorse a data standard whose only virtue was that it freed them from standards created by a commercial enterprise.

The real payback for SGML may come from these elements that are hard to place on a short-term balance sheet. It may come from converting your data, raising its level one more time, and knowing that the markup will not yellow and age like an old typescript or Multimate on 8-inch floppies, that the next release of someone else's markup language will not render three years of data obsolete.

Building an integration strategy around applications is like investing in depreciable goods—the half-life of an application is rarely longer than two or three years. Building an integration strategy around information that you control in a structured, open environment. makes your own assets appreciate and keeps them liquid.

Versatility and the ability to anticipate and respond to changing conditions are at the heart of the justification for large-scale commitment to SGML. You might look at it as "fortuitous" that two years after the start of the Pinnacles Initiative, the Web came on the scene offering even better return on the same investment. But the ability to use the World Wide Web, and the sophisticated search and navigation features of an SGML- and Web-compatible viewer with negligible added cost, is not fortuitous. It is the result of adopting data encoding that is flexible and adaptable over the longest time span.

This is not really the last word on costs and benefits and how to get the most out of your SGML-based production environment. The next four chapters continue this discussion, looking at the process of designing your system, making the transition, and what to expect once you are "there."

6

Where Is There?
Document Architecture

There are four major areas of concern in the design of an SGML production environment:

- Input—How do you get your data into SGML?

- Management—How do you manage your SGML text base?

- Output—How do you create print and electronic products?

and, underlying each of these:

- Data design—What kind of structure do you want underlying all these processes?

There is no area of input, management, or output that is not affected by the type of structure that you specify in your document analysis and create in your DTDs and, if you use one, in your document database, entity manager, or library of data structures. The type of structure you build into your documents—your document architecture—affects the most critical elements of your production process and your product itself. These must be reflected in your data design.

With these objectives in mind—what kind of products you produce and what kind of information architecture will allow you to do this—look at your current resources, your personnel, and your technical infrastructure, and then design the jobs that are needed in the new environment.

Finally, when you know what jobs will produce the products you want, and only after you know this, look to the list of new tools and your current technical infrastructure, and specify the technology for the new environment.

The ideal decision-making flow is:

- First, business/market objectives;

- Then, data structures;
- Then, jobs and functions; and
- Finally, specific tools and technology.

In reality, your data architecture will evolve with your system design and your understanding of the process and the new products and markets made possible by the technology. In reality, a prior investment or an existing form of organization may influence your objectives and the functions your team performs. In reality, planning is always an iterative process that loops back between ideal and real possibilities. Nevertheless, when planning and implementing your new environment, you should make the process fit the product and make the tool fit the process—not the other way around.

The previous chapter discussed how business and market objectives coincide with structured information systems. This chapter looks at designing data structures to fit your business and production needs. The next chapter focuses on designing processes for input, data management, and output; matching tools and technologies to functional specifications; and, lastly, getting the most bang for every buck invested.

DESIGNING YOUR DATA STRUCTURES

The ISO standard sets out what is legal and illegal use of syntax within a DTD and within a document instance, but this no more specifies the design of your data than a catalog of materials tells a contractor how high to build a wall and where to put a window. In between the building blocks and the building, there can be several layers of specification: zoning laws, building codes, design principles, modular designs, and architectural drawings. The same is true for document architecture. In between the ISO standard and the coded DTD, there can be any number of layers of specification and conformance.

As communities of interest develop the means to share SGML-encoded information, it is increasingly common to apply one or more layers of specification to the design of an individual DTD. The discussion that follows looks first at the major issues addressed in every design, then takes a brief look at some of the solutions developed by industry groups and communities of interest and, finally, describes the process for developing a document architecture through document analysis.

Basic Design Issues

What are the prevailing schools of thought on good design? We seem to be at a point where there are strong lessons about what *not* to do; there is some agreement over what you *should* do, but there is no consensus endorsing a single philosophy of document design. This summary introduces the issues involved in document architecture and some of the current thinking regarding them. What is right for one situation will not be right for another, but the primary design decisions must address the following:

- Function—What is the ultimate purpose of the information being encoded? Who is the audience, and what will they do with the information? Is it to create an online research archive? Is it for information sold and delivered daily?

- Usage—What is the purpose of the DTD within the publishing and information-handling environment? Is it for exchange of information? for input of new material or for data conversion? Is it for production of deliverable products or for storage and archiving?

- Boundaries of information—What is the universe of this DTD? What information does it cover and what does it exclude? Is it a subset or superset of an established DTD or library of DTDs? What is the *namespace*—the set of systems on which these names must be valid and unique—for this DTD and this document? What other namespaces need it acknowledge and respect?

- Granularity of identified objects—How far should the design go to identify objects? If the sole objective is for print publication, should it stop at the level of object identified by typography? What additional objects in the text should be identified—sentences, citations, parts of speech, dates, people, events, or concepts?

- Packaging—What objects get tied together, get handled together, and therefore need a common container? Will you import/export or check in/out clauses with their subclauses and head notes or will each of these be identified and handled separately? Should you support formal subdocuments or partial documents? Will the structure be flat or contain many nested levels?

- Process support—Will this DTD support document, data, job, workflow management, and tracking?

- Content models—How closely do you want to model the content that fills your structures? Do you allow a *mixed-content model* that permits text and text containers at the same level of hierarchy?

- Validation—What level of validation will this definition support? The parser validates SGML syntax and the containers for content through the content model. What else will the application validate?

- Structural flexibility and inheritance—How flexible should a document be in terms of its structure? Assuming each document component to have one and only one expression of structure, should this be a named element with its place in the structure defined or should it be inherited through its context?

- Search strategy—How will the document be searched—by algorithm or by code? How can the design be optimized for the type of search anticipated? Will queries use a sophisticated search engine? Will they rely on context and keywords?

- Hyperlink strategy—How are hyperlinks defined and identified? What provisions are made for links inside and outside this document and this namespace?

- Optional syntax—Which of the optional features of ISO 8879 should be supported? The major issue here is the use of permitted tag minimization, for example, omission of an end tag when the context makes it clear where the end tag would belong.

- Transitional strategy—Can you afford to implement your ultimate data design immediately, or do you prefer to get started with a lower level of coding and add value as the project matures? You need not reach the highest desirable level of coding in the first step. Transformation tools make it relatively easy to augment your data, once it is in SGML, but your initial design should have an eye toward the eventual goal.

Four issues—function, usage, information boundaries, and hyperlink strategy—are discussed in more detail below.

Function and Usage

"Form follows function" promotes good design in pottery and architecture and in documents as well. Here, too, the ultimate use of the information must be considered. That this would be so was not always accepted—there was an initial supposition that the entire architecture could be surmised from the basic materials, from the information itself.

The effect of divergent functions was demonstrated very clearly in an exercise performed for SGML '92 by Debbie LaPeyre of ATLIS Consulting, Yuri Rubinsky of SoftQuad, Dennis O'Connor of the Bureau of National Affairs, Steve DeRose and David Durand of Electronic Book Technologies, and Halcyon Ahearn; it was described by Ahearn (1993). Each of the panelists did a document analysis on *The New Yorker* magazine, each with a different objective in mind for the DTD. The result was five very different analyses.

One DTD was designed to conform to an industry standard DTD, a match that was difficult to justify because of the constraints of the standard. One DTD focused on content-specific tagging, one on print format, one on hypermedia, and one on database population. Ahearn concluded that the exercise illustrated

> ... the relationship between the design of an SGML document structure and the use or uses projected for the information. For example, to create the historical database application, I found content-specific naming of elements to be critical. For the hypermedia application, however, a shorter, simpler, and more generic set of element names sufficed. If the attributes needed for hypermedia were added to content-specific elements, these applications—and an online distribution system—might all be served.

Ahearn noted that if the exercise had not been speculative, the magazine staff would have set the requirements based on their vision of information function and usage and what they want in a publishing and editorial system. Diverse requirements are not irreconcilable but goals need to be articulated at the earliest stages of design.

Not only does the end use determine the shape of the design, but the stage of the production process also bears on certain design decisions. The Pinnacles Component Information Standard (PCIS) has one objective: to exchange information. While providing electronic data books to end users shapes the overall requirements, company-specific document type definitions are being developed to fulfill specific production and delivery requirements.

Tommie Usdin, of ATLIS Consulting and the Pinnacles Secretariat, writes:

> ... I make the distinction between Interchange, Authoring, and Display. All of these are varieties of *document* DTDs, optimized for different uses. It is rare that high-quality DTDs can be written that are optimized for all three uses of a document. It is becoming increasingly common for people to use different DTDs for these functions instead of using a DTD that is optimized for one function for all three.[1]

Not only the ultimate use of the information but also the stage in the production process can affect the design of a specific DTD. The discussion below on outputting to print describes some of the conditions that might lead to use of an output DTD that was separate and distinct, yet was part of an architecture shared with a storage or archival DTD. DTDs can be optimized for input, storage, data conversion, and output. If the DTDs share a common architecture, then they are just a transformation step away from each other.

---

[1]Private communication. For more information on PCIS, see the Intel case study in Chapter 4.

Information Boundaries

The boundaries of your data structures depend on the boundaries within which your information passes its useful life. If your document will live as a stand-alone unit, with no potential for recombination and interconnection with other documents, then a single DTD, with no specified relationship to other data structures, may be sufficient. Since you are using SGML, it is much more likely that your documents, even the stand-alone ones, have some relationship to each other and to information in the rest of the world.

For example, if your DTD targets a software user manual, it is likely that some procedures will appear here and in training materials, and possibly also in customer support handbooks. Glossary items and definitions may be used in context-sensitive online help and in printed reference material. If you want common data structures and shared content, then you must consider the information boundary for each of these types of output, even if the DTD is written for one output only.

While the DTD is always a discrete set of declarations, elements, and entities, there are different ways in which DTDs can share characteristics across discrete boundaries. These levels of shared characteristics include:

- Names
- Links
- Exchange elements
- Structural elements
- Structural modules or fragments

Sharing a common namespace means adhering to naming conventions for some or all of the named parts of a DTD which can include elements, entities, and attributes. Declaring use of the ISO-defined entity-set for Greek characters is an example of adhering to a shared boundary in terms of this namespace.

The ISO standard HyTime defines a set of attributes that describe link strategy. DTDs that incorporate these HyTime-defined attributes share a common information boundary in terms of their link strategy.

A tag library defines shared elements, a higher level of information definition. Sharing element definitions means sharing not only common names and common links but also common content models on the level of the individual element. In a set of technical documents, the structures of a reference manual and a user manual may differ even though they share common element definitions for glossary items and common entity definitions for tool names and menu selections.

Information boundaries that share hierarchical structures entail yet a higher level of common definition. For example, a shared hierarchy would define not only the element TOOLNAME, but the structure and content model of a parts list entry.

Structural modules or DTD fragments can be of any size or complexity and can include definitions of entire sections or constructs within a document, like the table models that are often incorporated into DTDs. In a corporate setting, a module might consist of a common definition for bibliographic entries or report title pages. Figure 6.1 indicates one of many possible ways that shared data structures and information boundaries can be affected by proximity.

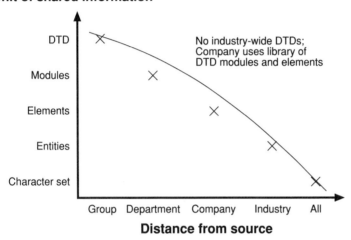

Figure 6.1 Shared information

In some cases, the information boundary might include the entire community of SGML applications. There is a debate in SGML technical circles over the method and advisability of applying consistent, standardized names to entities as well as to elements that will be shared by a community. One point of view is that exchange and reuse of information is best promoted by identifying a single set of entity names that will be used by all. The other point of view is that entities come in two varieties—internal and external—and that this feature should be exploited to allow local freedom of naming with community support of common names for only those entities imported from outside the local site.

The phrase "corporate gold standard" refers to a strategy for building a corporate document architecture promoted by Pamela Gennusa and Gregory Vaughn of Database Publishing Systems, Ltd. This method advocates using the same forethought and long-range strategy for DTDs developed for internal use as is applied to industry initiatives. This strategy regards corporate information resources as a microcosm of any of the industries developing common data architecture discussed in the next section and listed in *Resource Guide A.* The strategy advocates a thorough analysis of overall requirements and a shared information boundary within the corporation instead of a piecemeal, document by document, process by process, department by department development.

W ith out specifying the exact architecture to be applied, the gold standard specifies a central repository that holds a "cohesive model of corporate information," from which output and processing and delivery DTDs are derived. This model relies on industry standard fragments where applicable and in-house standards where applicable.

The past years have seen much refinement of the design strategies that deal with unclear, overlapping, and intersecting information sets. Your design process must include a clear definition of which boundaries you recognize and where you draw the line for the DTD under development.

Hyperlink Strategy

Not all strategies to designate links between pieces of text are created equal. In fact, this remains one of the most contentious areas of document design. The basic problem is this: While it is fairly simple to use the ID/IDREF features of SGML or the A and HREF features of HTML to link point *x* to point *y*, this strategy has several limitations.

First, these are one-way links and the converse link must be created and maintained separately. Second, these are hard-wired in the sense that if one end of a link is deleted, the application has no way to know that and therefore no way to prevent an error (Figure 6.2).

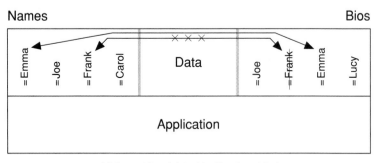

Link must be deleted for Frank, added for Emma. Link for Joe was overlooked

***Figure 6.2** Hard-wired linking*

Contrast this hard-wired strategy with what Exoterica calls "implicit link-ing." In implicit linking, the link is not directly point to point but is generated from the data, in this case, using OmniMark. Figures 6.2 and 6.3 illustrate the two strategies applied to the material in the Cinemania CD-ROM produced by Microsoft with help from Exoterica (see also the sketch in Chapter 4.) In the first edition of the CD-ROM, there was no Emma Thompson bio, so there was no link to a film biography. When a biography was added for the second edition of the ROM, with hard-wired linking, the entire database would have had to be searched for all links between her name and the new biography.

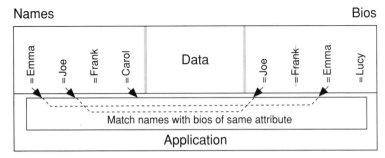

The application maintains the links.
No error messages, no missing links.

Figure 6.3 Implicit linking

The implicit link strategy lets the application tie the elements together based on end points with a common name—"this is a biography, this is an actress; if the name matches, create a link"—rather than making the data tie the links explicitly—"this point A links to that point B." With this strategy, changes to the database do not destroy the web of hyperlinks.

If this doesn't seem wonderful to you, consider the work involved to establish and maintain accurate matches for thousands of personal references and hundreds of biographies as Hollywood wrecks havoc with your carefully inserted pointers. In this case, the data would have to be searched for all references between names and biographies that no longer exist, as well as those newly created. Keeping a great mass of constantly changing information up-to-date using this type of link strategy would be a tedious and error-prone procedure. With implicit linking, the application polls actor names and actor bios and, if there is a match, generates a link. Thus, new names and biographies can be added, and old ones deleted, without any maintenance of links between the two.

This type of programmed linking can be done before the application is mas-tered for a CD-ROM or on the fly for live data.

HyTime is an extension of SGML, a set of rules for applying SGML, that describes three methods for designating links: by name, by position within a defined space, and by semantic construct. All these have the property ascribed to implicit linking above, that they can be maintained without hard-wiring data from point to point. If *finite coordinate space* is used as a HyTime-defined attribute, called an *architectural form*, link anchors can occur in any media, including voice, music, and still and moving pictures (Newcomb, Kipp and Newcomb, 1991). The finite coordinate space of HyTime adds another aspect to SGML-defined linking by specifying ways to link objects other than entire elements.

In HyTime, a named element is identified by a given attribute value, like "Article 55." A coordinate or node address is a relative designation like "first item in the second list." A link to a description is a link to a data point, not to a node, for example, to the "third word in the next list item." The first commercial, end-user product to employ HyTime linking is the Explorer browser from SoftQuad (see the Publications International sketch in Chapter 4).

Industry Standards

More and more industries are cooperating in the creation of a common information architecture based on SGML. The creation and promotion of an industry standard recognizes that some sort of natural information boundary surrounds that industry. The list of SGML industry initiatives now includes (in no particular order) pharmaceuticals, defense, law, finance, state and federal government, aviation, news media, aerospace and automotive engineering, academia, computer hardware and software, telecommunications, semiconductor manufacture, and, of course, plain old publishing.

Industry standards are appealing, offering the prospect of saving work and expense for all involved.

What all these efforts share is the incentive to get together and to figure out how to enable information sharing and reuse between parts of the industry. The goals can be specific such as standardizing new drug applications to a regulatory agency, or can be open-ended, such as eliminating redundant documentation between suppliers and users of component parts or sharing electronic texts so that each is able to use everyone else's markup for research and analysis.

Industry standards are appealing, offering the prospect of saving work and expense for all involved. In practice, it is not so simple to create a single model that achieves interchangeability and standardization and still gives each group the latitude to handle information in the way to which it is accustomed. For example, my documents may allow notes to appear anywhere within body text, but your documents may exclude them from within procedures. My documents may put AC voltage characteristics before pin-out tables, and yours may do the opposite. Some industries have standards for print documents, others have none. For this reason, it is becoming increasingly common for industry to concentrate on exchange issues and leave the individual companies to build their own, internal, DTDs for management and production.

The minimal objective of most industry initiatives is to standardize certain types of data representation so that it is easier to exchange information within the industry. For example, if we all call our part numbers with the same generic identifier <PN> and if <PN> has the same content model for each of us, then my specification sheets can slide into your engineering design system and into someone else's maintenance procedure. Some initiatives go further, attempting to standardize large portions of document architecture and even to establish standard DTDs.

The decision whether to be in compliance with an industry initiative, such as the American Association of Publishers or the Society of Automotive Engineers, is a business and marketing decision—it has to do with where your information is headed and who your audience is. Once that decision is made, you must still do a document analysis to determine the fit between your own information and the industry specifications, where their definitions leave off and your own begin. This analysis determines to what extent their specifications fit your requirements, if you can take pieces of an existing one—either your own or one in the public domain—or if you need to build your own using elements and entities that comply with the industry standard. Some industry standards go deeper into the design of a document than others.

The art of the industry standard has advanced further in the past few years than perhaps any other aspect of SGML information design. Each effort has contributed to our understanding of the best strategy for a given industry—some by their insights, some by their mistakes.

Following are brief descriptions of industry initiatives in the U.S. Department of Defense, the computer software industry, academia, and semiconductor manufacturing. They differ not only in the type of content described, but in the scope of the initiative and the design philosophy. See the section on *Groups Building Common Data Architecture* in *Resource Guide A* for complete contact information for these and other SGML industry initiatives.

CALS

CALS was originally Computer-Aided Logistic Support, or was it Computer-Acquisition...? In any case, it was then officially hyphenated to include both A-words. Currently, it stands for: Continuous Acquisition and Life-cycle Support. While the expansion of the initials has been unstable, the CALS concept has been consistent from its inception in 1985. The idea behind CALS is to cut expenses, reduce redundant labor, and improve delivery of goods and services throughout the U.S. military by creating an unimpeded flow of information between all the branches of the military and their suppliers.

The grand CALS vision—and it is grand—encompasses more than use of SGML as a text-encoding standard. There is an expanding set of CALS specifications that covers graphics, presentation and the IWSDB, the Integrated Weapons

System Database—a giant repository of up-to-date information containing all history, plans, specifications, parts information, and technical documents for all weapons systems. CALS created the Format Output Specification Instance, or FOSI, which uses SGML syntax to translate document instances to formatted pages. The idea behind the FOSI is that the translation to print, the composition format, should also be vendor- and platform-independent. (For more on FOSIs, see Chapter 7.)

The expectation at the time of the first release of the CALS SGML specification was that a DTD could be used off the shelf by those in compliance with the particular standard. The expectation was that one DTD per mil-spec would cover all requirements. Unfortunately, the sample DTD appended to MIL-M-28001, the SGML part of the CALS specification, was for MIL-STD-83784, which is a default standard for document *format* and had little to offer in terms of document structure and content. These are contained in service-specific regulations. While it was never the intent to cover all instances with the 83784 DTD because it was appended to the specification, this impression was widespread in the first years of the CALS initiative.

The DoD today, along with other industries, is establishing more flexible concepts of interchangeability that include libraries of DTD modules and fragments and common architectural concepts that ensure compatibility, interchangeability, and compliance to individual specifications. In this model (Figure 6.4), the DTD applied to a document is taken from a large set of DTDs designed to facilitate exchange. While a particular DTD from the library might cover only Air Force Job Guides, it has been designed recognizing the larger boundaries within which this information must exist. Thus, the constructs and definitions of parts within the Job Guide would conform to those used within an Illustrated Parts Breakdown (IPB) for the same piece of equipment.

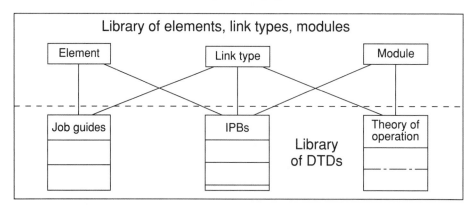

Figure 6.4 CALS information boundaries

DocBook and IBMIDDoc

The Davenport group is comprised of open-systems vendors, software vendors, and publishers interested in establishing DocBook as a common DTD for technical documentation. The group describes itself as a discussion group and is open to all participants, although only the group of Davenport sponsors formally votes on adoption of revisions of the DTD. Although the group has expanded its interests since its inception in 1991, the primary focus remains the creation and maintenance of the DocBook DTD.

The intent of the DocBook DTD is to create a superset of all software documentation requirements such that users can adapt it to their own needs by removing unneeded parts. What remains correctly models their local information, yet conforms to industry standards for exchange and reuse (Figure 6.5).

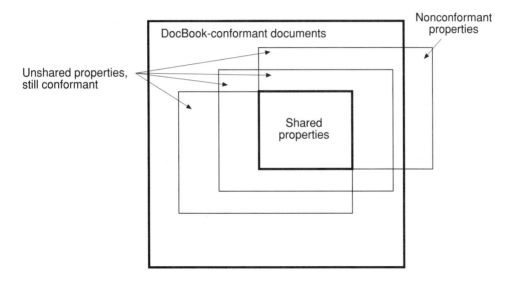

Figure 6.5 *DocBook information boundaries*

Sybase, Novell, Silicon Graphics, and most (not all) of the Davenport sponsors use DocBook for their technical documentation. See the sketch of Sybase in Chapter 4.

In addition to DocBook, the Davenport group sponsors working groups that are tackling standards for hypermedia in technical documentation in conformity with HyTime, standards for Unix manual pages, and a standard query language for SGML.

Another important public DTD for technical documentation is IBMIDDoc, which was developed by IBM for software product documentation. IBMIDDoc, which stands for Information Development Document, has been optimized for creation and exchange of technical documentation. Its modular design emphasizes information reuse, and it is a model for incorporation of HyTime architectural forms. IBM encourages use of IBMIDDoc to facilitate exchange of documentation with customers and clients.

The Text Encoding Initiative (TEI P3)

The image for TEI architecture given by Burnard in the keynote address for SGML '93 is that of a Chicago pizza: enough variety to satisfy any craving, with certain constraints.

"The Text Encoding Initiative," according to an introduction by Lou Burnard, who, along with C. Michael Sperberg-McQueen, is the editor of the standard, "is an international research project, the aim of which is to develop and to disseminate guidelines for the encoding and interchange of machine-readable texts." Its sponsors are the Association for Computers and the Humanities (ACH), the Association for Computational Linguistics (ACL), and the Association for Literary and Linguistic Computing (ALLC). Its widest applications today are colleges and universities, research institutes and archives, academic presses and organizations concerned with the long-term integrity of scholarly texts.

The image for TEI architecture given by Burnard in the keynote address for SGML '93 is that of a Chicago pizza: enough variety to satisfy any craving, with certain constraints. It is a pizza and remains a pizza, but you design your own meal choosing from three basic types of crust and several varieties of sauce, and you top it off from a long list of ingredients and condiments.

Burnard contrasted the Chicago pizza model with the Prussian model ("We know what's best for you, and you will do it our way"); the Waterloo model ("No one will ever understand our problems so we can't specify a common model"); and the Tower of Babel model ("We will use as many models as it takes to cover every possible instance"). In practice, the pizza model means that you choose the basic type of document from a discrete list that includes models such as prose, drama, and verse. All pizzas come with core (sauce) elements that are used across all documents. The topping consists of choices of link types, forms of analytical expression, and structural features.

Sperberg-McQueen elaborated on the philosophy behind the TEI P3 at the end of SGML '93. He said that the same DTD could not be optimized both for long-term storage and maintenance and for immediate output processing and that the TEI path was to optimize for the long term and encourage much adaptation and tweaking to accomplish immediate processing objectives. In his words, "Ignoring processing in the initial model gives better processing tweaking in the long run."

TEI P3 is the third release of the TEI Guidelines, published on May 16, 1994. The P3 Guidelines themselves are 1300 pages long in print and are also available in a number of electronic formats. Unlike other industry initiatives, the TEI focuses almost exclusively on content in a descriptive, not prescriptive, manner because it deals with established works, not works created as structured information. The specification contains much documentation and TEI history, plus

- Definitions of the base tag sets for prose, verse, drama, transcriptions of spoken text, print dictionaries, and terminological databases;

- Additional tag sets for linkage and alignment; simple analysis; feature structure analysis; certainty and responsibility; transcriptions of primary sources; critical apparatus; names and dates; graphs, networks, and trees; tables, formulas, and graphics; and language corpora;

- Auxiliary DTDs for independent headers, writing system declarations, feature system declarations, and tag set documentation;

- Essays on technical topics including conformance, modifications, interchange and multiple hierarchies; and

- A complete alphabetical list of all classes, entities, and elements.

The Guidelines are in widespread use throughout the academy, being used to encode and support research on Celtic verse, German philosophy, feminist novels—an ever-expanding list of texts, subjects, and intellectual life. See the sketch of the Women Writers Project in Chapter 4 and *Resource Guide A*.

The Pinnacles Group (PCIS)

The Pinnacles Component Information Standard (PCIS) recently published by the group of five semiconductor manufacturers known as the Pinnacles Group is an *exchange* DTD, not intended to define a document. The PCIS establishes rules for defining common objects found within component documentation but does not specify which pieces of information—which objects—must be included or what order or hierarchy they must follow. PCIS leaves each company at liberty to describe its own internal documents as internal requirements dictate while the community-at-large exchanges common data elements and incorporates them freely into local applications (Figure 6.6).

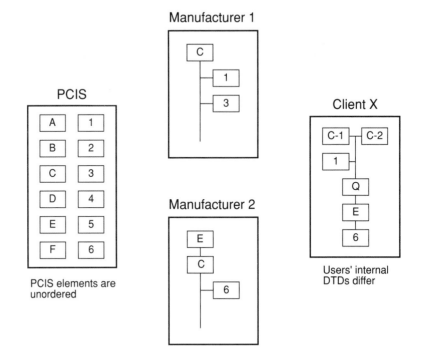

Figure 6.6 *PCIS information boundaries*

One of the primary motives behind Pinnacles was to provide a standard for-mat for printed and nonprinted information required by clients' computer-aided engineering systems. An information briefing published by the Pinnacles Initiative in October 1994 stated that the ability to import reusable data will

> ... increase the quality of product information by improving its accuracy, accessi-bility, and timeliness, as well as enabling CAD integration. Such improvements will help customers realize benefits in product identification and selection, reduced design-in and qualification cycle-times, enhanced product life-cycle man-agement, and many other areas.[2]

The engineers who will use the PCIS-encoded data can import it directly into local product databases and into product simulators. In this form, the data can be searched, queried, modeled, and compared. And, the information they receive

---

[2]Pinnacles White Paper, p.5. See the Intel case study in Chapter 4 and *Resource Guide A* for more information.

from each of the complying vendors is compatible and comparable. The Intel case study in Chapter 4 provides more background on the initiative and details on how CAD/CAE information is transferred through the PCIS model.

Lowest Common Denominator DTDs

There are several DTDs in common use, including hypertext markup language (HTML) on the World Wide Web, the International Committee on Accessible Document Design DTD (ICADD), and the Rainbow DTD, which have little document architecture to speak of because they represent primarily the format characteristics of a document. Architecturally, they are the mobile homes of the information landscape. Nevertheless, like mobile homes, they can play useful roles within a wider, SGML-based system and document design.

They are useful as:

- Lowest common denominator for cross-platform viewers;
- Simple output print format; or
- Intermediate conversion format, a stepping-stone to a more complex DTD.

Each of these DTDs and its application is discussed elsewhere in this book. The point here is to distinguish these standards that have limited roles from those standards that structure information and are useful for information processing.

The Method of Document Analysis

Document analysis is the first of the two stages required to create a DTD, the second being the actual coding in SGML. The purpose of document analysis is to build a model of document structure and content that can be translated unambiguously into an SGML document type definition (DTD). But don't let that objective mislead you into thinking that this is a mechanical exercise, with one "correct" outcome for any given document. There is a great deal of discretion in any document analysis process—in fact, you could say that discretion is the essence of document analysis.

The two critical types of expertise required for document analysis are expertise about your publication and your publication process and expertise about SGML design issues—not the mechanics of SGML coding, but the fundamental design issues inherent in choosing one type of structure over another. Document analysis, according to Debbie LaPeyre, of ATLIS computing,[3]

---

[3]Presentation at the SGML Forum of New York, January 18, 1994.

is a collaborative, interactive, iterative process: The SGML experts come in at the end. The most important people are the ones who now produce your documents: a typical group includes managers, systems people, editorial staff production workers, and a facilitator. A person can learn to code SGML in two weeks; what is more valuable is knowing how others have done it, knowing the implications of doing it one way or the other.

This modeling process, document analysis, should be accessible to all levels of participants, requiring a minimum knowledge of SGML and its syntax. The objective is to capture what is known about the document and its uses and to translate that into terms that an SGML programmer can then use to code the DTD. The process is analogous to constructing a set of specifications from a scale model, which is then turned into blueprints (the DTD) by an engineer or architect and, finally, into a building (the document instance) by a contractor.

People some-times see design alternatives in a picture that they cannot derive from a descrip-tion of the same relationships.

Tools that provide a graphic look at DTD structure are a boon both to those who are fluent in SGML syntax and to those who are not (and never will be). When the data is visually presented, we can see patterns and relationships that might not come to the fore when we are confronted with command line data. Another reason that visual tools can help us understand a DTD is that the sequence in which elements and entities are found in a DTD may be the sequence that is meaningful to an analyst; a tree shows hierarchy and inheritance, placing elements in their logical context, according to a user's view of structure. People sometimes see design alternatives in a picture that they cannot derive from a description of the same relationships. Graphic modeling tools can help in this process although they are not required.

There are several graphic DTD viewers and one, CADE Near & Far from Microstar, that writes DTD code based on the graphic view. Near & Far is a rela-tively new tool, and tool type, but it has been successfully integrated into pro-duction (see the Canadian Code Centre sketch in Chapter 4). While all the graphic tools add a powerful visual dimension to DTD writing and CADE also eases the burden of the syntax writer, knowing which pieces to put together, how to define them, and how to arrange them remains the real meaty part of DTD creation. Regardless of the tool used, document analysis must collect, collate and evaluate all that is known about a document type, its uses, and its production path.

Who Does It?

The document analysis team should be as wide as possible, including all those who influence the final publication. That group can include:

- Publications manager
- Product manager
- Editor

- Editorial supervisor
- Managing editor
- Production manager
- Production staff
- QA/QC
- Writer
- Typographer
- Layout and design staff
- Programmer

Unless at least one of the team members has experience with the process, it must include a facilitator and, unless one of the group is equipped to work a double role, a recording secretary as well.

It is odd, perhaps, that this group may have never sat down across a table before the document analysis process to discuss a publication. The object of including such a wide group, however, is not to perform an exercise in reengineering, although it does bear a resemblance. The objective is to include and anticipate all the requirements and exigencies that a document must fulfill during production, distribution, and normal use throughout its life span. If you do not include the people who shepherd it through each stage and some representative, at least, of those who will use it, the chances are you will not include all their requirements in the data design.

If you accept that the underlying data structure is the foundation on which the whole edifice of structured documentation rests, from its creation throughout its use, reuse, storage, and dissemination, it should not strike you as odd that those responsible for each of these steps in the process be represented at the table when that structure is designed and specified.

A final point about who should do document analysis: Involvement earns crucial buy-in—those involved from the outset, whose concerns have been incorporated into the design, are more likely to be enthusiastic supporters of the project throughout its life cycle. And this reduces the cost of later training because they are familiar with the concepts of structured information and the structures of their own DTD.

How Is It Done?

While this is still a nascent and inexact science, a methodology is being developed. The method that follows is adapted in small part from my own experience, in greater part from the experiences reported to me in the cases I have studied, and in greatest part from methodologies presented by Eve Maler and Jeanne El Andaloussi (1992, 1994), whose book on the subject is about to be published just as this book goes to press. I am also indebted to a lucid presentation of methodology given at the SGML Forum of New York by Debbie LaPeyre. While this method is derived from these sources, the authors are not responsible for this presentation.

In an idealized model, the document analysis procedure starts bottom-up in terms of requirements, and proceeds top-down in terms of design, looking first at the most salient features of document structure, like chapters and titles. Lloyd Harding, of Information Assembly Automation Inc., makes the case that this ideal is not always the best approach. He maintains that both are, at times, useful, the difference being:

- Top-down works well when there are few variations in leaf elements because you can quickly work down one branch of the tree.

- Bottom-up works when there are many varieties of leaves. This allows you to reduce the problem space early on by reducing the leaf varieties.

The process itself takes place over a series of meetings of the team described above. The discussion moves from the general to the particular, from a definition of objectives to specific choices, options, and alternatives for the DTD structure and content model. The last phase of the analysis is a testing phase, where the results are applied to a sample of the information being analyzed. The results of the test are fed back into the analysis, which leads to another iteration. When the analysis stabilizes, the results are coded in a DTD. The DTD itself is tested and revised until it meets production and product design specifications established in the document analysis.

The preliminary discussion establishes design and production standards. The discussion should identify and define the document life-cycle questions—Where does information come from? What do I do with it? Where does it go?—but in very concrete terms. This discussion must consider the media, structure, and system of markup of the source material; how it will be converted and when; and the media, structure, and system of markup of the final product. For print products, it must consider the requirements of the typographer and for electronic products, the requirements of the browser and search-and-retrieval engine. For archival products and databases, the discussion must consider the categories of information expected in the

General concerns and constraints that should be addressed include the type of document architecture—the issues described above—and how they relate to specific production questions. A typical discussion will cover:

- The size of the containers in which you will put your information—To what level of granularity should the document be coded?

- The type of objects to identify as objects—What will editors, users, and production staff need to identify, group, and retrieve?

- Future use of this material—What will ensure that you can derive all possible use of spin-offs and derivative products?

- Your production schedule—How long do you have for the analysis process and how long for production?

- Style guides and specifications that describe the document—These already describe structures and objects.

- The wider world of documents that may relate to this one—At what level do you need to subscribe to industrywide data architecture?

- Degree of rigor—Do you want highly rigorous specifications at the expense of ease, or can you live with a looser specification to gain ease of use?

Part of the problem with first-time document analysis is that the extreme practicality of these concepts—the extent to which your entire investment is in structured documents—may not be apparent until you have muddled through the process once and seen how these design decisions play out in the production process and in the final product itself. Hence the iterative nature of the process.

If your team is relatively raw and relatively new to document analysis, trying to do it by the book, without an experienced facilitator, will involve a great deal of trial and error and successive iterations and refinements until you get the product that you desire. This may not be a negative process, if you can budget the time for it. If time is limited, invest more in outside expertise. The cost of outside expertise is included in the budget estimates given in Chapter 5 because, if you need the budget estimates, you probably need an outside expert as well.

Maler and El Andaloussi have a methodology that starts with a preliminary discussion and proceeds through seven well-defined steps. LaPeyre breaks down basically the same process into four stages. Both roughly describe this sequence:

1. Discuss the goals and objectives of the document, the context in which it will be produced and used—this is the general discussion described above.

2. Identify and name the component parts of the document. At this point, look at only the biggest, most obvious shapes and containers. Take a step backward and squint to see just the big contours and not the details of the structure. Do not define the constituent pieces of your containers or how they fit together, only the containers themselves.

3. Create categories that organize these containers into structurally meaningful groups. These groups might be sequential (all containers that fit within front matter, body, and back matter) or might be thematic (all constituent pieces of an instruction set or procedure).

4. Define the smallest pieces, the "stuff" that fills each of the containers. "Stuff" differentiates and defines pieces that make up plain text, quoted text, citations, notes, lists, and instructions, to name just some of the possibilities.

5. Enrich the data set with nonprinting data fields, workflow- and process-related information, version and security levels, history, background, and commentary.

6. Finalize and test your analysis by applying it to a section or sample document. The more extensive the testing, the better.

The iterative nature and complexity of the process is not well captured in this oversimplified sequence. In practice, a discussion of categories (step 3) will lead to a revision of components and some overall objectives (step 1) will be revealed and revised in light of the analysis and classification of the data itself. Maler and El Andaloussi build at least one additional iteration of selection and classification into their basic sequence. "Enriching" the data may mean schematizing your workflow for document and job tracking or adding history and nonpublished data.

As with so many software development projects—and you *are* developing software—the cost of documenting the analysis is negligible next to the cost of not documenting it. Budget time and resources to record both what is said and done in document analysis sessions and what is encoded into the DTD. See Maler and El Andaloussi (1992) for a thorough description of tables, lists, and tree diagrams to accompany the analysis process. If this documentation is scrupulously maintained, it becomes the design specification for the actual coding of the DTD, which follows the document analysis.

Figure 6.7 illustrates two ways that a series of paragraphs could be represented during document analysis. One uses a relatively flat hierarchy, the other uses several layers of nesting.

You know that the iterative process is complete when your test document holds no more surprises and enigmas. The document or set of documents that you choose as your test vehicle is critical to the success of the enterprise. See the section *Planning a Pilot Project* in Chapter 8 for more discussion of sample documents.

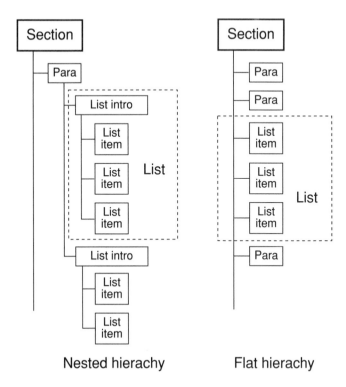

Nested hierachy   Flat hierachy

Figure 6.7 Text structure—two possibilities

Document Analysis and the Industry Initiative

One of the first decisions in any document analysis is whether to conform to an industry or an internal specification, to incorporate parts of an existing DTD, a DTD module, or to build your specification from scratch. If in doubt regarding how existing forms fit your data, the best approach is to do a preliminary document analysis, look at the results, compare your requirements with what is available and, on that basis, estimate the amount of customization or compromise required to make the two fit. One way to look at it is as you would any software build/buy decision.

In terms of the overall cost, once the industry standard is established, and there are costs involved in that process, conforming may save some effort because of the adoption of standards, but may cost some effort because of the requirement to track changes through an added level of design. Whether you are following the TEI, the DoD, or the requirements of your chosen compositor, the core element in the process is still document analysis, whether on macro/industry scale or on micro/document scale.

And what if there is as yet no standard DTD for your type of information? The creation of an industry standard involves, first, a broad analysis of industry requirements preliminary to creation of the standard and, second, a narrow analysis of project requirements for selective application of the standard.

There is no requirement that an organization participate in the creation of a standard. There is a definite price for participation, even if only the time and travel budget of representative members. In return, participants gain input into the direction that the industry takes for its data architecture and develop insider expertise in its application. (See the Intel portrait in Chapter 4.)

An Illustration

You can demonstrate the discretionary nature of document analysis to yourself if you consider as an exercise the section of this book that starts at the heading *The Method of Document Analysis* in Chapter 6. Straightforward and simple, right? Not really.

A document analysis of this section would need to answer these questions:

- Do we call the headings "headings" and indicate hierarchy by subordination in the document, or is one inherently a second-level head and one a third-level head?

- Could a third-level head follow a second-level head immediately, or must there be paragraphs (one or more?) in between?

- Are the lists extensions of the preceding paragraphs, or are they structurally independent?

- What metadata should be included with quotations? Should a citation be subordinate to a quotation? How will we link sources with citations? Will this cover sources cited more than once?

- Are numbered lists a variation on bulleted lists, or are they a distinct type of element?

- What constitutes a link anchor—words, sentences, paragraphs, or symbols inserted in the text?

- What kind of search mechanism will users rely on to find these topics? Do we need to encode keywords or will users rely on an index and search engine?

- What terms should be coded for index and glossary inclusion? How many occurrences, and which occurrences, of each term? How will this be handled by the print composition system and by the online browser? Does the browser compile an index that can link from one term to many anchors or must index entries be unique?

- Where in the text stream do footnotes come? Will the print composition engine and the online viewer work with that type of markup or do we need to transform it on output?

The list of questions and the structural possibilities could go on indefinitely—when you consider nonprinting data that could travel with this passage—like the author, the date of last revision, security level and so on—the possibilities are unlimited. There is no single "correct" document analysis for any document. What is correct is what achieves your business objectives, makes your production process efficient, and allows for future reuse, archiving, and retrieval. It is best to have the guidelines of a specific document architecture in mind and the guidance of an experienced information architect before tackling the analysis of an individual DTD.

It cannot be overemphasized that what you know about your documents and then inject into a design through document analysis is what you can expect to extract in production efficiency and in market value. This should be kept in mind during document analysis and during the design of your production environment.

Beyond Basic Design Issues

Text is the spine or frame on which the "document" is composed. So much of what we say when speaking of SGML is "text this, text that." In fact, we are using structured text as a script or storyboard for other media including pictures of all sorts and types, speech, video, animation, and music.

This short discussion of document architecture for tables, math, graphics, sound, and video is far from a thorough survey of current practice. It is here to introduce interested readers to SGML as an extensible text-handling language that describes all media, from multimedia to relational tables.

Tables

Traditional tables, which, by default, are tables in print, have the explicit and rigid structure of a database, yet, like any WYSIWYG document, they rely on format to convey meaning. In this sense, they have both a high and low structural aspect. This dual aspect of tables presents a particular challenge to data and application design.

Screen layout of tables in electronic books presents its own set of challenges. A display screen cannot present the equivalent of a paper page, nor should it. In print, a reader can flip through multipage tables and quickly zone in on the data requested, at the same time scanning for relationships between rows and column of data. On screen, readers lose the context, the meaning, and the ability to scan that they have with paper tables.

DTD table markup today employs two basic models: presentational and content. Presentational markup is based on table rows and columns. Although there are many variations on how to do this, basically each data point is marked up as an element nested within a row; sets of cells within rows are nested within columns. This type of markup makes it easy to derive a fixed, printed, or displayed form of the table.

Content-based table markup ignores the presentational aspect, treating the data points much like any other data sets within an SGML document and ceding control over how the table looks to the application (Table 6.1).[4]

Table 6.1 Sample table

PET	ARTISTIC ABILITY	STRENGTH OF VOICE
Cats	High	Soft
Dogs	Low	Loud

If the sample table were marked up according to the presentational model, the `<COLUMN>` element containing "Artistic ability" would contain `<ROW><CELL>` High `<ROW><CELL>`Low `</>` and so on. If the markup followed the content model, the DTD might define an element

```
<!ELEMENT PET - - (SPECIES, ART_ABLE, VOX)>
```

indicating that each `PET` element must contain one each of the species, artistic ability, and voice elements in that order.

A third way to look at tables is as fragments of relational data, actually relational database reports, that occur within documents. Lloyd Harding, of Information Assembly Automation, Inc., advocates handling tables in SGML as relational data, using SGML markup and incorporating existing relational tools, such as the report writer modules that are commonly bundled with relational software.

From this perspective, some of the compromises made today in the design of SGML tables do not make sense. Encoding just the appearance of the table would be the equivalent of trading in a report for the database that generated it. The relational perspective on SGML tables is attractive because structured documents, especially those that will have a life online, should not renounce the processing capabilities of data to achieve a good-looking presentation.

According to Harding, presentational tables can be standardized, and they provide convenient input processing but little or no internal or output processing

---

[4]This description of tables owes much to a poster presentation by Lloyd Harding, of Information Assembly Automation, Inc., at SGML '94.

since they provide a very low level of information. Content tables provide internal and output processing, but they inhibit input processing and are impossible to standardize. In contrast, relational tables can be standardized and they make possible processing at all stages of input, management, and output.

The most common approach today, however, is some form of row and column presentational model. This describes, roughly, the table model used in the CALS DTD and adopted by several application vendors. By using a common model for input and processing, application vendors have simplified some aspects of the tables question, but they have not solved it.

Markup overhead, the ratio of characters required to tag the data to the data itself, used to be considered a problem with tables in SGML. The markup overhead inherent in several levels of nesting can be avoided using techniques for tag minimization and SGML "shorthand"—short key sequences that stand in for longer strings of markup. Although this problem has been solved, the other design issues for SGML tables are still hotly debated.

The distance that we have yet to traverse to achieve a consensus on fully functional table design is a measure not of the shortcomings of SGML but of the relative youth of all online information. It is not only SGML applications that fall short of these requirements, but the extremes of structured and unstructured applications as well. Neither the WYSIWYG applications that format tables nor the databases that process them can do the dynamic reformatting required to achieve both ease of writing and ease of presentation. Chapter 7 looks again at tables in the context of current system design, and Chapter 10 looks to future solutions.

Math

There are two fundamental methods for working with math within SGML documents: The first incorporates non-SGML, math-specific markup within the SGML document; the second marks up the formula directly with SGML elements, attributes, and entities. Both methods are in use today; both have advantages and disadvantages.

The first method, incorporation of non-SGML markup, allows users to retain familiar processing tools, a clear advantage. Where T_EX has been applied and standardized, this method can be very effective.

The advantage of the second method, direct markup in SGML, is that a single SGML-based application can process, display, and parse the data. While this is possible in theory, the nature of mathematics presents certain practical difficulties. *Practical SGML* (van Herwijnen, 1994) is a good place to turn to appreciate the issues involved in a data design for mathematics within SGML. Eric van Herwijnen divides the approaches to math markup in SGML into those that encode presentation and those that encode semantics. He argues that, since math notation by its nature is incomplete and ambiguous, it is not possible to create a single DTD that specifies both the way a formula should look and how it can be computed. The harmonized math markup in ISO 12083 (the AAP DTD) takes the route of presentation.

A primary consideration for the design of an SGML-based system that will encode significant amounts of math is who will be doing the markup and what tools they are already familiar with. If the author is not doing the markup, the system must use a presentational model DTD or risk misinterpreting the author's intent. If the author marks up the text, then a familiar system will be appreciated. The proposed system for math in HTML3 leans heavily on the presentation model of T$_E$X. If this is approved and gains acceptance on the Web, it could become a general SGML standard for mathematical markup.

Pictures

SGML documents incorporate graphics by two methods: internally by declaration of a graphics notation and externally by reference to an external graphics file. Declaration of a graphics notation means that, although the data is in the same file as the SGML-tagged text, it is not SGML data and cannot be parsed. Since it requires a separate application for processing, there is little advantage in this method, and all current applications use the second method of inclusion by reference.

Inclusion by reference means that an element points to the name and location of a separate file that contains a graphic element. This separation of data for storage and processing does not necessarily mean a functional separation from the user's point of view. Input, management, and output applications, both print and electronic, routinely integrate text and graphics that are stored separately. The World Wide Web is one example of a browser that presents text and graphics as an integrated document when, in fact, each medium is stored separately.

From a functional point of view, the critical elements of graphic system design are naming, locating, and linking files in a way that is traceable and sustainable over time and across systems and creating a workflow process for doing so. All the factors must be considered in system design.

Sound and Video

Digital audio and video can be incorporated directly in SGML-encoded multimedia documents as a separate notation or indirectly, by reference and links to external files in the same manner as still pictures. These are documents only in the formal sense of the ISO 8879 definition of *document instances*. That the technology has outgrown the terminology indicates how far the original vision has expanded since the standard was first published almost ten years ago.

The case study of Cinemania describes one particular process of linking multimedia through SGML, and there are many other examples of the application of

SGML to multimedia. The HyTime standard prescribes general methods to do the same thing—link time-based sound and graphics to SGML-encoded text.

Everything Else

What else might you want to hang on your SGML skeleton? Two other significant areas where SGML goes beyond basic text application are the use of multiple character-sets and the use of interactive, logical components within a document.

In the United States, it is possible to be complacent about the set of 128 ASCII English language characters but, even here, the expansion in global markets is pushing us to recognize the need for smooth handling of multilingual and non-English characters. Text applications need to be able to specify multiple character-sets unambiguously when mingled in a single document and to specify replacement character-sets used in alternate versions of the document. SGML declarations can include public entity-sets and references to sets stored externally, public identifiers, which provide a framework for extending the characters used in a document or a version of a document.

Interactive electronic technical manuals, or IETMs, a term that comes from the DoD CALS initiative, use SGML syntax to encode logic. Much potential exists for development in this area, especially in the development of tools to simplify the writing and coding process.

7

Where Is There?
System Design

When considering your actual production system, it is convenient to follow the input–management–output division used throughout this book:

Here, however, where we are actually looking in depth at the real arrangement of work, these categories fail to reveal the complex nature of real, day-in/day-out production. While ideal workflow diagrams flow inexorably from left to right in neat, measured steps, real workflow flows from right to left as well in tight, predictable feedback loops and in loose, unanticipated change cycles.

More plans, more schedules, and more production scenarios run into trouble on the issue of review and revision than on any other issue—and that is *before* SGML is added to the loop. With its greater separation of function and specialized tools, SGML can add to the confusion or to the clarity, depending on how well the system is designed and implemented.

TYPICAL SCENARIOS

A real-life workflow diagram should be three-dimensional, adding the depth of the "human dimension." A simplified form might look like this (Figure 7.1):

1. Information originates in-house.

2. Writers work directly in an SGML editor.

3. Writers print draft-quality hard copy directly from the SGML editor for review, which goes to production editors and subject matter experts.

4. Hard-copy markup goes back to the writer, who inputs changes and makes modifications.

5. Quality assessment (QA) is done on-screen using an SGML editor.

6. Information is archived on a file server.

7. The database manager extracts the correct files for each publication.

8. Files are prepared for publishing with an SGML transformer.

9. File are down-converted to electronic publishing (WYSIWYG) format.

10. The publication is tweaked in the composition system, which prints a final review draft.

11. Final changes that would affect archival data are input twice, into the data files and into the composed pages. Cosmetic changes are input into the composition system only.

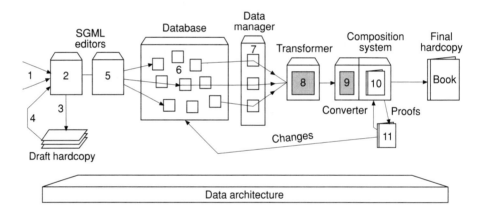

***Figure** 7.1 Workflow scenario: to print*

Or like this (Figure 7.2):

1. Information does not originate in-house; manuscripts come from multiple, outside sources.

2. Some converted in-house; some contracted out.

3. Inconsistencies brought to light during conversion require changes to the original document, the conversion program, and to the target DTD; change reports reviewed by project manager.

4. In-house editing done on documents in SGML, online; no hardcopy draft required because technical content reviewed prior to conversion.

5. Information archived in database.

6. Data manager extracts files for online publication.

7. Documents converted to browser format with style sheet.

8. Final QA done in viewer; errors fixed in database; document is re-exported and run through transformer.

9. After document passes final QA, files mastered on disk and CD-ROM.

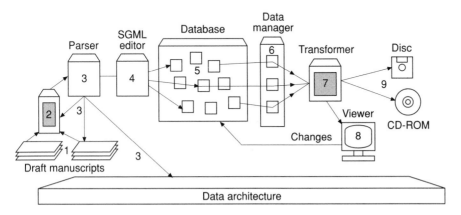

Figure *7.2 Workflow scenario: to screen*

Few people design a system from scratch; most start from an installed base of technology and expertise. How do you make the most of what you have, and how do you know when to jettison current processes and equipment in favor of new tools and techniques? There is no single prescription that will carry all businesses through this process. There is generic advice that applies to renovation of any information technology and is at least one principle that can be applied to all SGML systems.

DESIGNING THE PROCESS, CHOOSING THE TOOLS

First, the generic advice.

- Apply the same discretion that you would to any new technology purchase. Consider the platform, speed, function, ease of use, budget, ability to customize, strength of the company, and support policies during your evaluation. Use a representative sample of your own data to test any new technology. The sample should be representative in terms of size and complexity.

- Design around your needs, which means, primarily, around people—the skills you want them to have and to use—and around your intellectual product.

- Think scale, scale, scale, scale, especially for data-handling, search, and retrieval—the number of pages, chapters, books, and elements may have a determining effect on speed.

- Be demanding—Do your own needs analysis; don't start with the assumption that they built it, so you have to buy it. Tools are changing; if the tool you need is not there, ask for it.

- Be gradual, but look to the future—If you don't create a full system now, do what you can do to make the eventual conversion easier. A phased introduction is not only possible but, in many cases, preferable (see the section *Ways to Phase* in Chapter 8).

- Plan to change—Bringing in structured information is not a one-to-one swap with previous technology. Old jobs will be transformed, new ones will be added.

- Invest in planning—"Plan to plan" as Debbie LaPeyre says.

- Evaluate your current infrastructure—Start with what you have, know how to use, and like.

And one principle is SGML-specific:

- Consider your document architecture—What you can do and how you can do it is intimately connected with the structure and content of your data and its markup.

Inputting Information

The big decisions here are:

1. Do you "go native," using a native SGML editor, or do you write-to-convert using templates and styles in a WYSIWYG editor?

2. If you convert, how and who does the conversion?

3. If you go native, how native? Which type of editor—document- or data-centered?

A database can also be a front end for an SGML-based production system. In most cases, however, a database is not chosen as an input device—either the information already resides in the database or structured information is created elsewhere and then is mapped to the database.

Certainly, each type of tool has its appropriate area of application. Some environments thrive with a mix of tools, others require a uniform tool set. The discussion that follows provides some criteria for deciding which is best for your environment.

Native SGML Editors Versus Writing-to-Convert

One way to look at the trade-off between native and WYSIWYG editors is as a trade-off in where you put ambiguity. With a native editor, there is no ambiguity in markup at input, although there may be ambiguity for writers about the effect of what they do on the format of the final product. With a WYSIWYG editor, there is no ambiguity at input about *one form* of output markup, but there may be a great deal of ambiguity about structural markup and markup that would apply to other, nonprint, forms of output. While a WYSIWYG editor used in a write-to-convert scenario appears to specify both the data structure and its output characteristics, even a WYSIWYG editor can mark up a document unambiguously for one type of output at most.

The way around this trade-off is to give writers immediate feedback about the consequences of their work. If they use an SGML editor, writers need feedback on output format. If they use a WYSIWYG editor, writers need feedback on how their document will convert to SGML. Individual tools provide different types of feedback. The structured editors and packaged editors with conversion utilities described in Chapter 3 populate the spectrum between native and WYSIWYG editors. Each new product makes its own set of compromises between immediate structural validation and immediate output format definition and provides some degree of feedback.

Passage Systems' integrated SGML environment gives writers using an SGML editor a preview of output to print and output to screen while they are working on the input. Alternately, Passage Pro can give writers working on a WYSIWYG editor feedback on how their documents will convert to SGML. If this feedback is not an immediate technical capability, then the workflow process must allow for substantial feedback through other channels.

Factors to weigh when considering the cost of either a native SGML editor or a WYSIWYG editor with a template include the suitability of the material to conversion—can a template really cover, unambiguously, all the features that you want tagged in the structured file? Also, what access do your writers have to native editors? How diligent are they likely to be about using a template? How closely are they supervised? How closely do you want to supervise them?

There is no "right" answer here that will fit every situation. The key considerations are:

If they use an SGML editor, writers need feedback on output format. If they use a WYSIWYG editor, writers need feedback on how their document will convert to SGML.

- Your current investment in editing technology and your level of expertise with that technology;

- The type of markup required by your data design;

- The degree and type of control you can and wish to exercise over the input process;

- The relative cost of the technology available for your platform and the relative cost of conversion versus working in SGML;

- The preferences and preparation of the writers who will use the tools.

Current Investment

If you have been working with hot lead, then hanging on to your current technology is not a factor. If you have state-of-the-art workstations with high-end WYSIWYG publishers on all the writers' desks, and they all know how to use them, then you might consider ways to make the most of that investment, at least in the initial phase of your transition. You might make the input of information the last area to be converted to SGML-based production, using your existing knowledge of tools to compensate for the lack of native editors. While a prior investment might not determine your ultimate strategy, it must influence your transition strategy.

Data design

While data conversion is never 100 percent, some data designs are better targets for conversion than others. For example, content markup is more difficult to convert than structural markup. A "procedure" is a structural concept that will be relatively easy for conversion software to recognize if it has a title and numbered steps. The tool names and terms used in the procedure may be more difficult to recognize. If you are using your SGML data for job tracking and workflow management, you must consider the input interface for this nonprinting information.

SGML for prototype or one-of-a-kind documents is an underdeveloped field with limited possibilities. Currently, there is little available for modeling documents *as* you write them.

Process Control

The decision between native SGML tools and writing-to-convert is also a choice of how you want to exercise control over the data environment: If you use a native editor, the editing tool will exert control over the SGML syntax; if you write to a template in order to convert the data later, you must control the use of the template as stringently as the native editor controls use of SGML syntax.

If your data is not input on-site, you must balance the difficulties of enforcing adherence to a word-processing template against the difficulties of supplying SGML editing tools and training the off-site people in their use. The alternative to both of these options is not to expect a high level of structured input from your sources, but to raise the level of the data during or after the conversion process.

The managerial challenge is that there is no way to force anyone to use a non-structured editor as if it were a structured editor. Without that degree of enforcement, writers and editors must be trained and motivated to parse their material to the degree required by a structured editor.

On a managerial level, management must be able to distinguish what is worthwhile converting from what is better off left for manual cleanup.

Relative Cost

The initial cost of the technology is an important consideration, but you must also consider the relative cost of inputting information directly into SGML or adding a conversion step. In legacy data conversion, considered in detail in the next chapter, the factors that determine cost and method are the amount of data, the complexity of the target, the consistency of the source data, and the quality of the management and programming skill applied to the process.

Unlike legacy data, in a write-to-convert situation, you are not likely to have large quantities of information to convert at one time. Also, you can design your target and your source to make the most of the conversion process. Legacy data conversion, while it may be extensive, remains a finite process; in a write-to-convert scenario, the tools and processes that you develop may have an indefinite life span.

What remains constant between legacy and ongoing conversion is the degree of skill required both on a technical and a managerial level. On a technical level, building and maintaining a conversion program is a full-time job. Most writing environments go through constant, albeit slow, evolution that requires tweaking the document architecture and all its associated parts, including a conversion template.

The specific challenges for legacy data conversion are described in some detail in the next chapter. Off-the-shelf software starts, but does not complete, the process. Estimates for how long it takes to write a conversion program range from 2 to 15 weeks, depending on the skill and experience of the programmer and the complexity of the material.

Another consideration is whether you are investing heavily in legacy conversion. If your legacy conversion is done in-house, then, by necessity you have expertise and technical depth that can be applied to ongoing conversion as well.

The Writers

The final, and very strong, consideration when choosing writing tools must be the training and background and preferences of the writers themselves. The case studies in Chapter 4 illustrate that writers react sometimes positively, sometimes negatively to SGML editors. Many factors influence their reaction including how well they are trained, how well the system is designed, how well the process of writing is adapted to the new tools, and what they were using before the switch to SGML editors.

The managerial challenge is that there is no way to force anyone to use a nonstructured editor as if it were a structured editor.

Most writing environments go through constant, albeit slow, evolution that requires tweaking the document architecture and all its associated parts, including a conversion template.

These factors are discussed further in the section in this chapter on *Managing the Process* and in Chapter 9, *Being There.*

Choosing Structured and Write-to-Convert Tools

Native editors give you immediate feedback on data design; WYSIWYG editors give you immediate feedback on format. Write-to-convert and structured editors are beginning to populate the spectrum between these extremes with a variety of solutions and compromises. The various write-to-convert possibilities cover a range from using your own word processor with styles and templates, together with your own or an off-the-shelf conversion program, through word processors that come with conversion templates to SGML layers over conventional word processors which convert your data on the fly or during a separate output stage. Structured editors are getting more sophisticated in terms of SGML syntax and data management.

FrameBuilder from Frame and Tag Wizard from Nice Technologies combine highly structured editing with WYSIWYG styles. This brings back to the desktop direct control over format and adds real structural validation. Frame has tried to capture the best of both worlds in this product and, to some extent, has succeeded. By mapping DTDs and document instances to its own format, allowing work in a WYSIWYG environment, Frame has made working with structured documents much easier.[1]

What is lost in translation? Individual write-to-convert products may not support all features of SGML on both import and export. They may require a specific table model and they may not map to externally-defined entities. Alternately, they may do all-of-the-above, but so slowly that they are not practical in many production environments.

Getting a site up and running requires adaptation and mapping of a DTD to an internal format and an understanding of what that mapping means. These products do not necessarily lower the level of expertise required to install, configure, and manage SGML-based production but, by mapping the output to what the writer does at the input, it lowers the level of expertise required at each workstation and eliminates a separate output conversion step.

Individual products will continue to change, but one way to visualize the range of possibilities is the degree of direct mapping to SGML versus mapping to word-processor styles and also the degree of feedback between structured and formatted phases of the process. Today, the range of options includes products that:

- Use separate word processor and conversion tools and give feedback only at the output of the conversion process; until then, the degree of mapping is unknown;

---

[1]See the note in Chapter 3 on the new Frame+SGML product.

- Use integrated tools without validation feedback, and give feedback only after the conversion process; until then, there is no validation; and

- Use integrated tools that supply some validation feedback during the writing process.

Another consideration in the choice of production conversion tools is the variety of input formats. If you opt for a tool that integrates a specific word processor, obviously your conversion programming is valid only for input from that format or you must first convert your material into that format. Separating the word processor from the conversion tool gives you better leverage over a variety of input formats.

Choosing Native Editors

Early SGML editors and some customized and specialized editors today, such as those for HTML and the Web, are hard-wired to one DTD. As a minimum, any editor must accept the DTD or DTDs and the size files with which you will be working. Beyond the basic ability to load and to parse a file, the writer's interface is the most critical editorial consideration. In SGML-based systems that separate input and output functions, the input tool again belongs to the writer rather than to the designer or the production manager. The issues that matter for writers working in this environment are discussed at length in Chapter 9.

Is the basic input paradigm the one that you want, one that will be comfortable for your authors and editors? The answer depends on your staff—the answer might be emacs with SGML extensions, or it might be one of the native SGML editors, or it might be a customized version of one of these. Because of the relative youth of this technology, if you can specify it and you need it, and you are large enough, the tool vendors will build it.

In choosing a tool for writing-to-convert, we looked at the integration of validation feedback. In choosing native editors, we must consider the integration of output format feedback.

In general, there are two routes to higher productivity, and all SGML editors with a graphical interface choose from both, to some degree. You can raise productivity by restricting function to one, specialized portion of the process or you can raise productivity by increasing integration throughout the process. A closer integration of the action with the result is what made WYSIWYG desktop publishing a great tool for print pages. The ability to print formatted draft pages and the ability to view graphics in context with the editor are two ways to provide output feedback for the writer. Integrating the action with the result is the aim of integrated tool sets.

In SGML-based systems that separate input and output functions, the input tool again belongs to the writer rather than to the designer or the production manager.

Choosing Data Conversion Tools

While sometimes described as a simple mapping process, up-conversion to SGML is never a simple process. Chapter 8, *Getting There,* describes why this is so and where the problems arise. Here, suffice it to say that legacy data is never as consistent as you think it is and structure is never as unambiguous as you would like it to be. If you are converting recipes, it is difficult to distinguish quantities from measures; if you are converting legal codes, and you have specified that a paragraph starts a chapter, you can be sure that, at least once in your data, it starts with a note. In such cases, a conversion program can make a best guess at the right action, but a trained person must always make the final disposition.

> *legacy data is never as consistent as you think it is and structure is never as unambiguous as you would like it to be.*

If you are working with material written explicitly to be converted to SGML you can use document templates and style guides that streamline the task of conversion to a far greater extent than is possible with legacy files. In this case, the templates become software that must be carefully constructed and maintained along with the target DTDs and conversion programs. Despite the lack of a simple path, I suspect that far more data makes its way into SGML through conversion from a legacy format or a template than is written in native SGML.

At this writing, it is difficult to gauge the impact of the new, integrated conversion products because some of them have been shown but not released, others have been released but not long enough to be tested in production, and the others differ in many respects. DynaTag does not target a supplied DTD during the conversion process but makes one up to fit the conversion and does not provide document validation. It uses the Rainbow DTD as an intermediate format. SGML Author for Word uses SureStyle built on the FastTag engine. Passage Hub can be integrated into a Passage Pro production environment.

For the end user just beginning to work with SGML, the primary conversion decisions are not which tools to use since the tools are not mutually exclusive. One could argue that a healthy conversion environment is a heterogeneous conversion environment. For those just coming to SGML conversion, the primary decisions are about *who* should do the conversion—if the conversion should be done in-house or by contract—not necessarily which tools they should use. Many sites combine:

- Off-the-shelf software
- Home-grown software
- Service bureaus

Chapter 8 describes each of these options.

Managing Information

If a file is no longer in a one-to-one relationship with a document, if the physical and logical grouping of the "file" is a convenience for the operating system and nothing more, then the coherence and cohesion of your publication depend on the insight and foresight of the data management software as much as on the writer who wrote the pieces of it or the editor who checked the whole of it.

Here, the basic decisions are:

- Do you need a database manager or an entity manager or can you get by with file system management?

- If you need a document database, then do you want a relational tool, an object-oriented tool, or an SGML-based tool?

- Do you need document management and workflow?

Don't assume that you need a database manager just because you need SGML. If you did not need a document or workflow tracking system to manage your publications before, you might not need it now. If you did need it before, then even limited search and retrieval capability and some additional data recording and reporting may suffice. Many document and data management tasks can be programmed with a transformer, so review the capabilities and characteristics of transformation tools in Chapter 3.

The questions that sort out the various requirements are as follows:

- How much data will you handle and how complex is it?

- How do you slice and dice your data? How many sources does it come from, and where does it go?

If your work follows a traditional composition and writing pattern, with a one-to-one correspondence between authors and products, your need for a data manager may be low. If your product is closer to the data model than the text model, with a many-to-many correspondence between authors and products, your need for a data manager is certainly high. What SGML adds to the equation is the ability to query and extract from your data the pieces and parcels that compose just the product you want at the moment. If your reasons for adopting SGML include versioning, reuse, and recombination of data, then you must specify a data management system that can delivery these functions.

- How much workflow and job tracking do you want?

If you intend to use nonprinting and nondisplaying attributes to track work as it goes through the production process, you must specify the ability to store, query, and retrieve this information.

- How rich is your data set? What information do you want to extract from it?

Even if you are maintaining an archive where the output products themselves are invariant, as in an archive, there may be compelling reasons to collect data about your products. For example, if you produce and store articles that cannot be modified because of copyright and intellectual history, you may, nevertheless, wish to build an index of citations and cross-references that requires extracting information from data without modifying or manipulating the underlying files. See the Columbia University Press case study in Chapter 4, which describes how data collected about archived anthologies provided information that could not have been derived from a paper or file-based record; this information became the basis for several new products.

- What type of query and data extraction do you anticipate?

This, of course, is the key question in the evaluation of information retrieval software and is the subject of much debate and much current work. The key factor in a successful system design is to test the technology with the actual type of queries you will be using and to test it on a scale of data that represents a realistic approximation of the scale on which you will be working. Consider if the use of stop words is a factor and consider if the stop word list can be modified or turned off. Consider the speed of the search and the effect of missing hits and of false hits at the scale on which you may be working.

There are two kinds of trade-offs everyone lives with when searching for digital information. The first is the trade-off between coverage and precision: "Did I get every possible hit that I need?" versus "Did I get a large number of hits that I did not need?" Put another way, users trade the assurance that they have found everything there was to find for the annoyance of finding things that do not relate to their query. If they limit their annoyance, they pay by limiting their level of assurance.

The second trade-off is between search modalities built into the engine versus search modalities built into the data: "Do I use the cleverness of my search-and-retrieval engine to figure out that this book is about SGML because of the frequency with which the term is mentioned?" or "Do I rely on a list of keywords that state the subject of the book?" Most systems rely on one method more heavily than the other.

Search applications are distinguished by:

- How the search is specified—how easy, or intuitive;

- The speed of working with the scale of data that you manage;

- Precision/recall;

- Whether searches can be qualified by structure, for example, finding "tabby cat" in a figure caption or "cold, wet nose" in a list of symptoms;

Your choice of data management systems must also take into account your staff and the other tools that you use. Questions to ask when you consider a new system include:

- Who will be managing the data? What skills do they have?

If your staff includes people with programming backgrounds, you should be biased toward the tools that they are most familiar with and the tools used for the other data-handling applications for which they are responsible. See the Standard & Poor's case study and the Utah AOC sketch for examples of this type of integration.

- What special processing requirements do you have? Do you require loose-leaf publishing?

Loose-leaf publishing tracks the pages on which information appeared in a page-based composition system so that future versions can duplicate or track changes to this layout. A holdover from when the page was the most useful unit of data, loose-leaf publication is still a requirement for many publishers. While inserting pages is the proper work of the composition system, not the database manager, keeping track of those pages requires less effort with a database.

- What kind of database manager?

In the future, finer distinctions might be developed that indicate where an object-oriented, where a relational, and where a native SGML model are best applied. For now, the choice seems to be largely tool- and circumstance-dependent: Pick the tool that has the functions that you need and that integrates most smoothly with what else you have. Until the tools mature, and more experience is accumulated, the best advice seems to be to base a decision on the tool that meets your functional specifications rather than preselecting a group of tools based on the data-processing model.

The impact of HyTime on storage, management, and retrieval is just beginning. At this writing, the only integrated storage and retrieval system that incorporates HyTime entity management is Explorer from SoftQuad (see the sketch of Publications International in Chapter 4). With Explorer, comments that apply to a document are stored in a separate file from the published document, coded as SGML, and searched, queried, and retrieved in the same way as the document and concurrent with the document. This creates a shadow file that can fulfill many of the functions of a document and data management system, all within SGML.

At the present time, precedent, inheritance of technology, and expertise are large factors; also, integration with output and input tools is a significant factor.

The first rule, perhaps the only rule, for choosing document and data management software is: If you already have it and have the expertise you need to use it and it has the features that you're looking for, it's probably the right choice for you.

Outputting to Print

Down-conversion, in general, has a big payoff in SGML-based systems. Here, all the work of elevating your data to a higher energy level is released in the reverse process, that of taking structure and content markup and applying less rigorous, format-based markup. As Kate Hamilton puts it, "The files just slide into Quark." All the small work of composition—"What did the author mean by that funny symbol?" and "Is this indent part of a new section?"—has been done up front, while the file was in SGML.

The downhill conversion from SGML into print, while not energy-intensive like the trip uphill, is not without friction. A simple one-to-one mapping does not suffice. Either the compositor or the conversion tool must supply generated text, such as section and note numbers, tables of contents, and other generated lists and headers. Where elements change their format according to their context, the converter must read the hierarchy of the document and output format tags according to inheritance.

Illustrations and their placement are not fully specified in an SGML file. They are included, but usually by reference to an external file. Once the SGML file is in the composition software, unless the placement of the illustrations is extremely regular, they must be sized and positioned by hand.

Other considerations include tables and math. If your SGML is just a wrapper around another data format, like T_EX for math, then, on output, you must convert the data if the compositor will not handle it directly. The production of SGML-encoded tables is discussed in Chapters 6 and 7.

When the bulk of the formatting is handled in the down-conversion or filtering process, designers working with their design tool of choice find that the files have a regularity and a well-behavedness that other files, which never went through the structured state, never achieve.

The three stages of taking SGML to print, and the associated tools are (Figure 7.3):

1. Resolution of inherited styles and generation of text, usually by an SGML programming language, or database manager or transformation tool;

2. Application of format markup by a filter or conversion tool;

3. Definition of styles and composition of pages within the composition system.

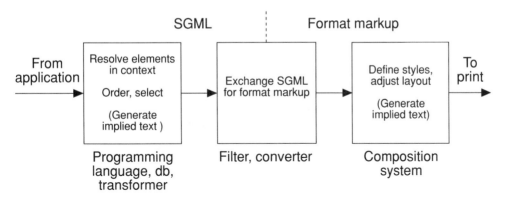

Figure 7.3 *Going to print from SGML*

All production systems must account for these tasks, even if you are setting up a print process to comply with an industry or corporate standard that mandates use of a Format Output Specification Instance (FOSI). When putting these stages together into an output system, the major variable, as with input systems, is where to resolve the ambiguity inherent in the transition from one form to another: in the prefiltering transformation, in the filter, or in the composition system.

There is an important difference, however, between this transformation and the one going into SGML. Going into SGML, certain types of ambiguity must be resolved by a person, with or without the aid of a tool; there are limits to automation. Here, when leaving SGML, automation can handle more of the task.

If your final design is regular, the final layout can be nearly hands-off. If your page layout involves irregular placement of graphics and layout elements that must be done by hand to achieve the desired effect, then you can automate the precomposition process to eliminate all but the tasks that are done by hand by preference.

Here, we will look in greater depth at what this stage must accomplish and at the design trade-offs that affect the whole process, looking first at use of standard composition tools and then at SGML-specific FOSI publishers.

Standard Composition

You can divide the tasks of an SGML composition system into two parts: those that are specific to SGML and those that are not. In the first category are the rendering of entities, elements, and elements-in-context into a form unambiguous to the composition system. A simple SGML-tag to format-tag conversion is not sufficient because an application that is not SGML-aware might not resolve inherited context and other structural features of SGML, such as marked sections and attributes, if they bear on final format. Tag minimization, the option of omitting SGML tags that are clear from the context, must be resolved for the translation process.

Tasks not specific to SGML that must be accomplished by the composition process are:

- Removal of nonprinting text;
- Manipulation of the order of the text stream;
- Generation of implied text; and
- Resolution of inconsistencies of usage.

Nonprinting text can include job tracking and history, comments and version-specific data. Manipulation of the order of the text stream may be a style or design requirement. For example, bibliographic style may call for the author first, then the title of a work, while page design may call for the title to come first, then the author.

Generation of implied text is the insertion of text strings, such as chapter, footnote, and list item numbers, that apply to the final composition, but that are not explicit in the stored data. The reuse of text in different contexts and its frequent revision are good reasons not to insert text that is dependent on the order of output into the storage format. Prefix and suffix copy, such as the string "Chapter" before the chapter number or a comma after a title in a bibliographic entry, may also be inserted by the composition system to give greater output independence to the archival data.

Some instances of inconsistent usage that are not caught by the parser can be remedied in the translation to the output format. For example, if bibliographic entries come both with and without commas after titles, this could be searched and corrected in the output transformation.

In putting together a system to perform these tasks, you can do more or less in the prefilter transformation and more or less in the composition system, by hand or by batch. How you balance the alternatives may depend on what is needed in a canonical archive: Do you need a document that represents the authoritative version of what was printed (what was printed, not necessarily the text from which it was generated)? If an authoritative form of the output version is required, then it might be desirable to do as much as possible while the data is still in SGML. The alternative is to create an output DTD and to do an SGML-to-SGML transformation between the storage or source DTD and the output DTD. In this case, you will have a design-ready document instance that can serve as an archive of the final print.

If the need for a canonical archive is not transcendent, you might still want an output DTD and a format-ready document instance to maximize the degree of automation in the output process. If automation is not an overriding concern, either because of the small quantity of material or because the final layout limits the degree of automation possible, then the prefilter transformation becomes less important.

Output Filtering, Transformation, or Conversion

There is much that can be done with the regularity of SGML using the text manipulation utilities sed, awk, and grep. Otherwise, your choice of text manipulation tools lies between the SGML-specific transformers and the non-SGML-specific capabilities of standard word processing and electronic composition. Figure 7.4 demonstrates the type of programming required for an output transformation. This program is written in OmniMark to go from SGML to RTF.[2] It takes the SGML DTD element DOC and its content model (the elements inside the parens), processes it (the lines beginning reset and set), and outputs RTF.

```
; The Document Element

element DOC; (FRONT, BODY, REAR?) +(FTNOTE|PGBRK|BRK)
   reset footnote-mark-number to 0
   reset footnote-number to 0
   set buffer docno to ""
   output "{\rtf1\ansi{\fonttbl" _
      "{\f20\froman Tms Rmn;}{\f2\fswiss Helv;}}%n"
      "{\stylesheet{\s242\sbasedon()\snext0 page number;}%n"_
      "{\sbasedon222\snext0 Normal;}}%n"_
      "\margl1440\margr1440\facingp\margmirror\widowctrl"_
      "\ftnbj\ftnrestart"_
      "\sectd\cols1 %n"_
      "%c}%n"
```

***Figure** 7.4 Sample output transformation script*

Composition

Choosing a compositor is one thing that the publishing industry knows how to do. The same questions of batch versus interactive versus rules-based publishing apply when the input is SGML data. The simplest method is to choose a composition system (in practice, to decide if you have any reason to change from the one you are currently using) and then, looking at your data design, your in-house expertise, and the tools described in Chapter 3, to determine the best method to translate from your data to your chosen composition system.

As you would with any composition system, you must consider who will do the design work, how it will be specified, and how it will be implemented. You must look at the requirements of your product and determine how much intervention is required on each page and how hands-off the process can be.

---

[2]Excerpted from the XGML OmniMark Sampler Version 1.0 translating a CALS-conformant MIL-M-28001A document into Rich Text Format.

If your current tools give you the pages that you want, if your staff is trained to use them and uses them well and efficiently, if the tools produce the print resolution and level of control over design that you want, then they will continue to do so when you feed them with SGML rather than with unstructured text. As Nelson Adams, of Adams & Hamilton, puts it, the best advice for publishers using SGML is to "Hire a good designer and make sure that your formatter is competent"—sound advice for *any* publisher.

What SGML adds to the choice of a composition system is the fact that the data going into the system will be regular and unambiguous. If your output can be described in the same terms, then a more automated, hands-off solution may be possible than was possible without SGML when most of the tweaking and normalization of the file was done at the last stage. For example, if your output pages are highly regular, when you standardize the input with SGML, you might not need an interactive page composition system. If your product will be irregular regardless of the input files, if graphics placement requires hands-on work, then the return on an interactive system will be better.

Special Considerations

Other considerations in choosing a composition system include tables, mathematical formulas, and loose-leaf publishing requirements.

There are various compromises current for encoding tables and table layout. What is specified in your DTD may or may not format easily. Often, to encode the sense of a table, designers skimp on layout specifications or, to fully specify the layout of a table, the content and structure are not fully specified. See the Butterworth case study in Chapter 4 for a description of how Butterworth produces extensive legal tables, and see the section on data design for tables in Chapter 6.

While loose-leaf publishing—defined as the tracking of page integrity from version to version—is possible by tracking pages without a database, it is easier with a database managing the pages.

The approach of Pager from Frame Technology is to insert the page break information back into the SGML file, and then break the SGML file up into smaller files, one per page. The Xyvision PDM approach is to maintain "div," or difference, files that track differences between this composition cycle and the previous one. Both are feasible without additional data management software as long as the loose-leaf requirement is not compounded by additional reuse and recombination requirements.[3]

---

[3]Thanks to Michael J. Maziarka, of XyVision and formerly of Datalogics, for this clarification.

Who Does the Work?

The final consideration in designing a system for going to print is this: Who is going to do this work? As Hamilton says, "We don't have a category for this work: It's not document creation, it's not typesetting—what is it? Or, more to the point, who is to be trusted with doing it?" Like other SGML-related tasks, this lies somewhere between traditional publishing concerns and traditional programming concerns. Clearly, how you answer this question for your production team must bear on the design of the system.

Is it easier to teach the ins and outs of publishing production work to a programmer or to teach programming to a publisher? There is no single answer to this question. How you settle the issue depends in no small part on the skills of your staff, how you judge their potential, the concurrent changes that you want to make in the workforce and the tools and training that you supply.

If you rely on staff with a publishing background, you may choose to automate less or to move the automation into the publishing tools with which they are familiar. If you rely on staff with a programming background, you may wish to automate as much as possible and to do it within the SGML environment.

Summary

Summing up this discussion, the manipulations that must be done to create formatted output files from SGML can be done more or less upstream, while the data is still in SGML, or all the way downstream, in the composition system. The factors that determine the design of a system are:

- Need for automation;
- Need for canonical archive;
- Special composition requirements such as loose-leaf and intensive use of tables and math;
- Limitations of the transformer and composition system;
- Nature of final layout; and
- The skill set of those who do the work.

FOSIs

A Format Output Specification Instance, known with affection as a FOSI (rhymes with "bossy") is essentially a set of rules for text composition written in SGML created for the U.S. Department of Defense's (DoD's) CALS initiative. Formally, a FOSI is an SGML-marked-up document that uses the DoD's Output Specification (OS) as its DTD. The OS document type definition and every FOSI instance use the same syntactic structures as any other DTD and document instance—elements, attributes, and entities.

FOSIs map SGML documents to appearance-based markup ready for composition by a FOSI-capable system. The objective of a FOSI is to extend the generality of SGML markup to composition, originally for print, but they are also applicable to on-screen composition. FOSIs use the same constructs as documents but apply them to format instead of to structure and content.

For example, a FOSI FONT element with a size attribute looks like:

```
<FONT size="16pt'>
```

Industries and individual companies outside the CALS initiative have adopted FOSIs—see the case study of Ericsson in Chapter 4. Currently, however, only two composition vendors have tools that handle FOSIs directly.

Paul Grosso, ArborText, explains that every FOSI contains two basic types of information: page layout and style (Grosso, 1993). Page layout can vary from section to section, for example, single-column with no running header for title pages and two-column with a header for the body.

FOSI styles define the classic features of composition: font, leading, quadding, spacing, and so on—there are about 125 such characteristics. FOSI style applies to elements-in-context (e-i-c), for example, NOTES in the context of body text have one style and NOTES in the context of tables have a different style. The FOSI can also define a distinct style based on first or last occurrence (first item in a list, last item in a list) although not based on arbitrary occurrence.

Grosso (1993) gives an example of style (Fig. 7.5) where the element is TITLE and the context is SECTION. Note that the syntax is the syntax of any SGML document: e-i-c and FONT take the place of element names, GI (for generic identifier) and INHERIT take the place of attribute names, and TITLE and 14pt are attribute values. Optional sections describe features such as counters, tables, footnotes, and graphics.

```
<e-i-c gi="title" context="section">
    <charlist>
        <font inherit="1" size="12pt" weight="bold">
        <leading lead="14pt">
        <quadding quad="center">
        <presp minimum="4pt" nominal="6pt" maximum="8pt">
        <postsp minimum="12pt" nominal="14pt" maximum="16pt">
        <span span="1">
```

Figure 7.5 An example of FOSI style

FOSIs in Production

The FOSI composition system applies format characteristics and translates the file to a printer description language such as HPCL or PostScript in a hands-off process. If changes in the text are required, they are made in the source file and the process is repeated. This means that changes can be incorporated into the source up to the last possible moment because composition is completely automated. Unlike unstructured electronic composition systems, there is no last-minute, final tweaking of the composed document.

FOSI publishing changes the type of expertise required to produce a printed page. SGML programming takes the place of an output filter or transformation or conversion, followed by design and composition.

Because the composition occurs in the structured environment, the composition system (the FOSI) must also consider that any change affects the data design at the other stages and, conversely, any change at the other stages of publishing—input or management—has a potential impact on composition. Hence the emphasis at FOSI sites on clear procedures for the maintenance of the DTD and output specification instance.

Like any SGML document, or for that matter any program, the flexibility and utility of the FOSI is contingent on the particular application. A thorough knowledge of the production environment and of the associated DTD is critical to the success of the whole. For a section of a document or a chapter of a book to be processed and printed, that section must be defined as a valid "document" in the document type declaration of the DTD. Otherwise, the entire document would have to be processed to print one section.

Since the FOSI was created to cover specific technical publications, its flexibility is limited. In the same article on FOSI capabilities, Grosso states that the FOSI cannot specify:

- Semantics of interactive electronic access and navigation;

- Semantics for database load/unload processes;

- Composition of right-to-left or vertical text;

- Presentation of complex mathematics;

- Newspaper or magazine-quality page layout;

- Format for specific tag instances.

To FOSI or Not to FOSI?

The advantage of a FOSI is that it retains the application, vendor, and platform independence of SGML all the way to the final output. The same set of format rules, defined once, can be applied consistently to an entire class of documents, and multiple sets of format rules can be applied to a single document. In practice, most implementers have not chosen to go this route, finding conversion to application-specific composition systems to have largely the same function and to be easier to work with except in applications where appearance is tightly controlled, such as the military and certain corporate environments.

The divorce of content from output has meant that products are one-time, finite, deliverable goods with limited shelf life, so that the ability to make a final product look exactly the same regardless of platform has relatively little market value. The early assumption—that platform independence had to extend to the final product—could be regarded as a carryover from the time when the final product was the essential, archival master. Once this archival function is transferred to the information, independent of format, keeping a tight reign on appearance and ensuring that it stays identical across varying conditions and output devices becomes much less important.

The failure of FOSIs to be widely adopted means that there are limited tools for creating them, no method to verify their effectiveness short of trial and error, and relatively little expertise available in their application. Of the arguments in favor of FOSI-based publishing, all but one—portability to standards-based publishing systems—apply equally well to nonstandard, local, proprietary style sheets and transformations. And, ironically, while FOSIs are also vendor-independent, the limited number of products offered creates a de facto dependence.

Users want variation, diversity, and competitive excellence that cannot easily be translated into interchangeable markup. They want to use the output product with the most unique bells and whistles. Output products, not archives, are the deliverables, so why worry that, at that stage, data will no longer translate into data for someone else's output application? The source will translate, so why worry about the end product?

In terms of what you get for your investment, keeping the data in an application-neutral markup for an additional step does not buy as much flexibility relative to the investment as does an application-neutral format for source data. The fundamental question is this: Is the look of a product tied intrinsically to the information or does the look of a product belong with the application used to create it?

> *Most users have concluded that it is the information, not the appearance of the information in any one product, that must be kept application-independent.*

Most users have concluded that it is the *information*, not the appearance of the information in any one product, that must be kept application-independent. In other words, they have concluded that the value of application independence lies with the information, not with its appearance. As long as the source is transportable and unchanged by whatever products are derived from it, it matters little if the products are created on proprietary applications and are therefore not transportable after the format has been applied.

Most users of SGML have not adopted FOSI publishing, making the decision based on simplicity of system design and ease of production. But, the question of who controls the look of the product, the information producer or the information consumer, is likely to heat up as distribution of format-independent structured information increases. See the discussion *To All-of-the-Above* later in this chapter.

Outputting to the Screen

The discussion of preparation for output—where you need to disambiguate and where you want to automate—applies to the screen as well as the printed page. The difference is that the destination, instead of being a composition tool, is a browser.

Chapter 3 presented a brief characterization of the extensive browser features available for online publication of SGML-encoded data. The question remains: How do you integrate this information and make a selection? Fortunately, it is not always necessary to restrict yourself to just one delivery vehicle. It is possible to customize a browser for CD-ROM sales to the high end of a market and to take a derivative of the data and the access features and deliver it to the low end of the market via the World Wide Web, where the reader chooses the browser. The very basis of the Web is that it allows the same data to be delivered through multiple, competing viewers and platforms with a wide spread in display capabilities.

While SGML leaves you great freedom to choose multiple electronic delivery modes, you must still make choices. This discussion divides the criteria into three major areas of concern:

- Structure, scale, and acrobatics;
- Production model; and
- Cost, audience, and distribution requirements.

Structure, Scale, and Acrobatics

Many choices about search and retrieval and navigation characteristics can be reduced to a discussion of scale: On a small scale, tricks and acrobatics—the Acrobat viewer from Adobe or similar picture-based viewers—are fine. Acrobat and its like capitalize on the work done in preparing documents for print and use the same markup to display the document on the screen. What they get is an image that duplicates the printed image and the ability to display the WYSI-WYG image on another computer.

What these page-based viewers do not provide with WYSIWYG navigation is search and retrieval or the ability to find your way around that is suitable to any document longer than one or two pages. What might be appropriate for a short advertising brochure, where much effort is encapsulated in the design and layout, is not necessarily appropriate for a collection of specification sheets, where the ability to search and navigate is critical. Acrobat's page metaphor allows the user to scan a page as if looking at a newsprint-sized sheet through a display-screen-sized hole. This arrangement maintains the look of the page, but it can cut off columns at awkward points and throw together pieces of unrelated stories. It puts together pieces of information in an arrangement that works well in print but that does not maximize the small area and relatively poor resolution of any computer screen.

To scale up, browsers must operate on document structure, whether or not that structure is supplied by SGML. Hypertext links and dynamic tables of contents that transcend the page metaphor can be added to page-based browsers, but the value of coding added in a browser is then output-specific and is not reflected back in the source data.

Production Model

If you have eliminated from consideration the browsers that do not take advantage of document structure, that do not scale up, the next step is to look at the production model required by the browser and how it fits into your situation. How much effort you want to spend getting your data in to the browser depends in part on the life span of the data—will it be out of date tomorrow or is it a permanent archive? You might want to compromise some richness of display, navigation, and search and retrieval with data that is replaced on a regular basis, if it means a hands-off conversion to the browser format. Will the data be heavily annotated, with layers of links and connections that you will want to preserve through successive build cycles?

Other production considerations include whether the text can be edited and modified once in the browser, if those changes can be reexported as SGML, and if a style sheet can translate the viewer format to print.

Cost, Audience, and Distribution Requirements

Your choice of a browser should be based on what you know about:

- Size of audience

- Segmentation of audience—do they require different versions or views?

- Sales and price model

- How ease of use affects your market

- How search and retrieval and navigation affect ease of use for this market

- Special requirements, like multimedia or multibyte character-sets

- Platform required by this audience

Browser Selection Summary

We have grouped the qualities of a browser into three areas, according to the scale and structure of your data, your production requirements, and your audience. How do these qualities combine into real products and real presentation strategies?

Kent Summers, Director of Marketing at Electronic Book Technologies, did an Electronic Document Delivery survey of 15 corporate and commercial publishers using five different products. He presented the results at a Seybold Seminar in March, 1994. The types of publication ranged from entertainment to reference, from sales and marketing to record-keeping, and the results of the survey were as diverse as the subjects. The areas that showed the greatest distinction between the five products were:

- Cost of getting material into the browser;

- Richness of search and retrieval and navigation features;

- Cost of distribution;

- Platform availability; and

- Relationship to print.

On this last point, some users said they chose a browser because of its fidelity to a print image; others chose a browser because they were not held to the same format maintained in print.[4]

Fortunately, output to a browser is not an either-or decision. Electronic data is easily ported to multiple delivery platforms.

The basic trade-off is often ease of entry versus ease of use. You must balance your own equation, putting money for conversion and configuration and the basic cost of the browser on one side and, how often the material is updated, what should be recovered, and on the other side the distribution and usage requirements of the audience.

Bob Glushko, of Passage Systems, cautions that it is important to look at value as well as features. It is worth looking at those viewers not specifically designed for SGML, like SmarText from Lotus. Although these browsers accept page-based frozen data, if the delivery requirements are met, and they offer savings in production and distribution, there is no reason not to consider them. In other words, do not provide a Cadillac solution for someone who just needs to cross the street.

To make a good decision, it is necessary to understand the requirements of the market, as well as your own production requirements. See the case study on Columbia University Press in Chapter 4 for a summary of a successful market survey designed to identify just these market characteristics.

Fortunately, output to a browser is not an either-or decision. Electronic data is easily ported to multiple delivery platforms. Distributors routinely offer a variety of output and viewing formats. The best example of this is the variety of viewers available for the World Wide Web.

The open, standard data format of the Web means that HTML or SGML data is not attached to a browser—when a better browser or a better platform comes along, users will chose it with no loss of data integrity or portability. It should be

---

[4]Kent J. Summers, *Electronic Document Delivery Customer Survey*, presented at Seybold Seminars, March, 22, 1994.

stated, however, that browsers that require proprietary extensions run the risk of becoming just another browser using a proprietary formatting language. Conversely, creating Web data to be displayed in one and only one Web browser runs the risk of obsolescence when the next browser or browser upgrade comes along with a different data type. If all Web data were to include proprietary extensions, the Web would no longer be an open, nonproprietary system. Instead, the data format would be owned and controlled by the toolmakers and information would no longer be freely interchangeable outside of a single vendor's tool set.

Getting on the Web

There are three basic strategies for getting SGML-encoded data onto the Web. Doubtless, more will be developed in the near future. Today, these strategies are 1) conversion; 2) extension; and 3) direct delivery.

The conversion strategy includes the obvious option of down-converting SGML data to HTML. Going from SGML to HTML is not only easier and more easily automated than other conversions, but it implies that information will be maintained in SGML. HTML itself is not suitable for most data archives because it cannot support a complex or long document type.

A variation on the conversion strategy is to convert SGML on the fly, on demand. This means that search-and-retrieval and query software can operate directly on SGML archives, but retrieved information is "dumbed-down" to HTML for delivery and presentation as it is needed.

The Web as an extension of a local SGML document is not, strictly speaking, putting SGML on the Web, but it combines the use of SGML resources with the worldwide, instant delivery of the Internet.

The third strategy is to make full SGML resources available directly along with SGML-capable Web browsers. Today, Panorama from SoftQuad is the only such browser, but there is no reason to suppose that it will remain so. NCSA and SoftQuad maintain[5] a list of public Internet SGML archives that can be viewed online with Panorama.

To All-of-the-Above

The title of this section refers to the various methods of linking text marked up with SGML to output specifications that fully describe the appearance of the material in more than one form

While originated for printed technical manuals, FOSIs can be written for screen display with the same caveats as for print. DSSSL, which stands for Document Style, Semantic, and Specification Language (and rhymes with "whis-

---

[5]There is a link to this list on your disk, in *Resource Guide A*.

tle"), was approved in February 1994. It is complementary to SGML and generalizes the work of an OS and a FOSI—that is, it specifies how to take information marked up for structure and content and render it in a variety of media. There are, as yet, no applications for DSSSL and little sense of if and how it will be implemented.

So far, the only instance where format portability has been wildly successful has been the HTML of the WWW, where the markup is so limited, mixing structure with format, that the viewers can interpret it unambiguously. Other format specification methods standardize output to some degree using non-SGML style sheets and standard conversion template. These include style sheets that would travel along with the document and give the end user an easy set of controls over appearance.

The proliferation of cross-platform electronic delivery, coupled with the release of products that use DSSSL or advent of another standard for style and appearance, may turn the tide the other way. One of the more interesting discussions about the Web is who should control the appearance of the document, the writer/publisher or the reader? Should a reader be able to render a document in any way—to look like *The New York Times* or like *Wired*—or should the author be able to lock the document to a predetermined style?

An interesting experiment in SGML style-sheet-based publishing was reported by François Chahuneau of Advanced Information Systems, S.A. in France, which built a style sheet for the DynaText SGML browser using its interactive style sheet editor, InStEd. The style sheet resolved many of the same issues for on-screen use that need to be resolved for print, such as generated text and inherited format. Then, instead of using the text in DynaText, they exported it in the MIF format to FrameMaker. They refined the style sheet in FrameMaker, saving their work to a style template. When new text is exported from the same DynaText style sheet, it can be brought into the enhanced template without further formatting.

This experiment, called "Gateway," is the prototype for a product that will use the database and SGML-aware features of the DynaText style editor to support import of files directly into FrameMaker, Interleaf and Microsoft Word.

The experiment used a 10-Mbyte legal text with 300,000 elements. Using SGML transformation and processing built on custom C programs and an SGML parser, Chahuneau reports that it took about one month of labor to bring the book into the Miles 33 format. He estimates that the Gateway process, going to the .MIF format, will produce equivalent results in one week.

This is, of course, just an experiment, but the author points out that the process—using an SGML-aware tool to resolve a document instance for browsing and to transform the same document instance into a flat file ready for mapping directly into a composition system—while not compliant with DSSSL, uses the same processing model as we can expect from products that take advantage of the new standard.

Should a reader be able to render a document in any way—to look like The New York Times or like Wired—or should the author be able to lock the document to a predetermined style?

PUTTING IT ALL TOGETHER

Mary Laplante, Executive Director of the vendor consortium SGML Open, likes to explain the difficulty some companies have experienced when putting together an SGML production system by quoting this observation, which she attributes to Fred Dalrymple, who worked on the Open Software Foundation SGML implementation:

> The Dalrymple Observation: Companies no longer expect to have on staff a person who integrates applications—they expect software to work off the shelf, and they do not expect to "tinker." Ten or fifteen years ago, the expectation that new electronic formats required specialized integration would have been commonplace. Today, many companies are surprised that this is so and are unprepared for it.

The Technical Agenda of SGML Open provides a forum for vendors to "collaborate in establishing pragmatic technical guidelines which assure interoperability, without limiting the breadth of SGML." The first interoperability technical resolution adopted by the consortium, in September of 1994, described a "standard convention for specifying the location of file-based objects external to a document—other text, graphics, and media—in a way that can be supported by any conforming application." In practice, this means that the way an entity identifier is mapped to a system-specific file name is consistent from application to application.

Other interoperability items on the SGML Open Technical Agenda include:

- A definition of interoperability
- Documentation guidelines for markup definitions
- Guidelines for RFP writers
- Research into areas such as table interoperability

The cooperation among vendors and the trend toward more integration means that, the Dalrymple Observation aside, more is available off-the-shelf than ever before. Integration is a valuable commodity, whether you do it with your own in-house tinkerers or by purchasing a higher level of integration in the products that you select.

And even if you do plan to grow-your-own integration, it is not a bad idea to start with a good core dump from someone who has been through it before. The consultation might be the equivalent of a chat with the investment counselor at the local bank, or it might be like hiring a full-time analyst. The field of SGML-based technology is expanding and changing rapidly. Unless you can cost-justify an in-house expert who goes to the conferences, reads the published papers, follows comp.text.sgml and the other lists devoted to structured information, you will need to pay, on an occasional basis, someone who does.

Putting together the pieces of an SGML-based production system into a coherent and cost-effective whole is a process that differs at each site, but there are some considerations and generalizations that apply across the board.

How the *process* fits with the tools and the data design must be considered at every juncture. Will your editorial staff work online? Will your reviewers see hard copy or not? Will they see complete works or fragments? Who will do the transformation and conversion work? These are the process questions that should drive your system design.

Exactly what SGML brings to the picture that was not there before depends on your implementation and your objectives. These can include:

- Increased use of on-screen review and revision, leading to greater need for procedures and tools for job tracking;

- Increased use of partial documents, leading to greater need for formal document management; and

- Increased use of existing and new feedback loops from composed/viewable documents through previous production stages.

How this process feels to workers and managers is discussed in Chapter 9.

It's the Data...

Document architecture and document analysis determine what you can and cannot do with your information throughout the production process, and they determine what your customers can and cannot do with it once it is in their hands. A simple illustration of this point is the coding of italic words and phrases. Say, for example, that examination of a document reveals these uses of italics:

- Emphasis
- Publication names
- Latin or other foreign language
- No-reason italics—those that don't fit any of the above

If the document analysis team decides to make coding or data conversion simple by using a generic emphasis tag for everything italic, the decision may speed initial production, but at what price? If the team uses markup to distinguish these items, the decision increases the ability to query and rearrange the data. For example, making it possible to do a simple query like "Show me all references to 'SGML' in a publication title" creates a powerful tool for writers, production, editors, and quality control.

The case study of Columbia University Press is a real-world demonstration of the determining power of the underlying data design. This example shows both the influence on the production process—initially, in this case, a disruptive influence—and the influence on the products produced—in this case, a creative and positive influence. Lack of involvement by document experts meant that early production runs had difficulty meeting the fine distinctions of format called for by the information, but fundamentally sound coding made it possible to analyze the data in ways that led directly to new, spin-off products.

The way the data design handles partial documents is another example of how data design and production systems must be synchronized. One of the issues here is the extraction for processing of document fragments that are part of a compliant DTD but not compliant on their own—in other words, how do you work on part of a document? The Parlance relational database from Xyvision resolves this issue by wrapping a set of tags around the fragment while it is checked out for editing and stripping the tags away when it is redeposited for storage.

Document architecture determines what data management applications can do to reuse information across media and in different contexts. Eliot Kimber, who wrote IBMIDDoc at IBM with Wayne Wohler before going to Passage Systems, explains two mechanisms for reuse built into the design of that DTD—first, a content model that differentiates between introduction, body, and summary; and second, "retrieval alternatives" that link different versions of the same element. To create media-specific outputs, you select from a type of content or a retrieval alternative.

The lesson should be clear and simple: The capabilities of your production environment and the long-term value of your information assets depend directly on the quality and thoroughness of your data design.

Mapping the Payback

Where and how your investment will pay you back is a complicated question, but there are two generalizations that relate SGML investment and payback.

First, as costs are moved up front in the production process, payback is separated from investment. Too often, SGML is "sold" by demonstrating a payoff without detailing the up-front work that makes it possible. If you look at the map of the SGML universe, the payback increases in the middle sections, in document and data management, and gets more intense as you move to the right, to the output side (Figure 7.6). Most investment in production costs is in the first half of the cycle, in pushing that data uphill into the higher-energy state, in doing careful, up-front data analysis, and in doing precise data management.

The production benefits are spread across the cycle. Many sites, like Ericsson, experience increased efficiency in writing with SGML but this is contingent on the type of information, the baseline against which productivity is measured, and on increased demands on writers that make relative productivity hard to measure. Other sites, like Standard & Poor's and Butterworth, increase efficiency across the board. And yet others, like Adams & Hamilton, see more efficiency at the output stage only. The payback for production depends too much on prior conditions and on the type of system created to generalize further.

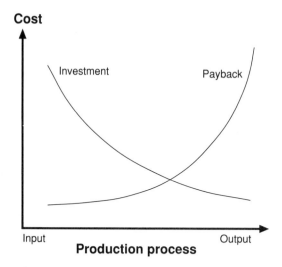

Cost

Investment

Payback

Input

Output

Production process

Figure *7.6 Investment and payback*

The major benefits of SGML, in most cases, derive from the ability to manage information for reuse, either in different versions of the same product or in new products. The long-range payback from conversion insurance, which is hard to pin down on a balance sheet but is nonetheless real, is that you raise your data up once and only once and continue to benefit from that investment.

Second, capturing information where it resides, when it is most easily available, is optimal. For example, if you want content markup, get it at the source—the author of the content. If you need design input, capture it at the output stage, but give typesetters and compositors the source information that they need to create a design. This generalization has what I call "Kate's Corollary" after Kate Hamilton: It costs more to inject missing information the further along you go in the process. If you do not capture the author's intent, unambiguously, in a form that can translate throughout the process—that the funny character with the circle over it is a Sanskrit *a*—then the longer it takes to inject this knowledge into the file, the more will be added to the bottom line.

Injecting information into the product earlier in the cycle requires investing in structured editing and writing tools that allow authors to identify their intent without ambiguity and investing in the planning, training and document analysis that will make that a reality.

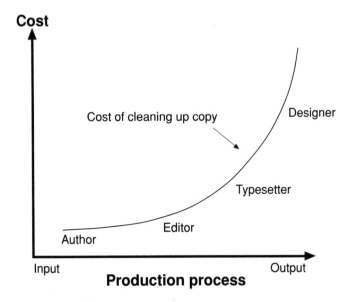

Figure 7.7 *The cost of cleaning up copy*

Other Considerations

As with data design, most of the discussion has been about text—generating it, tracking it and formatting it for some output. System design, like data design, must also incorporate nontext elements.

Where Are the Pictures?

So, where do the pictures come in? Graphics handling is a concern at each stage of production, but too often pictures never really get their due until the production process as a whole is considered.

Graphics have their own granularity—generally, one per file is acceptable. Each graphic has a unique identifier on that file system and a known format, so that many of the issues that occupy our concern for text are settled by default for graphics. The easy answers for graphics are:

- Input—By external entity reference within the SGML text file

- Management—On the operating system file directory system

- Output—Position as you would any graphic in an electronic publishing system

In practice, graphics handling involves several more complex procedures. These are apparent only when you examine the production *procedures,* as opposed to the production technology, and when you consider production on a large scale. Three additional issues to consider are:

- Preview of graphics for writers, editors, and reviewers
- Complex graphics management requirements
- Format compatibility through the production process

The first issue in system design for graphics is preview during the writing process. Indicating the correct external entity may be sufficient for the computer to understand what is intended, but what about the author, the reviewer, and the editor? When writers need to preview graphics or refer to graphics during the writing process, the production environment must provide a viewer for graphics, either the same application that composes the text or a second application that can be invoked separately.

Depending on your exact requirements, you may or may not need more than invocation of a separate graphics viewer. Writers may also require the capability to edit, annotate, print draft, and designate final output position for graphics that affect their composition. While these are not baseline requirements for an SGML editor, they can be fundamental requirements for an integrated, SGML-based publishing environment.

There are several workflow issues that come into play when designing a system to handle graphics. While small publications with low potential for reuse and few graphics may not require special handling, large complex systems almost certainly will.

Naming, locating, and linking graphics files constitute a process that starts simply and grows exponentially with complexity and revisions. Names must be unique within a given namespace. Tracking locations and links that connect graphics must adhere to the same design criteria as any other SGML link scheme. The scheme must allow for revision, maintenance, and change within any piece of the whole.

Some implementations benefit from using several versions of the same picture, each in a different format. Often, a low-resolution bit-map image is used for identification and position, a high-resolution bit map for print, and a vector image for online display. These requirements are not directly related to SGML, but they are concurrent with document and data management and with large-scale, complex electronic publishing.

The file system may or may not be an adequate manager for the graphics if, in conjunction with SGML, you adopt heavy reuse of graphic as well as textual information. If the file system is your storage and retrieval system and you are working with large numbers of large files, file identification can be a time-consuming task. Image management systems provide thumbnail images that can be viewed quickly at low resolution to verify the identification of graphic elements. There is nothing inherent in SGML-based production that requires more image management than a well-defined file-handling system but, if you raise the ante on reuse and recombination of text elements and your products are image-intensive, then you have also raised the requirements for your image-handling technology.

A final consideration in terms of graphics in SGML-based publishing is that when you separate the input, management, and output functions of your information-processing system in your move to SGML, it is only the text format that is system-, application-, and operating- system-independent. You must ensure that the graphics format at input and the format required by the preview viewer you use in input, the storage system you use during management, and the composition and output system are all the same or compatible or translatable.

The separation of function in terms of graphics can be exploited if considered as an integral feature of the production process.

And Tables?

The data design choices for tables determine the production system and what it can do. Each type of markup has advantages and deficiencies that were discussed in Chapter 6. It is relatively easy to create an input and output model for presentational markup, but it inhibits revision and retrieval. Problems in revision and retrieval are more stubborn because they point to the inherent anomaly of using SGML for a presentation-based scheme. As with any other data, including math and graphics, what is not encoded in SGML cannot be processed with SGML-based tools. Standard processing techniques, such as Boolean searches, are not possible on presentational tables because the data points are defined only by their relative position. If you change position, you change meaning.

The table content model enables revision and retrieval by standard means but can require large numbers of models and model names for complex tables. The content model makes it more difficult to build input and output applications that meet expectations for format.

An example of how people compromise using existing tools and data design methods is presented in the Butterworth case study. The study reports how the staff use the vendor's WYSIWYG table editor because it is convenient for input. To produce the complex print layout required for their books, they insert compositor-specific processing codes because there is no direct translation or transformation between the WYSIWYG input scheme and the parameters required for effective layout of the pages.

SGML as an Occasional Requirement

Most SGML implementations today are consonant with large-scale information-handling requirements. This is partly because the reasons for adopting SGML are more pronounced, the more data you are handling. This is partly because the entry cost is high and you need to be moving large quantities of data before it pays off. But there are many people who have occasional or small-scale requirements to supply or to handle SGML data. How does the scale of production affect the design of a smaller system?

Data design is the issue that is most difficult to scale down. If you are producing on contract to an outside client, you will produce to their design, so that costs are confined to learning the design, not creating it. For internal use, economically justifiable small projects would require one of the following: that the expertise exists to create a DTD using in-house resources; a simple DTD exists already; a format-based DTD is used as an initial step toward structured information with the understanding that a series of transformations will bring the information up to a higher level at a later date; or the entire project is considered a training expense, and some of the cost of data design is allocated to training.

Given an existing data design, producing SGML as an occasional requirement could require no more than an input system and enough knowledge to understand the structural requirements of the supplied DTD. In such an instance, or where you expect to produce to a series of such requirements, analysis tools and the skills to use them have a high premium.

If formatted hard copy is also part of the requirement, then porting the data to a composition system is also required. The size of the project should determine the degree of automation involved. If the scale is small, there is less incentive to automate the conversion. If the scale of the project puts it within the range where conversion automation makes sense, then the same options apply as for any other conversion.

The alternative, to create the deliverable hard copy in a WYSIWYG editor, then port it to SGML, appears simpler initially, but ultimately it encounters all the problems of any up-conversion. There is no way to know how the initial hard copy will convert to a structured editor until it is converted and, because you are adding structure and complexity and a new kind of information to the document as you convert it, it is highly unlikely that the content and structure of the original hard copy can remain unchanged. The net result of such a process remains that the SGML file must be created before the hard copy can be finalized—in which case, you are better off creating it first and then deriving the hard copy from a known, good source.

In other words, even for small production environments and occasional requirements, it does not pay to ignore the logic of SGML. SGML is and remains a data description format, not an output format. Trying to avoid the issue by working in a nonstructured environment and going to the higher structure on output is apt to cause more problems than it solves. The preferred solution, as for large-scale solutions, is to create the structured data, and then the output form.

8

Getting There
Labor, Data, and Technology in Transition

This chapter is about getting from here to there.

People tend to think of the transition to SGML as being a mechanical process, like replacing a monitor or a mouse—just install the equipment and away you go. But the tools play a relatively minor part in the transition. The major concerns are training, data conversion and, of course, integration and timing of the whole. Creating a gradual, nondisruptive transition is a major factor in keeping costs down, products flowing out the door, and making SGML a feasible technology. This chapter talks about each of the components of a smooth transition and about creating a transition plan to ensure that all the pieces don't break while you're putting them together. This chapter looks at:

- Planning—The big picture
- Labor—Training, hiring, and rearranging
- Data—Converting legacy data
- Pilot projects and transition plans—Ways to phase in new tools and processes

THE TRANSITION PLAN

The phrase "long-range plan for SGML implementation" is redundant—there is no short-term version. Just as needs assessment and system design must encompass a large vision of corporate or group information-handling requirements, so the transition plan and implementation require a wide view of enterprise goals and priorities and schedules.

Prerequisites for the transition plan are a needs assessment and buy-in, if not across the organization, then at least in the implementing group. Part of the purpose of the transition plan itself is to ensure that initial buy-in spreads throughout an organization. Assuming that these prerequisites have been accomplished, the elements required in a transition plan are individual plans and schedules for:

- System and data design
- Workforce training and hiring
- Data conversion design and implementation
- Equipment introduction and integration
- Pilot project design, implementation, and assessment

While transitional plans are, by their nature, site-specific, this generic summary traces the outlines that must be addressed in every plan. In addition, it sketches a pattern that is likely to form in any specific plan. This pattern, in its most generic form, looks like Figure 8.1. While, for clarity of concept and presentation, the elements in Figure 8.1 lay out cleanly and neatly, in practice, the pattern is not so neat and clean. While some of the processes have arrows showing that they extend in time, in practice all of these processes extend over time. In practice, there is feedback and interaction between system design and data design, between pilot projects, conversion planning, and equipment installation, between equipment installation and training.

	EARLY PHASE	*MIDDLE PHASE*	*LATE PHASE*
Labor	Concept training	Technical training	Operational training
Data	Design (doc analysis)	Pilot project	← Conversion →
		Conversion planning	
Equipment	System design	Initial install ←	→ Final install

Figure 8.1 The pattern of the transitional plan

Note that this sketch of a transitional plan does not address the types of tools and processes being introduced. There is a surprising, startling even, diversity of approach in terms of the specific *content* of the initial system being brought in. For example, one group chooses to phase in product line by product line, across the workforce. Another group attacks all product lines but brings new technology and processes to one division at a time. Yet other groups address only one aspect of SGML-based production—this aspect can be data input, data management, or data output.

Data and system design were discussed in the two previous chapters. The balance of this chapter looks at the other elements of the transition plan.

LABOR

Preparing your workforce for a transition to SGML consists of two components: raising the skill level and reevaluating and reshaping your workflow processes.

Training and Hiring

If you are going to produce and maintain higher-energy data, you need "higher-energy" labor to do so. The new skills are:

- Writing and editing structured documents
- Input template creation and maintenance
- Conversion filter creation and maintenance
- Transformer creation and maintenance
- Document analysis—how to facilitate and document
- DTD (FOSI) coding and maintenance
- Document and data management
- Page composition from structured documents
- Porting to electronic presentation devices
- QA/QC of new products and new procedures
- Operational skills related to all new software

In addition to these new skills, your current skill set for management must expand to cover the new requirements and the new environment. This means acquiring new skills through hiring new staff and through training current staff.

There is no general rule that states which skills can be brought in by training and which require hiring. Much depends on the background and training of current staff and on the current production design.

Interestingly—some might say perversely—the intense focus on WYSIWYG, on working directly with the final page image, over the past five years may prove to have been counterproductive for writers who are now asked to back away from design issues and return to a concentration on document structure. This is the contention of Peter Jerrum, who managed the technical writers at Novell during the early stages of SGML adoption. Jerrum feels that WYSIWYG is responsible for a natural selection against those with a predisposition for working with structure. Instead of working with outlines and abstract relationships, the state-of-the-art writing software in the WYSIWYG years gave an advantage to those who organized their work in visual patterns instead of in rule-based structures.

Whether or not these old skills have been selected out of the technical writing workplace, the new environment does call on new and different capabilities. There is no evidence that these new capabilities exceed those of any qualified writer working in a well-designed environment and given proper tools.[1]

---

[1] Chapter 9 examines the writer's perspective in detail.

Managers who have gone through this process agree that some employees will make the transition more easily than others and that it is difficult to know, in every case, who will pick up the new technology and run with it. All agree that an understanding of structure and basic document architecture is essential for everyone involved with the production process.

Who will need training and what kind of training and how much? There are three basic types of training: conceptual, operational, and technical.

Conceptual Training

Everyone will need some level of conceptual training. Conceptual preparation need not be abstract or removed from the nitty-gritty of everyday production, but conceptual training is distinct from job- or skill-specific training. Conceptual training gives the Big Picture of what this new stuff is and why the company is bringing it in. Small pieces of the picture, like, "You can no longer change a template without formal review and sign-off" make much more sense when trainees see for themselves where the template fits into the large scheme of things and how minor changes to a template might have major ramifications for online books and other products.

Even for those whose contact with structured information will not include designing data structures, a smooth transition demands that they understand the basic concepts behind structured information. All levels of an organization do have the potential to contribute to design models. Whatever manipulation was done on a text in an unstructured environment represents some knowledge of the text and some expertise that should be represented in the final data model. This is what draws together the broad-based teams required for document analysis. So, in addition to functional, "this is now your job, do it this way," kind of training, be prepared to provide some conceptual training to all levels of your staff. It need not be long and involved and can be integrated with the training in specific functions and tools, but it needs to be done.

Management will have (should have) acquired a sufficient level of conceptual training during the assessment and design phases. Any part or level of management that somehow avoided this, even if not directly involved in operations, should be up to speed on the basic concepts before the system goes into production. One of the most frequently mentioned characteristics of a successful implementation is buy-in at the top levels. Management will not buy in if it does not understand what it is buying. Understanding maintains buy-in even as real-world complications force changes in well-laid plans.

What constitutes a sufficient level of conceptual understanding? I would like to think that this book would be a good start. But a solid understanding of structured document concepts usually requires an iterative look at theory and applications and back to theory and then back again to applications. Very few people

One of the most frequently mentioned characteristics of a successful implementation is buy-in at the top levels. Management will not buy in if it does not understand what it is buying.

grasp the full implications of structuring written communication in this way on the first go-round. Providing written material and a stand-up training session, with chances for questions and answers tailored for the specific type of operation, is ideal. (See *Resource Guide A* for a list of training courses.)

Operational Training

There is no single prescription for training someone to use a piece of software effectively—obviously, how much and what kind of training is required depends on the tools being brought in and the background of those who will be using them. In this area, you can get specific guidance from the vendors of these tools. Without exception, SGML vendors offer training on their products and usually negotiate this with the equipment contract.

If not provided by the vendor, invest in training an internal trainer and budget the time for that person to carry through the training mission. The tools that demand training are those that are new to your structured information environment, all of them. That is, don't look on your new editor as the only tool that requires training if you have also installed a new data management system, are outputting text to three simultaneous formats, and are using new conversion software to do so.

Beyond getting the proper job- and skill-specific training, it is important that this training be applied on top of a conceptual base, that it be provided at the right time, and that it be provided with training on the new workflow procedures that are discussed in the following section.

Technical Training

Technical SGML training consists of learning the SGML syntax delineated in ISO 8879, learning how to design and interpret documents and document type definitions coded with SGML, and learning the tools and techniques used in various stages of SGML-based production. These tools and techniques include converting, parsing, and transforming coded documents using the DTD utilities described in Chapter 3.

People coming from publishing as well as from software engineering can be successful SGML techies. In fact, there are several former technical writers and editors among the most respected cadre of SGML technical experts.

The most difficult type of training to acquire today is training on structured document design and management. What is rare is not the knowledge of how to do this, but the knowledge of general principles of how to do this—principles that can be transferred and applied to the next context as well as to your own. What you cannot be taught in a set curriculum, you will acquire, however, over time and will slowly build in-house, as it pertains to your own data set. Or you can hire the expertise from outside to come and look at your data with your internal document experts. You will go through the same cycle, but it will be shorter and require fewer, less drastic revision cycles.

Training Sequence

Providing the right training, in the right amounts and to the right people, is a critical part of your transition. Timing that training so that it has the maximum impact is important as well. Offering detailed training too soon, before the new process is real or before the new concepts are understood, is not as effective as offering the same instruction closer to going into production. The ideal sequence for preparing a work group is:

- Introduce new concepts;
- Provide initial technical training;
- Let operators try the new techniques in a non-mission-critical setting;
- Provide the bulk of the detailed, job-specific training when the opportunity to put the new knowledge into use is immediately available.

This sequence is not unique to SGML training—it is a good practice for training on any new technology.

For the most part, available SGML-related courses offer conceptual and technical training. Operational training on tools is the province of individual software vendors and system integrators. Operational training on new procedures and processes must be provided in-house.

A shortage of people for hire with SGML skills has been a hallmark of this technology since the late 1980s. Employment agencies are becoming more knowledgeable about the field as demand increases. In addition to traditional recruiting venues, many positions are listed on the Internet discussion forum, comp.text.sgml (see *Resource Guide A* for more information).

Workflow

Workflow transition may require putting in place new procedures for:

- Writing, editing, and production
- Transfer of manuscripts, drafts, and reviews between work groups
- Maintaining and upgrading the basic data design

The process of writing will change, editing will change, design and composition will change. What these will look like is described in the next chapter. Do not assume that providing training and tools will suffice—workers must also have the procedures in hand to coordinate the new efforts. The transition period must account for preview, review, and revision processes that encompass all aspects of the new information products.

A writer preparing a document with an appearance-based editor has the means at hand to check his or her work—the way it prints is the way it will appear to readers. An editor or QC supervisor has the means at hand to check the work of that writer in the form of the printed draft and well-established review procedures.

In contrast, a writer preparing a document with an SGML-based tool may be preparing that document to print in any number of versions, to go online through multiple, diverse viewers, and to be archived where it will be searched with engines of varying capabilities. This writer has some tools at hand to aid in this process—a parser will check SGML syntax, as a minimum. Integrated tool sets may provide some feedback on the impact of conversion to different formats. Changes in *process* as well as changes in technology must provide the balance of the previewing and checking required.

Editorial and QC procedures can change drastically in the transition to SGML. When a file is no longer the definitive container for a document, you must ensure that editorial and QC procedures adapt to the change. For example, if your documents are now assembled from a document database instead of from static files, you must develop new procedures to check them for accuracy and completeness. Today, there are no tools designed for the intermediate processes. There is no specific editorial (as opposed to writing) interface. Yet editors must access the work and access it in such a way that the ultimate configuration and cohesion can be checked and corrected.

Any change in the way a document is put together or processed or understood or constructed affects it throughout its life—that is the strength of the system, that is the intelligence that you want to put in once and use many times. By the same token, if you expect structures to hold up to many uses in many parts of the production process, you must expect to coordinate any change to these structures.

The formal engineering change request/engineering change order (ECR/ECO) process, familiar to those who have worked in a commercial manufacturing environment, is well suited to the document production environment when the document is an SGML document. When you consider processes and procedures for creating and maintaining style sheets, conversion templates, DTDs, and databases, keep in mind that the structured document that goes online becomes software.

See the case study of Ericsson in Chapter 4 for an example of the type of new processes you may need to establish during the transition period.

LEGACY DATA CONVERSION

Data conversion has always been a major expense, if not *the* major expense, in new technology adoption. In fact, this is one of the primary reasons that companies with foresight are investing in SGML in the first place—not because it costs so little to get your data *into* it, but because it costs so little to get your data *out* of it.

Conversion Cost Factors

If the original exists in electronic form with a visual markup scheme or template and that visual scheme makes clear to the reader all the elements of the text structure that the reader needs, what else must be supplied for a conversion to an explicitly structural form of markup? The answer is: a great deal. If you understand why legacy data conversion is expensive and difficult, you understand much about SGML.

If you understand why legacy data conversion is expensive and difficult, you understand much about SGML.

The conversion utilities that come with most high-end word processors translate smoothly between high-end word processors because they are converting *like* quantities: The information marked up in one system is, for the most part, equivalent to the information marked up in any other. This is not the case for high-end composition systems, and it is not the case for SGML.

The information required for SGML markup is *different information* than that required for other markup schemes—it is more explicit, more complete, and more consistent. While some of this missing information can be inferred from the source, much of it cannot be inferred. The complexity that prevents simple, unambiguous, and cheap conversion can be divided into four classes:[2]

- Complex and ambiguous mapping
- Incomplete and inconsistent sources
- Content tagging
- "Gotchas"—tables, cross-references, and generated text

Underlying each of these types of complexity is the fact that the SGML markup simply contains more information than other forms of markup. As Mark Gross (1993) puts it, "SGML requires not only explicit structure, but also consistent structure... Writers don't plan for their materials to be taken apart at a later time for use in a database, but that is what you are doing when you convert them to SGML."

Complex and Ambiguous Mapping

While many features of the source document map unambiguously to features of the target document, it is those that do not that determine the expense and difficulty of a conversion. A simple example of a complex and ambiguous mapping is use of italics in the source that maps to emphasis, foreign language, cross-reference, technical term, and so on in the target.

---

[2]I owe much of the information in this discussion to various presentations by Mark Gross, of Data Conversion Laboratories, his article in *Technical Communication* (1993), and the unpublished data conversion handbook prepared by DCL for its customers.

Incomplete and Inconsistent Sources

Any source which is not an authoritative source may be incomplete. For example, typesetting tapes used to create a print edition may have been patched with shorter files that were never incorporated into the main tape. The same can be true of any source that is not itself the final product.

Consistency, as designed into the DTD, may or may not have been present in earlier documents. For example, a DTD can mandate a level-two head before every level-three head, but not all previous documents may have done this consistently. If this is the case, and it almost always is the case, then the legacy documents need to be reworked to conform to the new, more consistent design specification. Until the source is partially converted and you get your first error reports, you may not know how many and where these anomalies occur, since this level of consistency has not been required.

Hand-massaging of page composition is a constant, not an exception, in electronic word processing and desktop and electronic publishing. Even the least elegant layout requires some tweaking and manipulation of styles to prevent awkward page breaks, tables that do not fit where they should and columns that do not line up.

In addition to adding stricter standards for consistency, converting to SGML reveals all the little "cheats" done to get a document out the door. There are many ways to achieve a single visual effect. If no one is checking the source code, then what appears as a heading may be the result a word-processor style or a unique combination of format characteristics. At the eleventh hour, a writer or production person will do whatever is required to the markup of an appearance-based document to get the look of the piece right on the page. This is as it should be—until you need to use a computerized algorithm to convert that document. At that point, every point-size change, every modification of a style sheet, every liberty taken with spacing and alignment becomes a new case for the converter to categorize and translate.

Content Tagging

Content tagging adds markup to elements that were not tagged in appearance-based formats. In appearance-based markup, the same string of characters can indicate a tool name or process (example: "weekly calendar" might be the name of a tool—the "weekly calendar tool"—or the name of a process or the product of that tool as in, "To create a weekly calendar..."). When the writer created the source document, the writer knew what was a tool name and what was a title, what was a part number and what was the index entry on p. 37. But word processors, even those using styles, do not capture this information.

Content-based tagging requires experts or expert-system inference. Even when using string and pattern matching to identify text in the source document, the source may refer to the same thing in more than one way, which is very hard for any system to catch. Some conversion programs identify likely objects by computer and prepare exception reports for humans experts to review.

Markup of nonprinting metadata also falls into the category of content tagging. Metadata such as who last checked a document or where a module is used has no bearing on the appearance of a document but is useful for data and workflow management.

"Gotchas"—Tables, Cross-References, and Generated Text

Tables are notoriously hard to mark up and hard to translate from one system of markup to another. Table troubles include:

- Columns that are spaced, not tabbed
- Information that spans columns
- Spanning that is not clearly delineated
- Hard returns for row and line endings
- Multipage tables: Is it one table read across or down or is it two tables?

For more on the general problems of coding tables in SGML, see Chapter 6.

Cross-references are one of the neat structural entities where you expect to have a smooth carryover from WYSIWYG to structured information. Without explicit tagging, however, the transition can be quite difficult. Data Conversion Laboratories (DCL) ranks typical references, in descending order, from the easiest to the hardest to convert:

- see figure 5.2
- see fig. 5.2
- see illustration above
- for more information, see 5.2.3
- for situations over 1.22, see sections 4.3 and 5.1
- see illustration 3 in the next section
- as indicated in the diagram

A thorough approach to conversion, according to DCL, requires tagging all possible references, ranking them in probability order, and providing sorted exception lists for manual review.

A final "gotcha" is generated text, such as page, chapter, and figure numbers, supplied by a composition system. Since the composition system created these on the fly, they may be difficult to recreate with certainty in the converted file.

An index reference page number generated by a composition system must be reverse-engineered by the conversion software. Unless the index reference string is explicitly delineated at start and end points, it may be difficult or impossible to infer the correct placement of an index reference anchor from a page number given in an index. The conversion must change page number references to location references and match ID/IDREFs, or indirect links between object and reference. If the conversion is from unpaginated typesetting tapes, the composed index that references page numbers may be useless for automated conversion.

Who Converts?

Controlling the cost of automation for a project of a given complexity is a question of balancing expertise against cost. In most cases, there is greater expertise to be had through contract services, the cost of that labor will be higher, and the time required to achieve the same degree of automation will be less. How, then, do you decide who does the conversion?

It is not unusual for a site to have considerable conversion expertise and experience in-house that can be applied to SGML legacy data conversion. The advantage of using in-house expertise is that these experts already know your data and, assuming that they are brought up to speed on SGML and are involved in the process of creating the target DTD, they know the target as well.

Using in-house expertise cuts down on the inevitable communication gaps that can spring up in an off-site conversion. Although they can tailor a process to fit your needs, in-house experts will lack, initially, the cumulative experience gained by others of taking data into a structured format. Even though your experts are experts in your data and have written filters and converters from Wang to T$_E$X to Quark and back, don't expect them to crack the legacy-to-SGML nut in one fell swoop. You cannot expect to produce a conversion path without significant investment in time and diversion of significant resources from other projects.

Service bureaus use available commercial software plus what they have nurtured and grown on their own. What they do not have is the knowledge of your data and what you want done with it. Communication, therefore, between conversion service bureau and client, is essential to a successful project. Choose a firm with which you are comfortable and one that paints a realistic picture of the conversion process, a process that works best when plotted with multiple iterations, tests, revisions, and reviews.

A mark of a solid conversion bureau is one that knows when to write clever conversion routines and when to send the data offshore to be rekeyed. Mark Gross, President of Data Conversion Laboratories, puts it this way: "Anything *can* be converted. The question is, at what price?" His job, the job of any conversion project supervisor, is to restrain the programmers from writing routines that apply to such a limited piece of the data that the effort will never have a payback.

Regardless of *who* does the conversion, the technique for doing it will most likely be a combination of the techniques described in Chapter 3, including the use of an intermediate conversion step between appearance-based and structural

Mark Gross, President of Data Conversion Laboratories, puts it this way: "Anything can be converted. The question is, at what price?"

markup. The rule of thumb is: If it gets the job done, use it. If you contract out, the contractor will use the most efficient method available, including rekeying, OCR, other-people's-off-the-shelf, C routines, Rainbow, batch files, word-processing macros, as well as their own software library. If you build or buy your own conversion software, you will most likely do the same.

The new conversion tools described in Chapter 3 may bring down the level of expertise and setup required for data conversion, but they are all too new to the marketplace to say with certainty what their impact will be.

Legacy Conversion Pricing

Each of these methods of conversion may prove to be cost-effective at different points in your transition and for different types of data.

Figure 8.2 shows the basic relationship between cost per page and number of pages converted for manual (brute force) data entry and for automated conversion: Point A is the crossover point where automated conversion becomes more cost-effective than manual data conversion. Three factors affect where point A lies for any given project. These factors are:

- Total number of pages converted
- Complexity of conversion effort
- Degree of automation applied

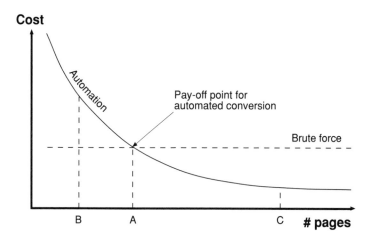

Figure 8.2 Basic data-conversion cost comparison

If the number of pages equals B, there is no payback for automation. If the number of pages equals C, automation is worthwhile. Clearly, automation pays off for large conversion projects and does not pay off for small conversion projects. Assuming that the amount and complexity of the data to be converted are fixed, the key variable—the one over which you have the greatest degree of control—is the amount of up-front effort that goes into the automation: How much is customized for your data and how skilled is the labor that performs this customization? Do you want 50 percent accuracy or 85 percent accuracy or 98 percent accuracy?

The alternatives can be considered as points on an automation continuum with the following range:

Most automated:	External contractor
	Off-the-shelf software
	In-house programming
	Scan hard copy, proof, and code
Least automated:	Rekey data by hand (brute force)

Figure 8.3 demonstrates the effect of the complexity of the data design and the degree of automation on the cost-effectiveness of the project. The greater the complexity in the data design, the more pages must be converted to justify the effort. The degree of automation has the same effect on the crossover point—the more automation applied, the more pages must be converted before the payoff point is reached.

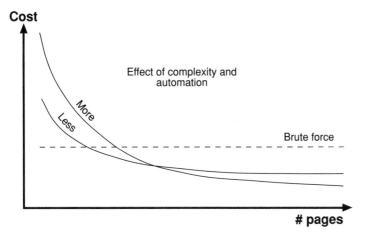

Figure 8.3 *Cost comparison with degree of automation and complexity*

To sum up, the point where automation begins to pay off depends on the number of total pages, complexity of data design, and sophistication of automation. More complex data will require greater volume to compensate for a high degree of automation; less complex data will require less volume before a high degree of automation pays off. Both the degree of automation and the complexity of the data design are variables.

We can learn more about the crossover points by looking at some actual numbers.

One way to analyze conversion costs is to compare the cost of up-front automation (programming plus purchase or licensing of code) with the cost of processing the job. The cost of manually rekeying data and adding SGML markup is about $5–10 per page, high for keyboarding unless you consider the complexity of the markup. The cost of rekeying 100 pages at this rate would be about $800. The cost of automated conversion, *per page*, might be lower, but the setup cost spread over so few pages raises the price to about $15 per page.

For example, the cost of converting a page might be $2.50; the cost of setup might be $4000. In this case, the project must do 1600 pages before the cost of setup is exceeded by the cost of work. If the project converts 100,000 pages, the cost of setup becomes less than 2 percent of the total cost of the job.

Data Conversion Laboratories and Avalanche each has a different estimate of the critical crossover points at which its services and software become more cost-effective than rekeying and at which its method becomes the most cost-effective possible (Tables 8.1, 8.2). Interestingly, each considers its own option to have the greatest start-up cost but the lowest costs for large amounts of data.

Table 8.1 Data conversion costs—service bureau[3]

PAGES TO CONVERT	COST PER PAGE ($)
Less than 1000	15 or more
1000–10,000	5–15
10,000–50,000	3–5
50,000–100,000	2–4
More than 100,000	0.75–3

Table 8.2 Data conversion costs—commercial software[4]

PAGES TO CONVERT	COST PER PAGE ($)[a]
Less than 1000	61 or more
1000–10,000	6.60–61
10,000–50,000	1.80–6.60
50,000–100,000	1.20–1.80
More than 100,000	less than 1.20

[a]*Assumptions for commercial software pricing are as follows: Cost of cleanup personnel is $796/week (includes benefits and overhead); cleanup rate of 1500 pages per week (an 85 % + rate in conversion application); average cost of fully configured application is $60,000.*

[3]Reproduced with permission from Data Conversion Laboratories.

[4]Provided by Avalance, makers of FastTag conversion software.

Keep in mind, while looking at these figures, that actual conversion costs are determined by the complexity of a task, the amount of effort spent programming a conversion and the expense of that effort. Estimates on actual jobs from these and from other sources may vary greatly.

The cost of scanning and proofing can be about half that of rekeying if the original is a good prospect for scanning—not everything is. Pages that mix portrait and landscape on a page, with narrow margins and ransom-note typography, are not good prospects for OCR. You can scan it, run OCR software on it, clean up the OCR, and run conversion filters and algorithms to recognize visual structural clues and insert appropriate tags. By the time you have finished, however, it would have cost half as much to rekey the material with an SGML or ASCII editor inserting markup as you go.

It is common to have OCR accuracy of 98 percent, but two errors every 100 characters is far below the accuracy of a professional typist. Spell checking will catch some errors, but not all. Starting from a paper document, in either case, whether scanned or rekeyed, the material must be proofed against the original.

There are some additional conversion pricing caveats that you should keep in mind:

- These figures are ballpark. The true cost of automation depends on the actual source, method, target format, structure, and content required. These figures do not consider the complexity of illustrations, poor source material, equations, and extensive tables.

- These sets of figures should be read and interpreted separately because each was derived differently and it is impossible to normalize the expectations and assumptions in terms of the degree of complexity involved.

- Data conversion can be significantly less expensive if the degree of automated conversion is less. In other words, if the expectation is that there will be a greater amount of manual cleanup, the total cost for smaller amounts of data is much less per page than indicated in these figures.

- Conversion as part of an ongoing production process has other cost factors, and this type of conversion is not being considered in this discussion.

- Data design is a variable that can be optimized for data conversion. This may or may not jibe with other requirements.

- Data can be converted to a simple DTD on the first step and upgraded in later transformations.

If these factors do not dictate your conversion path, there are three final considerations that may settle the question.

The first consideration is the relative experience or inexperience of in-house programmers, the cost of their time and the cost of not having their time to spend on other efforts where they may have greater expertise. If you have in-house or contract experts who know your data and your data design and these same experts have experience in writing conversion scripts, your costs can be significantly less.

The second key consideration is that conversion automation always reaches a point of diminishing returns where the effort to reach a programmatic solution is more expensive that a manual one. A highly expert conversion might accomplish 99 percent automation; if the last 2 percent incur half of the programming effort, then it might have been more cost-effective to settle for 97 percent automation. Knowing "when to say when" and when to clean up remaining problems manually is one of the benefits of extended conversion experience.

A final consideration is whether you are preparing to move into ongoing conversion as a production method for new data, as well as for legacy data. If so, the cost of acquiring conversion expertise should be spread across a production training and hiring budget as well as a legacy conversion budget. In this case, you have an additional incentive to acquire your own conversion code and in-house expertise, whether you develop code from scratch, build it on top of off-the-shelf software, or license custom software developed for you from a contract with a conversion house.

Legacy Conversion Procedures

Legacy conversion merits intensive planning. It is a major expense; in many cases legacy data conversion is the single greatest cost of moving to SGML-based production.

The basic process includes these steps:

- Analyze source data and media, and target data design.
- Define conversion strategy (degree of automation and who will do it).
- Do a pilot conversion, review, and repeat.

Expect to perform each of these in successive iterations as you refine your conversion procedure and understand and improve your technical capabilities.

Analyzing Source and Target

Source data analysis determines which data to convert and in what order, the complexity of that data and any special problems it presents, and which medium to use as the source when more than one form of the data is available.

If this is a large conversion effort, then, by necessity, the conversion will be phased over time. The selection of the first data is based on which is needed most urgently and which will be representative of what is to follow. An initial assessment should eliminate automated conversion for all print data that is not a good source for OCR. While, theoretically, anything can be scanned, recognized, and cleaned up, in practice, the cost of doing so for some material is greater than the cost of rekeying with new markup.

Once the data is identified, the analysis must identify the factors that will have an impact on the degree of automation that is feasible and cost-effective. This analysis looks at the conversion cost factors described above and categorizes the text according to the types of mapping, consistency, completeness, content tagging, and the presence of graphics, math, and tables.

The last part of the source analysis is an examination of available media, in cases where the source is available in more than one form. For example, data that was previously published in book form exists on the page, on typesetting tapes and, perhaps, in one or more word-processing files. Each source has its advantages and disadvantages from the perspective of conversion.

Print media must be scanned and recognized or rekeyed, then proofread just to capture the original character stream. The advantage of print is that it is the authoritative form. All changes, by definition, are contained in print. Typesetting tapes and word-processing files cannot be relied on for the complete character stream of the files they hold. Any one tape may or may not contain the final version of the job. A final print run may be composed of various generations of files and tapes, with small patches and updates coming in pieces over the final stages of production. Reassembling the canonical text in electronic form from typesetting tapes may not be feasible, even if the tapes and files are available.

DCL schematizes source material in an "ease of conversion entropy hierarchy," which fits roughly into our scheme of high-energy data: The higher the initial energy, the easier it is to convert it. Material that is handwritten, on microfilm, typed, or printed falls below ASCII text on the energy scale. Above ASCII are:

- Word processing, no styles
- Typesetting, no tags or macros
- Word processing with styles
- Typesetting with tags or macros
- SGML-like tagged text

Analysis of the target is an assessment of the target DTD in terms of the ease of conversion. What determines ease of conversion is the complexity of the structure as well as the amount of required content-based tagging.

The objective of a conversion strategy, at the highest level, is to segregate those portions of the source that have a low return on automation and to estimate the optimum degree of automation on the balance of the material.

How, precisely, to derive a strategy from an analysis of source and target is more an art than a science. Good management of the conversion process must comprehend that it is not always desirable to automate everything that can be automated and must put the brakes on those who would spend 20 hours programming to find and fix an anomaly that occurs twice in 10,000 pages.

The conversion strategy should also take account of the fact that it need not happen all at once. Information converted to a simple structured design can be transformed and enhanced at later stages. This conversion-then-transformation approach spreads costs over a greater period of time and can accommodate changes and refinements in the data design that occur after the initial conversion.

Another advantage of the conversion-then-transformation approach is that heterogeneous word-processing, appearance-based, markup goes into a single, open format. From there, a single converter can bring the documents up to SGML. This reduces the conversion overhead in heterogeneous data environments.

When you have a rough idea of the amount of automation you want in your conversion, the next step is to price alternative sources and do a pilot conversion.

Pilot Conversion

Regardless of the method selected, converting a prototype section of the data is a necessary part of the preconversion process. The pilot includes not only the programming and automated processing of a sample section of the document, but also the review of the results. The review process must include parsing all material and proofreading all scanned materials. In addition, the pilot sample must be carried through the full production process to test the converted material in each environment, whether that includes a document database, composition system, or on-screen viewer.

Making sure you got it right and feeding the results back into the data design, system design, and conversion strategy is not a trivial process. Repeating and refining the conversion will, eventually, lead in to the first phase of the conversion.

The best policy for this, as for the entire transition effort, is to expect to work in phases, giving yourself enough time for each. Leaving enough time for planning and testing saves time in the long run, at the end of the project, when your deliverables are not pilots, but the real item.

PLANNING A PILOT PROJECT

A data-conversion pilot may be only one aspect of an all-encompassing pilot program that is the shakedown cruise for the entire transition to SGML-based publishing. The structure and nature of an SGML pilot shares much with a trial of any new technical process. What follows is an outline of some of the SGML-specific aspects of such a trial.

Before you begin:

1. Decide on pilot program goals.
2. Choose pilot document.
3. Set tentative budget and schedule.
4. Decide on technical requirements.

Pilot Project Goals

The types of project goals that you might see in an SGML pilot include:

- Trial document analysis, trial DTD
- Test data markup by editor or by conversion
- Convert from different types of legacy data: text, word-processor or type-setting files
- Preview material in online viewer or viewers
- Output to a composition engine
- Evaluate production methods and division of labor for new tasks
- Evaluate pilot data for first deliverable
- Review system design
- Evaluate cost of coding, producing pilot

The most important goal of this as of any pilot is *not* to ensure "success" at any cost. The pilot succeeds if it reveals strengths and weaknesses in the initial design. A pilot project that heaves up problems at every turn, that costs too much and takes too long, is a *good* pilot. Glossing over the problems or setting the goals for the pilot too low thwarts the purpose of the whole project.

The pilot is the time and place to highlight and identify the wrinkles and curves, not to smooth them out or tuck them away out of sight. Finding mistakes and incompatibilities is the purpose of the pilot. Exploit the weaknesses, magnify them, and solve them before you go into production.

Criteria for Selecting a Pilot Text

Choice of an appropriate data set is crucial to the success of the pilot. The objective is to choose a text that has all the problems and anomalies of the larger work but is manageable in a short time frame. The text used in the pilot should meet the following criteria:

- Of lasting value, taken from actual production data
- Do-able in a realistic time frame
- At least 1 percent of the whole, never less than 50 pages
- Of representative complexity

While most pilots will start with a text of less than 1,000 pages, it is important that the sample be representative yet, at the same time, not so long that the length itself will interfere with the objectives of the pilot.

Technical Requirements

The technical requirements for the pilot should match this phase of implementation. If this phase of the implementation concentrates on one phase of production, then the pilot should as well. For example, if the first stage of implementation concentrates on data input methods, then the composition engine and viewer used to test trial data may not be critical.

In addition to the tools brought into a pilot program, technical requirements include the technical skills to design and test the data. If the pilot includes a document analysis, trial data conversion, and output to print and browser, the following would be required:

- Document type definition
- Conversion algorithm
- Write-to-convert template
- Output filter to print
- Output filter to browser

Implementation Sequence

A simple sequence for a pilot that focuses on data input and output, not data management, might include the following:

1. Set pilot project goals.

2. Get ballpark pricing for technical requirements (tools and skills).

3. Set pilot program budget and schedule.

4. Choose pilot data.

5. Evaluate and purchase tools, required contract, or consulting labor.

6. Create DTD.

7. Code document.

8. Filter to print and to online.

9. Test pilot material in viewer.

10. Evaluate pilot in light of goals, budget.

WAYS TO PHASE—SAMPLE TRANSITION PATTERNS

There are several ways to stage a successful, gradual transition to SGML. The sequence of bringing things online must consider all three basic components: technology, data, and the people who make it all work together.

What all scenarios have in common is a reluctance to plunge blindly ahead and a preference for taking many small steps over fewer large ones. Broadly, these scenarios can be divided into those that start with:

- The full production process, one product at a time
- The full production process, one work group at a time
- One part of the production process at a time

It is the last scenario, one part of the process at a time, that is difficult to conceive at first glance, but it is in wide practice and is an excellent method to spread costs while gradually gaining expertise and refining data designs and methodologies.

A phased introduction starting with data input might be as gradual as starting to use templates with your current editor or upgrading your current editor so that you can use templates. This is a relatively small step that prepares writers and editors and quality control to think beyond the immediate goal of how something looks on a page. Alternately, it could start with a relatively simple data design, adding components for automated workflow and sophisticated data management when the basic process is in place.

For data management, it might mean design and use of a DTD that identifies objects and components that will form the significant units of a later data management system. You would be producing and using SGML before the data management system is in place, retaining the operating system file as the basic container of your data management system. And, on the output side, a phased introduction might mean bringing in a new composition system and gaining proficiency with it before designing the data structures that will ultimately port to that system.

Alternately, phased transition can mean identifying one product or category of information that is most needed/has the highest return and converting the entire process for that one product. Briefly, some of the transition sequences described at the case studies are:

- Butterworth—Developed SGML-based production for one product at a time; for first product, brought in new composition system, then did data conversion and data management, and lastly, added editorial input of new data.

- Columbia University Press—Introduced SGML for typesetting and CD-ROM production, then as a data management system, and lastly as an editorial input system.

- Ericsson—Introduced SGML first as an editorial system, then as an output specification.

- Standard & Poor's—Introduced SGML as an input editorial system and as a data management system; some impact on output technology.

- Sybase—Introduced SGML to improve production, leaving writers' input tools basically unchanged.

- Publisher's International—Introduced SGML for data management first, without significant changes to input and output technology.

- Canadian Code Centre—Introduced SGML-based document production in one division while a second division brought in data, document, and project management software. After each division has developed some expertise, they will switch and help each other during the next round of introductions.

Getting into SGML as a part of an industrywide initiative can have a substantial impact on the transition process. For a description of model industrywide planning and cooperation, see the case study of Intel in Chapter 4, which had two years of expertise in data design and analysis before specifying its own internal system.

What remains? Only the conventional wisdom of how to phase in any new technology—cover your bases with the same redundancy, backup, and support that you would when bringing in any new production system and expect that the most profound changes will be in the process and manner of work, not in the new technology. The new work environment is described in the next chapter.

9

Being There
SGML-Based Production

The key to understanding the changes in the writer's environment and to changes throughout an organization, from copy editor to top management, is structural awareness—that SGML-encoded text is no longer an undifferentiated mass, distinguished indirectly by its typography. This has ramifications throughout an organization.

This chapter discusses the issues that arise in an SGML-based production environment from the point of view of managers, writers, and production personnel. The largest section of the chapter is devoted to the question of writing with SGML which benefited from an excellent and thoughtful discussion among technical writers that occurred on the Internet.[1] The initial discussion centered on the inability of any technology, SGML included, to allow a writer to write one text and reuse it in different contexts without revision and modification. What ensued was a detailed discussion of the writing process and how it is affected by structured information technology.

At the end of the chapter is a short section that considers subcontracting for SGML services.

MANAGING SGML

In SGML-based systems, jobs change.

Put most plainly, when documents are coded in SGML, parsed, and online—whether just for production or for final delivery—they have, in effect, ceased to be "documents" as we know them and have become software.

---

[1]The discussion started on comp.text.sgml, the SGML discussion and news forum on the Internet, and moved over to techwr-1, the technical writers' listserv newsgroup.

This change highlights divisions in the workforce that the advent of word processors and desktop publishers tended to blur. WYSIWYG tools bundle many functions into one tool—you can write, edit, draft, review, archive, transmit, design, compose, typeset, and produce the document in one file with one application. As a result, the job descriptions of the people who perform these tasks have tended to melt together.

In contrast, the specialization of SGML-based applications returns an advantage to an older, more distinct division of function. While it is still possible for a single person to do all these tasks, the distinction between input, processing, and output tools, together with the separation of content from any one, fixed, format, confers an advantage on a degree of specialization that WYSIWYG was driving out of fashion.

The manager trying to anticipate what the new environment will bring should read carefully the case studies in Chapter 4 and take note of the conclusion of the Butterworth case study: Upper management cannot rely on technical personnel to make technical decisions, but must become informed and involved.

There are some general points that clarify the new demands and responsibilities placed on management by the new production environment. This discussion expands on several issues that describe the managers' new role:

- Redefining old jobs, adding new ones
- Changing workflow
- Fine-tuning the process for maximum efficiency
- Maintaining buy-in

Redefining Old Jobs, Adding New Ones

Who does the work in the new environment, and how is the work divided up? Are these new jobs programming or publications or something else? The new jobs created at most sites include:

- Participating in and leading document analysis
- Creating, managing, and maintaining DTDs
- Writing and managing data-conversion programs
- Document database management

The ideal candidate for these new positions has a background both in publishing and in programming or a strong background in one and the ability to understand the other. Generalizing from the experience detailed in these and other case studies, it is best to discount no one from consideration but to begin the training and evaluation process and see who the crossover candidates are.

Data design requires participation in document analysis by the entire staff, an exercise in communication that may be new in itself. At sites where the division of labor has not changed from pre-electronic-typesetting days, it is an innovation in itself to sit a senior editor across the table from a typographer and direct a discussion between them. The facilitator or leader of the document analysis group must ensure that participants have a common vocabulary and understanding of the process and its implications for their roles in production.

While the jobs of DTD coding, data conversion, and data transformation are closer to programming than to publishing, an understanding of the impact of each on the product and the production process is essential. In coding, conversion, and transformation, a knowledge of document structure is essential. Is it easier to teach a programmer about documents or a publications person about programming? In this new field, no one should be excluded from consideration, whether their background is in publishing or in programming since document analysis and document architecture require participation by people with both sets of skills.

Changing Workflow

There are three key workflow issues that managers should consider:

- Production change management
- The underlying data design
- Feedback and revision cycles

Change Management

Once the document is analyzed, coded, and produced, it has, in fact, become software. From then on, the process of managing that document has as much to do with software engineering processes as it does with traditional document management processes. As software, changes to one aspect of the online document have ramifications throughout the production process and on the final product itself. The case study of Silicon Graphics (SGI) (Glushko and Kershner, 1993) described how a change in a conversion template would "ripple into the DTD and the software for format translation and online presentation."

One way to handle changes in data design is copied from the process for engineering changes in a controlled manufacturing process. The change is not incorporated willy-nilly as soon as someone on the floor discovers the need for it—you don't make up a new tag or element or change a conversion algorithm on the spot without going through the procedure. There is a process of review and documentation that accompanies the change, usually initiated by a formal engineering change request.

The request is usually reviewed in two stages by a delegated committee that determines the priority of the request and if it merits further consideration. From there, it can be put on a rush basis for high priority or review, rejected for lack of substance, or sent for a thorough review by each affected department. The review process typically results in modifications to the change request. The full review then goes back to the review body, which decides its fate. If it is adopted, then an official engineering change order is issued that specifies the change and that becomes a permanent part of the process documentation.

Such a procedure does not eliminate the midnight rush to press with all the pressure of encountering the unforeseen through the eyes of a sleepy and stressed-out staff, but it does solve the problem of undocumented changes rippling through the daily production workflow.

But not every production glitch can wait for a formal review and change cycle. Not every instance can be anticipated and controlled before a document goes into production. The most highly-seasoned professionals in this business report that a DTD, a conversion template, and an output specification can never be finished— there will always be new conditions or requirements that initiate change. How can the writer or supervisor build in flexibility to meet the unforeseen instance? How can you adjust to meet the new requirement?

Design for Change

You may want to build your DTD to anticipate unanticipated constructions. This is not as impossible as it sounds. Document architecture varies in flexibility.

Say, for example, that the DTD defines bulleted lists and procedures, but that the author has used an unanticipated structure, a bulleted list within a procedure. If you build the elements—list items and procedural steps in this case—and do not restrict where and in what order they appear, then the unanticipated bulleted list within a procedure is legitimate. Of course, your output formatter may not have the appropriate style for it—which brings us back to the original point: that all pieces of the production process are tied together through the data design.

The degree of flexibility that you build into the DTD should be a reflection of your writing environment. Just be sure that if you build in flexibility, that you have flexibility throughout the process. Alternatively, you may want to build a data design and a production process that is optimized for quick or temporary responses to production problems.

Feedback and Review

The toughest part of putting together an SGML production environment may be providing for feedback and revision, both internal and external. The review and revision cycle for the product itself, the text being written or edited, is changed by a structured environment. Where, in the past five years, WYSIWYG tools have compressed all functions into one application, and jobs have shifted accordingly, SGML tools tend to have the opposite affect—splitting functions into separate areas of expertise. Regardless of how you change your workforce to take advantage of the new production environment, it is critical to provide the technical capability for review and revision at each stage. The critical element, which only a structured editor or a tightly integrated process can supply, is feedback on the structural aspects of the document that have ramifications for the later stages of the production process.

For example, a writer using an SGML editor may no longer be required to produce final print pages but may be required to write separate versions for print and online use. "The key problem of the writer," according to Jon Bosak, Information Architect at Novell, is "no immediate feedback that they are doing it right." While the writer may not be preparing final pages, he or she should have easy access to a preview of what a final page would look like. While the process of compiling the final electronic book may not occur until the writer has handed off the text to another production team member, he or she should have easy access to a model or preview of the impact that his or her coding will have on the final online book.

Although the final format may not be applied until a largely hands-off translation is used, once the information has been reviewed, validated, archived, and retrieved, technical and editorial reviewers must have access to online tools that will help them review the material; alternatively, a preliminary compilation must produce a close simulation of the final product.

Fine-Tuning the Process

The move from typesetting to desktop and electronic publishing often blurred the traditional division of labor, eliminating the intermediate jobs of copy editing and some typesetting functions. When cleanup was required, say a stray quotation mark was missing or a non-English character was required, the assignment to put in the correction migrated from the author to the editor, to the typesetter, in some cases all the way to the final designer, but it is very expensive to have designers clean up copy.

Chapter 7 on system design considered "Kate's Corollary": The further along in the production process that information is injected, the higher the cost of adding it. Reorganizing around SGML and structured information can be an opportunity to reapportion the responsibility for content and format, as Kate Hamilton puts it, to ensure that "content settles down independent of the format." In an ideal workflow, the writer and editor finish before they hand it over, instead of relying on designers and typesetters to fill in what is missing. In an unstructured environment, a typesetter must ask: "This looks like a fourth level head, but it's the only one. What is it?" With SGML, this aspect of the file, as least, is clean and well defined when the file goes to production. As Kate Hamilton said:

SGML shows where the responsibility lies, and from a process point of view, that's necessary. It identifies the structure of the process: you know when content, structure, design are each done; [you can] work in whatever way, but when each person hands work over, they have to hand it over with all the information necessary for the next person.

Maintaining Buy-In

Not all reports from the field are of smiling, structured-information workers, eagerly awaiting the release of the next DTD. Sites that report success and those that report failure in adapting to the new tools are in agreement over the key variables for achieving worker buy-in. These are:[2]

- Lack of training
- Inadequate time given for tasks
- Feeling of losing control
- Goals ill defined, low sense of accomplishment
- Lack of user involvement

From a manager's perspective, defining goals that match the new alignment, the new division of labor, is primary.

Perhaps the primary complaint is that when new goals are not defined to fit the new tasks, the workers, writers primarily, see only the greater demands of the new system and do not share in its greater rewards. Writing with SGML requires discipline and effort and can engender strong feelings regarding ownership of information.

From a manager's perspective, defining goals that match the new alignment, the new division of labor, is primary. When divvying up responsibilities, the manager should redesign each job for a sense of accomplishment. This demands some creativity and willingness to change on the part of the manager because, in many regards, the benefits of structured information accrue to the organization rather than to the individual. If no thought is given to such a redefinition, for authors, this can mean new responsibilities without new rewards—a situation that can lead to intense discomfort with the new system.

Writing with SGML is demanding. Bob Glushko of Passage Systems was correct when he wrote of the implementation of SGML at SGI: "More precise structural tagging requires more work." This should not be a surprise—greater efficiency and flexibility, new products to offer, does not mean a free lunch. What is key for a manager is to realize that writers must be given a sense that the added work required to make a document parse and flow smoothly through the new production system is recognized and credited to their effort.

---

[2]Some of these were listed by the Center for Information Technology Services of the University of Oslo, Norway, in a presentation at SGML '94. Others are from my own observations and interviews.

The worker's sense of accomplishment can be further undermined by the perceived loss of control over the information produced. Melanie Yunk says that, at Intel, as is common elsewhere, writers manage their own products, their own word-processor files, on the desktop of their computers. With a document database approach, where their product is managed from a central repository, she anticipates that the hard lesson for writers will be that "the information does not belong to you, it belongs to the company."

Writers need to have a clear stake in the company goals to maintain their sense of control over their work. Goals must be redefined as creation and delivery of information instead of publishing, as providing the basis for a wide range of publications, not just a set number of pages. And workers need to see their part in producing better, customized, up-to-date products. It is the ultimate job of the manager to tie the benefits listed in the first chapter of this book into the job description of each person contributing to the new process and to make the benefits to customers and to the market important to each person necessary to achieve those benefits. The writer's point of view is discussed next.

WRITING SGML

In the first five, six, seven years of the standard, most experience in writing with SGML was accumulated through writing technical and engineering data. Since World War II, it has been these technical writers who have provided the bridge between those responsible for creating technical innovations and those on the receiving end of that innovation. It comes as a shock to some of us that, this time, it is our own tools that are being reinvented.[3] But it is not only technical writers who are affected by the move to structured information.

If you consider the widespread use of SGML in the humanities and the polymorphous diversity of the WWW, it is possible to say that there is no limit to the subjects that are covered in SGML-encoded documents.

While the applicability of SGML is not limited by subject matter, I would limit this discussion on writing to those writers creating documents of known structure. There is very little accumulated experience in the use of structured edi-

---

[3]If this section is written with a personal, tone, it reflects the fact that here, I am in my own neighborhood—this is where I live. It was as a technical writer and technical writing manager that I first encountered SGML, and it is as a writer about technology that I care about the tools that I use and the power that I have in my place in the working world. More than that, SGML, and the controversy over its use for writers, touches the very reason why I write and write about technology—it is on the cusp, the meeting edge, between the human and the technical, between language and computation. Today, it defines the field on which the two meet.

tors and SGML to create original works of fiction.[4] Even writing nonfiction without an established DTD presents a special set of circumstances—see the description of the simultaneous development of a new type of document and DTD in the Ericsson portrait.

The discussion that follows applies to writers working on new works, or revising existing works, where a model of structure exists and the usual type of document analysis can take place.

What Are The Issues?

Virtually no one reports that structured writing fails to make an impact on writers. Where the reports vary is in the evaluation of that impact. The discussion regarding the role of the writer in an SGML-based production environment can be characterized by several, sometimes contradictory, assertions and assumptions, by complaints and by praise.

First, the complaints:

1. SGML is a top-down technology where the writer is not a programmer, is not the architect of the DTD and is, therefore, constrained by what the DTD programmer has wrought.

2. SGML-based editors interrupt the writer's flow of thought with beeping reminders of structural requirements that are not relevant to the immediate task.

3. SGML limits the way things look in final form, and this constrains writers.

4. SGML cannot anticipate all the tags and constructs needed, even for a work of known structure.

5. SGML presents no advantage, so there is no reason to change the way you work.

6. Even with SGML, it is necessary to write independently for each output medium.

7. The writer needs to determine how things look during the writing process, but SGML-based tools restrict this.

---

[4]The rumor has circulated that Margaret Atwood wrote her novel *Cat's Eye* in SGML. I wrote to the source and received the polite reply that, while the book was typeset from SGML, the markup had been applied during production, not during the writing process. The only case of fiction written directly in SGML that I can confirm is the short work *Christopher Columbus Answers All Questions* by Yuri Rubinsky, President of SoftQuad and one of the most persistent and articulate spokesmen for the adoption of SGML. This notable work does not constitute a precedent, but this, too, can change.

8. The writer is constrained in what he or she writes, in the actual content and framework, by writing in an SGML environment; it limits expressiveness and creativity.

The first five complaints concern the way SGML is implemented and are not symptomatic of the basic nature of the technology. It should be abundantly clear from the case studies in this book that SGML need not and should not be implemented in a top-down manner, without the essential participation of all available writers.

If an editing tool constantly beeps, interrupting the writing flow, there are several solutions. The most fundamental is to reexamine the data design, to see what is required. The most immediate is to use an editor that allows rules to be turned off or overridden on a temporary basis. If the complaint persists, it is undoubtedly a symptom of inadequate training and inadequate understanding of the various roles of SGML syntax, document architecture, and application requirements.

The idea that SGML limits the way things look is quite simply a misconception, a generalization based on the way SGML has been used in limited contexts. While some sites use SGML to constrain format, using it as an automated style guide, there is no requirement that it be used in this fashion.

This brings up the related question of copy fitting: changing the words so that they fit the page. Again, there is no reason why this is any more or less possible when the master file is in SGML. At the final composition stage, the copy can always be made to fit the design of the page. Since the composed page is not the master file, the copy-fit changes are not automatically reflected back in the master. This is no greater problem with SGML-based systems than with typewritten or word-processed pages that are later composed on separate systems.

Can a DTD faithfully and completely describe every tag that would and should be used in every context? Can it anticipate every combination and construct that a writer will need, even for documents of known and predetermined structure and content? Much depends on the generality and flexibility of the basic document architecture. A good data design can remain stable through several generations of application upgrades.

While every DTD is subject to change, the good news is that change is possible. Altering a data design entails some technical and administrative overhead, but much less so than implementing a change to a software application that is not subject to influence by the writer.

The fifth point, that SGML presents no advantage to the writer, could indicate that a needs assessment was not properly done and that, indeed, SGML is not appropriate for this particular situation. Alternatively, it could point to a situation that calls for structured information, but one in which the implementation was not done well. A third possibility is that the writers, like those at Ericsson, see no advantage for themselves while the company as a whole is reaping a large benefit.

The sixth point, that even when using structured information technology it is necessary to rewrite for each independent output—once for online books, once for help systems, once for print, and so on—confuses what SGML makes possible with what it requires. Structured information applications make it possible to write in a modular fashion with different outputs in mind. Eliot Kimber, a former technical writer who was one of the two key developers of the IBMIDDoc, a DTD for technical documentation, explains that the architecture of the DTD allows a writer to write a single passage with the consideration that the full description will be printed—introduction, description, conclusion—while only the middle, descriptive paragraph will be extracted for the online help system.

SGML offers many other methods to simplify and track multiple outputs from a single source. In each case, the method must be thought out before the writer plunges into the task. Structuring a document and coding that structure with SGML markup does not magically transform books into help files, but if there is a practical way to reuse some portions of text, SGML markup allows applications to do so.

The last two points raised by writers anxious about the impact of SGML on their work deserve extended discussion because they touch on the fundamental nature of structured information and of the writing process itself.

WYSIWYG Wars

The question here is whether or not the lack of a perfect mapping between the writer's screen display and the subsequent page is an impediment to good writing.

"WYSIWYG Wars" is my term for the arguments for and against a writing environment where the writer has direct, immediate control over every detail of the appearance of the final page or screen. "Wars" may sound melodramatic, but the debate reaches a religious intensity when fueled by theories of "how we think" and it is on this turf that much of the battle between open standards and proprietary data formats is being waged.

The question here is whether or not the lack of a perfect mapping between the writer's screen display and the subsequent page is an impediment to good writing. Let's look more closely at what the lack of WYSIWYG in SGML means for those doing the writing.

Actually, let's look at what it does *not* mean. It does not mean that the screen of a writer using SGML looks like a primeval data terminal with no buttons, icons, or graphic aids. For many writers, the switch *to* WYSIWYG was concurrent with the switch to a graphical user interface. The switch away from strictly WYSIWYG is not concurrent with a return to character-based terminals and the merciless C: prompt. Leaving WYSIWYG does not mean that the screen of a writer has no visual clues indicating how things relate to each other on the page. This misconception is a throwback to the preadolescent days of the SGML tools market. Today's SGML editing tools, in their late teens perhaps, offer abundant on-screen formatting.

In addition to on-screen format that gives implicit, visual clues to structure, writers can get explicit structural representations of their documents and their document types using any of the SGML editors or structured editors and any of the DTD viewers. Some of these even allow cut-and-paste editing directly on the graphic view of the document. See the screen shots of these products in Chapter 3.

So, where's the rub? The persistent question is whether the lack of *complete congruity* between final page and writer's screen is an impediment to writing and to production workflow. Is that level of visual feedback is an integral part of the act of writing? It certainly was not an integral part of writing during the 500 years between the invention of the printing press and the invention of desktop publishing.

Writers working in a corporate or collaborative environment need to know the effect of what they do on the final publication. This feedback is attainable through integrated technology and through integrated work processes. Writers also need feedback from others, from reviewers, on their work while it is in draft form. Like many writers, reviewers have become accustomed to drafts that have the format of a polished product and often do not give their full attention to drafts that appear too far from final. Writers need to be able to present their work-in-progress in a format that is close enough to final to elicit the appropriate feedback.

The core of the matter is this: All nonfiction writers—and, with few exceptions, writers of fiction as well—think of structure.

If a draft printout from a structured word processor is not enough, the author must be able to send this unfinished fragment through the output transformations to get an interim, review manuscript. Fundamentally, this is a workflow issue and can be addressed as such by closer integration of tools and by new tool types that make it easier to translate from structural markup to any given output format.

The last question is fundamental for writers because it asks if there is a basic difference between how we think and work in an unstructured word processor and how we think and write in a structured editor. The question is: When we work in a WYSIWYG environment, are we working more with visual clues, as opposed to an SGML-structured environment, where the clues are abstract and nonvisual?

And what of the idea that there has been a natural selection among technical writers against those who "think structured" in favor of those who "think visually"? This is an interesting assertion, but when you look at the guts of the writing process, the dichotomy is not such a deep, sharp divide as it is made out to be. I question if there is a fundamental opposition between those who "think structure" and those who "think pictures." The core of the matter is this: All nonfiction writers—and, with few exceptions, writers of fiction as well—think of structure. The real divide is not between structured or unstructured thinking during the act of writing, but between structure expressed unambiguously in an abstract language that the computer can compute and structure expressed in sometimes imprecise, ambiguous visual clues that a computer cannot always interpret.

So, the WYSIWYG Wars—supposedly uptight, rigid SGML in a shoot-out against the permissive pretty-picture editors—is not so much a question of structured versus visual ways of thinking (Sparta versus Athens?) but of how structure is expressed. Does the author express it through typography or through explicit markup with typography as an option? When posed in this light, the difference between SGML editors and unstructured editors becomes one of historical evolution and emphasis rather than fundamental opposition. It is a question of *What kind of structure are you comfortable working with? What kind of structure do you need to carry over your publication into multiple media?*

The writing process does change with a structured editor but, far from giving something up in terms of visual clues and feedback, I would make the case that SGML markup is a tool that we can use to gain greater control over our product. If the write-to-convert and structured editing tools that map to a specific output format are successful, they will demonstrate that the whole notion of an opposition between structured and visual thinking was a red herring to begin with.

Let's leave the WYSIWYG Wars behind and look at the other essential characteristics of an SGML editor from the perspective of the writer.

> There is more in SGML markup than the minimum required to make a text look good in print. That extra, that higher energy, that added value, is most useful when it comes directly from us—from the writer.

Writing Down the Structure

Writing down the structure, to borrow a phrase from Natalie Goldberg (1986), is the opportunity in SGML-based applications to enclose more in our work than the words, their absolute arrangement in a file, and their relative arrangement on a display or output medium. As this book has repeated many times, there is more in SGML markup than the minimum required to make a text look good in print. That extra, that higher energy, that added value, is most useful when it comes directly from us—from the writer.

The argument that I am going to put forth here is that structured word processing—and today that means SGML-based technology—provides tools and techniques that we as writers can use to our benefit.

Now, the praise for SGML:

1. SGML-based technology gives us useful tools that can help us visualize and manipulate the structure of our work during the writing process.

2. SGML markup gives us a way to identify objects and to add metadata, to our documents without burdening our prose.

3. SGML markup gives us a way to identify explicit connections between objects as we write, connections that will work across diverse media.

4. SGML markup and SGML-based technology saves writers and editors from tedious, repetitive tasks such as cross-referencing and repetitive formatting.

5. SGML gives us control over how our material appears across diverse media, especially electronic books.

6. The idea that we think visually instead of structurally, or that the two are not wedded, misses the essential nature of the WYSIWYG versus SGML debate and of the writing process itself.

Working directly with SGML or through a tightly-controlled mapping process we can add to our documents:

- Links
- Objects
- Relationships

In many cases, these would be clear to a human reader by context, by typography, or by the words themselves. When we make these explicit with SGML markup, we allow computer applications to distinguish them unambiguously as well. And there are instances where SGML markup aids the human reader as well, where our explicit content and structure translate into direct benefit in the production process and the final product.

If linking is done schematically, that is, structurally, the writer can add a glossary item and the links to the proper terms will be supplied by the application. At the time the word is first used, the writer may not know to what an object will be connected. It may not be connected to anything yet, but, the writer knows that it is an object and that it could be linked. With a properly constructed document architecture and application, the writer can mark it once, *at the time of writing*, and the link will be there later, when needed.

In the writing process, you would note to yourself "This is a term," then you would pull down a list of elements or attributes that describe what type of term it is, select the proper one, and apply it. In this way, SGML can be a way to *quit* worrying about structure. Without the ability to mark the term "HyTime" as a glossary term during the writing process, the writer must keep a separate list of potential glossary terms throughout the writing process. Surely this interrupts the flow of composition at least as much, if not more, than pulling down a list and choosing the appropriate item.

Why identify objects more explicitly than can be done with language alone? One reason is that the computer can then manipulate the objects in an explicit, controlled, and predictable manner in electronic books and document databases. An additional reason is that those who follow you in the production process—editors, reviewers, designers, typographers, programmers—can also identify and manipulate the objects in an explicit, controlled, and predictable manner.

In technical writing, for example, the same word sequence can identify a command, a menu item, or a tool name. Yet these objects must be distinguished for glossary entries, appendices, procedures, updates, changes, indices, hypertext links, catalogs, and, not least of all, format. If my tool's name is Weekly

Calendar, then I can write about a specific weekly calendar and about the Weekly Calendar tool. If my Weekly Calendar (tool name) is an element or an entity, then I am not constrained in my format, punctuation, or choice of words or phrasing. I can write about the feature, the tool, the menu choice, without constraint (if this meets other requirements of usage) because, having identified each reference as the correct type of entity, the computer will keep track of which is which in case one is changed, reformatted, or rearranged. Without a structured editor, I would have serious, immediate constraints in my use of syntax and format because I had to rely on these essentially secondary characteristics to tell the computer which was a description, which a reference, which a piece of jargon, and so on.

When you put your text in containers and define objects within those containers—as SGML does—then the computer can know what you are talking about. Before, it saw only an undifferentiated text string. Now that you have told it what's what, you can use the computer to manipulate these structures. I don't know how this plays out for poets but, for technical writers, this is simply a better way to do what we do.

Many word processors and desktop publisher employ these features of a structured editor, albeit in their own proprietary format. If you automatically generate tables of contents, use the outline function of your word processors, use embedded cross-references and index entries, you are making the structure of the document explicit. These features say nothing about the typography of the document and they are not intrinsically WYSIWYG features—they mark up structure and content, not format.

The Structured Editor

Let's look, from the writer's perspective, at the essential features of a structured editor.

Controlled Tag Set

The controlled tag set limits the structural elements that can be used in a document to those defined in the DTD. In this manner, SGML gives us the ability to enforce corporate styles or rules that we, perhaps, didn't enforce before. It also reminds us why we did not do so.

Next to the desire to edit someone else's copy, there is no greater desire on earth than to create a new style tag that will make some anomalous construction fit the look of the publication. Who among us has not, when nearing deadline, found or created the first and only instance of a bulleted list within a procedure? And who has not engendered a new style tag to fit this instance?

How would this differ under SGML structured editing? In SGML implementations, the work of figuring out what to do with the bulleted list within a procedure should be done up front. What, with unstructured editors, manifests as a problem in typography at the end of the process is actually a problem in structural definition and, as such, should be addressed in the document analysis that precedes the writing of the DTD.

Should writers be able to invent new styles like bulleted list within a procedure on the fly? Nothing really prevents this—just be sure that, if you build in flexibility, you have flexibility throughout the process. SGML forces you to articulate the decision-making process, and it pushes this process up front and forces you to live by the rules that you set, until you change those rules. If this is a constraint, it is no greater a constraint than what you will find in any corporate or technical or industrial style guide worth the paper it is printed on.

Note that the limitation on named structural elements does not apply, necessarily, to attributes, the structural modifiers. A data design can build in the ability for writers to apply descriptive terms of their own invention to pieces of text delimited as an element.

Context-Sensitive Markup

Context-sensitive markup is not only easy to describe, it is easy to accept.

Context-sensitive markup means that only the element tags appropriate for where you are in the document show up on the tag list. For example, if you are on the cover page, you will not be able to select a chapter title—it will not show up on the list of available tags. If you are working in a chapter, you will not be able to select a publication title element.

This has obvious benefits, not the least of which is the sheer reduction in volume of available tags. When there are only a dozen appropriate choices, why page-down through the whole list of 200 style tags? So, context-sensitive markup not only goes far to enforce good usage, it just plain saves time.

Structural Validation (Parsing)

Structural validation is the formal vetting of the document in terms of the document type definition. Because this is at the heart of so many of the ramifications of writing with SGML, relatively little need be said of it here. In trying to assess how your own personal writing process may be affected by using a structured editor, the only general comment I can make is to try to think of it as an editor—granted, it is an automated one, one that brooks no argument—but the relationship is not unlike the relationship of a writer to a copy editor and an enforcer of corporate style.

This is where the writer comes up against the intelligence, perspicacity, wisdom, experience, and all-around smarts that were built into the data in the design stage, in the document analysis. Who did it, and did it get adequate input from writers? This is a large determinant in whether or not writers will be happy writing to this DTD. (Managers, take note: Writers participating in document analysis are not getting the afternoon off. Consider, instead that they are working simultaneously on all the documents that will be written to that DTD.)

Navigational Tools

Navigational tools, like context-sensitive markup, are a feature of working in a structured environment that should be cause for universal celebration. Consider the added convenience, now that your editing tool knows the difference between footnotes and captions, between instructions and descriptions. Then, imagine how much easier it is to find instances of particular usage and application.

With structured markup, you have the freedom to arrange your text and to navigate according to all markup elements. You can go to the next instance of TOOLNAME in a procedure and you can use a dynamic table of contents to navigate and even to edit the actual text of the document.

Some Conclusions

SGML markup and SGML-based technology can be a great asset in the writing process. If it does not seem like that yet, it is because we are still not clear about the role of these tools and how to use them, data designs and the processes for creating them are still evolving rapidly, and the tools themselves are not mature.

We Always Created Structure

We always created structure and format; we just threw out the structure when we put our thoughts into complete, grammatical sentences. We kept only the format. If we keep the structure as well, just look what we can do with it! From the writer's perspective, "What You See Looks Like the *Structure* of What You Write" is at least as significant as "What You See Is An Exact Replica of What Will Print." The problem is not to "adjust" to thinking structurally, but to learn how to express structure in explicit and unambiguous terms rather than visual terms that may or may not be precise.

We Rarely Created Form

Unless you have been writing in stone or hand-setting your own type—and the writers considered here have rarely done so—it's hard to claim that SGML has taken away an essential characteristic of our craft, our art, or our science. Separation of functions has been accepted since the advent of specialized publishing technology. After only five years of widespread WYSIWYG technology, it is hard to argue that taking away absolute fidelity to the final page disturbs the fundamental act of writing.

Of course, the vast majority of documents like proposals, reports, and letters were never formally published, but were handwritten or typed so that the writer might have had full, final control over format. These formats are not so demanding that they cannot be matched with SGML editors. Today's SGML editing tools have much more on-screen and draft format control than the average typewriter.

It Is Not That Simple

That being said, the issue of writing with SGML is not as clear-cut as stated by DeRose and his collaborators in their seminal articles on markup systems (Coombs et al.; DeRose et al., 1990, 1987), which claimed that descriptive markup is the easiest, best, and clearest method of writing. This was an early, optimistic, and largely theoretical appraisal. The years of actual work with such systems and the evolving set of tools available have not altered the fact that, as Glushko and Kershner (1993) pointed out at Silicon Graphics, "More precise structural tagging requires more work." While writers need not be technical SGML experts, they must be aware of the explicit structure of the document architecture.

But The Tools Are Catching Up

The problem is not how to adjust to thinking structurally, but how to express structure in explicit and unambiguous terms both in code and, where required, in immediate visual terms.

What does seem to be a compelling argument for graphic interfaces and control of on-screen format is that writers—this one included—do like to fiddle with the look of the page, to rearrange ideas visually at the same time as they rearrange them thematically, linguistically, and structurally. Future tools that divorce content, structure, and on-screen and final format might give writers more leeway to fiddle than is possible even with WYSIWYG systems. See the section on new tools in the next chapter.

It Is Up To Us

The red flags being raised over SGML are not wholly without merit—it is a critical juncture for writers. If we throw up our hands at this and say that we cannot get involved, that structuring information is not what our writing is about, we could limit our future role. The most disturbing misconception about writers and SGML is the assumption that writers are not doing and cannot do DTD design and document analysis. This is simply not a true reflection of how the workplace is adapting to SGML. Academicians, writers, and editors are in the forefront of document analysis and DTD design and implementation, not only in

Future tools that divorce content, structure, and on-screen and final format might give writers more leeway to fiddle than is possible even with WYSIWYG systems.

individual companies but in the collective work being done by the OSF, the Davenport group, the TEI, and others. Unless writers as a whole self-select out of this, like a type shop hanging on to hot lead, I do not know of any reason why we cannot make this the means by which we become more essential to the whole product development cycle.

With structured information, more of the work of writing happens up front, in document architecture and document analysis. The tools and techniques for achieving this are still evolving, but there is certainly no reason to oppose an entire class of technology on the grounds that it restricts a writer's freedom.

The fear that SGML limits creativity and takes control away from the writer is an abiding one and a serious one. Even the mildest hint that SGML presents limitations on a writer's ability to work, the perception that it offers no payback, no benefit to the writer, can lead to serious disaffection and unwillingness to meet and contribute to the goals of the larger group.

Whatever else I can say to a writer, I must say this: If you don't tag it, someone else will.

Management must do its part to ensure that this buy-in happens, and writers must do their part as well. As writers, if we abnegate this responsibility, in fact, if we do not take it for our own, it will be taken from us, and we will indeed find ourselves in situations where our control over our work can be diminished.

Writers must participate in the work of document analysis; they must learn the fundamental principles of working with structured information; they must be structure-aware; and they must have a sense that they are contributing to better products, which are more highly customized, more accurate, more timely, and more usable. And writers must be given recognition for their part in this because jobs do change with this new technology.

Whatever else I can say to a writer, I must say this: If you don't tag it, someone else will. New products like electronic books and new production methods like document databases require the structured dimension and will achieve it. If you do not understand the basic concepts of your document architecture, if you do not understand the interaction between the document type and the data markup, if you do not understand where data markup leaves off and application design takes over, you will be at the mercy of those who do. The workplace around us is changing, again, and this time it is our tools—not the data analyst's, the compositor's, the editor's, or the accountant's—it is our tools that are at the center of the transformation. And we, the writers, had better understand the change and start demanding what we need from these new tools and processes.

PRODUCING SGML

There is a close relationship between who does the work and the design of the system.

Beyond what was detailed elsewhere, in the case studies and the sections on system design, there are a few generalizations about production with SGML that bear emphasis here.

The Work Load Moves Up Front

More of the work of producing a given product is moved up front into prep work, leaving less to do in the final stages of production. This up-front work includes everything from the original document analysis to the coding of the document, whether in an SGML editor or by conversion from another format.

When the file comes to final production, it is more highly specified and defined. All characteristics that will eventually be distinguished in the output format are identified unambiguously in the SGML source file.

The movement of the labor of identifying and coding this material up front, closer to the source in the original writer or editor, changes the timing of the entire production cycle. When the production of typeset copy required laborious handwork searching for anomalies and figuring out ambiguities left in the file by writers and editors, it required keeping the work in production for a longer time span.

Although, ideally, all editorial changes would be made before the file was sent to production, the length of time required for production, as well as the hidden inconsistencies of the files, worked against this. As a result, editorial changes were routinely entered into the file in the final production format. The combination of rapid typesetting and earlier detection of anomalies and ambiguities means that the real editorial work can happen in the archival master copy before it goes to the final format. The file spends less time in the output format, so double entry of changes or translation from output format back into archival format are smaller concerns.

This change in timing leads to changes in orientation toward master file and output.

SGML Changes Job Descriptions

SGML creates new categories of production work and changes the job description of those who perform this work. Preparing hard copy for a composition system used to mean hand markup of typesetting codes in the margin of a manuscript. This editorial judgment is still required but is best inserted before the transformation for the composition system. The final preparation for composition is now more like a programming task than an editorial task.

Unlike page layout, designing and producing on-screen output does not have centuries of development as a guide to good quality and useability. Nowhere is this process better described than in the article "Developing a CD-ROM" by James Raimes of Columbia University Press (Raimes, 1994). He tells potential designers to budget plenty of time for planning, for checking every detail on every screen, and for testing the product both inside the house and outside.

Not every production person is ready, willing, or able to change a job description to cover the more technical aspects of producing structured information, but some individuals will grow to fit the new aspects of the job.

The Coded Archival Data Is the Essential Product

The old attitude to master files used to be that the output was the product. Now, the output in a particular format is *a* product, but the essential asset is the archival data used to produce that output.

This change, in turn, manifests as a different attitude toward the entire production cycle, which relates to the all-important fiddle factor.

Properly Understood, SGML Can Enhance Fiddling

When the data archive is the essential asset, it is okay to fiddle with the output for a specific product. Adding hard returns, forcing page breaks, moving margins, adjusting leading, can be done freely in an output file without fear of corrupting data that will be translated into other media.

SGML Changes Relations with Contractors

Going to SGML-based production has a further impact in respect to contract services. In general, integration is highly desirable, making it difficult to contract for some aspects of production. This is discussed further in the next section.

SUBCONTRACTING SGML

In addition to the usual incentives to subcontract part of the information creation and production process, subcontracting can be an important part of a transitional strategy for the adoption of structured information. Using service providers instead of bringing new technology in-house can defer, minimize, or confine to one area the training required of in-house staff. As areas of the in-house staff gain expertise in SGML, subcontracting can be reduced. While there are added incentives, there are also added cautions beyond those that apply in all subcontracting situations.

The impediments to successful subcontracting are the same issues that can complicate in-house production if not considered carefully during design. These include:

- Shifts in the division of labor that make it less clear where one job's responsibilities end;
- Need for coordination of all aspects of production around the data design;
- Provision for adequate feedback on the consequences of changes in any one part of the process; and
- Changes in workflow to ensure effective and efficient review cycles.

With these caveats, many aspects of SGML production can and are routinely subcontracted. These include:

- Data conversion
- Data design
- Data management
- Typesetting and final production.

Conversion of legacy data is probably the most common subcontract item and is covered extensively in Chapters 6, 7, and 8. As a production issue, problems in subcontracting data conversion usually arise from less than perfect communication between vendor and client.

Data design here includes hiring both an outside expert to facilitate document analysis and an outside expert to code or maintain a DTD. This, too, is common. What is less common is the subcontracting of the entire process, including the document analysis. The case study of Columbia University Press illustrates one instance where this was effective, at least as a transitional strategy.

Long-term data management is less common. The Columbia case provides an example where this was effective, although probably not indicative of the Press's long-term direction.

Ironically, typesetting and final production are among the last areas to see extensive subcontracting. It is ironic because SGML started as a means to make production subcontracting more fluid and available. Demand for typesetting direct from SGML markup is changing this picture.

Another area that has seen little subcontracting is writing—it is harder to use a writing subcontractor effectively when the in-house system is SGML. SGML moves the responsibility for structural coding onto the writer so that it is difficult to keep a subcontractor current with all phases of the data design. While this may change as expectations about structural awareness and training among subcontractors rise, it is not considered effective to subcontract writing today. Generally, files produced on the outside must be considered as legacy data that will need a full conversion effort.

If you subcontract some portion of your DTD writing, which is likely at least initially, use a service provider for data conversion, and send your SGML files

Ironically, typesetting and final production are among the last areas to see extensive subcontracting.

outside to be typeset or mastered for CD-ROM, in effect, you have subcontracted much of the process, albeit not to a single vendor. The difficulty will be, as always, coordinating the programming required to keep the data constructs synchronized between DTD, a conversion template, and an output filter.

A final consideration of costs should include the cost of future maintenance and revision. One of the advantages of SGML is ownership of the format of the data. To some extent, this is only realized when the bulk of data design and maintenance is in-house.

10

And Beyond
SGML Today and Tomorrow

IS SGML THE LAST STOP ON THE MARKUP EXPRESS?

SGML, at some point, took off from the original vision of its progenitors and became a whole new way of doing business. It is a measure of just how well this new notation fits its subject matter that applications are going in ways that the framers of the system never intended. While the original emphasis was on information reuse and on generic, vendor-independent coding, the newest applications for SGML are in information processing, storage, search and retrieval, and time-based multimedia. The ramifications of this markup system are more profound, and exciting as new types of tools become available.

How fast the use of SGML is expanding is difficult to measure and how long it will continue to do so is in the realm of projection and speculation. Market surveys of SGML have had a difficult time tracking dollars spent for SGML-based publishing because they have based their analysis on sales of commercial, off-the-shelf publishing tools. The difficulty extrapolating from these figures to useful measures of SGML is that large applications may rely heavily on custom programming and spend relatively few dollars on commercial, off-the-shelf software. The ratio of dollars spent on off-the-shelf products versus custom applications is rising which indicates increasing maturity in the marketplace.

One simple measure of the increasing popularity of SGML is attendance at the Graphic Communications Association's SGML Conference, held each year in the early winter. Conference attendance has risen by approximately 50 percent each year (Figure 10.1) from fewer than 100 attendees in 1989 to over 700 in 1994.[1]

---

[1]The GCA conference is both a technical and an educational event, so the relationship between industry growth and attendance may change as the technology becomes more accessible.

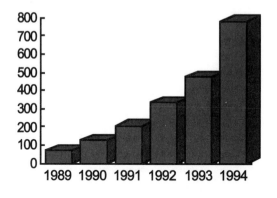

Figure 10.1 Attendance at the annual GCA SGML conference

This wait-and-see attitude has occurred along-side steady growth. In the long run, the slow, steady incubation of the first years may turn out to have been best for the industry.

We know that use of SGML has been expanding rapidly, but where is it on its development curve? Will growth flatten out or continue to shoot up? If the worth of publicly held stock in SGML tool companies is any indication, prospects for growth have never been better.

The "Sounds Good, Maybe Later" tag that used to be pinned on SGML reflected a sense that the technology was not yet ready for prime time, that the smart money was waiting to see what the rest of the industry did before making a commitment. This wait-and-see attitude has occurred alongside steady growth. In the long run, the slow, steady incubation of the first years may turn out to have been best for the industry. The technology, the expertise, and the tools now available are built on a decade of experience and are robust enough to sustain the current accelerated pace of adoption.

Today, no other data format describes text the way SGML describes text. No other data format makes possible the manipulation and processing of text that SGML makes possible. In 1992, Reynolds and DeRose, writing in *Byte* Magazine, had the audacity to state that "Some industries have *not yet* formally adopted SGML." Soon, this statement may no longer be true.

If SGML fails to continue to expand, it will be because its best features become embedded in proprietary applications. But, if Whiz-Bang Software International develops a better SGML, even if it separates content from format and allows you to process language as you have processed data, by definition, it will not have vendor independence. Let us hope that the vendors with the greatest ability to sidestep ISO 8879 by developing competing "standards" instead bend their extraordinary resources to developing applications for, not against, SGML.

NEXT-GENERATION TOOLS

Tools for working with SGML-encoded data have had their own development curve which at times seemed to lag the use of the standard and now leads it. New tools are announced quarterly. These not only extend and enrich the features of the existing tools, but extend and enrich the types of tools themselves.

What might the next generation look like?

There will certainly be some integration of input, output, and management functions or, at least, some blurring of the boundaries between these functions from the user's point of view. It is hard to imagine the same degree of flexibility in a single, off-the-shelf tool that is achieved by integrating a selection of tools, unless that tool was for a specialized application.

A new wave of editors and integrated tool sets with novel solutions to the need for format independence and output preview is emerging. It would be a boost to the industry to offer real, flexible structured writing in a quasi-WYSIWYG environment, but we need new writing metaphors as well. Word processing was built on top of the typewriter metaphor, which was built on top of the printing press metaphor.

SGML writing tools should get a fresh look at the user interface. The next round of tools should be built borrowing whatever works from database, word processing, graphic design, hypertext, multimedia, and CASE tools. After all, the real WYSIWYG is no longer type on a piece of paper but the look and feel of information on the screen. We need more tools for the creative and the imaginative process, not only the process of re-creating predetermined structures.

A naive observer might say that by offering Intellitag and SGML Author for Word, Novell and Microsoft have shown their support for SGML. A cynic would say that this write-to-convert category, populated as it is by the giants of WYSIWYG word processing, is an attempt to maintain control of the billion-dollar information creation market in proprietary internal formats while giving lip service to the demand for structured, open, nonproprietary solutions.

Which is true? It is far too early to tell.

From an analyst's perspective, it would be interesting and encouraging to see products from these vendors that make it easy to import SGML files *into* their WYSIWYG tools for final page composition and production as well as tools that attempt to create structured documents in an unstructured environment.

Editorial and QC procedures can change drastically in the transition to SGML. When a file is no longer the definitive container for a document, you must ensure that editorial and QC procedures can follow the change. When your documents are assembled from a document database instead of from static files, you must develop new procedures to check them for accuracy and completeness. Today, there are no tools designed for the intermediate processes. There is no specific editorial (as opposed to writing) interface. Yet editors must access the work-in-

> *SGML writing tools should get a fresh look at the user interface. The next round of tools should be built borrowing whatever works from database, word processing, graphic design, hypertext, multimedia, and CASE tools.*

process and access it in such a way that the ultimate configuration and cohesion can be checked and corrected.

Tools should be built for proofreaders that take special advantage of structured information. A proofreader should be able to query a text for every *second* instance of a citation not in a footnote and every internal reference to the third level headings.

How can the ease of using paper tables be equaled, or surpassed, on a small computer monitor? Before looking at data models and application design, let's look at the solution from the user's point of view: How *should* tables work online?

Electronic tables should have the flexibility and dynamics of online graphics and the processing power of a database with dynamic queries, search and retrieval, and flexible output. Readers should be able to choose position, size and dimension for cells, rows and columns, and collapsing and expanding the whole or sections of the whole. It should be possible to scroll, pan, or zoom into data as if the data were being scanned with a camera. It should be possible to set data ranges directly or as the result of a query, and it should be possible to construct tables from subsets on the fly. It should be possible to adjust screen format or export data to a graph or chart.

Today, applications are still at the beginning of the developmental curve for electronic tables. Often SGML is "dumbed down" to a presentational model because the applications available have not developed suitable ways to handle the richer information set. To reach an acceptable solution, SGML data design must encode the structural relations between data points, and SGML-aware applications must provide the flexibility to use this data.

We may see more tools that target specific markets. For example, Utah is indicative, toolmakers may begin to develop SGML brief writers or general tools with specialized templates for single applications. This pattern would parallel the way databases and spreadsheets are sold as custom tools for specialized markets like accounting and inventory management.

Off-the-shelf data conversion has not yet reached its full potential. The type of work that is being done on natural-language processing may expand the extent to which content markup can be generated automatically. The introduction of new tools that use multistep conversion and transformation and the integration of conversion with editorial tools may change the economics of data conversion.

The expanding use of SGML will not dissolve reliance on proprietary, format-based word-processing tools. SGML-based applications will coexist with these tools. As the market for SGML-based tools expands and matures, more major vendors will offer serious products in both arenas—their own proprietary arena, where they control the format, and the public, standards-based arena. Application-independent data forces product designers to earn their customers' support with each new release. When the data format is nonproprietary, licensees upgrade to a new release or switch applications when it serves their needs, not

> *Electronic tables should have the flexibility and dynamics of online graphics and the processing power of a database with dynamic queries, search and retrieval, and flexible output.*

> *Application-independent data forces product designers to earn their customers' support with each new release.*

from a fear of being left behind in an unsupported data format. To the extent that this encourages companies to produce usable—not merely feature-laden—applications, consumers will benefit.

CHANGES IN THE APPLICATION OF SGML

How might SGML itself change in the future? There will be amendments to the standard. It is not in the scope of this book to look at specific proposed changes, but anyone can monitor the discussion and respond when requests for comments are circulated.[2] What follows is a brief discussion of ways in which the application of SGML may change in the near future.

Technical Issues

This is a formative time in document architecture. For those with the skill and the vision, this is a period when innovation in design can change the way an entire industry looks at its data. The change in design methods for interchangeability and reuse since the issuance of the first CALS specifications is nothing short of a transformation. Each new initiative, such as the Interactive Electronic Technical Manual, the Text Encoding Initiative, and the Pinnacles Component Information Standard, has contributed to a reinvention of what document architecture means. While the pace of reinvention may slow down, there is no reason to believe that it will halt in the near future.

On a less global scale, there are several areas where change is imminent.

In terms of tables, we have a perverse (and temporary) situation, where a smart technology looks dumber than a dumb technology. SGML applications and data design must coordinate and clarify in what instances it is sufficient for tables to look good with all the presentational flexibility of unstructured publishing, and in which cases it is necessary to have the computational capabilities of a structured database. The technical committee of SGML Open, the vendor consortium, has tackled the table question and it seems certain that a higher-level consensus than exists today cannot be far behind. The solution may be as simple as the suggestion of Lloyd Harding, Information Assembly Inc., that SGML-based tools incorporate relational table writers and generators from existing database technology. Or the solution may involve completely new approaches to the problem.

---

[2]See the Internet sources and the contacts for the ISO in *Resource Guide A*.

The first product of the consortium Technical Committee was a resolution on entity management.[3] The use of entities is an expanding paradigm within SGML. This was the message delivered by Charles Goldfarb, one of the IBM members of the ANSI effort, who wrote the seminal book on SGML programming, *The SGML Handbook* (Goldfarb, 1990), at the SGML '93 conference. During this address, Goldfarb announced the release of public domain tools for HyTime, the time-based extensions to the SGML standard, and stated that his work on HyTime has led him to new insights into the importance of entity management in SGML.

To date, the emphasis has been on SGML elements used to delineate text structure. If HyTime engines become integrated into a new generation of applications, the next phase of development will see an equal emphasis on SGML entities used to delineate text storage. Where storage has been defined by file structure and by traditional data managers, we may see new applications that define storage in purely SGML terms.

Nontechnical Issues

SGML is still a field held back primarily by a shortage of skilled practitioners. This is not in any way a criticism of those in the field—we just need more of them, at every level.

We need more and better trained programmers, engineers, and scientists; we need college and university and engineering school and library school and technical school courses that bring SGML into the fold of legitimate computer science applications.

We need a better understanding of what to do with SGML, especially in the humanities, where some of the best minds are a tad leery of the ability of technology to help them in their work yet where some of the richest potential exists for using computer-processable text to explore language and culture. We need to make the most of the extraordinary convergence of technical know-how and linguistic ability that SGML has inspired. Previous waves of technical innovation have been overpopulated with those uninterested in intellectual life not carried out by computer. Here, finally, we have a technical field that has established major channels of communication between the worlds of technology and language.

We need to overcome the misconceptions that promote SGML as either all-powerful or all-threatening. We need better understanding of structured information among users, particularly on the Web. It's great that you do not need to know anything about structured information before you use the Web, but many

---

[3]See *Resource Guide A* for SGML Open contact information to obtain a copy of the resolution.

Web users mistake its power and performance for the power and performance of proprietary applications. Users commonly attribute the interchangeability and compatibility of the Web to a single browser and ignore the data standards that make it all possible.

A popular application, mixing open and proprietary data standards, can extend the proprietary capabilities at the expense of long-term data independence. It is not just structural rigor and richness that the Web needs to absorb from SGML, but an awareness of the importance of open, nonproprietary data formats. In ten years, it will not matter if we are marking up files according to HTML10 or according to arbitrary DTDs. It will matter if the data format is read only by NetWebAPP Release 10.3 and is controlled by NetWebAPP Mega Corp, or if all vendors can offer competing applications filing every user need by complying with an open, nonproprietary data format.

As is often the case, the technical solutions are the easy ones; the solutions that require reorganization of our way of doing things are the hard ones.

CLOSE

We need most of all a recognition that text has come home to the computer to stay and not just as an intermediate stop on the way to a printing press, although printed books will always be with us. In fact, we will cherish words in print more than ever for what they hold that is distinct from the screen. We will have greater numbers and variety and control over them because, in so many instances, the computer can pare and shape what goes into print to an unprecedented degree. Specialized, high-quality, small-quantity publishing is more feasible than ever with SGML. The homecoming, the integration of language onto the computer, is a landmark event, not because it will disrupt previous channels of cultural transmission but because it will allow new ones to form.

The homecoming, the integration of language onto the computer, is a landmark event, not because it will disrupt previous channels of cultural transmission but because it will allow new ones to form.

Text on the computer will be processible text, text that you can sort, query, link, split, suppress, and recombine as freely as in now done with data. The biggest splash made by text on the computer will be when the technology and the use of the technology make possible widespread creation and distribution of viable electronic books, books that will grow increasingly distinct from books in print.

There was an unspoken, but very powerful, sense among the early hypertext vendors that whoever got the product right—the products were essentially browsers built on proprietary data formats—would have the world beating a path to their doorstep. The notion that there had to be a better way to present text on the computer was a sound one; the notion that any one product could be so attractive as to become a magnet for the world's data was not a sound one. What we see today, with the emergence of SGML as the preeminent format for electronic text, is that the "killer app" is not an "app" at all, but a data format.

There is nothing magical about encoding with SGML. It does not free us from the constraints of language. It does not change "the way we think." As has been pointed out, an SGML textbase does not change the requirements for good usage, and it does not transform a user manual into a help system or a reference book into a troubleshooting procedure. SGML markup can be a tool of analysis that reveals and makes more accessible the work of the original authors. The great promise and opportunity of SGML is not that the machine will acquire, encode, and manipulate its own, artificial, intelligence but that it will adequately record, encode, and process our own human intelligence.

The strength of SGML is that it works with language, it does not reinvent it.

Resource Guide A
Keeping Pace with SGML

This is a selected guide to SGML-related resources. I have included here items of particular use to those getting started with SGML and items likely to remain current through the life span of this print edition. Likewise, I have restricted both this *Resource Guide* and the one that follows to those listings with which I have some familiarity and which I have been able to confirm. The result, while necessarily U.S.- and Canada-centric, is a better editorial selection. The online *ABCD... Resource Guides* will be updated at regular intervals. They can be found at www.thomson.com under Web Extras.

Please note:

- Tools, tool vendors, and some commercial services are covered in *Resource Guide B*.

- Assume that addresses are in the United States unless otherwise stated.

- Phone numbers are for the United States or Canada, area code first, unless a country code is given after a plus sign (+). Those in the United States and Canada should dial 011 instead of the plus, while others should note that the international country code for the United States is 1.

TRAINING

There are many colleges and universities—CalPoly in San Luis Obispo, UCLA, the University of Massachusetts at Amherst, Eastern Washington University, the University of Alabama at Huntsville and Bowling Green University among them—where students are known to be working on theses and projects related to SGML and structured documents. None of these offers a regular curriculum or degree in the area.

Most SGML vendors and consultants offer training. Some train only on their own products and some cover topics of general interest. Increasingly, commercial training firms include SGML in their schedule.

There is little available from noncommercial institutions—the exceptions are listed below. Even here, many noncommercial organizations subcontract their training to vendors (which does not mean that the training is not valuable, only that expertise in SGML remains highly concentrated.)

University of Wisconsin

The College of Engineering at the University of Wisconsin offers training in SGML and SGML-based production systems. Current offerings run approximately three times a year. Creating the Structured Document Environment provides a background for understanding and managing SGML production systems, emphasizing the conceptual side of SGML systems, including needs analysis and system requirements. Implementing an SGML Publishing System provides the technical background required to start building an SGML-based publishing system (also offered as a live satellite teleconference).

Richard Vacca
University of Wisconsin
Department of Engineering Professional Development
432 North Lake Street
Madison, WI 53706
800/462-0876
800/442-4214 (fax)
608/262-4341
rpvacca@facstaff.wisc.edu

Electronic Publishing Special Interest Group (EPSIG)

EPSIG is a joint effort of the GCA Research Institute and the Association of American Publishers, Inc. The group currently offers courses on the World Wide Web and ISO 12083, an application of SGML published and maintained by EPSIG. See also the information on EPSIG under *Groups Building a Common Document Architecture*.

EPSIG
C/O GCARI
P.O. Box 25707
Alexandria, VA 22313-5707
703/519-8184
703/548-2867 (fax)
document@well.sf.ca.us

Graphics Communications Association (GCA)

GCA offers an expanding schedule of courses in conjunction with, and independent of, its yearly conferences. The offerings for 1995–1996 include basic and advanced courses on SGML, DTD development, HTML and the Internet, HyTime, management strategies and the Pinnacles Component Information Standard.

GCA
100 Daingerfield Road
Alexandria, VA 22314-2888
703/519-8160
703/548-2867 (fax)
blake@access.digex.net

The Text Encoding Initiative (TEI)

The TEI offers workshops and tutorials periodically, both independent of, and in conjunction with, conferences of its sponsoring organizations. The sessions introduce principles of text markup and the TEI application of SGML. TEI has also conducted a TEI metaworkshop to train the trainer—sessions designed to prepare individuals as instructors in TEI-compliant markup. See the contact information for the TEI under *Groups Building a Common Document Architecture*.

In addition, the Center for Electronic Texts in the Humanities (CETH) holds the Summer Seminar on Methods and Tools for Electronic Texts in the Humanities, cosponsored by the Centre for Computing in the Humanities (CCH), University of Toronto. The Seminar is held in Princeton, New Jersey in June of each year. The directors of the seminar are Susan Hockey, CETH and Willard McCarty, CCH.

The Center for Electronic Texts in the Humanities
169 College Avenue
New Brunswick, NJ 08903
908/932-1386 (fax)
ceth@zodiac.rutgers.edu
ceth@zodiac.bitnet
http://cethmac.princeton.edu/CETH

PUBLICATIONS

Robin Cover's definitive SGML bibliography lists over 500 books and articles and is updated regularly. Earlier versions are available in print, among them a series of articles in *<TAG>* (see *Periodicals* below). Of course, the most up-to-date version is the one online at http://www.sil.org/sgml/biblio.html

The online bibliography has abstracts and live links to the full text of many of the cited works.

Another online bibliography entitled Methods and Tools for Computing in the Humanities has been compiled over several years by Susan Hockey, Center for Electronic Text in the Humanities (CETH), and is available at the Web site: http://cethmac.princeton.edu/CETH/bib.html

I list here a very small selection of the most significant books, periodicals, and miscellany.

Books

These are the standard technical reference works on SGML, plus two new books on HyTime and Peter Flynn's book on the World Wide Web, selected from a multitude of Web books because of the author's thorough knowledge of SGML.

Martin Bryan (1988) *SGML: An Author's Guide to the Standard Generalized Markup Language*. Addison-Wesley, Wokingham, United Kingdom and Reading, Massachusetts.

Steve DeRose and David Durand (1995) *Making Hypermedia Work: A User's Guide to HyTime*. Kluwer Academic Publishers, Dordrecht, Netherlands, and Boston, Massachusetts.

Peter Flynn (1995) *The World Wide Web Handbook: A Guide for Users, Authors, and Publishers on the Internet*. International Thomson Publishing, London.

Charles Goldfarb (1990) *The SGML Handbook*. Clarendon Press, Oxford, England.

Eric van Herwijnen (1994) *Practical SGML*, 2nd ed. Kluwer Academic Publishers Dordrecht, Netherlands, and Boston, Massachusetts.

W. Eliot Kimber (1995) *Practical Hypermedia: An Introduction to HyTime*. Charles F. Goldfarb Series on Open Information Management. Prentice-Hall Professional Technical Reference, Englewood Cliffs, New Jersey (forthcoming).

Joan Smith and Robert Stutely (1988) *SGML: The User's Guide to ISO 8879*. Ellis Horwood, Chichester, United Kingdom.

Periodicals

CALS/Enterprise Integration Journal covers, in its own words, "information management, interoperability, and best business practices" related to the Department of Defense's CALS initiative. It publishes an excellent *Reference Guide* in March of each year that lists many points of contact as well as vendors and consultants working with CALS SGML and related applications.

CALS/EI Journal
14407 Big Basin Way
Saratoga, CA 95070-6008
408/867-8600
408/867-9800 (fax)

<TAG>, the SGML newsletter, is the only periodical dedicated to SGML. For many years, it has been the definitive hardcopy publication.

<TAG>
SGML Associates
6360 South Gibraltar Circle
Aurora, CO 80016-1212
303/680-0875
303/680-4908 (fax)
brian@sgml.com

Seybold Report on Desktop Publishing, Digital Media, and *Seybold Report on Publishing Systems* all report regularly on SGML, especially the *Report on Publishing Systems*. These are among the few periodic media to report reliably and consistently on SGML. Mark Walter is the senior editor who covers SGML.

Seybold Publications
P.O. Box 976
Media, PA 19063
800/325-3830
215/565-2480 (Walter)
610/565-1858 (fax)

The Gilbane Report on Information & Document Systems covers the indicated topics and covers SGML very thoroughly.

Frank Gilbane, Editor
One Snow Road
Marshfield, MA 02050
617/837-7200
617/837-8856 (fax)
frank_gilbane@CAPV.com
http://www.CAPV.com

Release 1.0, the publishing industry newsletter from Esther Dyson, is an excellent source of news and analysis on SGML. Dyson is on the board of Industry Advisors for SGML Open.

Esther Dyson, Editor
Edventure Holdings
104 Fifth Avenue, 20th floor
New York, NY 10011
212/924-8800
212/924-0240 (fax)
edyson@eff.com

Miscellany

The TEI makes available a "Gentle Introduction to SGML" which is notable for its literacy as well as its kindness. Sources for TEI material are listed under *Groups Building a Common Document Architecture.*

Many vendors have produced monograph-size introductions to SGML.

The SGML Software Market Report from InterConsult has taken on the difficult task of measuring this industry. Although the way it defines "dollars spent on SGML-related technology" is not accepted by all, it is still the only show in town providing this depth of market research. Excerpts are freely available; the full report is costly.

David Goodstein
InterConsult
37 Sherman Street
Cambridge, MA 02140
617/354-0400
617/354-0940 (fax)
dhg@world.std.com

Exoterica sells a Conformance Test Suite as part of *The Compleat SGML* CD-ROM which includes approximately 2300 conforming and nonconforming documents. The CD-ROM also contains a hypertext-linked version of the SGML standard, ISO 8879. The sample documents are cross-referenced to the relevant sections of the standard. See the Exoterica listing in *Resource Guide B* for contact information.

SoftQuad provides a CD-ROM called *The SGML World Tour* that contains a dozen hyperlinked articles designed to answer questions from beginners, experts, and executives. It points to other resources and contains an acronym list with over 550 entries. Created from a single set of SGML source files, the CD-ROM can be used on UNIX, DOS, Microsoft Windows, and Apple Macintosh systems and can also be output to Braille and computer voice. See the SoftQuad listing in *Resource Guide B.*

CONFERENCES

Increasingly, conferences on subjects as diverse as judicial administration, hypertext, and medieval manuscripts have taken on the air of SGML conferences, and so it is quite impossible to list all conferences with a strong SGML component. The listing below includes the major yearly gatherings.

There is no trade show devoted exclusively to SGML-related technology, although SGML Open has held SGML Open for Business seminars at different sites which combine presentations and tabletop demonstrations. The vendor consortium has recently announced a new conference, Inter.Com.95, "focusing on business solutions and trends in the electronic and online publishing market." Check with SGML Open for future dates and locations.

User groups often sponsor local and regional events.

Graphic Communications Association (GCA)

The GCA sponsors many SGML events, including *the* annual conference called SGML '9X, usually held in Boston in December. These conferences are the primary gatherings for those advancing the theory and practice of SGML. There is a short time slot reserved for tabletop vendor displays and there are training workshops held in conjunction with the conference.

In addition to the U.S. conference, GCA runs an annual SGML conference in Europe in the spring, in Asia in the fall, and a conference on HyTime, held for the past two years in the summer in Vancouver, British Columbia. Documation is a GCA-sponsored conference in the spring of each year that focuses on document management and replaces the earlier TechDoc conferences.

GCA
100 Daingerfield Road
Alexandria, VA 22314-2888
703/519-8160
703/548-2867 (fax)
blake@access.digex.net

Seybold Seminars

The biannual Seybold Seminars, held in Boston in the spring and San Francisco in the fall, have the best collection of SGML vendors and related sessions of any conference not explicitly devoted to SGML. The seminar is actually a free trade exhibition and a paid conference program held concurrently, covering publishing, printing, and graphics. In recent years, many SGML vendors have chosen Seybold for product announcements and presentations.

Seybold Seminars
P.O. Box 5856
San Mateo, CA 94402-0856
800/488-2883
415/525-0199 (fax)

CALS

There are CALS conferences held around the globe, from Europe to the Far East. The U.S. CALS conference is held by the National Security Industry Association in the late fall of each year.

NSIA
1025 Connecticut Avenue NW #300
Washington, DC 20036
202/775-1440

Web-Related

Since May 1994, Web conferences have been held regularly. There is an International World Wide Web Conference Committee (IW3C2), and the latest information on conference schedules can be found at http://www.w3.org/hypertext/Conferences/. The groups currently organizing the conference are the Massachusetts Institute of Technology (MIT)—Laboratory for Computer Science and the Open Software Foundation (OSF) Research Institute. For those rare birds who need this information yet have no easy Web access, contact information for the cochairs is given here.

Albert Vezza
MIT Laboratory for Computer Science
545 Technology Square
Cambridge MA 02139
617/253-5851
617/258-8682 (fax)

Ira Goldstein
Open Software Foundation Research Institute
11 Cambridge Center
Cambridge, MA 02142-1405
617/621-7340

TEI-Related

There are many TEI-related conferences during the year. The main conferences are held by the sponsoring organizations, the Association for Computers and the Humanities (ACH), the Association for Computational Linguistics (ACL), and the Association for Literary and Linguistic Computing (ALLC). The TEI Steering Committee members for these organizations are listed here with affiliation, phone, and e-mail contact information. Full contact information for each of the Steering Committee members is provided on the TEI Web site, http://www.uic.edu/orgs/tei/ See also the general TEI contacts given below.

Susan Armstrong-Warwick (ACL)
ISSCO, University of Geneva
+41 22 705-7113
susan@divsun.unige.ch

David Barnard (ACH)
Computing & Information Science
Queen's University
613/545-6056
barnard@qucis.queensu.ca
http://www.qucis.queensu.ca:1999/~barnard

Susan Hockey (ALLC)
Center for Electronic Texts in the Humanities
908/932-1384
Hockey@Zodiac.rutgers.edu
http://cethmac.princeton.edu

Nancy M. Ide (ACH)
Department of Computer Science

Vassar College
914/437-5988
ide@vaxsar.vassar.edu

Judith Klavans (ACL)
914/478-5737
klavans@cs.columbia.edu
http://www.cs.columbia.edu/~klavans/home.html

Antonio Zampolli (ALLC)
Istituto di Linguistica Computazionale
+39 50 560481
glottolo@icnucevm.cnuce.cnr.it
glottolo@icnucevm.bitnet

In addition, there is a rich array of conferences on electronic text, a recent example of which is the Electric Scriptorium: Electronic Approaches to the Imaging, Transcription, Editing and Analysis of Medieval Manuscript Texts. This was announced as "A Physical/Virtual Conference," sponsored by the Calgary Institute for the Humanities and the Society for Early English and Norse Electronic Texts. Watch the TEI listserv, given below, for announcements.

GROUPS BUILDING COMMON DATA ARCHITECTURE

This section provides contact and background information for groups building a common document architecture in SGML. Table A.1 correlates initiatives with names, acronyms, and communities.

Table A.1 Collaborative initiatives in SGML

INITIATIVE NAME	FULL NAME	DTD NAME	COMMUNITY SERVED
ATA 2100	Air Transport Association Digital Data Standards for Aircraft Support	ATA 2100 (currently 12 DTDs, was ATA 100)	Civilian aviation
CALS	Continuous Acquisition and Life-cycle Support	CALS DTDs (there are many)	U.S. military, its suppliers, and other similar initiatives
Davenport	(A small town on the California coast)	DocBook	Technical software documentation
EDGAR	Electronic Data Gathering and Retrieval	EDGAR	Securities and Exchange Commission
EPSIG	Electronic Publishing Special Interest Group of the American Association of Publishers	ISO 12083 (was AAP DTD)	Journal, book, and magazine publishing
IBMIDDoc	International Business Machines Information Development Document Type	IBMIDDoc	Technical software documentation
ICADD	International Committee on Accessible Document Design	ICADD	All those providing information to print-disabled public
MERS	Multiagency Electronic Regulatory Submission (was known as CANDA)	CMC (Quality section of CANDA) in development	Pharmaceuticals, computer-assisted new drug applications
Pinnacles	Pinnacles	PCIS	Semiconductor manufacturers
SAE J2008	Society of Automotive Engineers J2008	SAE J2008	Automotive engineering
TCIF	Telecommunications Industry Forum	TIM (telecommunications industry markup)	Telecommunications
TEI	Text Encoding Initiative	TEI	Academic, scholarly research
TMC T2008	Truck Maintenance Council T2008	TMC T2008	American Trucking Association
UTF	Universal Text Format	UTF	News media
World Wide Web	Hypertext markup language	HTML2, HTML3	Internet users

Air Transport Association (ATA 2100)

This initiative used to be known as ATA 100, but the specification became so large that a new specification just for electronic document delivery was created. ATA 100 continues to regulate the content of the manuals. The new specification is ATA 2100 Digital Data Standards for Aircraft Support. It contains approximately 12 SGML DTDs, covering all civilian aircraft manuals, plus documentation on the DTDs, implementation guides, and a tag glossary.

The specification was published March 1, 1995. It is available on paper or CD-ROM and will be revised yearly. In addition to SGML, it covers standards for use of SQL and CGM.

Air Transport Association (ATA)
1301 Pennsylvania Avenue NW, Suite 1100
Washington, DC 20004
800/497-3326 (to order ATA publications)
http://air-transport.org/ata/home.htm

Continuous Acquisition and Life-cycle Support (CALS)

The CALS vision includes all weapons-system-related information from conception through deployment and specifies use of many standards in addition to SGML.

In the SGML realm, there is a repository and library of DTD modules and fragments. A growing number of individual DTDs and FOSIs address particular document types in particular services. The Interactive Electronic Technical Manual (IETM) is an important contribution to electronic text that has come out of the CALS effort. All these are available from the online NTIS FedWorld bulletin board:

703/321-3339 (modem)
http://www.fedworld.gov

The Industry Steering Group (ISG) is the civilian voice of CALS. The current chair is General James A. Abrahamson, now with Oracle Corporation.

Industry Steering Group
202/775-1440
202/775-2309

Elaine F. Litman
CALS Director
Department of Defense
703/756-2554
703/756-5682 (fax)

Hatd-copy CALS documents are available from:

National Technical Information Service
5285 Port Royal Road
Springfield, VA 22161
703/487-4650
703/321-8547 (fax)

See also CALS publications.

The Davenport Group

The Davenport Group promotes use of SGML for shared, linked technical documentation. There are currently two Davenport projects. The first is the ongoing maintenance and application of the DocBook DTD for software documentation. The DTD, its documentation, sample documents, and much discussion concerning its use and development are available from the O'Reilly & Associates Internet site.

The second project is the Davenport Advisory Standard for Hypermedia (DASH) which promotes use of HyTime architectural forms for compound documents created from dissimilar DTDs. In other words, if you do not use an industry standard DTD, such as DocBook, you can incorporate the DASH architectural forms so that your document can be indexed, cross-referenced, and linked to others using the same conventions, regardless of the specific document type employed.

The meetings of the Davenport group are open to all, but voting on revisions to the DocBook DTD is limited to sponsor members. As of this edition, the sponsors are Jon Bosak, Novell; Ralph Ferris, Fujitsu OSSI; Lee Fogal, Digital Equipment Corporation; Eduardo Gutentag, SunSoft; Steve Hiebert, Hewlett-Packard; Murray Maloney, SCO; Conleth O'Connell, HaL Computer Systems; Nancy Paisner, Hitachi Computer Products; and Terry Allen, O'Reilly & Associates.

There are directories for DocBook and DASH at the O'Reilly ftp site.

ftp://ftp.ora.com/pub/davenport/
http://www.ora.com/davenport/

Electronic Data Gathering and Retrieval (EDGAR)

The Securities and Exchange Commission (SEC) has been phasing in electronic filing of required reports since 1992. By May 1996, electronic filing will be mandatory for every corporation filing with the SEC. EDGAR filings can be by direct transmission, diskette, or magnetic tape.

The Internet EDGAR Dissemination project, which is subcontracted to Mead Data Central, makes available all electronic SEC filings as text files through ftp or e-mail. The same files are available with or without SGML headers. The markup in all cases is SGML-like even if not parsed. Mead also sells the service on subscription.

At the Town Hall site, MDC provides tagged sample files and tag descriptions. The DTD is available on request.

Mead Data Central, Inc.
4200 Wilson Boulevard, Suite 950
Arlington, VA 22203

EDGAR Dissemination Customer Service
800/542-9246
http://www.town.hall.org
gopher.town.hall.org
mail@town.hall.org

Electronic Publishing Special Interest Group (EPSIG)

EPSIG is a membership organization responsible for development and maintenance of the ISO Standard, 12083:1993, a DTD initially known as the AAP DTD. Originally sponsored by OCLC (Online Computer Library Center), it is now managed collaboratively by three groups: the Association of American Publishers (AAP), the Graphic Communications Association Research Institute (GCARI), and McAffe & McAdam, Ltd.

EPSIG runs a series of training sessions on the DTD.

EPSIG Membership Office
c/o GCARI
P.O. Box 25707
Alexandria, VA 22313-5707
703/519-8184
703/548-2867 (fax)

IBMIDDoc

IBMIDDoc was written by Wayne Wohler and Eliot Kimber for IBM (Kimber is now at Passage Systems). From the readme file in the SGML archive at ifi.uio.no in pub/SGML/IBMIDDOC:

> The IBMIDDoc application is designed to be as flexible as possible. Toward this end it is designed to be both extensible and subsettable...The basic premise of IBMIDDoc is that concrete applications are unified by the use of common archi-

tectures, which enables much processing to be defined at the architecture level rather than at the concrete GI [generic identifier or element] level, making it possible to reuse the same base processing for a variety of special-purpose applications.

The DTD and documentation are copyrighted by IBM but are available without charge, and IBM encourages their use, hoping to facilitate information interchange with clients, customers, and suppliers. It was designed for software documentation and will be extended to cover hardware documentation.

For more information, see the SGML archive and numerous threads in comp.text.sgml or contact Wayne Wohler (contact by e-mail strongly preferred!).

Wayne L. Wohler
Dept. 5BN/026N
ISSC Corporation
5600 North 63rd Street
Boulder, CO 80314
wohler@vnet.ibm.com
IBMMAIL: USIB29WX@IBMMAIL

International Committee on Accessible Document Design (ICADD)

ICADD was formed in October 1992. The ICADD DTD is a simple DTD, within a few tags of HTML2. It maps complex structural markup or format markup to media such as Braille, voice synthesis, or large print that are more accessible by the print-disabled. The ICADD markup can be incorporated into any DTD as SDAs (SGML disability attributes) to automate the conversion to these alternate media. (See the description of ICADD in use at UCLA in Chapter 4.) There are public scripts available to convert ICADD/SDA markup to Braille and other formats. ICADD is also part of ISO 12083 (see EPSIG above).

George Kerscher, Director, Research and Development, Recording for the Blind and Dyslexic (RFB), chairs the committee. His e-mail address is cbfb_gwk@selway.umt.edu and the e-mail address for ICADD is icadd@asuvm.inre.asu.edu. The general contact address for RFB is:

Recording for the Blind and Dyslexic
20 Roszel Road
Princeton, NJ 08540
800/221-4792
609/452-0606
609/520-7990 (fax)

Multiagency Electronic Regulatory Submission Project (MERS, CANDA)

The MERS Project is an international effort initiated in January 1994 and composed of representatives of the Drugs Directorate of Health Canada (HPB), the Food and Drug Administration (FDA) of the United States, the Therapeutic Goods Administration (TGA) of Australia, the Medical Products Agency (MPA) of Sweden, and the Medicines Evaluation Board (MEB) of the Netherlands.

The objective of the group is to develop standards for submission, review, and management of electronic regulatory information. The first DTD, covering the Quality (Chemistry and Manufacturing, CMC) portion of a new drug application, was in prototype in July 1995. When the CMC DTD is complete, the group expects to develop DTDs for the clinical and safety sections of new drug applications.

This effort follows earlier work supported by the GCA and several pharmaceutical companies which demonstrated the feasibility of computer-assisted new drug applications using SGML. That effort was called CANDA using the generic name for electronic drug applications.

PharmaSoft of Sweden posts project updates on http://www.pharmasoft.se

HPB in Canada provides project management.

Robert Kapitany, Ph.D., Project Manager
Bureau of Human Prescription Drugs
Health and Welfare Canada
Health Protection Branch
1600 Scott Street, Holland Cross, Tower B, 3rd Floor
Ottawa, Ontario K1A1B8
Canada
613/941-1351
613-953-5840 (fax)
bkapitany@hpb.hwc.ca

In the United States, contact:

Carl J. Berninger, Ph.D.
U.S. Food & Drug Administration
Stategic Systems Staff, Office of the Commissioner
16B-45 HF-21
5600 Fishers Lane
Rockville, MD 20857
301/857-1461
301/594-0829 (fax)
berningc@fdacd.bitnet
cberning@cpcug.org

The Pinnacles Group

The Pinnacles Group is a consortium of five semiconductor manufacturers who joined together to write the Pinnacles Component Information Standard (PCIS), an exchange DTD for manufacturers, suppliers, and their clients. The initiative is described in detail in the Intel case study in Chapter 4.

For information on the Pinnacles Component Information Standard, contact:

The Pinnacles Secretariat
c/o The ATLIS Consulting Group
6011 Executive Boulevard
Rockville, MD 20852
301/816-4231
301/468-6758 (fax)
pcis@access.digex.com

For information regarding membership or other aspects of the Pinnacles Group, contact:

Bob Yencha
Sr. Systems Analyst
National Semiconductor
207/775-8736
b_yencha%spc.dnet@gpo.nsc.com

Society of Automotive Engineers (J2008)

SAE J2008 was recently approved as a Draft Technical Report. It was written by the Data Model Working Group, a task force of the Vehicle Electrical and Electronic Diagnostics Committee. There are no documentation standards in the automotive industry comparable to those in military and aircraft manufacturing, so this DTD is not document-based. Instead, this DTD is based on a relational data model built according to the basic categories of automotive maintenance such as make, model, year, system, and subsystem. The intent of the standard is that individual service providers will map their own document type definitions to SAE J2008.

SAE J2008 is copyrighted by the SAE and will not be released in the public domain. The specification includes a family of standards with character-sets and graphics as well as documentation, samples, and conventions for use of the DTD. It will remain a Draft Technical Report until 1998, at which time it will come up for ballot as a permanent standard.

The Truck Maintenance Council of the American Trucking Association sponsors a similar initiative called TMC T2008.

Publications can be ordered from:

SAE Customer Service
412/776-4970

For SAE-related information, contact:

Kristi Hansen
Technical Standards Developer
Society for Automotive Engineering
3001 West Big Beaver Road, Suite 320
Troy, MI 48084
810/649-0420, ext. 3101

For SGML-related information, contact:

SAE, Data Model Working Group
Dianne Kennedy, Chair
SGML Resource Center
146 North End Avenue, Suite 100
Elmhurst, IL 60126
708/941-8197
708/941-8196 (fax)
dken@mcs.com

Telecommunications Industry Forum (TCIF)

The Information Products Interchange (IPI) committee of TCIF has selected SGML as the document interchange standard in the telecommunications industry. TCIF is affiliated with the Alliance for Telecommunications Industry Solutions (ATIS). The Telecommunications Industry Markup (TIM) DTD is the latest version of the TCIF standard. As this goes to print, the DTD is in "draft for ballot" status and is being tested by the IPI committee.
A copy of the latest TIM DTD can be retrieved from ftp://ftp.bellcore.com/pub/world/TCIF

TCIF
1200 G Street NW, Suite 500
Washington, DC 20005

Diane Tucker, Chair
IPI Committee
BellSouth Telecommunications, Inc.
205/977-7337
205/977-2246 (fax)

Text Encoding Initiative (TEI)

The TEI is sponsored by the Association for Computers and the Humanities (ACH), the Association for Computational Linguistics (ACL), and the Association for Literary and Linguistic Computing (ALLC) and is funded by these groups as well as by public and private foundation grants. Management is by steering committee of the sponsors, and there is an advisory board of scholars.

TEI-related documents available online or from the editors have recorded the development of the initiatives and each release of the guidelines, P3 being the current release. The full bibliographic entry for the print edition of P3 reads:

> ACH/ACL/ALLC (Association for Computers and the Humanities, Association for Computational Linguistics, Association for Literary and Linguistic Computing). Guidelines for Electronic Text Encoding and Interchange (TEI P3). Edited by C.M. Sperberg-McQueen and Lou Burnard. Chicago: ACH/ACL/ALLC, April 8 1994. 2 volumes, xxvi + 1290 pages.

The guidelines are also available online in a variety of formats, including Web-accessible hypertext, from a variety of sites.

The online sources for the P3 Guidelines include:

http://www.uic.edu/orgs/tei/
ftp://info.ex.ac.uk/pub/SGML/tei
ftp://ftp-tei.uic.edu/pub/tei/
ftp://ftp.ifi.uio.no/pub/SGML/TEI/

To get the guidelines sent as e-mail, send a message to listserv@uicvm.uic.edu with the message line: `get P3SG DOC` For the listing, send the message line: `index tei-1` For the entire set of P3 files: `get P3ALL $PACKAGE`.

The editors of the guidelines are:

C. M. Sperberg-McQueen
Computer Center (M/C 135)
University of Illinois at Chicago
1940 West Taylor Street, Room 124
Chicago, IL 60612-7352
312/413-0317
312/996-6834 (fax)
u35395@uicvm.uic.edu
u35395@uicvm.bitnet

Lou Burnard
Oxford University Computing Services
13 Banbury Road
Oxford OX2 6NN
United Kingdom
+44 1865 273238, 273200
+44 1865 273275 (fax)
lou@vax.ox.ac.uk

Steering committee members from the three sponsoring organizations and their contacts are listed under *TEI-Related Conferences*.

Truck Maintenance Council (T2008)

The Truck Maintenance Council is the maintenance arm of the American Trucking Association. The Council's DTD, T2008, is closely modeled on the SAE J2008 DTD with these differences: The TMC DTD incorporates HyTime linking, a different numbering scheme, and different navigational capabilities required by the complexity of truck maintenance. The standard is being developed by the S.5 Task Force which has groups working on the DTD and on data modeling. The Task Force expects to publish the standard by June 1996. The chair of the Task Force is Jim Cade. For information on the DTD, contact Thom Locke.

Thom Locke
AI^2, Inc.
Medallion Center, Suite 8
Merrimack, NH 03054
603/429-3003
603/429-3339 (fax)
thoml@ix.netcom.com

Universal Text Format (UTF)

The UTF is an industry DTD intended for news services, newspapers, and news archives. This DTD has a simple tag structure with much accommodation for tagging of content. This is a draft (as of this writing) standard of the Newspaper Association of America, International Press Telecommunications Council.

International Press Telecommunications Council
Attention: David Allen
8 Sheet Street
Windsor, Berkshire SL4 1BG
United Kingdom
+44 1753 833728
+44 1753 833750 (fax)
100321.2156@compuserve.com

Newspaper Association of America
Attention: John W. Iobst
11600 Sunrise Valley Drive
Reston, VA 22091
703/648-1000
703/648-1333 (fax)

World Wide Web (HTML)

The World Wide Web is a set of communication and data standards that make possible a global, multimedia hypertext on the Internet. The data standard for the World Wide Web is hypertext markup language (HTML), which is an SGML application.

Originally, HTML was not tightly controlled but, with the proliferation of the Web and demands for greater performance and higher standards of interchange, a group was formed to standardize the DTD. This group is the W3 Consortium (W3C) run by the Laboratory for Computer Science at the Massachusetts Institute of Technology in collaboration with the European Laboratory for Particle Physics (CERN) and the French National Institute for Research in Computing and Automation (INRIA).

HTML2 is considered a codification of current practice and is just now being officially balloted. At the same time, HTML3 is already under test and contains many rich additions in terms of math, tables, and presentation capabilities. Several applications that take advantage of these new capabilities are available in beta release. The sites below contain all the contact information for the latest draft of both specifications as well as background information, discussion groups, beta applications, and documentation.

http://www.w3.org
http://web.mit.edu
http://www.cern.ch
http://www.inria.fr

MIT Laboratory for Computer Science
545 Technology Square
Cambridge MA 02139
617/253-5851
617/258-8682 (fax)
http://www.lcs.mit.edu

For more on HTML and the Web, see the case studies of the Electronic Volcano and Intel in Chapter 4.

ONLINE RESOURCES

Most, but not all, of these require Internet access, at least for e-mail. Some, like the CALS BBS, can be accessed either on the Internet or through direct modem dial-up.

The online *ABCD... Resource Guides,* an updated version of this guide plus the guide to tools and vendors can be found at http://www.thomson.com under Web Extras.

Newsgroup and Archive

The most important online discussion group for SGML is comp.text.sgml, moderated and maintained by Erik Naggum on facilities provided by the University of Oslo.

The archive for comp.text.sgml, also maintained by Naggum since March of 1991, is at ftp://ftp.ifi.uio.no in /pub/SGML/comp.text.sgml. Access the archive through WAIS as comp.text.sgml.src In addition to the Usenet discussion, the archive contains the full text of major articles (see /pub/SGML/comp.text.sgml/features/) and several publicly available software programs, including parsers and editors, sample documents, and DTDs. A mirror site is ftp://sunsite.unc.edu/pub/packages/SGML (see the Oslo mirror subdirectory).

If you have e-mail, but no access to the Usenet, you can receive and post articles using Naggum's mail-to-news and news-to-mail service. To subscribe, send a note to comp-text-sgml-request@naggum.no.

Robin Cover's Resource Directory

This Web site maintains an extensive directory of resources, both on and off the Internet. While the site is supported in part by SoftQuad and the Summer

Institute of Linguistics, much of the information and the links are contributed voluntarily, so that the coverage, while generally good, is necessarily uneven.

In its own words,

> This WWW document attempts to embed links to the SGML archives within descriptive prose, and within a subject-oriented document hierarchy. The links point to other WWW servers, GOPHER servers, and ftp servers, as well as to important SGML documents archived locally. The SGML Web Page also includes an annotated and linked bibliography for SGML, with over 500 entries.

The latest edition of the Cover bibliography on SGML is available on the server. That and the extensive scope of this directory have made this an important HTML site for SGML information:

http://www.sil.org/sgml/sgml.html

Tools

Steve Pepper's *Whirlwind Guide to SGML Tools* is a periodically-updated guide to tools and vendors. It lists tools by category and gives contact information for each company. The coverage of European companies is extensive. The Guide is available in HTML and text format at http://www.falch.no/~pepper/sgmltool/ and other mirror sites.

Another good source for online information on vendors is the SGML Open home page at http://www.sgmlopen.org. All members who have home pages are linked directly to this site.

This guide and the guide to vendors and tools in *Resource Guide B* of this book are available in SGML at http://www.thomson.com under Web Extras. We plan to update the online guides regularly and may extend them to areas not covered in the print edition, so check the Web site for the latest information.

Listservs

Listservs are discussion groups that communicate through Internet e-mail sent to a distribution list. There are many listservs dedicated to technical subjects or to keeping up with one type of product. I have included only those with the most general appeal.

Caution: There are always two addresses associated with a listserv. One is the address for submissions. Whatever is sent to this address is distributed to the entire list. The other is the administrative address. This is the proper destination for requests to be added to, or deleted from, the list.

SGML-l

This list has sporadic activity. To subscribe, send the command `subscribe sgml-l YOURNAME` in an e-mail message to listserv@dhdurz1.bitnet or to listserv@vm.urz.uni-heidelberg.de

Davenport/DocBook

This list has much activity and ongoing discussion concerning the development and deployment of the DocBook DTD. To subscribe to the mailing list, send an e-mail message to listproc@online.ora.com with the command `subscribe davenport`

TEI

To subscribe to the mailing list, send mail with the line `subscribe tei-l your.name` to listserv@uicvm.bitnet or to listserv@uicvm.uic.edu. The list itself is tei-l@uicvm.cc.uic.edu.

WWW-HTML

This is a general discussion group about HTML. To subscribe, send mail to listserv@info.cern.ch with the message `SUBSCRIBE WWW-HTML your full name` in the body of the message. The list itself is www-html@info.cern.ch and there is an archive at http://gummo.stanford.edu/html/hypermail/www-html-1994q2.index.html.

SGML Newswire

The Newswire is a public-relations and news distribution service provided by Avalanche (Interleaf) which mails notices of significant industry events and articles to people in the news media. The Newswire distributes a periodically updated "hitlist" of contacts for stories or case studies about SGML. The current list manager is Sue Martin-Gamble. To subscribe, send e-mail to the address below.

303/449-5032 Ext. 109
303/449-3246 (fax)
sgmlinfo@avalanche.com

ORGANIZATIONS

Users' Groups

The International SGML Users' Group was started in 1984 and now has chapters in Australia, Belgium, Canada, Denmark, Finland, France, Germany, Ireland, Israel, Italy, the Netherlands, Norway, Sweden, Switzerland, and the United Kingdom, as well as at least ten local and regional chapters in the United States. There are two Special Interest Groups—SIGhyper and the European Workgroup on SGML.

SGML Users' Group
Pamela Gennusa
P.O. Box 361
Great Western Way
Swindon, Wiltshire SN5 7BF
United Kingdom
+44 1793 512515
+44 1793 512516 (fax)
plg@dpsl.co.uk

There is no official point of contact in the United States, but the following is given for New York:

SGML Forum of New York
Bowling Green Station
P.O. Box 803
New York, NY 10274-0803
212/691-4463
212/691-1821 (fax)

Many academic, trade, and industry associations now have SIGs (Special Interest Groups) in SGML.

SGML Open

SGML Open is a vendor consortium dedicated to educating the public about SGML and coordinating technical issues between vendors. In its own words, the mission of the consortium is to "accelerate the adoption of SGML, especially within commercial industries."

Consortium membership has grown rapidly since its establishment in January of 1994. From an initial base of 30 sponsor members, in a year and a half, it has grown to 41 sponsors, 13 associate members, and 4 subscribers. Membership fees are on a sliding scale, according to company revenues and grade of membership.

Recent members include Novell, one of the world's largest mainstream software companies, and Corel Corporation, a supplier of desktop publishing tools.

The SGML Open Web page is linked directly to members' home pages.

Mary Laplante, Executive Director
910 Beaver Grade Road, #3008
Coraopolis, PA 15108
412/264-4258
sgmlopen@prepnet.org
http://www.sgmlopen.org

The Graphic Communication Association (GCA)

GCA has supported the development of SGML since before SGML was SGML. It underwrote some of the original work by the convener of the ISO committee, James Mason, and provided the framework for some of the original collaborative work that went into the draft standard. The GCA Research Institute continues this tradition with its sponsorship of HyTime, ISO 12083, registration of public identifiers, and other efforts.

The conferences and training offered by GCA are listed in those categories above.

Norm Scharpf, President
GCA
100 Daingerfield Road
Alexandria, VA 22314-2888
703/519-8160
703/548-2867 (fax)

The International Organization for Standards (ISO)

The Internation Organization for Standards is the publisher of ISO 8879:1988, *the standard.* The group within ISO responsible for the standard is called ISO/IEJ JTC 1/SC 18/WG 8, sometimes abbreviated to Working Group 8. The charge of the group is:

To produce standards for languages and resources for the description and processing of compound and hypermedia documents, including:

- Standard Generalized Markup Language and support facilities;

- Document processing architecture and formatting for documents represented in SGML;

- Final-form document architecture and Standard Page Description Language;

- Font architecture, interchange format, and services; and

- Hypermedia document structuring language and application resources.

For more information on the WG8, see:

http://www.ornl.gov/sgml/WG8/wg8home.htm
ftp://ftp.ornl.gov/pub/sgml/WG8

The convener of the group is:

Dr. James D. Mason
Oak Ridge National Laboratory
Information Management Services
Bldg. 2506, M.S. 6302, P.O. Box 2008
Oak Ridge, TN 37831-6302
615/574-6973
615/574-6983 (fax)
masonjd@ornl.gov

The standard itself is available electronically on *The Compleat SGML* from Exoterica (see *Publications* for information on the CD-ROM and *Resource Guide B* for Exoterica contact information). To obtain a print copy, send $38 to ISO or contact your local standards organization. The standard is also incorporated in its entirety in the Goldfarb *SGML Handbook.*

International Organization for Standards (ISO)
1 Rue de Varembe
Case Postale 56
CH-1211
Geneva 20
Switzerland
+41 22 242340
+41 22 333430 (fax)

Alternate sources for the standard within the United States are:

American National Standards Institute (ANSI)
11 West 42nd Street
13th floor
New York, NY 10036
212/642-4900
http://www.ansi.org

National Institute of Standards and Technology (NIST)
U.S. Department of Commerce
Technology Administration
Gaithersburg, MD 20899-0001
301/975-2000

MISCELLANEOUS

Groups Standardizing on SGML

This list grows daily. The items below are selected for the express purpose of impressing people with how widespread is the use of SGML. This list is by no means comprehensive and should under no circumstances be read as a list of *all* the groups, companies, and institutions using SGML. Furthermore, inclusion on this list does not imply that the entity uses SGML exclusively, but indicates only that it is employed for a significant portion of the group's information resource processing, publishing, or archiving.

U.S. Government Agencies

Department of Energy
Environmental Protection Agency
Library of Congress
Government Printing Office
Patent and Trademark Office
Internal Revenue Service
Treasure Department
Social Security Agency
Defense Mapping Agency

In addition, all aspects of defense and defense documentation, including the Defense Logistics Agency, use SGML.

The IRS was one of the first government agencies to adopt SGML. (Yes, there is a DTD for your 1040!) A random sample of documents available from the IRS in SGML includes publications such as *Withholding of Tax on Nonresident Aliens and Foreign Corporations* and *Tax Guide for Aliens, Scholarships and Fellowships*.

For use of SGML in the judiciary, see the case studies on the Utah Administrative Office of the Courts and Butterworth Legal Publishers in Chapter 4.

It is not known if the National Security Agency (NSA) has adopted SGML in any capacity but, in 1995, it assigned an employee to work with SGML Open to become familiar with the industry and the technology.

Other Government Agencies

International CALS has contacts throughout Europe as well as in Japan, South Korea, Taiwan, and Australia. FUSION (Canada) is a joint government/industry venture with a CALS-like agenda. The acronym stands for Focused Use of Standards for Integrating Organizations and Networks.

In addition, there are initiatives under way at the European and Japanese patent offices, the Australian Tax Office, and the Australian Stock Exchange; there are several government initiatives in Taiwan; and Singapore has adopted SGML as its national data standard.

Companies, Corporations, and Institutions

The companies/organizations/projects profiled in case studies in this book are:

Adams & Hamilton
Butterworth Legal Publishers
Canadian Code Centre
Columbia University Press
The Electronic Volcano
Ericsson, Inc.
InfoUCLA and ICADD
Intel Corporation
Microsoft's Cinemania
Publications International, Ltd.
Standard & Poor's
Sybase
Utah Administrative Office of the Courts
The Women Writers Project

Academic institutions and presses with major initiatives in SGML are too numerous to mention. They range from the Royal Institute of Technology in Stockholm to the University Press of New England. At this stage, there are few major colleges or universities without an ongoing SGML project.

The following private and public corporations are among those that make use of SGML:

Aérospatiale
Allen-Bradley
American Chemical Society
American Mathematical Society
American Physical Society
AT&T Global Business Communications Systems
Bellcore
Boeing Computer Services
Boston Computer Society Magazines
British Airways
Bull S.A.
Bureau of National Affairs

Canadian Standards Association
Candle Corp.
Caterpillar Inc.
Clark Boardman & Callahan
Commerce Clearing House
Cray Research, Inc.
Cubic Defense Systems
Diebold Inc.
Digital Equipment Corporation
Dow Jones & Co.
Elsevier Science
Fluke Corporation
Ford Motor Co.
Freightliner Corp.
Fujitsu, Fujitsu America, Inc.
GE Aircraft Engines
GE Medical Systems
General Dynamics
General Motors
Grolier Inc.
GTE Government Systems
Hewlett-Packard
Hitachi America Ltd.
Honeywell
Houghton Mifflin Co.
IBM Corporation
IEEE (Institute of Electric and Electronic Engineers)
Intergraph Corporation
Lawrence Livermore National Lab
Lufthansa
Mead Data Central
MITRE Corporation
Mobil Oil
Motorola Government Systems & Technology Group
Nihon Unitec Co. Ltd.
Northern Telecom
Novell, Inc.
Oscar Mayer Foods Corporation
Polaris Industries
Pratt & Whitney
Recording for the Blind and Dyslexic
Semiconductor Research Corp.

Shell International Petroleum
Silicon Graphics, Inc.
Simon & Schuster
Tandem Computers, Inc.
Teradyne
Thomson Professional Publishing
TRW
United Airlines
Uniscope
US Air
Wessels, Arnold & Henderson
Xerox Corporation

Archives Created in SGML

A catalog of the work available in SGML, either in the public domain or published commercially, would require an entire volume on its own. I have included a sample here to indicate the types of work available.

British National Corpus (BNC)

The BNC has just been released for the European Union on three CD-ROMs containing over 100 million words from over 4000 different British English texts. Each text has been tagged with TEI-compliant SGML. The design of the data favors linguistic analysis—each word has a part-of-speech tag automatically assigned, with software developed for the project by the Unit for Computer Research in the English Language at Lancaster University.

The work was produced by a coalition of dictionary publishers and research groups over a period of three years. In a statement released by the group:

> It provides a unique and authoritative view of the state of the English language today, with carefully balanced representation of as many different varieties of English as possible. It can be used to exercise NLP systems of all kinds, as a fertile source of real life examples for language learners, or simply to explore the way the language is currently used.

British National Corpus
Oxford University Computing Services
13 Banbury Road
Oxford, OX2 6NN
United Kingdom
+44 1865 273280
+44 1865 273275 (fax)
natcorp@oucs.ox.ac.uk
http://info.ox.ac.uk/bnc

Human Relations Area Files

Twenty-two institutions sponsor this Yale University-affiliated archive which includes over 1 million pages of information on human culture indexed into over 700 categories. In the 1960s, the HRAF resembled a card catalog for a good-sized library. The project has since outgrown the bounds of conventional paper indexing and is comfortably housed in SGML.

Electronic HRAF 800/520-4723
hrafsir@yalevm.cis.yale.edu

Novell Technical Documentation

Novell Electronic Publishing has made available some of its documentation sets without charge on the Internet, together with a free version of the DynaText 2.2 viewer for Windows. In addition, the server contains the Hebrew Bible, the New Testament, the Book of Mormon, the Koran, and the complete plays of William Shakespeare in a simple SGML markup created from public domain ASCII files that can be viewed with the same browser.

The document sets can be installed on a local drive or a network. When installed, the religious texts require 21 Mbytes and the Shakespeare about 24 Mbytes.

To download the viewer and the collections, ftp to ftp://ftp.novell.com and look in the /pub/epub directories. The files and viewer are also available in the novlepub area of Netcom.[1]

The Patrologia Latina Database

Published privately by Chadwick-Healey, the electronic database covers 2000 years of the theological writing of the Latin Fathers to the thirteenth century. The database is encoded in TEI-conformant SGML, which the editors identify as a critical element in its design as it permits searches on single words and phrases in context, in proximity, and through Boolean operators.

Chadwyck-Healey Inc.
1101 King Street
Alexandria, VA 22314
800/752-0515
703/683-7589 (fax)

---

[1]View these same files in Panorama at http://www.oclc.org:5046/oclc/research/panorama.

The Women Writers Project

See the sketch of the Women Writers Project (WWP) in Chapter 4. The URL for the WWP World Wide Web page is

http://www.stg.brown.edu/projects/wwp/wwp_home.html

Text requests and comments can be e-mailed to the WWP office at wwp_orders@brown.edu or sent by surface mail to:

Women Writers Project
Text Requests
P.O. Box 1841
Brown University
Providence, RI 02912

Resource Guide B
Tools and Vendors

This is a selected guide to SGML-related tools and vendors. As with *Resource Guide A*, I have concentrated on those tools and vendors with a substantial presence in the United States. While this omits many resources available to the European community, it permits me to provide a more informed guide for readers. The online version of this guide will be updated regularly, so check the Thomson Web Extras (www.thomson.com) for the latest releases. See the online tool resources mentioned in *Resource Guide A* for a wider selection of European companies.

All lists of tools and vendors incorporate editorial decisions about what to include and how to categorize the inclusions. Tools and whole classes of tools evolve rapidly, especially those at the center of the move to electronic information delivery, as these tools are. The primary criterion I have applied for inclusion in this list is the ability to read and parse SGML syntax. Many excellent information managers and viewers can make use of SGML-encoded data, but have no special provision for doing so. These products are not included in this list. Where applicable, I have indicated if a product incorporates a validating SGML parser.

Tools that require a second product as a base are listed with that base product as an add-on except where the base product is offered by a different vendor.

I have included Web products that recognize SGML as well as HTML and products that are HTML-only versions of SGML-capable tools.

The product tables have summary product information arranged by category and alphabetically within each category. An alphabetical list of vendors and a summary of noncommercial software follow the product tables.

PRODUCT TABLES

The products are listed alphabetically, grouped in the following categories:

- Data Design and Validation
- Editors
- Conversion and Transformation
- Information Management
- Composition Systems
- Viewers
- Integration Platforms
- Web-Specific Tools

In addition to the columns indicating availability in Windows and Macintosh PC platforms, I have abbreviated some manufacturers platforms as follows:

AIX, MVS	IBM RS6000, minicomputer, and mainframe operating systems	Int	Intergraph Clipper
DEC	Digital Equipment Corporation VAX/VMS or Alpha workstation operating systems	SCO	Santa Cruz Operation Unix
DG	Data General	SGI	Silicon Graphics IRIX
HP	Hewlett-Packard HP-UX	Sun	Solaris, Sun OS

Data Design and Validation

	VP	Win	Mac	Unix & other platforms	Notes, add-ons, requirements	Vendor
Balise	✔	✔		AIX, DEC, Bull, DOS, Sun	An SGML processing tool; developer and runtime; API; C/T	AIS
HyMinder	✔			Linux, Sun	A HyTime engine; validates, processes HyTime DTDs, documents; object-oriented API	Techno
Mark-It	✔	✔		AIX, DEC, DOS, HP, MIPS, Sun	Full or runtime versions; parser and document analyzer; C/T; Write-It add-on editor for PC, Sun	Sema
Near & Far	✔	✔		HP, Sun	Graphic tool to view, write, revise DTDs; CADE add-on is Lotus Notes document analysis template	Microstar
Near & Far Lite	✔	✔			DTD viewing only	Microstar
OmniMark	✔		✔	AIX, DEC, DOS, HP, Int, OS/2, SCO, SGI, Sun	Scripting language plus validating parser; C/T	Exoterica
ZifTech Viewer	✔	✔			Graphic DTD viewer	ZIF

VP: Validating Parser   (x): Not released   C/T: Conversion and transformation   C: Client

Editors

	VP	Win	Mac	Unix & other platforms	Notes, add-ons, requirements	Vendor
Adept Editor	✔	✔		AIX, HP, OSF, Sun, Ultrix	Add-on for DTD, FOSI editing, compilation; add-ons announced with support for HTML and for electronic review	ArborText
Author/Editor	✔	✔	✔	AIX, DEC, HP, Int, SGI, Sun	Sculptor for scripting; Rules Builder for DTD compilation	SoftQuad
ClearCheck				Ultrix	Enforces controlled English; integrates with Adept Editor (ArborText) or standalone on DEC Ultrix	Carnegie
ESSE	✔	(✔)			Edits, validates DTD in text format	Lexicon
FrameBuilder		✔	✔	AIX, HP, SGI, Sun	Application development tools include parser; superseded by FrameMaker+SGML	Frame
FrameMaker+ SGML	✔	(✔)	(✔)	(Sun, HP, AIX)	Drawing tools, composition, exports PDF, HTML; link and entity reference management	Frame
Grif SGML Editor	✔	✔	✔	Sun, AIX, DEC, HP	API for composition formats; can upgrade to Grif Symposia	Grif
Grif Symposia	✔	✔	✔	Motif	SGML or HTML output; edit, update documents on remote server	Grif
InContext	✔	✔			Uses Microsoft Excel for table editing; includes DTD editor, spelling, grammar checker	InContext
Intellitag	✔	✔			Write-to-convert, superseded by WordPerfect add-on	Novell
Interleaf 5 <SGML>	✔			AIX, DEC, DG, HP, Sun	Requires Interleaf 5 and Toolkit; includes composition, add-ons for CALS publishing, conversion	Interleaf

Editors (continued)

	VP	Win	Mac	Unix & other platforms	Notes, add-ons, requirements	Vendor
Microsoft SGML Author for Word	✔	✔			Requires Microsoft Word 6; setup maps styles to DTD; conversion parses, annotates original document; third party add-ons for input conversion (Interleaf Sure Style); SGML cleanup (SoftQuad Enactor)	Microsoft
Near & Far Author	✔	(✔)			Requires Microsoft Word 6; composes pages	Microstar
Smart Editor	✔	✔			Requires DTD-specific integration; database-model editing	Auto-Graphics
SoftQuad Enactor	✔	(✔)			Requires Microsoft SGML Author for Word	SoftQuad
TagWizard	✔	✔			Requires Microsoft Word 6; composes pages; also edits HTML	NICE technologies
WordPerfect 6.1 for Windows SGML Edition	✔	(✔)			Produces composed pages; DTD editor, interactive validation	Novell
WriterStation	✔	✔		OS/2	API toolkit add-on	Frame

VP: Validating Parser   (x): Not released   C/T: Conversion and transformation   C: Client   ✔: Conversion step required

Conversion and Transformation

	VP	Win	Mac	Unix & other platforms	Notes, add-ons, requirements	Vendor
Balise	✔	✔		AIX, Bull, DEC, DOS, Sun	An SGML processing tool; DynaText/Balise Toolkit will provide composition; DDV	AIS
Context-Wise Auto Tagging Engine		✔		DOS	Parser optional	U.S. Lynx
Data Conversion Lab	✔	✔	✔	✔	Service bureau; custom software	DCL
Docucon	✔	✔	✔	✔	Service bureau	Docucon
DynaTag		✔			Optional style editor can generate DynaText style sheets; batch mode on some Unix platforms	EBT
FastTag	✔	✔		AIX, DEC, DOS, HP, OS/2, SGI, Sun	Converts to/from multiple formats	Avalanche
Hammer	✔	✔		AIX, DEC, DOS, HP, OS/2, SGI, Sun	Transformation tool; library of output filters	Avalanche
Lynx Autotransformer		✔		DOS	Parser, editor, tape-handling, graphics modules	U.S. Lynx
OmniMark	✔			AIX, DEC, DOS, HP, Int, OS/2, SCO, SGI, Sun	Programming language; DDV	Exoterica
Passage Hub	✔			SGI, Sun	Conversion with feedback, but without Passage Pro's interactive debugging	Passage
Sema	✔			all Unix, also DEC, DOS	Full or runtime versions; Write-It add-on editor for PC, Sun; DDV	Sema

Conversion and Transformation (continued)

	VP	Win	Mac	Unix & other platforms	Notes, add-ons, requirements	Vendor
SGML Instance Imager		✔		DOS	CALS SGML to Frame composition format; requires customization	U.S. Lynx
TagWrite	✔			DOS	Also bundled with Corel Ventura	Zandar
SureStyle		✔			Requires Microsoft Word 6; applies style for pre-conversion to SGML Author for Word and HTML	Avalanche

VP: Validating Parser (x): Not released C/T: Conversion and transformation C: Client

Information Management

	VP	Win	Mac	Unix & other platforms	Notes, add-ons, requirements	Vendor
ActiveServer	✔	C		AIX, DEC, SCO, Sun	ActiveSearch is the Windows client	Active Systems
Astoria	✔	(C)		(Sun)	Object-oriented management with search-and-retrieval; integrates any editor	Xerox / XSoft
Basis SGMLserver	✔	C		AIX, DEC, HP, MVS, MIPS, Sun, SGI	Relational search, query, retrieval built on BASISplus engine	IDI
DT-Balise	✔	✔		(some Unix, DOS)	Manages DynaText books;	AIS
DynaBase		(C)		(AIX, HP, SGI, Sun)	Workflow and document management; Balise (AIS) add-on for composition; ArborText add-on for editing; builds DynaText indexes	EBT
Information Manager	✔	(C)		(AIX, HP, OSF, Sun)	With customization, integrates writing, review, query, workflow, data management	Texcel
Open Text	✔	C	C	DEC, HP, IBM, SCO, SGI, Sun	Operates on native SGML; can index other formats as well	Open Text
Parlance Document Manager	✔	C		AIX, DEC, Sun	Manages data and workflow	Xyvision
Passage Pro	✔	(✔)		SGI, Sun	Workflow and data management integrates any editor, composition, conversion tools	Passage
SGML/Store	✔			Sun	Automatic database loading, search with query engine, uses Balise for transformation and processing	AIS
WorkSmart	✔	C		HP, DEC, Sun	Work management uses SGML	InfoDesign

VP: Validating Parser   (x): Not released   C/T: Conversion and transformation   C: Client

Composition Systems

	SGML input	Win	Mac	Unix & other platforms	Notes, add-ons, requirements	Vendor
Adept Publisher	✔	✔		AIX, HP OSF, Sun, Ultrix	FOSI publisher; includes Adept Editor	ArborText
CAPS	✔			Sun	Batch and interactive; InContext editor is add-on	XSoft
Corel Ventura	✔	✔			Contains TagWrite from Zandar for input filtering of SGML	Corel
DeskTopPro	✔	C	C	DG, Sun	SGML input, interactive or batch pagination	Penta
DynaPage	✔			(Sun)	Incorporates Balise from AIS; requires DynaBase or DynaText	EBT
Pager	✔			DEC, Sun	Batch composition	Frame
SGML Composer	✔			DEC, HP, Sun	FOSI publisher	Frame
SGML Enabler	✔		✔		Outputs Quark extensions	SoftQuad
Xyvision Parlance Publisher	✔			AIX, DEC, Sun	OmniMark input translation; supports looseleaf publishing	Xyvision

(x): Not released   C/T: Conversion and transformation   C: Client

Viewers

All viewers, except as noted, require input setup of some degree to import SGML data; those indicated require programming level effort.

	SGML input	Win	Mac	Unix & other platforms	Notes, add-ons, requirements	Vendor
DynaText	✔	✔	✔	AIX, DEC, HP, SGI, Sun	Style sheet editor required; DynaPage add-on will create print style sheets; on-the-fly conversion to HTML by DynaWeb add-on	EBT
Explorer	✔	✔			No input transformation required	SoftQuad
FolioViews	✔	✔	(✔)	DOS	Views Toolkit is an OmniMark input transformation script	Folio
Grif Active Views	✔	✔	(✔)	AIX, DEC, HP, Sun	Uses Grif editor with API	Grif
GTI Publisher	✔	C		HP, SGI, Sun	Design, compile, distribute on CD-ROM direct from SGML; distribution for Windows users	Jouve
Guide Professional Publisher	✔	✔			Not sold singly; distribution license sold with suite of tools including editor, indexer, filter; supports conditional logic	InfoAccess
HyperWriter for SGML	~	✔		DOS	Requires programming to accept arbitrary DTDs; OmniMark input script	Ntergaid
Latitude	✔	C	C	All Unix; terminal, DOS clients	Integrates Open Text search & retrieval engine with SGML or WYSIWYG viewer	Open Text
Olias		✔		Sun	Add-ons convert to SGML; create document libraries; access Web, remote documents	HaL
Oracle Book	~	✔	C	Motif client	Includes scripting language for SGML input; add-on includes set scripts	Oracle
Panorama Pro	✔	✔			Works with HTML Web browsers	SoftQuad
WorldView	✔	✔	✔	AIX, DEC, HP, Sun	A distribution system with production, viewing, linking; toolkit	Interleaf

(x): Not released   C/T: Conversion and transformation   C: Client

Integration Platforms

	VP	Win	Mac	Unix & other platforms	Notes, add-ons, requirements	Vendor
Information Manager	✔	(C)		(AIX, HP, OSF, Sun)	Includes customization, integrates writing, review, query, workflow, data management	Texcel
JCALS	✔	(C)		DEC, HP, Sun, other	Integrates hardware and software components from many vendors for complete CALS-compliant publishing[1]	CSC
Passage Pro	✔	(✔)		SGI, Sun	Integrates arbitrary editing, viewing, composition applications with data conversion, data and workflow management	Passage
WorkSmart	✔	C		DEC, HP, Sun	Workflow, task and data management	InfoDesign

VP: Validating Parser   (x): Not released   C/T: Conversion and transformation   C: Client

---

[1] Available on limited basis to CALS suppliers.

Web-Specific Tools

	Win	Mac	Unix & other platforms	Notes, add-ons, requirements	Vendor
BASIS WEBserver			AIX, DEC, HP, SGI, SCR4, Sun	Built on BASIS Server; store HTML or simple SGML files; query with BASIS Plus	IDI
Cyberleaf			AIX, DEC, HP, Sun	Web viewer, editor, manager; converts SGML to HTML	Interleaf
HoTMetaL Pro	✔	✔	AIX, DEC, HP, SGI, Sun	Incorporates a validating SGML parser.	SoftQuad
InContext Spider	✔			Web editor with Spyglass Enhanced Mosaic browser; validating SGML parser	InContext
Olias			Sun	Add-on Filter Development Kit converts to SGML	HaL
Panorama Pro	✔			SGML viewer works with Mosaic from NCSA, Spyglass, or with Netscape	SoftQuad
Symposia Pro	(✔)	(✔)		HTML editor; edit document on remote server; validating SGML parser	Grif

(x): Not released   C/T: Conversion and transformation   C: Client

VENDOR DIRECTORY

Please note:

- Addresses are in the United States unless otherwise stated. Many organizations have regional offices but I have listed only one address for each company, with the exception of U.S. contacts or distributors for European firms.

- Phone numbers are in the United States or Canada, area code first, unless a country code is given after a plus sign (+). Those in the United States and Canada should dial 011 instead of the plus, while others should note that the international country code for the United States is 1.

- A plus sign (+) between two products indicates that the base product supports add-on modules from another product category.

- An asterisk (*) indicates that the company offers more than one product in that category.

- Items in parens (x) were announced or in beta but not released as of August 1995.

Abbreviations used in the directory are:

- Data Design and Validation (DDV)
- Editors (Edit)
- Conversion and Transformation (C/T)
- Information Management (Man)
- Composition Systems (Comp)
- Viewers (View)
- Integration Platforms (Int)
- Web-Specific Tools (Web)

Active Systems
11 Holland Avenue, Suite 700
Ottawa, Ontario K1Y 4S1
Canada
613/729-2043
613/729-2874 (fax)
sales@ctmg.isis.org
> Man

Advanced Information Systems, S.A.
(A.I.S. Berger Levrault)
35 rue du Pont
92000 Neuilly-sur-Seine
France
+33/1 46 40 84 00
+33/1 46 40 84 10 (fax)
balise@ais.berger-levrault.fr
(A wholly owned subsidiary of Berger-Levrault; distributed in the U.S. by EBT)
  DDV, Man*, (C/T+Comp)

ArborText, Inc.
1000 Victors Way, Suite 400
Ann Arbor, MI 48108-2700
313/996-3566
313/996-3573 (fax)
info@arbortext.com
www.arbortext.com
  Edit+DDV(+Web), Comp+Edit

Auto-Graphics, Inc.
3201 Temple Avenue
Pomona, CA 91768
800/776-6939
909/595-7204
909/595-3506 (fax)
info@auto-graphics.com
www.auto-graphics.com
  Edit

Avalanche Development Company
947 Walnut Street
Boulder, CO 80302
303/449-5032
303/449-3246
sgmlinfo@avalanche.com
(Avalanche is a wholly-owned subsidiary of Interleaf, Inc.)
  C/T*

Carnegie Group, Inc.
5 PPG Place
Pittsburgh, PA 15222
800/284-3424
412/642-6900
412/642-6906 (fax)
info@cgi.com
  Edit

Computer Sciences Corporation (CSC)
Integrated Systems Division
304 West Route 38
Moorestown, NJ 08057
800/522-5701
609/988-4400
609/988-8410 (fax)
   Int

Corel Corporation
1600 Carling Avenue
Ottawa, Ontario K1Z 8R7
Canada
800/772-6735
613/728-8200
613/728-9790 (fax)
www.corelnet.com
   Comp

Data Conversion Laboratory (DCL)
184-13 Horace Harding Expressway
Fresh Meadows, NY 11365
718/357-8700
718/357-8776 (fax)
   C/T

Docucon, Inc.
7461 Callaghan Road
San Antonio, TX 78229
210/525-9221
210/525-0507 (fax)
docucon@docucon.com
   C/T

Electronic Book Technologies, Inc. (EBT)
One Richmond Square
Providence, RI 02906
401/421-9550
401/421-9551 (fax)
info@ebt.com
www.ebt.com
   View+Web(+Comp), (Man+Edit+Comp+Web), C/T

Exoterica Corporation
1545 Carling Avenue
Suite 104
Ottawa, Ontario K1Z 8P9
Canada
800/565-9465
613/722-1700
613/722-5706 (fax)
info@exoterica.com
    DDV, C/T

Folio Corporation
5072 North Information Way (300 W)
Provo, UT 84604
800/543-6546
801/229-6710
801-229-6790 (fax)
sales@folio.com
www.folio.com
    View+C/T

Frame Technology Corporation
333 West Can Carlos Street
San Jose, CA 95110-2711
800/843-7263
408/975-6000
408 975-6600 (fax)
comments@frame.com
www.frame.com
ftp.frame.com or 192.111.118.8
(Datalogics is a Frame Technology Company; at this writing, Frame will be
merged into Adobe Systems, Incorporated.)
    Edit*, Comp*

Grif S.A.
Immeuble "Le Florestan"
2, boulevard vauban
Boite Postale 266
St Quentin en Yvelines
78053 Cedex
France
+33/130121430
+33/130640646 (fax)
grif@grif.fr
www.grif.fr
    Edit, (Edit+Web), View, (Web)

HaL Software Systems
3006A Longhorn Blvd., #113
Austin, TX 78758
512/834-9962
512/834-9963 (fax)
olias-info@hal.com
www.hal.com
  View+Web

InContext Systems
2 St. Clair Avenue West, Suite 1600
Toronto, Ontario M4V 1L5
Canada
416/922-0087
416/922-6489 (fax)
http://incontext.ca
  Edit, Web

InfoAccess, Inc.
2800 156th Avenue SE
Bellevue, WA 98007
800/344-9737
206/747-3203
206/641-9367 (fax)
infoaccess@infoaccess.com
  View+Edit+C/T

InfoDesign Corporation
One Prince Street, Suite 300
Alexandria, VA 22314
703/519-9656
703/827-5548 (fax)
sales@idc.com
  Man, Int

Information Dimensions, Inc. (IDI)
5080 Tuttle Crossing Boulevard
Dublin, OH 43017-3569
800/328-2648
614/761 8083
614/761-7290 (fax)
www@idi.oclc.org
www.idi.oclc.org
(IDI is a subsidiary of OCLC)
  Man, Web+Man

Interleaf, Inc.
Prospect Place
9 Hillside Avenue
Waltham, MA 02154-9524
800/955-5323
617/290-4961 (fax)
i-direct@ileaf.com
www.ileaf.com
comp.text.ileaf
(See also Avalanche)
    Edit+Comp+C/T, View+Edit, Web+View+Man

Jouve Software, Inc.
500 East Main Street #328
Branford, CT 06405-2929
203/488-6625
203/481-1133 (fax)
    View

Lexicon Systems, Inc.
6165 Lehman Drive, Suite 204
Colorado Springs, CO 80918
800/700-2712
719/593-8971
719/593-9268 (fax)
merff@lexisys.com
    (Edit)

Microsoft Corporation
One Microsoft Way
Redmond, WA 98052-6399
206/882-8080
206/936-7329 (fax)
    Edit+Comp

Microstar Software Ltd.
34 Colonnade Road North
Nepean, Ontario K2E 7J6
Canada
800/267-9975
613/727-5696
613/727-9491 (fax)
cade@microstar.com
www.microstar.com
    DDV*, (Edit)

NICE technologies USA
2121 41st Avenue
Suite 303
Capitola, CA 95010
408/476-5872
408/476-0910 (fax)
nice-sales@netcom.com
http://infolane.com/nice/nice.htm
(Headquarters are in Gex, France)
 Edit+Comp

Novell, Inc.
1555 North Technology Way
Orem, UT 84057
800/451-5151
www.novell.com
(WordPerfect is a division of Novell, Inc.)
 Edit, (Edit)

Ntergaid
2490 Black Rock Turnpike, Suite 337
Fairfield, CT 06430
800/254-9737
203/380-1280
203/380-1465 (fax)
75160.3357@compuserve.com
 View

Open Text Corporation
180 Columbia Street W.
Waterloo, Ontario N2L 3L3
Canada
519/888-7111
519/888-0677 (fax)
info@opentext.com
www.opentext.com
 Man, View+Man

Oracle Corporation
500 Oracle Parkway
Redwood Shores, CA 94065
800/633-0676
415/506-7000
415/506-7200 (fax)
www.oracle.com
 View

Passage Systems
10596 North Tantau Ave.
Cupertino, CA 95014
408/366-0300
408/366-0320 (fax)
info@passage.com
www.passage.com
   C/T, Man, Int

Penta Software, Inc.
107 Lakefront Drive
Hunt Valley, MD 21030-2259
410/771-8973
410/771-4020 (fax)
   Comp

Sema Group Belgium
Rue de Stalle 96
B-1180 Bruxelles
Belgium
+32 2 333 53 24
+32 2 333 55 22 (fax)
info-markit@sema.be
info-sgml@sema.be
   DDV+Edit, C/T

SoftQuad, Inc.
56 Aberfoyle Crescent
Toronto, Ontario M8X 2W4
Canada
800/387-2777
416/239-4801
416/239-7105 (fax)
www.sq.com
sales@sq.com
   Edit(*), View*, Comp, Web*

TechnoTeacher, Inc.
P.O. Box 23795
Rochester, NY 14692-3795
courier:
3800 Monroe Avenue
Pittsford, NY 14534-1330
716/389-0961
716/389-0960 (fax)
www-info@techno.com
ftp.techno.com
www.techno.com
　　DDV

Texcel International B.V.
Texcel House
Fountain Court
28-32 Frances Road
Windsor, Berkshire SL4 3AA
United Kingdom
+44 753 833111
+44 753 854090 (fax)
sales@texcel.no
　　(Man), (Int)

U.S. Lynx, Inc.
853 Broadway
New York, NY 10003
212/673-3210
212/673-5261 (fax)
solutions@uslynx.com
　　C/T*, C/T+Edit

XSoft
10875 Rancho Bernardo Road, Suite 200
San Diego, CA 92127
800/428-2995
619/676-7700
619/676-7710 (fax)
info@xsoft.xerox.com
www.xerox.com/XSoft/XSoftHome.html
(A division of Xerox Corporation)
　　Man, Comp+Edit

Xyvision, Inc.
101 Edgewater Drive
Wakefield, MA 01880
617/245-4100
617/246-6209 (fax)
info@xyvision.com
www.xyvision.com
    Man, Comp

Zandar Corporation
P.O. Box 480
Newfane, VT 05345-9985
802/365-9393
802/365-4974 (fax)
    C/T

ZIFTech Computer Systems, Inc.
120 Herchmer Crescent
Kingston, Ontario K7M 2V9
Canada
613/531-9226
613/531-8003 (fax)
70444.126@compuserve.com
    DDV

NONCOMMERCIAL SOFTWARE

The tools in the public domain include several parsers plus editors, conversion engines and utilities, DTD viewing and analysis tools. These are available from the SGML archive maintained by Erik Naggum and its mirror sites.

```
ftp://ftp.ifi.uio.no/
ftp://sunsite.unc.edu/pub/packages/SGML
```

There are simple versions of commercial products from the following vendors available on the Internet without support or paper documentation:

Grif S.A.
+33/130121430
+33/130640646 (fax)
grif@grif.fr
www.grif.fr
    Symposia SGML and HTML Editor

Microstar Software Ltd.
800/267-9975
613/727-5696
613/727-9491 (fax)
cade@microstar.com
www.microstar.com
    Near & Far Lite DTD Viewer

SoftQuad, Inc.
800/387-2777
416/239-4801
416/239-7105 (fax)
www.sq.com
sales@sq.com
    HoTMetaL Editor, Panorama Viewer

Glossary
Talking SGML

This glossary contains definitions of terms, explanations of usage, and expansions of acronyms used throughout *ABCD... SGML*. Product and vendor names and acronyms defined in the text are indexed.

ANCHOR

End-point for a hypertext link. An anchor can be a section of text, a point between text elements, a graphic or a specific position on a graphic, or any other defined element of the target whether the target is text, sound, video, or any other media.

APPLICATION

Applications are software programs. They are to be distinguished from *data* which can be created and processed by a software application and the *format* of the data. For example, a word processor is an application; a writer uses the word processor application to create data stored in files, typically in the format native to that word processing application.

With proprietary word-processing technology, the data format, and the application used to create, manipulate, and store that data format are synonymous. Thus Word Processor *MinesBest* creates, manipulates, and stores data in *MinesBest* format.

With SGML-based technology, the application and the file format are not synonymous. While an SGML application may translate data into its own, internal format for more efficient processing, data is input, output, and stored as SGML.

APPLICATION PROGRAMMING INTERFACE (API)

APIs are sold as an option with many off-the-shelf software tools and are used to customize those tools for specific implementations.

ASCII

American Standard Code for Information Interchange. ASCII assigns a numerical value to numbers, letters, punctuation, and other symbols, like the dollar sign, used in typography. Computer systems can exchange sequences of ASCII codes, then translate the ASCII values into their own, internal system for representation and processing. Standardization ensures that the defined characters translate reliably between systems.

ATTRIBUTE

A term defined by the SGML standard. Attributes are characteristics or variables that modify elements, that is, they differentiate between elements. The document type definition specifies which attributes an element can have and which values an attribute can have. Attribute values can be supplied by an author, a processing application, or can be implied by position in a text stream.

BINARY LARGE OBJECT

Text or graphics in binary format stored as one object by a relational database. The database maintains information about the object in its own, relational table structure and it can manipulate and process the object as one unit.

BITMAP

Electronic images—either text or graphics—defined and stored as patterns of picture elements. Bitmapped graphics can represent text or art, but the computer sees only a pattern of dots. In bitmapped graphics, the word *cat* is a pattern of black and white and would not be recognized by a search for the string of letters c, a, t.

BROWSER

Computer application used to view electronic books. Synonymous with viewer. Browsers and viewers come with a range of features but all provide some ability to link and display text in a nonsequential manner.

CAD/CAE

Computer-aided design/computer-aided engineering. A class of computer applications used in architecture, manufacturing design, and engineering.

CASE

Computer-aided software engineering. A class of computer applications that assist a programmer in the creation of applications.

CD-ROM

Compact-disk read-only memory. A distribution media for electronic information such as digital music, video, computer applications, and data.

CHUNK

A nontechnical term that in hypertext circles generally means a portion of text, or other information, defined in such a way that the computer can do something with it. For example, if a glossary term and definition are considered one chunk of data, then applications can be developed that sort and retrieve a term and definition as one unit.

COMPOSITION SYSTEM

A software application for composing text and graphics in preparation for print.

CONTENT MODEL

Part of the element declaration defined by the SGML standard. The content model specifies what other elements or what types of data are possible, required, or optional within an SGML element. The content model can also specify order.

CONVERTER

A computer program that converts data from one format to another format. The data can be graphics or text.

DATA

In the context of this book, data is information stored, exchanged, and processed in digital form on a computer. In restricted contexts, the term *data* refers to information defined by discrete database fields in contrast to *text* of arbitrary length and complexity defined by SGML.

Live data is information that is updated or replaced on a continuing basis outside the control of the local computer application.

DATABASE (DB)

Database. A type of computer application that stores and processes information organized in table-like structures consisting of defined records and fields.

DESKTOP PUBLISHING (DTP)

A class of computer applications for desktop computers. Desktop publishing software prepares text and graphics for print by applying typographic characteristics and by specifying page layout.

DOCUMENT ANALYSIS

A stage in the development of an SGML document type definition. Document analysis defines the goals for the DTD and produces the specification used to code the DTD.

DOCUMENT ARCHITECTURE

The design principles on which a DTD is based. For example, modular document architecture assembles DTDs from sets of elements and entities that can be reused in different contexts.

DOCUMENT INSTANCE

The formal term given by the SGML standard to a unit of information defined by one document type definition. If the DTD defines a memo, then each memo is a document instance; if the DTD defines a dictionary entry, then each entry in the dictionary is a document instance. Document instances are not limited to text, they can contain any digitally-encoded media such as sound or graphics.

DOCUMENT STYLE, SEMANTIC, AND SPECIFICATION LANGUAGE (DSSSL)

An ISO standard that complements SGML, specifying the rules for a nonproprietary language to describe the appearance of text in various media.

DOCUMENT TYPE DEFINITION (DTD)

The set of rules and descriptions that together form a template for the structure and content of a document marked up with SGML. A single DTD can be a model for many documents of similar structure and content. The SGML specification allows infinite variety in the construction of DTDs and, therefore, of documents. A DTD can be rigid, requiring conformity between documents or a DTD can be loose, allowing a great deal of variation between documents.

ELECTRONIC DATA BOOK (EDB)

Term used in certain industries for documentation and data delivered electronically, not in print. EDBs may contain information used directly by computer applications, such as calibration parameters for the application, information that would not appear in a printed manual.

ELECTRONIC DELIVERY

Delivery of information on the computer screen. Information delivered electronically may originate and be disseminated in any media such as disks, CD-ROMS, or network file servers.

ELECTRONIC PUBLISHING (EP)

The preparation of text and graphics for print by means of specialized computer applications called electronic or desktop publishers.

ELEMENT

A term defined by the SGML standard. Elements and their content are defined in the DTD. They are the basic units, or building blocks, of a document instance. An element consists of a pair of tags marking the element's start and end plus the contents of the element. Elements can contain other nested elements and elements can contain defined types of data, such as ASCII characters and entities.

ELEMENT DECLARATION

An entry in a document type definition that defines an *element* by pairing a label (a *generic identifier*) with a type of content (the *content model.*) For example, the declaration for a tool name element might give it the generic identifier **TOOLNAME** and specify that the content of the **TOOLNAME** element must be defined characters or entities.

ENTITY

A term defined by the SGML standard. Entities are short text strings defined within a document type definition. They are used in SGML documents and document type definitions to take the place of other objects. Those other objects can be typographic characters, thus the entity *–* is a substitute for the symbol "–". *Parameter* entities can take the place of a set of elements or entities in a DTD thus becoming a shorthand for describing the content or use of those objects without listing each one in each place where it applies. Document type definitions can include *external* entities defined in other, referenced files.

FILE FORMATS

See *Applications* and *Format.*

FILE TRANSFER PROTOCOL (FTP)

Set of communications protocols used to transfer files between computer systems.

FORMAT

Text format is the appearance of that text on a printed page. Typically, text format refers to a set of typographic and layout characteristics including page width, typeface, and so on.

Data format refers to a method of organizing that data for processing and storage on a computer. Data format may refer to the filing system used by a disk drive and operating system (*file format*) or to the markup system used by an application such as a spreadsheet or word processor.

FORMAT OUTPUT SPECIFICATION INSTANCE (FOSI)

Format Output Specification Instance. Application of SGML markup to a document instance to describe the appearance of that document.

GENERIC IDENTIFIER (GI)

A term defined by the SGML standard. The generic identifier is the name of an SGML element as defined in a DTD. The DTD assigns GIs to content models in the element declaration.

GRANULARITY

The scale of a typical unit of information. Thus markup that identifies paragraphs as the smallest unit would be one level of granularity while markup that identifies parts of speech would be a different, finer level of granularity.

HARDCOPY

Information in print.

HYPERTEXT MARKUP LANGUAGE (HTML)

Hypertext markup language. The document type definition created for the World Wide Web.

HYTIME

Hypermedia/Time-based Structuring Language, ISO 10744:1992. An SGML application that specifies design principles and methods for document type definitions. HyTime promotes exchange and linking of documents without restricting their structure and content by creating a superset of definitions that can be applied to any document type.

INTERACTIVE ELECTRONIC TECHNICAL MANUAL (IETM)

Term defined by the U.S. Department of Defense for technical manuals that use conditional, branching logic in an electronic delivery system. The IETM adjusts its output in response to user input.

LEGACY DATA

Data in an application-specific format inherited by a system that no longer uses that application. Thus when you stop using *BrandX* word processor, or when *BrandX* upgrades to *BrandX.1,* all the information in *BrandX* format becomes legacy data that cannot be used by the new or upgraded application until it is converted.

LINK

A connection between two pieces of information. In electronic texts and information systems, links are not physical like a piece of chain or wire, but are pointers, much like cross references in a printed text. Computer applications use these pointers to present first one piece of information then another to the reader, even when the pieces are in different physical locations such as different files or remote computer systems.

MAPPING

A programmed correspondence between information in different formats used for translation and data conversion.

MARKUP

Notation added to text that does not become part of the text stream, but remains distinct, usually indicating some treatment of the text. Hardcopy markup indicates the correspondence between sections of text and typography. For example, a title might be marked up as "Big, bold, and centered" and then formatted in this manner when typeset.

Markup of electronic text supplies information about the text that can be used by processing applications. For example, markup that indicates "The string of text between these two points is a product name," can be used by an application to extract the name for a list of products and to format the name accordingly.

MARKUP LANGUAGE

A systematic approach to markup that sets up rules and standards so that a processing application can interpret the markup consistently.

METADATA

Information about information. Typically, metadata classifies and categorizes a piece of information that is stored separately from the metadata. For example, if the original information is the character string "111850," metadata in a relational database might identify this as the date of birth field in a biographical record.

MIL-SPEC

Military specification. Mil-specs for documentation describe the content and format of that documentation. New mil-specs created through the CALS program also describe the electronic format of the data and how it is to be stored and transmitted.

NESTING

Embedding one object within another indicating hierarchy. In a traditional outline, detailed information is nested within more general information in successive levels of hierarchy, thus level 1. is nested within level A. which is nested within level I. This is indicated visually by successive indentations; the lower an item in the hierarchy, the greater the indentation. Nesting is used in structured information to indicate hierarchy and subordination.

OUTPUT SPECIFICATION

An SGML document type definition that defines how a document instance appears.

PARSER

An SGML parser is a software program that reads, interprets, and processes SGML document instances and document type definitions. A *validating* parser does the same and, in addition, locates and reports errors in markup. A DTD is validated against the rules of the ISO standard; a document is validated against the rules of the applicable DTD. See Chapter 3, page 46 for a detailed description of what a parser does in an SGML-based production system.

QC/QA

Quality control/quality assurance.

SPEC

Specification.

STANDARD GENERALIZED MARKUP LANGUAGE (SGML)

An international standard published by the International Organization for Standards (ISO) as ISO 8879:1986, "Information processing—text and office systems—Standard Generalized Markup Language (SGML)." SGML sets up rules for defining markup so that the markup can be added to information which can, as a result, be processed and exchanged by the widest variety of computer applications. There are no restrictions on the type of information processed or the type of information supplied through SGML markup.

STRUCTURED INFORMATION

All information has some structure; this usage implies that structure is applied explicitly in a manner that a machine can interpret and process. Structured information need not be as regular as data in a database which typically are discrete pieces of information in a precise, repetitive pattern. Thus, structured information need not restrict the content, organization, or consistency of a text, although some degree of consistency can augment the processing power of applications that make use of the markup.

STYLE

See *template*.

TAG

A term defined by the SGML standard. Tags are the markup strings that name and delineate SGML elements.

TEMPLATE

A mold or pattern, like a cookie cutter, used to create multiple objects of like form. In electronic publishing and word processing, a template is a collection of *styles*, each style being a specific set of typographic characteristics. For example, a heading style might specify "12 point optima bold, flush left." A template would contain all the styles required to specify the appearance of one document including headings, body text, footnotes, and so on. Templates can also specify the appearance and arrangement of text and graphics in a browser.

Conversion templates specify the styles required to map one type of markup to another type of markup.

TEXTBASE

Text that is structured and marked up in a manner that can be identified and processed by a computer application without ambiguity. Typically, text in a textbase is less regular than data in a database.

TRANSFORMER

Computer program that changes one type of SGML markup to another type of SGML markup or that modifies a document instance without degrading its structure. See Chapter 3, page 64.

VALIDATION

See *parser*.

VIEWER

See *browser*.

WORD PROCESSOR (WP)

A computer application for the creation and modification of human language. Text created on a word processor can be read on the computer screen, stored in digital format on a number of media, transmitted to other computer systems or applications, or translated to a printer language to be printed on paper.

WORLD WIDE WEB (WWW, THE WEB)

A set of Internet protocols and standards for data and communications. Together, these systems form a distributed hypertext linking disparate, remote computers into a single, connected, electronic library accessible to millions of people world wide. The primary data standard for the World Wide Web is an application of SGML called hypertext markup language or HTML. Information encoded in SGML can also be read and distributed on the Web.

WORM

Write once, read many. A digital storage and distribution media that, like ink on paper, becomes a permanent record once data is recorded.

WYSIWYG

What you see is what you get. Acronym applied to electronic publishing systems that display text and graphics on the screen precisely as they will print on the page.

References

Ahearn, H. (1993) *SGML and the New Yorker*. Technical Communication, Second Quarter, pp. 226–9.

Berkner, D.S. (1994) *CD-ROM Marketing: A Case Study Scholarly Publishing*, 25 (2), 113–125.

Bryan, M (1988) *SGML: An Author's Guide to the Standard Generalized Markup Language*. Addison-Wesley, Reading, MA.

Burnard, L. (1991) *TEI EDW26: An Introduction to the Text Encoding Initiative*. August 6, 1991 (revised, May 1992). (See Resource Guide A for ordering information.)

Chahuneau, F. (1994) *Practical Approaches to SGML Page Composition*. Proceedings, SGML '94.

Coombs, J., A. Renear and S. DeRose, (1987) *Markup Systems and the Future of Scholarly Text Processing. Communications of the Association for Computing Machinery*, 30, 933–47.

DeRose, S., D. Durand, E. Mylonas and A. Renear, (1990) *What Is Text, Really?* Journal of Computing in Higher Education, 1(2), 3–26.

DocBook 2.1. Copyright *1992*, 1993 HaL Computer Systems International, Ltd., and O'Reilly & Associates, Inc.

Flynn, P. (1995) *The WorldWideWeb Handbook: An HTML Guide for Users*. Authors and Publishers, International Thomson Publishing, London.

Ford, A. (1994) *Spinning the Web*. International Thomson Publishing, London.

Glushko, R. J. (1989) *Transforming Text into Hypertext for a Compact Disc Encyclopedia*. In Proceedings of the ACM Conference on Computer-Human Interaction-CHI '89, pp. 293–298.

Glushko, R. J. (1992) *Seven Ways to Make a Hypertext Project Fail*. Technical Communication, 39; 226–230.

Glushko, R. J. and K. Kershner, (1993) *Silicon Graphics' IRIS InSight: An SGML Success Story*. Technical Communication, August, pp. 394–402.

Goldberg, N. (1986) *Writing Down the Bones*. Shambhala Publications, Inc., Boston.

Goldfarb, C.F. (1990) *The SGML Handbook*. Clarendon Press, Oxford, England.

Gross, M. (1993) *Getting Your Data into SGML*. Technical Communication, August, pp. 219–225.

Grosso, P. (1993). *The Output Specification, FOSIs, and their Design and Processing*. TAG, July 20.

Hammer, M. and J. Champy, (1993).*Reengineering the Corporation*. Harper-Business, New York.

Herwijnen, E. van (1994) *Practical SGML*, 2nd ed. Kluwer Academic Publishers, Boston, Dordrecht, London.

LaPeyre, D. (1994) DTD, *Application and System Utilities*. Proceedings, SGML '94.

Maler, E. and J. El Andaloussi, (1994) *Methodology for Developing DTDs*. Proceedings, SGML Europe '94, pp. 85–95.

Maler, E. and J. El Andaloussi, (1992) *Developing the OSF recommendations*. <TAG>, 5(11).

McFadden, J. (1994) *Applying SGML to Multimedia Viewing Technology*. slide presentation.

Newcomb, S., Kipp, N. and V. Newcomb, (1991) The "HyTime" Hypermedia/ Time-based Document Structuring Language, Communications of the ACM, 34(11), 67–83.

Owens, E. (1994) Talk given to the SGML Forum of New York. June 14, 1994.

Raimes, J. (1994) *Developing a CD-ROM*. Scholarly Publishing, 25(2), 107–14.

Reynolds L. R. and S. J. DeRose, (1992) *Electronic Books*. "Byte," special section on "Managing Infoglut," June 1992.

Schettini, S. and L. Alschuler, (1994) *SGML is Here to Stay*. "Publish," June 1994.

Sperberg-McQueen, C. M. and E. Brennan, (1994) *SGML and the TEI*. Presented at Literary Texts in an Electronic Age: Scholarly Implications and Library Services Data Processing Conference, April 10.

Sperberg-McQueen, C. M. (1994) *Databases, Document and Workflow Management*. Proceedings, SGML '94.

Swank, R. and S. Chapman, (1994) *Case Study: Maintaining and Developing a Dynamic SGML Environment at Ericsson*. Presented at Bellcore's Electronic Delivery '94.

Index